The Chartulary or Register of the Abbey of St. Werburgh, Chester

REMAINS

Historical and Literary

CONNECTED WITH THE PALATINE COUNTIES OF

Lancaster and Chester

VOLUME 82.—NEW SERIES

MANCHESTER:

Printed for the Chetham Society

1923

The Chetham Society.

COUNCIL FOR 1921–1922.

PROF. JAMES TAIT, M.A., LITT.D., F.B.A., PRESIDENT.

WILLIAM FARRER, ESQ., D.LITT., VICE-PRESIDENT.

REV. H. A. HUDSON, M.A., F.S.A.

T. CANN HUGHES, ESQ., M.A., F.S.A.

MAJOR WILLIAM LEES, J.P.

COLONEL JOHN PARKER, C.B., F.S.A.

PROF. F. M. POWICKE, M.A., LITT.D.

J. PAUL RYLANDS, ESQ., F.S.A.

HENRY TAYLOR, ESQ., M.A., F.S.A.

PROF. T. NORTHCOTE TOLLER, M.A., LITT.D., LL.D.

W. ASHETON TONGE, ESQ.

PROF. T. F. TOUT, M.A., D.LITT., F.B.A.

JOHN MOODIE, ESQ., HON. TREASURER,
Williams Deacon's Bank, Manchester.

ERNEST BROXAP, ESQ., M.A., HON. SECRETARY,
Riversdale, Kersal, Manchester.

[3]

The
Chartulary or Register
of
The Abbey of St. Werbur
Chester

EDITED WITH INTRODUCTION AND NOTES

BY

JAMES TAIT, Litt.D., F.B.A.,
President of the Society

PART II

PRINTED FOR THE CHETHAM SOCIETY

1923

PREFACE

THE present volume completes the publication of the Chester Chartulary, the first part of which appeared three years ago   It includes more than five hundred documents (a few being specially numbered as not in the abbey register), and of these sixty-four are full texts with witnesses, gathered from various sources to replace the usually meagre abstracts of the register   The general proportion is slightly less than in Part I., but while that included no more than four taken from surviving originals, and one of these of contested authenticity, thirty-two, exactly half the total number of complete texts in the present part, are copied from originals.   Of the thirty-two, twenty-four form part of the Mainwaring collection of charters which Sir Harry Mainwaring, when giving up Over Peover recently, placed in the John Rylands Library, Manchester, on loan for an indefinite period, for the use of students.[1] Ormerod and his editor Helsby do not seem to have had access to these deeds, and did not make full use of the transcripts of many of them which the antiquaries of the seventeenth century have left   Until the middle of the eighteenth century they belonged to the Kermincham branch of the Mainwarings, which had acquired the abbey manor of Barnshaw-cum-Goostrey and with it the deeds relating to the various estates included in the manor   On the sale of the manor to the main line between 1752 and 1757[2] the charters were transferred to Peover   There is reason to believe, however, that some deeds which originally formed part of the collection had become

[1] A useful handlist of them has been printed by Dr R Fawtier in the *Bulletin of the John Rylands Library*, vol vii (1922-3)
[2] Ormerod, iii 132

separated from the rest either at the Dissolution or during their stay at Kermincham   For the eight original charters of abbey holdings in Lees and Cranage which were acquired by the late Mr R H Wood, formerly secretary of the Chetham Society, must almost certainly have been associated with them at one time, as Lees and Cranage were within the jurisdiction of the manor of Barnshaw-cum-Goostrey, and both collections include grants in Lees by Gralam de Rundchamp (Nos. 737 and 758) These eight charters were seen and used by Helsby, but his abstracts are far from satisfactory, and we are glad to be able, by the kindness of Mr J Hatton Wood, their present owner, to give full and careful transcripts of all

These thirty odd parchments, recording the thirteenth-century acquisitions of the abbey in a group of little townships on and around Rudheath in central Cheshire, which by a singular chance have been preserved (almost as fresh as when they were written), while so many hundreds have perished, are fairly typical of the contents of the present volume   With few exceptions, the Rhuddlan grant of Ranulf Blundeville (No. 598) is one, the charters of kings, earls, and high ecclesiastical authorities are confined to the earlier part of the chartulary   Gifts, sales, and exchanges by the lesser landowners of Cheshire form the bulk of the transactions recorded in this, which therefore furnishes more detailed information on the genealogy, local topography, and agricultural economy of the county   Almost every page bears testimony to the energy and activity of that stout upholder of the abbey's claims and interests, Abbot Simon de Albo Monasterio (1265–1291), in the period following the Barons' Wars   The extent to which religious houses were liable to suffer at the hands of covetous magnates " in tempore turbacionis " is well illustrated by the one-sided agreement of 1258 between Simon's predecessor and Roger de Mold, the steward of the earl of Chester, which even half a century later wrung a hot protest from the scribe of the chartulary (No 535)   In the litigation with Basingwerk Abbey in 1287 over the advowson of West Kirby (No. 513) presentations made ' during the time of war ' were disregarded.   Even in time of peace a watchful eye and a firm attitude were needed

The heirs of benefactors were sometimes disposed to whittle away
what they considered excessive generosity. In two such cases
abbot Simon himself had to come to terms with the discontented
heir, surrendering the lordship of Old Withington, which had
been granted to the abbey in 1267 as a dependency of Chelford,
perhaps the most important acquisition of the thirteenth century
(Nos 563-64), and about ten years later half the Cranage mine
on Rudheath which Robert de Croxton had given (No 740a)
Expensive litigation with neighbouring landowners over rights of
pasture in the waste and the like was sometimes necessary (Nos
691, 694-95, 837)   The suit between abbot Thomas II. and the
holders of the master cook's fee over the kitchen perquisites of
their office, heads and tails of fish, pieces of the back bones of
pigs and oxen, skimmings of fat, etc., provides the most enter-
taining document in a somewhat austere collection   Ormerod
devoted considerable attention to it in his *History of Cheshire*,
but we are able to give a better text and to make an important
correction of the date to which he assigned it (pp 353-55).

In this and the preceding part there are materials, unfortunately not very easy to handle, for a study of the separate
endowments of the various departments of the monastic economy,
infirmary, wardrobe, almonry, and so forth.   The agreements as
to burial rights with the hospital of St. John, the nuns of St. Mary,
and the friars preachers form an interesting group (Nos 522–26)
They make it quite clear that the only original parish churches
of Chester and its suburbs were St. Werburgh's and St. John's.

Attention may also be drawn to the identification of the
present Holm House farm near Ince with the Alrichesholm of
the Chester and Stanlaw chartularies and the evidence thereby
afforded that the hundred boundary has been diverted at this
point since the thirteenth century

The grant of lands in Ulster to the monastery by John
de Courcy in the reign of Henry II , in return for the provision
of a prior and monks for a new abbey at Downpatrick (No 886),
was known to Dugdale from one of the manuscripts of the
chartulary, but the lands do not seem to have been identified or
their later history traced.

For other points of interest in these charters the reader must be referred to the notes which have been appended to many of them and to the Addenda and Corrigenda, which would not have been so numerous had not the book, for reasons of economy, been set up at once in page

In taking leave, with somewhat mixed feelings, of a work which has occupied much of my time for the last six years, I cannot refrain from expressing a hope that it may help to bring to the Society a larger number of members in Cheshire than it has possessed in recent years   There are still many unprinted documents relating to the abbey in the British Museum, the Public Record Office, and elsewhere, including a rental of its estates in the fifteenth century and a court roll of the early sixteenth, and if adequate support is given, it may be found possible to print a volume of these at some not too distant date

My obligations to the Council and Librarian of the John Rylands Library and to Mr Hatton Wood have been already recorded. Mr W. Fergusson Irvine and Mr. R Stewart-Brown have again kindly read my proofs, preserved me from not a few errors, and furnished even more additional matter than my notes and addenda expressly indicate   Mr John Brownbill has made transcripts and searches for me with his usual skill and care.

JAMES TAIT.

WITHINGTON,
   MANCHESTER,
     February 20th, 1923

ADDENDA ET CORRIGENDA

Page iv, line 29   A Ralph justice (*iusticia*) witnesses two charters of Ranulph II , *c* 1150   (Stenton, *Danelaw Charters*, 363 , *Spalding Chartulary* (College of Arms), f 447)

Page v, line 1   In Harley MS 2074, f 30 (142) Randle Holme records a 'Convencio facta A D 1202 coram Philippo de Orreby, tunc existente iusticiario Cestrie, aliisque baronibus et fidelibus domini comitis inter Gilbertum Pica, etc' Unfortunately no more is quoted and Holme may have made a mistake in the date This was evidently Canon Morris's authority for dating Orreby's justiceship 1202–29 in his *Chester in Plantagenet and Tudor Reigns* Mr Stewart-Brown informs me that he believes he found proof that Orreby was justice on November 13, 1207, but has lost the reference

Page v, line 5   Draycot attested as justice a charter dated 1239 (Shakerley (Vernon) MS 3, f 238) and was still acting in July 1240 (*Rot. Parl* i 81a) Was John de Lexington his colleague or deputy in the preceding February ? Draycot is known to have had two colleagues, John Gobaud and Simon of Norwich, during part of his term of office (MS Coll of Arms, i D 14, No 45)

Page v, line 9   Ormerod's statement (ii 78) that Sir Walkelyn de Arderne discharged the office of justice between 1252 and 1258 is unsupported by evidence there, and as the justices of those years are known, Arderne can at best have only been acting as deputy The assertion in the next paragraph that Roger de Mainwaring was justice in 1232–33 is a mere slip

Page xi, line 10-13   If Æthelred acquired Lindsey in the strict sense only in 679, the inference here made falls to the ground, for Threckingham is in Kesteven

Page xlv, footnote 5.   The reference should be to No 6, though No 12 shows the same system in force under Ranulf II

Page xlviii, line 17   For Simon, a later chancellor, see Orm ii 486

Page 9, line 11   The Chartulary has EAston, not Easton, the 'E' being intended as a correction of the 'A'

Page 29, line 16   See No 782

Page 38, No 4   Cf Dugdale, *Mon Angl* IV 20

Page 46, line 2   I have, however, since found a deed in which a William de Punterleia of the text is William Punterlin on the seal (Shakerley (Vernon) MS 3, f 226)

Page 66, line 42   Dr A G Little, who has kindly examined the photographic facsimile for me, writes   " The writing certainly looked like that of the middle of the twelfth century, but my impression was that there was a suggestion of artificiality about it, as though the scribe were copying something not quite in his usual style   It might be an ' attracted ' script, but I could not find any conclusive indication "   Apropos of this, it may be pointed out that Mr Gilson's view that the writing is considerably later than 1150 (which would make the document either a forgery or a mere transcript) is not, as he seemed to think, consistent with that of Mr Crump, who accepts the ostensible date

Page 89, line 3   For ' ann, iuel ' read ' anni uel '

Pages 91-92   For ' Hente ' (de Boydell) read ' Heute '

Page 94, No 46   The seal was attached in Erdeswick's time and apparently bore a stag (Harl MS 506, fo 46 (92))

Page 95, line 18   For a Hamelin de Bardulf who witnesses a charter of Earl Ranulf II , see F M Stenton, *Danelaw Charters* (British Academy), 362

Page 124, line 16   Dr Farrer tells me that I have done injustice to Ormerod here and that Sir Robert Touchet *was* son of Thomas

Page 131, line 13   John de Giuges here is probably the same person as the John de ' Ginoes ' who witnessed No 80, and one or both names must be misreadings, perhaps of Ginges

Page 131, footnote   For ' Robert ' read ' Roger '

Page 142, No 127   For the use of the ordinary form of enfeoffment in the grant of churches see Stenton, *Danelaw Charters*, lxxiv, and cf No 120

Page 165, No 194   Rugeram is an ' un-name ' for Ingeram or Engeram

Page 171, line 1   Mr Charles Johnson suggests that the eyre in question was that of 53 Henry III (1268–69)

Page 179, No 248   Add reference to No 207 for Lyme Wood

Page 202, line 13.   For ' R[ogero] ' read ' R[oberto] '

Page 206, No 309   For a contemporary agreement between William de Bunbury and Stanlaw Abbey as to the rights of the latter in this neighbourhood see *Whalley Coucher Book*, 1 29

Page 214, line 8   For ' the second William Lancelyn ' read ' the first William Lancelyn '   There was no William in the direct line before William (son of Robert II), who died in 1283   Cf No 689 *n*

Page 218, No. 331   A fuller copy enrolled on the Cheshire Domesday Roll was dated 53 Henry III (1268–69), " coram Thoma de Boulton tunc Iusticiario Cestrie, Thoma de Meyngarin, Petro de Ardena, Willeimo

ADDENDA ET CORRIGENDA

Patrike, Willelmo de Boydel, Thoma de Orreby, Roberto de Stokeport, Roberto Extraneo, Ricardo de Wilburham tunc vicecomite Cestriscire, militibus, Roberto de Monte Alto, Hugone de Corona, Hugone de Pulford, Eadm[undo] Fiton, Thoma de Audelim, Radulfo de Vernon, et aliis baronibus, militibus et libere tenentibus ibidem existentibus " It ends after antecessorum suorum   " prout ex inspectione cartarum ipsarum quas predictus Willelmus inspexit, audiuit, manibus propriis tractauit, etc " (MS College of Arms 1 D 14 (1580), No 52   I owe this transcript to Mr Stewart-Brown)

Page 222, No 335   Mr. Earwaker dated this grant earlier, " certainly before 1250," and seems justified by Abbot Simon's enfeoffment (c 1270) of Robert de Mascy with the moiety which the abbey held in demesne at an annual rent of 8s for all services (*East Cheshire*, 1 266)

Page 234, line 11   Insert a comma after Sage

Page 239, line 5   For " 456 " read " 460 "

Page 242, Nos 372-73   Cf No 605

Page 248, Nos 387-9 n   For " William Lancelyn II " read " William Lancelyn I "   Cf correction to p 214   *Botta* in these abstracts may be the scribe's error for *bovata*

Page 250, line 28   For " Nos 642, 652-53 " read " Nos 645 n , 656-657 "

Page 255, line 17   This conjecture is improbable

Page 256, line 7   Here and elsewhere " grant in fee farm " would be more strictly correct

Page 257, line 8   An inquest held Tuesday after Ascension Day 16 Edw I (1288) states that " Dominus Hugo de Dutton tenet quartam partem feodi unius militis in Nesse inveniendo duos homines fediles " (*sic*)— Ches Plea Roll, No 6, m 1 d

Page 262, line 10   There was a house in Elton in the eighteenth century which was called ' The Rock,' which we may perhaps connect with ' iuxta petram ' in this deed   *Ex inform* Rev J G Slater of Ince.

Page 264, line 26   Ormerod (ii 26 n) gives the names of the witnesses to this charter from an *inspeximus* by the Black Prince   Rob de Brescy, Ric de Kyngeslegh, Jac de Pulle, Will de Hellesby, Will de Trofford, and Ric. Marshall of Elton   James de Poole died before December 22, 1307 (*ib* ii 419)

Page 266, line 7   If the Thomas de Elton here mentioned were the grantor of Nos 432-35, the identification of this Hugh de Pulford with the rector of c 1220 would be a little difficult

Page 269, line 14   As the charter of Humphrey II de Bunbury mentioned in the note to this entry (a grant of a moiety of Lachford to Henry, son of Gilbert de Malpas) is prior to 1209, when the abbey's possession of Alrichesholm is first recorded, it is just possible that the exchange was effected with this Humphrey and not with his grandfather In that case the William Patrick who confirmed it would be the son of the William who died in 1184 and elder brother of Robert de Patrick (see p v *supra*)   This second William attested the Lachford charter

Page 273, line 6   The father of the grantor was perhaps the grantee of No V in *Journ Chest Arch Soc* N S x 18, for the date ot which cf No 357 *n* above

Page 275, line 34   In Wallasey charters copied by Richard Kuerden and Christopher Towneley (*penes* Dr W Farrer) Mr Irvine finds Alan de Waley occurring as late as 1230 and his son Robert flourishing *c* 1240–1245

Page 275, line 35   A Gilbert de Barnston, brother of Hugh, flourished *c* 1260–70 (W F I)

Page 288, line 29   In a county court held on December 21, 1311, the abbot's claim to exemption from attendance at the iter of the Justice of Chester for lay tenants on the glebe of Chirchotheheth (described as a vill of a carucate of land) was rejected on the verdict of a jury (*Chester Plea Roll*, 24, 5 Edw II m 15 *d*)

Page 293, No 510   The full text of this quitclaim is given here from Harl MS 2148, f 24 (in a record of a plea in 1289)

*Placita die Martis post Ascensionem Domini
anno H xlvij° tempore W La Zuche*

Omnibus Christi fidelibus ad quos litere presentes peruenerint Ric' de Kirkeby salutem in Domino   Nouerit universitas uestra me concessisse et pro me et heredibus meis in perpetuum omnino quietum clamasse et hoc presenti scripto meo confirmasse domino Th[ome] abbati sancte Werburge Cestr' et conuentui eiusdem loci et eorum successoribus omne ius et clamium quod habui uel aliquo casu contingente habere potui in ecclesia de Kirkeby cum pertinentiis uel in eiusdem ecclesie aduocacione cum omnibus terris, tenementis et libertatibus dicte ecclesie pertinentibus   Ita quod nec ego nec heredes mei nec aliquis ex parte mea uel nomine meo uel heredum meorum aliquid iuris uel clamii in predicta ecclesia uel eius aduocacione cum pertinenciis exigere poterimus uel decetero uendicare   Et ad maiorem securitatem habendam presenti quiete clam[ancie] sigillum meum apposui   Hiis testibus   domino W la Zuche tunc iusticiario Cestrie, domino R de Pulford constabulario, domino Ricardo de Wilburgham, militi[bus] , Ricardo de Orreby, camerario Cestrie, Stephano clerico tunc uicecomite Cestrisirie, Rogero de Dunuill', Patricio de Hesilwell', Philippo de Baumuile, Iohanne de Wetenhale, B de Melys, et aliis

Et ut perpetue commendaretur memorie ad instanciam parcium decretum fuit istud scriptum hic irrotulari et in rotulo qui uocatur Domesday

Page 295, line 25   From an original writ of 1205 in the British Museum (Wolley Charters, v 27) it appears that the abbot of St Evroult had laid a complaint before the Pope against the abbot of Chester and others for injuries received in relation to the church and manor of Kirkby and the chapel of Woodcote (*sic*)   The nature of the offence is unluckily not indicated.

Page 295, line 29   Thanks to the kindness of Mr Stewart-Brown I am able to amend Ormerod's account of this suit by comparison with the original report in *Chester Plea Roll*, No 3, m 6 The abbot of Basingwerk claimed that the action was one *de iure mixto cum possessione*, but it was decided purely as a possessory case. It was admitted that the last three presentations had been made by the abbot of Chester, but Basingwerk rested its case on the fact that the last of these, that of Ralph de Mold in 1265, was made in time of war and so invalid This was so far admitted that the decision was given for the abbot of Chester on the ground that the last presentation in time of peace, that of Richard de Coudray, had been made by his predecessor abbot Roger (the inversion of Roger and Walter in Ormerod's list of rectors, vol ii p 486, is due to a slip in the Plea Roll) The suit was heard in January-February 1287 At some date before 1310 two-thirds of the demesne tithes of the parish were appropriated to the fabric of the abbey and known as le Bordland Harl MS. 1994, f 8 (265)

Page 296, last line   My argument in favour of a later date than Ormerod's for this quitclaim is somewhat weakened by failure to discover his authority for the presentation of a William as rector by Chester Abbey in 1287 which I accepted in my note Is it possible that he misunderstood the statement made in the suit of that year (see previous addendum) that Basingwerk presented a William on the death of Ralph de Mold, whose disallowance by the abbot of Chester led to the action ?

Page 297, line 16   In Wallasey charters copied by Towneley (*penes* Dr W Farrer) which Mr Irvine dates *c* 1250, he has noted charters mentioning Robert, son of Herbert de Meles, and witnessed by Bertram de Meles and Richard, son of Herbert de Meles In the *Cheshire Sheaf*, Series III No 4038, Fulk de Meoles is described as aged 50 in 1309

Bertram, son of Henry (not John as stated by Ormerod) succeeded (*aet* 22) as next heir to Bertram de Magna Meoles early in 1295 (*Cal Inq* iii No 222)

Page 298, line 36   'The original,' i e the original of the grant of Caldey hundred to Merton

Page 299, line 5   The 10s was included in the grant in 1545 of £19, 10s od to the Dean and Chapter (R S-B).

Page 301, line 26   There is an article on the Friars Preachers of Chester by C F R. Palmer in the *Reliquary*, vol xxiii pp 97-103

Page 302, line 33   Robert de Mold's stewardship ended before 1211 See No 598, which his ~~brother~~ and successor Roger witnesses with Roger the constable (*d* 1211)

Page 304, line 39   The date given by the ' Annals ' is confirmed by an entry of the final concord in Eaton MS 28 (old xxi 5), f 106

Page 305, No 532   The MS at Eaton Hall containing extracts from the Domesday roll gives (f 106) this as a final concord of 42 Hen III , but does not mention the concessions wrung from the abbey

Page 305, line 33   The site of Spon chapel was identified by Mr T Cropper on Spon farm, Spon Green, in Buckley (*Cheshire Sheaf*, III ser vol vi p 10)   It is said to have been built by the abbey on its manor of Bistre (*supra*, p 31) and was in the parish of Mold (Thomas, *Hist of St. Asaph* (1874), 606)

Page 311, Nos 542-43   If Ormerod is correct in his affiliation of Reginald le Brun to the Croxtons, his relationship to the Robert le Brun of No 542 is not clear   A Robert le Brun of Brun or Bruen Stapleford granted Allostock to Robert, son of Picgot, about the same date (*Ancestor*, ii. 140)

Page 318, line 37   That Richard de Wybunbury was sheriff of Cheshire in 1236 appears from a dated document in Orm 1 xxxvi, and in 1239 from a Norley deed in Shakerley (Vernon) MS No 3, f 238   For his holding office in 1244, see No 753a

Page 324, No 565   Mr Irvine tells me that there are deeds extant relating to the family of Mugebroc or Midgebrook.

Page 336, line 31   The authority followed by Ormerod for the existence of a Birkenhead chapel in Wallasey is distrusted by Mr Irvine

Page 339, line 27   Mr Irvine is inclined to identify the Walter Livet of this entry with Walter Linet or Lynnet who was mayor of Chester in 1246 and 1257–60, and would date this grant 1260–65, in the time of abbot Thomas I

Page 340, line 10   There can be little doubt that the ' Ricardus clericus ' of this deed was the Richard Clerk who was mayor of Chester 1261–67

Page 349, line 21   Poimton may possibly stand for Poynton here

Page 350, line 18   Reginald de Lein (seal) occurs 1315 as Reginald de Thleen (Aston deeds)   Does this represent Lleyn, the peninsular part of Carnarvonshire ?

Page 352, line 33   An alternative suggestion might identify Pulle with Bachepool (Orm 1 372, ii 776), but the difficulty in either case is that no separate hamlet of Poole with arable fields seems to be recorded.

Page 356, line 18   See preceding addendum

Page 357, line 26   For a charter of Philip de Newton dated 1244 and another of his son William, see the *Ancestor*, vi 33

Page 364, line 24   Mr Irvine is inclined to regard ' decanus ' as a surname, Dean, but the previous entry tells the other way, unless we suppose an omission   •

Page 368, line 26   Backford Cross is marked on the Ordnance map. The cross itself has vanished

Page 375, line 34   For a perambulation in 1271–72 between Bidston and the abbot's vill of Noctorum (Knocktyrum), see Orm , *Domesday*, 17.

Page 379, line 5   " A ' certain road ' is the road leading from the Mill dam past Spital Station   About 400 yards west of the station on the road is still to be seen the ' old ditch,' which formerly drained Spittell

Green (which before its enclosure began at this point) This ditch runs S S E directly to the head of Crosdale (or Crowsdale), thus completing the encirclement of this piece of waste " (W F I)

Page 380, lines 40-41 " The old rectory of Bebington is now called Bebington Hall Probably the site of this messuage and toft is approximately marked by the modern house called Abbots Grange " (W F I)

Page 381, line 2 " According to the Tithe Map there was formerly a ' field ' which lay to the south of the church, bounded on the east by Bromborough Road, on the west by the road leading from the church to Poulton, and on the south (roughly) by the formerly existing railway from Storeton quarries to the river bank This ' field ' was called in 1840 ' Birches,' a name which is probably a corruption of le Bruche The leper houses can hardly be other than the Spital which formerly stood on the site of Spital Old Hall (see No 91 *supra*) If these identifications are correct, Poulton Millway is probably represented to-day by Bromborough Road At the same time one would expect it to be called Bromborough Millway There was a windmill in Poulton, close to the farm now called Windy Harbour, so Poulton Millway may be represented by the road leading from Bebington church to Poulton, which was on the *west* side of the Birches " (W F I.)

Mr Stewart-Brown clinches the identification of the ' leper houses ' with the Spital by reference to a grant made by Edward I to the ' fratres de domo leprosorum de Bebynton ' quoted in Tanner's *Notitia* under Babington

Page 387, bottom. Ranesfield occurs as Ransfield in an original survey of *c* 1755 among the Mainwaring papers It was a large, formerly arable, field, lying, with another called the Seeches, south of Bromborough Hall grounds

Page 393, line 23 The *inq p. m* of William Lancelyn (I.) shows that he was lord of.⅓ fee of Manley under the lord of Dunham (*Cal Inq* ii 298)

Page 398, line 7 Le Portforthe occurs in the license to the abbot to enclose the waste of Hulse from Ra de Vernon and his wife Joan (*D K* 36 *Rep* 495-96)

Page 401, line 3 The duplication only extends to the quitclaim of the rent Curiously enough the scribe of the chartulary has duplicated the grant of the lordships and gives the rent only in No 758

Page 404, Nos 742-43 Leycester inserts a second Gralam in his pedigree of the Rundchamps of Lostock, but this is doubtful (*Ancestor*, ii 148)

The Wulfric ' man ' of the abbey in Windgates may be the Wulfric de Lache of No 766*a* Windgates was close to Lache Dennis and Crooked Lache (Nos 737, 748) The latter Wulfric was no doubt the Wulfric de Lache who gave a salthouse in Middlewich to Liulf the sheriff (Harl MS 2074, f 87 (190)) In Ormerod's pedigree of Cranage (iii. 127) Wulfric de Lache is identified with Wulfric father (*rectius* grandfather, *ib* 210) of

Liulf, in that of Croxton he is made grandfather of an earlier Liulf and removed to the time of Edward the Confessor and William the Conqueror (see pp 123, 235 above)

Page 405, footnote 2   The scribe of the chartulary does not always distinguish ' n ' and ' u,' but the original charters show that Craulache and Craunache were the two types of the name now spelt Cranage

Page 408, line 1   This charter refutes Mr Bird's scepticism (*Ancestor*, ii 148) as to the existence of a Richard father of Gralam de Rundchamp (Orm 1 670)   Richard married Mabel de Mainwaring (*Journ Chester Arch Soc* N S xiii 98)

Page 411, line 18   There seems to be no other evidence than this charter for Robert, son of Liulf, having had an interest in the Mainwaring moiety of Winnington

Page 427, line 9   Legends on seals   S' H   NETABL' and S' FELICIE BONETABL'

Page 454, line 12   The Chartulary abstract ends   Hec conuencio irrotulatur in Domesday

Page 467, line 10   Alexander le Beel, son of William le Beel and Agnes Arneway, was rector of Holy Trinity Church, Chester (*Journ Chester Arch Soc* N S ii 152-54, a deed misdated 1293 instead of 1283)

CONTENTS

	PAGE
PREFACE . .	(xxv)
ADDENDA ET CORRIGENDA . . .	(xxix)
CHARTERS AND OTHER DOCUMENTS	257-479
THE KITCHEN	257
THE ALMONRY .	260
THE INFIRMARY . .	271
THE FABRIC .	275
CHESTER .	276
STORETON	281
VARIOUS TITHES	282
EXCHANGE WITH COMBERMERE ABBEY	285
BRUERA AND LEA CUM NEWBOLD	287
WEST KIRBY . .	289
HILBRE CELL . .	296
PAROCHIAL RIGHTS . .	299
NESTON CHURCH	302
CHURCH LAWTON . .	309
GOOSTREY . .	310
TILSTONE FEARNALL .	313
WINNINGTON .	315
CHELFORD .	319
PRESTBURY	327
WALLASEY	335
CATTENHALL	337
RHUDDLAN . .	338
THE ABBOT'S CHAMBER, CHESTER CHARTERS	339
THE COOK'S FEE . .	353
NEWTON AND UPTON	356

	PAGE
WOODCHURCH	359
MOSTON	366
CHORLTON AND BACKFORD	368
LITTLE SAUGHALL	372
BIDSTON AND SAUGHALL MASSEY	375
POULTON AND BEBINGTON	376
EASTHAM AND NETHERPOOL	383
IRBY AND THURSTASTON	387
BROMBOROUGH	388
MANLEY AND HELSBY	390
HULSE	394
CRANAGE	400
LACHE DENNIS AND LEES	406
BARNSHAW AND GOOSTREY	416
PLUMLEY	431
IDDINSHALL	434
CHURCH LAWTON	437
SAIGHION	451
COTTON ABBOTS AND WAVERTON	454
CHRISTLETON AND HOOLE, ETC	456
WERVIN	459
PICTON, CRABWALL, AND BLACON	461
CHESTER	464
LANCASHIRE	470
IRELAND	471
ST WERBURGH'S AND STOKE PARISH	473
POYNTON CHAPEL	474
TRENT FERRY	475
RABY FULFORD BRIDGE	477
THE ABBEY CLERK IN THE EXCHEQUER	479
INDEX	481

De Coquina

409. Grant by Sir Hugh de Dutton, kt , to abbot Walter and the convent of a toft in Ness (Wirral)   1228–40.

Hugo de Dottona miles dedit abbati[1] Waltero et conuentui vnum toftum in Nesse super le Houtrake longitudinis x perticarum latitudinis iiii perticarum, liberum ab omni seruicio seculari

This grant carries back the tenure of Ness by the Duttons of Dutton to a date a century earlier than the earliest evidences known to Ormerod (ii 541)   [See Addenda]

410. Quitclaim by Hugh (*rectius* Richard) de Coudray and Matilda his wife, daughter of Geoffrey the cook, to abbot S[imon] of 2s of yearly rent which he used to pay to them for their share of 2 oxgangs of land in Ness, together with the said oxgangs which the abbot of Chester had of the grant of the said Geoffrey   Similar quitclaim by Ellis de Chorlton and his wife Agnes, another daughter of Geoffrey. 1265–91.

[2] Hugo de Coudrey et Matilda vxor eius, filia Galfridi coci, quietos clamauerunt S[ymoni] abbati Cestrie ii solidos annui redditus quos dictus abbas eisdem reddere solebat pro porcione sua de ii bouatis terre in Nesse, vna cum dictis bouatis quas abbas Cestrie habuit ex concessione dicti Galfridi   Item Helyas de Thurlston[3] et Agnes vxor eius, altera filia Galfridi coci, simili modo quietos clamauerunt alios ii solidos annuos de dicta terra vna cum eadem terra, vt patet in sua carta

For Richard de Coudray (whose Christian name the scribe doubtless miswrote under the influence of the preceding deed) and his

[1] Harl MS 2062 inserts Cestrie
[2] This entry, which has no rubricated heading, is placed at the foot of the page   It is incorporated in the text later (No 698) with slight variations of wording, but without correction of the mistake in Richard's name. Ellis is described as venator
[3] *Rectius* Churlston   Chorlton (in Backford par) appears as Cherlston in No 667

father-in-law, the master cook of the abbey in the time of abbot
William Marmion, see Nos 631–6 and Orm ii 384–5 Ormerod
does not notice Geoffrey's gift Geoffrey's sister Agnes married
William, son of Richard de Ness (No 634)

411. Grant by Alice, formerly wife of Gilbert Bloye, to the
kitchen (of the abbey) of an acre of land in (? Little)
Saughall called Middle Acre in We Furlong, which she
formerly held of the abbot, together with a plot called the
kitchener's croft   ? 1265–91

Alacia quondam relicta (*sic*) Gilberti Bloye dedit et quietam
clamauit coquine vnam acram terre in Salhale que Media Acra in
Weforlong' appellatur, quam prius de abbate tenuit, vna cum
placea quadam que dicitur croftum coquinarii.

Alice Blay or Bloye inherited a third part of Little Saughall which
she ultimately gave to the abbey (Nos 678–86) in abbot Simon's
time   For a gift in Chester see No 623*a*

412. Grant by the same to the kitchen of a selion in (? Little)
Saughall next to the acre which she formerly gave   ? 1265–
1291

Alacia relicta quondam Gilberti Blay [1] dedit coquine vnam
sellionem in Salhale propinquiorem acre terre quam ante dedit
coquine ex parte boreali

413. Grant by Roger, son of Roger de Copston, to the abbey of
3 butts near the vill of Shotwick in exchange for as much
land in Shotwick, with easements, and free access with
carts through his garden to the kitchen grange, the road to
be 9 feet wide

Rogerus filius Rogeri de Copston dedit tres [2] buttas iuxta
villam de Schetowyca in escambium pro tanta terra in Schetowyca,
cum pertinenciis et aysyamentis, et liberum introitum et exitum
per medium gardinum suum ad grangiam coquine cum carrectis
quandocunque necessarium fuerit. Et quod illud iter sit nouem
pedum in latitudine

An Adam de Copeston and Henry, chaplain of Copeston, are
mentioned in connexion with Shotwick and the abbey in 10–11 Edw
II (Orm ii 562)

[1] Omitted, and inserted in later hand
[2] duabus in heading here and in Harl 2062

414. Grant by abbot Walter of the church of Shotwick for the augmentation of the convent kitchen for six monks whom he added to the wonted number 1228–40

Abbas Walterus dedit ecclesiam de Schetowyca cum pertinenciis ad incrementum coquine conuentus pro sex monachis quos acreuit ad solitum numerum monachorum.

Licence for the appropriation of the church of Shotwick for their own uses had been given to the monks by bishop William between 1214 and 1223 (No 110)

415. Grant by abbot Roger to the convent, for the increase of its kitchen and for raising the number of monks to 40, of the chapel of Wervin, also of 5 marks to be taken yearly from the vicar of Eastham and 1 mark from the vicar of Bromborough, 4 of which marks to remain to the chamber of the convent to find mattresses and coverlets and 2 to the charities of the convent, viz. 20s for the repayment of the Neston debt and ½ mark for the feast of the Invention of St Stephen (3 Aug), remission of what he should take from the chamber, for the convent's tunics, and of what he used to take from its garden, and grant of 20s to the prior, 2 marks to the infirmary, 10s. to the sacrist, 40d (to be taken annually from Newcastle[-under-Lyme ?]) to the monks celebrating in chapter, and to the altar of St Mary by the choir all that messuage near the cemetery which he bought from Norreys (No. 479). 1240–49.

Abbas Rogerus dedit conuentui, ad incrementum sue coquine et in augmentum numeri monachorum usque ad xl, capellam de Wyruin Item dedit conuentui v marcas annuatim percipiendas de vicario de Estham et vnam marcam de vicario de Bromburg', ita quod iiii de illis marcis remaneant camere conuentus ad inueniendas stragulas et coopertoria, et due caritatibus conuentus, videlicet xx solidos pro restitucione debiti de Neston et dimidiam marcam pro festo Inuencionis sancti Stephani Item remisit quicquid ipse deberet percipere de camera conuentus, ad augmentum tunicarum conuentus, et quicquid solebat percipere de orto conuentus Item dedit priori xx solidos, et infirmarie duas marcas, et sacriste decem solidos, et monachis in capitulo celebrantibus xl denarios de nouo castro annuatim percipiendos , dedit eciam altari sancte Marie iuxta chorum totum illud mesuagium iuxta cimiterium quod emit de Norreys. Quere de hoc inter cartas operis ecclesie   Item quere de terris in Neston inter cartas ecclesie de eadem

De Eleemosinaria

416. Grant by William, son of Simon clerk of Thornton (le Moors), to the almonry of 2½ selions in Elton, namely 6 butts next the land of Richard the marshal, etc , and 2 butts in Whitfield and a ½ selion next Richard the marshal's land, i e. near the boundary of Ince, paying to him 1d. yearly. Late 13th century

Willelmus filius Symonis clerici de Thornton dedit elemosinarie duas selliones et dimidiam in Elton', scilicet sex buttas iacentes iuxta terram Ricardi marescalli et extendentes se uersus bruerium, et duas buttas in campo qui vocatur Wytfelt, et dimidiam sellionem iacentem proximam terre Ricardi marescalli, scilicet iuxta metam de Ynis, reddendo sibi vnum denarium annuum

The relationship between the grantors of lands in Elton to the almonry of the abbey is of some importance for the genealogy of the families of Elton of Elton and Thornton of Thornton Ormerod and Helsby conjecture (ii 16–17) that the William de Thornton father of Hawise the grantor of No 426 was a younger son of Sir Peter de Thornton (d. 1280) and that John de Elton, son of William son of the parson (persone), who granted No 430, was the grandson of a younger son of Thomas de Elton, the first of his house, persone, it is suggested, being " intended for Symone (sic) subsequently mentioned," i e in the chartulary from which they are quoting (ib ii 26, 28). The William son of Simon the clerk of Thornton who is the grantor of Nos 416–24 is described as son of Simon de Elton in the confirmation of his grants by his son John (No 425) The identification of this Simon de Elton, the clerk of Thornton, with the parson of No 430 seems probable and, if correct, adds a name to the list of rectors of Thornton le Moors (Orm. ii 19)

Helsby's long note on the relations of the Thorntons and the Eltons (ib p 26) is ingeniously worked out, but in the fifth line from the end he has by a slip made Matilda, sister of Hawise de Thornton, a daughter of Thomas de Elton instead of William de Thornton (cf p 28)

417. Grant by William, son of Simon clerk of Thornton (le

Moors), to the almonry of 4 butts in Elton, in the Moorfield, paying to him 1d yearly

Willelmus filius Symonis clerici de Thornton dedit elemosinarie iiii buttas in Elton iacentes in campo qui vocatur Morfelt, reddendo sibi vnum denarium annuum

418. Grant by W[illiam], son of Simon clerk of Thornton (le Moors), of 6 seliions in Elton, i e 2½ in Broomfield and Bottomfield, 1 called Flaylont and another called Crougreflont, etc , paying to him 1d yearly

W[illelmus] filius Symonis dedit elemosinarie sex selliones in Elton, scilicet vnam et dimidiam in campo qui dicitur Brom, et vnam in campo qui dicitur Bothum, et vnam que iacet inter terram que fuit Th[ome] et terram que fuit Marg[erie] et extenditur usque ad magnam viam, et vnam selionem que vocatur Flaylont et vnam que vocatur Crougreflont et dimidiam selionem que iacet uersus metam de Ynis, reddendo sibi vnum denarium annuum

The separate naming of so small a field division as the selion, an unusual feature, is said to point to " an open arable field of restricted area" (Gray, *English Field Systems*, 255)   Nine such fields in Elton are mentioned in these charters

419. Grant by William, son of Simon, to the almonry of 1½ seliions in Elton, of which one lay in Longthornfield

Willelmus filius Symonis dedit elemosinarie vnam selionem in Elton in campo qui dicitur Longethorn [1] et dimidiam extensam uersus bruerium

419a. Grant by W[illiam], son of Simon, to the almonry of 3½ seliions in Elton, paying to him 1d. yearly.

W[illelmus] filius Symonis dedit elemosinarie tres selliones et dimidiam in Eltona quarum vna iacet inter selionem Margerie et terram ecclesie, et alia inter terram Thome et terram Margerie, et tercia et dimidia in campo qui vocatur Brom, reddendo sibi vnum denarium annuum

420. Grant by W[illiam], son of Simon, to the almonry of 3 half seliions in Moorhillfield, and 1 seliion called " Roggedelond," and a ½ seliion extending towards the marsh beneath Flaye-

[1] Longothorn, MS   Corrected from the heading

lond selion, and a ½ selion extending to the highway between Ince and Elton near the Stone, paying to him 2*d*. a year.

W[illelmus] filius Simonis dedit elemosinarie 3 dimidias selliones in campo de Morhul cum prato adiacente, et vnam sellionem qui vocatur Roggedelond, et vnam dimidiam sellionem extensam uersus mariscum de subtus sellionem que vocatur Flayelond, et dimidiam sellionem extensam ad magnam viam inter Ynes et Eltonam iuxta petram   Reddendo sibi duos denarios annuos

Though it is not distinctly stated, these selions, like those granted by the same donor in preceding charters, were in Elton   [See Add.]

421. Grant by William, son of Simon (to the almonry), of a selion in Elton called Much Headland between the village and Bottomfield, paying to him 1*d* yearly

(20) *d*]   Willelmus filius Symonis dedit vnam sellionem in Eltona que vocatur Muche Hadlond, iacentem inter villam et campum qui uocatur Bothum,[1] iuxta terram Ricardi de Torperlegh', extensam ad magnam viam uersus domum H. de Eltona, reddendo sibi vnum denarium annuum

Richard de Tarpoiley himself gave land to the abbey (No. 431).

422. Grant by W[illiam], son of Simon, of a selion extending to the almonry selion, and another extending to the marsh, and a half selion in Crowgravefield, etc , paying to him 2*d* yearly.

W[illelmus] filius Simonis dedit elemosinarie vnam sellionem extensam ad sellionem elemosinarie iuxta Stanewaye, et aliam extensam uersus mariscum, et dimidiam sellionem in campo de Crowegraue, et vnam buttam super eandem sellionem extensam, reddendo sibi duos denarios annuos.

423. Grant by W[illiam], son of Simon, to the almonry of a selion and a half in Broomfield, and a selion towards the marsh, paying to him 2*d*. yearly

W[illelmus] filius Symonis dedit elemosinarie vnam sellionem et dimidiam in campo qui uocatur Brom, et vnam sellionem uersus mariscum, reddendo sibi duos denarios annuos

424. Grant by William, son of Simon, to the almonry of 13 selions and 15 butts in Elton, i e 3 selions in Broomfield,

---

[1] The end of this word is doubtful in the MS , but presumably it is the Bothum of No 418

7 butts in Moorfield, 1 selion in Bottom, 1 selion between the land that was Thomas's and Margery's land, 1½ selions called Flahelond', a half selion and 6 butts extending towards the heath, 1½ selions in Crowgrave and 2 extending towards the marsh, a half selion extending towards Spertes Deynes, 2 half selions near Stanewaye, 1 selion called Longthorn, and 2 butts in Whitfield, paying to him 1*d* yearly

Willelmus filius Symonis dedit elemosinarie tres selliones in Eltona in campo qui uocatur Brom, et vii buttas in Morfeld, et vnam sellionem in Bothum, et vnam sellionem iacentem inter terram que fuit Thome et terram Margerie, et vnam sellionem et dimidiam que vocantur Flahelond', et dimidiam sellionem et sex buttas extensas uersus bruerium, et vnam sellionem et dimidiam in Crowegraue, et duas selliones extensas uersus mariscum sine prato, et dimidiam sellionem extensam uersus Spertes Deynes, et duas dimidias selliones iuxta Stanewaye et vnam sellionem que uocatur Longethorn, et duas buttas in Witfeld, reddendo sibi vnum denarium annuum

425. Grant by John, son of William son of Simon de Elton, to the almonry of all lands, etc , which his father gave to it in the teiritoiy of Elton, with a quitclaim of 12*d* rent reserved for them, and of his own gift 2½ selions in Elton

Johannes filius Willelmi filii Symonis de Eltona dedit elemosinarie omnes terras et tenementa et possessiones cum omnibus pertinenciis quas pater suus prius elemosinarie dedit in territorio de Eltona   Insuper quietos clamauit duodecim denarios annui redditus in quibus elemosinaria sibi tenebatur pro predictis   Item dedit duas selliones et dimidiam in Eltona, quarum vna iacet inter terram Rogeri de Trohford' et terram Ricardi filii Roberti et alia uocatur Brodelond in campo de Assefeld, et dimidia sellio extenditur uersus bruerium iacens inter terram elemosinarie et terram Radulphi filii Willelmi

Roger de Trafford may be the landholder of that name who was living in 1306–7 (Orm. ii 45)   Cf No 434.

426. Grant by Hawise, daughter of William de Thornton, of 6½ selions in Elton, viz , one called Dritegravelond and another Crabbelond, 2 half selions near Wallewaye, 3 selions in Aysefeld, and ½ selion in Crabbefurlong, paying to her 1*d* yearly.   ? 1292–*c* 1310

Hawisia filia Willelmi de Thorntona dedit sex selliones et dimidiam in Eltona, quarum vna vocatur Dritegrauelond et alia Crabbelond, et due dimidie selliones iacent iuxta Wallewaye, et tres selliones iacent in Aysefeld, et dimidia sellio in Crabbefurlong, quam Ricardus Gemme quondam tenuit, reddendo sibi vnum denarium annuum

For Hawise de Thornton see Orm ii 26 and above, No 416 *n*

427. Confirmation of the preceding grant by Sir John de Arden (Arderne), kt   ? 1292–c 1308

Johannes de Ardena, miles, dedit et confirmauit sex selliones et dimidiam in Eltona quas Hawisia filia Willelmi de Thorntona contulit, liberans ab omni seruicio

Elton was in the Aldford fee, of which the Ardens or Ardernes were from the 13th century the chief lords (Orm ii 24)   Ormerod (ii 77) identifies the grantor with the first Sir John, but this is quite inconsistent with his date for Hawise de Thornton (*ib* 17)   He is probably the second Sir John, though the third is just possible

428. Licence by Sir John de Arderne, kt , to dig, without the supervision of his bailiffs, 30 cartloads of turves each year in Elton Moss and to carry them to Ince   ? 1292–c 1308

Johannes de Ardena, miles, dedit licenciam et potestatem fodiendi, etc , et capiendi xxxᵗᵃ carectatas turbarum singulis annis quacunque parte in Eltonmos sine visu balliuorum et per terras suas cariandi ad Ynes quocunque tempore anni, et si contingat hoc inundacione aquarum vel alio modo anno aliquo impediri, quod defuit anno sequenti suppleatur   [See Addenda]

429. Grant by Sir Peter de Arderne, kt , to the almonry of a plot in Elton. *c.* 1265–92.

Petrus de Ardena, miles, dedit elemosinarie quamdam placeam in Eltona iacentem inter terram que fuit Willelmi de Thorntona, quam elemosinaria tenet, et vetus fossatum versus brueram, liberam ab omni seruicio

For William de Thornton see above, p 260.

430. Grant by John de Elton, son of William son of the parson, to the almonry of meadowland in Elton

Johannes de Eltona, filius Willelmi filii persone, dedit elemosinarie in Eltona pratum iacens inter Welle et sellionem dicte elemosinarie, et illud pratum quod iacet propinquius iuxta pratum Ade de Hapesford.

See note to No 416

431. Grant by Richard, son of Ralph de Tarporley, to the almonry of half a selion in Elton, paying to him yearly a pair of white gloves

Ricardus filius Radulphi de Torperley dedit elemosinarie dimidiam partem sellionis in Eltona iacentem iuxta le Hoklone et extensam vsque ad brueram versus Thorntonam, reddendo sibi annuatim par albarum cirotecarum.

Richard's land in Elton is mentioned in No 421.

432. Grant by Thomas, son of Alexander, to the almonry of 6 selions in Elton called Seven Lands

Thomas filius Alexandri dedit elemosinarie sex selliones in Eltona que vocantur Seuenelondes, incipientes de subtus le Longethorn et extensas usque ad brueram

433. Grant by Thomas de Elton, son of Ralph de Helsby, to the almonry of a half selion, with a meadow adjacent, in Elton *c* 1268–95

Thomas de Elton filius Radulphi de Hellesby dedit elemosinarie quamdam dimidiam sellionem cum quodam prato adiacente in Eltona in campo versus mariscum de Hellesby, iuxta terram H. de Donuile

The grantor was ancestor of the Eltons of Elton (Orm ii 26).

434. Grant by Thomas (de Elton), son of Ralph (to the almonry) of 4 selions in Elton *c* 1268–95

Thomas filius Radulphi dedit quatuor seliones in Eltona in campo versus Thorntonam, quarum vna extenditur ad terram elemosinarie que vocatur Seuenelond[es], duo iacent inter terram Ricardi clerici de Cestria et terram domine Juliane,[1] quarta iacet inter terram dicti Thome et terram Ade filii Rogeri de Trowefordia

435. Grant by Thomas (de Elton), son of Ralph (to the almonry), of 3 half selions (in Elton). *c.* 1268–95.

---

[1] Corr from domini Juliani. Helsby conjectured the lady Juliana (de Elton) to be wife of the donor

Thomas filius Radulphi dedit iii dimidias seliones iacentes inter sellionem elemosinarie ad crucem et Egmundisheuede.[1]

436. Grant by Ralph the chaplain, son of Hugh de Pulford, to the almonry of 2 selions in Elton

(21)] Radulphus, filius Hugonis de Polford, capellanus dedit elemosinarie duas seliones in Elton, quarum vna iacet proxima terre que fuit Thome de Elton, et alia extenditur uersus crucem super bruerium

Hugh de Pulford, the father of the grantor and of his brother Henry who confirmed his gift (No 437), is doubtless the Hugh, clerk of Pulford, who was the grantor of No 438, and who may perhaps be identified with the Hugh who was rector of Pulford, c 1220 (Orm ii 859)   [See Addenda]

437. Confirmation of the preceding gift by Henry, brother of the grantor, who also confirms a gift of 1½ selions by Walter the almoner's serjeant (No. 439) and quitclaims his homage and service

Henricus filius H[ugonis] de Pulford dedit elemosinarie ii seliones in Eltona quas Radulphus capellanus, frater suus, ante dederat, et aliam selionem et dimidiam propinquiores campo qui vocatur Egmundesheued, quas Walterus seruiens elemosinarii ante dederat, et homagium et seruicium quod idem Walterus sibi pro predictis debuit quieta clamauit

438. Grant by Hugh, clerk of Pulford, to Walter the almoner's serjeant, of 1½ selions in Elton, near the almonry land in Egmundshead, paying to him and his heirs yearly a pair of gloves

Hugo clericus de Pulford dedit Waltero seruienti elemosinarii vnam selionem et dimidiam in Elton propinquiores terre elemosinarie in Egmundesheued, reddendo annuatim sibi et heredibus suis par cirothecarum in festo sancti Johannis Baptiste

See the preceding entry

439. Grant by Walter de Ince,[2] the almoner's serjeant, to the almonry of the land bought by him from Hugh de Pulford (No 438)

Walterus seruiens elemosinarii dedit elemosinarie vnam

---

[1] Egesmondesheued, Harl 2062   [2] Supplied from the heading

selionem et dimidiam in Eltona quas emit de Hugone de Pulford, reddendo annuatim eidem H[ugoni] par cirothecarum in festo sancti Johannis Baptiste

440. Confirmation by earl Ranulf III of 2 oxgangs in Elton which Peter the clerk gave to the monks (No 396), and a toft in the village, and six launds which Ellis held with one of the aforesaid oxgangs, with all the liberties of the vill. 1208–28

Ranulphus comes confirmauit duas bouatas terre in Elton, quas Petrus clericus monachis dedit cum omnibus pertinenciis, et vnam toftam in medio predicte ville, et vi landas quas Helias tenuit cum vna predictarum bouatarum, cum omnibus libertatibus predicte ville

For Peter, clerk to eail Ranulf, who founded the family of Thornton (or le Rotei) of Thornton, see above, p. 166

441. Quitclaim by Philip de Orreby of half a crannoc of wheat and half of barley which were rendered to him yearly for common in the wood of Alvanley 1216–c 1229

Philippus de Orreby quietum clamauit dimidium cranocum [1] siliginis et dimidium ordei que sibi annuatim reddebantur pro communa habenda in bosco de Aluadeleya.

John Fitz-Alan, who as superior lord confirmed the elder Philip de Orreby's purchase of Alvanley (Orm ii 75), succeeded his brother William as lord of Clun and Oswestry in Shropshire and Dunham on the Hill in Cheshire in 1216 The grantor must be the justiciar, who resigned his office at Easter 1229, for his son and namesake predeceased him (ib.).

442. Grant by Thomas le Tinker and Beatrice his wife, for the almonry, of a plot in Northgate Street, Chester, with its croft, rendering to the abbot $4\frac{1}{2}d$ yearly Cf No 451

Thomas le Tinker et Beatrix vxor eius dederunt vnam placeam terre in Northgatestrete cum suo crofto, iacentem inter terram Symonis Spendeloue et terram Aubrey sororis dicte Beatricis in aumentum elemosinarie, reddendo abbati iiii denarios annuos et obolum

443. Grant by William the cutler (cf Nos 360–1), for the almonry, of all his land outside Northgate, rendering $9d$ yearly to the abbot Before 1291.

[1] A varying measure Crannocs of 2 and 4 bushels occui

Willelmus cultellarius dedit in aumentum elemosinarie totam terram suam (extra portam aquilonalem iacentem) inter terram Johannis de le Ruyding et terram Agnetis Pele, reddendo annuatim abbati ix denarios ad festum apostolorum Petri et Pauli

444. Grant by Ralph Trane, for the almonry, of a plot outside Northgate, paying 12*d* yearly to the abbot   Before 1291.

Radulphus Trane dedit in aumentum elemosinarie quandam placeam terre extra portam aquilonalem, iacentem inter terram quondam Johannis le quaireyer et terram quam Johannes de Bache de monachis tenuit, reddendo annuatim xii denarios abbati in festo sancti Martini

445. Grant by Ralph Norman, for the almonry, of all his land outside Northgate, with garden and croft, paying 9*d* yearly to the abbot   Before 1291

Radulphus (filius Johannis) [1] Norman dedit in aumentum elemosinarie totam terram suam extra portam aquilonalem cum gardino et crofto, iacentem inter terram quondam Johannis fabri et terram Eduse Maluodan, reddendo annuatim ix denarios abbati in festo sancti Martini

Ralph Norman made a grant to another Chester citizen in 1292–3 (*Journ Chester Arch. Soc*, N S, x p 48).

446. Grant by Richard, son of Richard (Saracen), to Alan de Trafford of certain land of his in Northgate Street lying over against the churchyard of St. Werburgh next the market place, paying yearly 2½*d* as Landgable and 12*d* to himself and his heirs

Ricardus filius Ricardi dedit Alano de Trovford quandam terram suam in Northgatestrete, iacentem contra portam cimiterii sancte Werburge propinquiorem foro, reddendo annuatim ii denarios et obolum de Longable ad Ascensionem Domini et xii denarios sibi et heredibus ad Natale Domini et ad Natiuitatem sancti Johannis Baptiste per equales porciones

For the Traffords of Bridge Trafford see Orm ii 43   For Landgable, p. 255

447. Grant by William, son of Alan de Trafford (to the convent), of the land in Northgate Street bought by his father from Richard, son of Richard Saracen (No 446), paying yearly 2½*d* for landgable and 12*d* to the said Richard or his heirs Before 1291 ?

[1] The fuller form is given in the heading.

Wıllelmus fılıus Alanı de Trovford dedıt totam terram suam quam pater suus emıt de Ricardo fılıo Rıcardı Saracenı ın North-gatestrete, reddendo annuatım ad longable ıı denarıos et obolum ad Ascensıonem Domını et dıcto Rıcardo uel heredıbus suıs xıı denarıos ad Natale Domını et ad Natıuıtatem sanctı Johannıs Baptıste per equales porcıones

448. Confirmation by Wılliam Patrıck (of Malpas) of an exchange between hıs relatıve Humphrey (de Bunbury), kt , and the monks by whıch he gave them, for Peckforton and 4 ox-gangs ın (Lıttle) Stanney, the mıll of Stanney [1] and Alrıches-holm wıth ıts appurtenances ın marsh and meadow on the sıde of Stanney and on the sıde towards the Mersey ; also the whole meadow and marsh and the stream as ıt runs ınto the Mersey   ? Before 1184   [See Addenda]

Wıllelmus Patrıcıus confirmauıt escambıum Umfrey cognatı sui, mılıtıs, quod fecıt cum monachıs, dans eıs pro Pecfortona et ıııı bouatıs ın Staneya molendınum de Staneya et Alrıchesholm, et quıcquıd pertınet ad eam ın marısco et prato ex parte uersus Staney, et ex altera uersus Merse , dans ecıam totum pratum et totum marıscum et totam aquam sıcut decurrıt ın Merse

The Patrıcks were lords of a moıety of the barony of Malpas, and theır share ıncluded Peckforton, a manor acquıred by the abbey from an under-tenant of theır ancestor Robert Fıtz-Hugh ın the last years of the ıı th century (above, pp 19, 34)   Its acquısıtıon was naturally an object of ambıtıon to the lords of the adjoınıng manor of Bunbury, who were related to the Patrıcks.   Humphrey [de Bunbury], who achıeved thıs by an exchange wıth land ın hıs Wırral manor of Lıttle Stanney, whıch ıs here confirmed by the superıor lord, Wıllıam Patrıck, may safely be ıdentıfied wıth the Umfrıdus mıles de Boneburı who, wıth hıs son Wıllıam, wıtnessed a deed whıch Mr Jeayes dates *temp.* Stephen–Henry II (*Cat of Derbyshıre Charters,* 530), and Wıllıam Patrıck must be the lord of Malpas who dıed ın 1184 (*Ann Cestr* 32) The pedigree of the Bunburıes ın Ormerod (ıı 395, 253), ıt ıs true, contaıns no Humphrey at thıs date, and makes Wıllıam, who was lord of Bunbury, *temp* Rıchard I and father of a Humphrey, who dıed wıthout ıssue, a son of Henry, who ıs placed ın the reıgn of Stephen. It would seem that a generatıon has been omıtted   Thıs ıs confirmed by a charter of Humphrey II , who refers to Humphrey hıs grand-father (Harl MS 2074, f 139 (235) , cf Orm ı 602).   The early date

[1] At some unknown date Lıttle Stanney mıll came agaın ınto the possessıon of the Bunbury famıly and was bought wıth theır Stoke and Stanney estate about the mıddle of last century by the Dean and canons of Chester, thus at last revertıng to St Werburgh's (*ex ınform ,* W F Irvıne)

assigned by us to the exchange is supported by the fact that Alrichesholm was in the possession of the abbey before 1209 (No 307)

The presumption that Alrichesholm (Aldricheholm in the Whalley Coucher Book) is the Holm of Nos 449–50, and therefore represented by the existing Holm House farm, which occupies the position roughly indicated in the present charter, is converted into practical certainty by the inclusion of " (Little) Stanney cum le Holm " in an arbitration between the abbey and the rector of Stoke about the end of the 13th century (No 888)   Holme House farm is now in Eddisbury hundred, not in Wirral, but it is still partly in Stoke parish, and the westward loop of the Gowy, the boundary between the hundreds, in which it lies, no doubt represents an artificial deviation of the main channel of the stream and of the hundred boundary   A possible explanation of the deviation may be found in discontent on the part of the monks with the settlement of 1279 (No 308), which left the road from (Alriches)holm to the abbey mills of Ince, further down stream, to run partly over Stanlaw land   The deviation put Holm on the Ince side   It may not, however, have been made by the abbey itself   The inclusion of Holm House in the adjoining manor of Thornton le Moors (in Eddisbury hd) can hardly be explained except by an alienation from the abbey between 1279 and the Dissolution, and the deviation may have been effected by its new lords

In dealing with this problem I have been much helped by Mr Fergusson Irvine's great topographical knowledge

449. Quitclaim by William de Holm of all his land in Holm (in Wirral [1]), which he formerly held of the monks.

Willelmus de Holm quietam clamauit totam terram suam in Holm quam de monachis quondam tenuit

450. Grant by abbot Simon and the convent, for the increase of the almonry, of the whole land of le Holm near Ince Mills with approvements, as Tarvin Water (Gowy) and a ditch enclose it   1265–91

Abbas Symon et conuentus dederunt ad incrementum elemosinarie totam terram de le Holm iuxta molendina de Ynes cum approuiamentis, sicut eam aqua de Teruein et fossatum includit (*sic*)

Among the original charters seen by Randle Holme was   " carta de Holme-Hows data elemosine per abbatem Symonem " (Harl MS. 1994, f 8 (265)

[1] From the heading

451. Grants by abbot Simon and the convent of the pensions
from the churches of Christleton, Astbuiy, and Handley
(cf No 399), for the increase of the chamber, of the house
of William de Trafford, etc , to the almonry (with remission
of 3s 4½d. from 4 houses outside Northgate (Nos 442–5)),
of 1 mark from a house over against the abbey gate to the
infirmary, of 4s to the kitchen from the 8s. which the
kitchener was bound to pay to the abbot from the chapel of
Wervin, and the remaining 4s to the refectory   1265–91

Abbas Symon et conuentus dederunt ad incrementum camere [f 24
pensiones de Cristelton, videlicet xxiii solidos, de Asteburi xii
solidos, de Hanleye 1 marcam   Item dederunt elemosinarie
domum Willelmi de Trovford et terram Symonis Breuitoris extra
portam aquilonalem, et xii denarios annuos de quadam domo in
Ynes quam capellanus tenere solebat, et eciam quandam placeam
terre in Ynes propinquiorem elemosinarie quam Hugo Kenil quondam tenuit   Item remiserunt iii solidos annuos et iiii denarios et
obolum de quatuor domibus extra portam aquilonalem, scilicet
Willelmi cultellarii, Radulphi Norman, Radulphi Trane et Willelmi
le Tinker pro terra Willelmi de Walton   Item dederunt infirmarie
vnam marcam de domo contra portam abatie, et coquine conuentus
pro festo Trinitatis iiii solidos de illis octo quos coquinarius abbati
soluere tenebatur de capella de Wiruin, reliquos uero iiii refectorio

INFIRMARIA

452. Grant by Guy, son of Hamon, to William of the cellar, and
Margaret his wife, of certain land of his in the North street
of Chester, paying to Guy and his heirs 4s. yearly   c. 1240–
1260

Guydo filius Hamonis dedit W[illelmo] [1] de celario et
M[argarete] [1] vxori sue quandam terram suam in vico aquilonali
Cestrie.   Reddendo inde annuatim Guydoni et heredibus suis iiii
solidos pro omni seruicio

The grantoi witnessed a charter of about 1240 (*Journ Chestei
Arch Soc* N S. x p 22), and another about twenty yeais later (*ib*
p 32)   See also No 637

453. Confirmation by Guy, son of Hamon, of the bequest to the
abbey of the land transferred in No 452

[1] Extended from the heading (Marg). Might be Margeria

Guydo filius Hamonis concessit et confirmauit legacionem terre
que quondam fuit sua quam Willelmus de celario legauit cum
corpore suo monachis Cestrie, que iacet in vico aquilonali, reddendo tamen sibi et heredibus suis iiii solidos annuatim

454. Quitclaim to the abbey by Robert le Mercer and Margaret
his wife, formerly wife of William of the cellar, of all right
and claim in the land bequeathed to the monks by the said
William (No 453), Margaret swearing on the relics not to
contravene this quitclaim and the fact being enrolled on
the king's rolls   For this the monks gave them 8 marks.

Robertus le Mercer et Marg[areta] vxor sua que quondam fuit
vxor W[illelmi] de celario quietum clamauerunt abbati et conuentui omne ius et clamium quod habuerunt in terra quam
W[illelmus] de celario eis legauit, necnon predicta Marg[areta]
tactis sacrosanctis iurauit quod nunquam contra istam quietam
clamacionem veniet per se uel per alium, et hoc irrotulatum fuit
in rotulis regis   Pro hac quieta clamacione monachi dederunt eis
viii marcas

The grantor is probably the Robert le Mercer who was often sheriff
and mayor of Chester from 1251 to 1294 (Orm ii 207, *Journ Chester
Arch Soc*, N S x 24)

455. Quitclaim by Robert le Mercer, junior, of the land which
he held of the monks, near the land of William de Newton
in the North street   Cf No 640

Robertus le Mercer iunior quietam clamauit terram quam de
eis tenuit, iacentem iuxta terram Willelmi de Neuton in vico
aquilonali

456. Obligation of Robert le Mercer for a yearly payment of 14s
for the land in the North street formerly belonging to
W[illiam] of the cellar and his wife Marg[aret], which he
held of the monks

Robertus le Mercer fuit obligatus in xiiii solidis soluendis
annuatim monachis Cestrie pro terra in vico aquilonali quam de
eis tenuit, que quondam fuit W[illelmi] de celario et Marg[arete]
vxoris sue

457. Quitclaim by Robert le King and Marg[aret] his wife of all
right in the land which William of the cellar bequeathed to
the monks, for which they received 40s.

Robertus le Kyng et Marg[areta] vxor eius quietum clamauerunt totum ius et clamium quod habuerunt in terra quam W[il-
lelmus] de celario monachis legauit, vnde xl solidos receperunt

Robert le King was possibly a third husband of Margaret, formerly
wife of William of the cellar

458. Grant by John, son of Nicholas son of Herbert, of 3s to be
taken yearly for the infirmary from land in Ironmonger
Street [See Addenda]

Johannes filius Nicholai filii Herberti dedit iii solidos annuatim
percipiendos infirmarie de terra que iacet in Irnmonger strete inter
terram que fuit Ade de Paris et terram Hospitalis sancti Johannis.

459. Grant by William Clerk, mayor of Chester, of all his land
lying outside Northgate to the infirmary ? 1244

Willelmus clericus maior ciuitatis Cestrie dedit totam terram
suam infirmarie, iacentem extra portam aquilonalem iuxta terram
quam Robertus Bras monachis dedit

William Clerk was mayor about 1244 (*Journ Chester Arch Soc*,
N S x, 26, with too late a date), and according to Canon Morris (*Chester*,
p. 575) in 1251. Cf No 390

460. Grant by Isoult, formerly wife of Suan the clerk, to the
infirmary of her land outside the Northgate (cf No. 360).

Ysolda quondam vxor Suani clerici dedit terram suam extra
portam aquilonalem cum gardino et crofto infirmarie

461. Grant by Lucas, son of Simon, of his land outside the
Northgate

Lucas filius Symonis dedit terram suam extra portam aquilonalem, iacentem inter terram Hugonis fabri et terram Alani filii
Eilwini

462. Quitclaim by Simon, son of Robert the baker, of half his
land outside the Northgate

Symon filius Roberti Pistoris quietam clamauit medictatem
terre sue extra portam aquilonalem versus aquilonem, iacentem
iuxta terram Thome incisoris.

463. Grant by Thomas, son of Robert the chamberlain, to the
infirmary of 6d of annual rent on the feast of St Werburgh

C

in the summer to be taken from the land which Felicia de Paris held of him in the street over against the abbey gate.

Thomas filius Roberti camerarii dedit infirmarie vi denarios annui redditus in festo sancte Werburge, percipiendos in estate [1] de terra quam Felicia de Parys de se tenuit in vico contra portam abbathie

464. Quitclaim by John le Quarrey[e]r (No. 444) of a plot of land outside the Northgate with 2 selions adjoining, paying yearly to the abbot 6*d*   Before 1291

Johannes le quarrey[e]r quietam clamauit quamdam placeam terre latitudinis xxv pedum extra portam aquilonalem cum duabus selionibus adiacentibus, iacentem inter terram eiusdem fabrice et domum dicti Johannis, reddendo annuatim abbati vi denarios in festo apostolorum Petri et Pauli.

465. Quitclaim by Leuka, daughter of Anketil, to Gilbert, son of Geoffrey de Spalding, and his (? her) sister Guinild, of a messuage outside the Northgate, etc , and the messuage of Bache with all the land adjacent and a furlong near the churchyard of St Thomas.

Leuka filia Anketilli quiete clamauit Gilberto filio Galfridi de Spalding et Guinilde sorori sue quoddam mesuagium extra portam aquilonalem iacens inter terram Ricardi filii Martini et [terram] Roberti filii Matilde, et mesuagium de Bache cum tota terra adiacente et cultura iuxta cimiterium sancti Thome

The similarity of the bounds, etc., in the grant by Leuka's sister, Geva below (No 467), would suggest a simple confirmation of this, were it not that the grantee is there Gilbert, son of Richard   It would perhaps be rash on the strength of a like similarity of bounds to suggest the identity of the Gilbert Gast of No 466 with the Gilbert, son of Geoffrey of Spalding, of the charter before us   A Gilbert de Spalding occurs in a deed dated by Mr Irvine *c* 1240 (*Journ Chester Arch Soc* , N S x p 22)

Bache was an early possession of the abbey (Orm. ii. 773)   The chapel of St Thomas stood outside the Northgate (Orm. i 352)   It does not perhaps appear so early as Ormerod asserts (see above, p 132).

466. Grant by Gilbert Gast and Gunwara, his wife, to the fabric

[1] *Sic.* No doubt for in festo s. W in estate percipiendo» The inversion is found also in Harl 2062

of the abbey of all their land outside the Northgate, renewed
by Gunwara after her husband's death

Gilbertus Gast et Gunwara vxor eius dederunt fabrice ecclesie
totam terram suam extra portam aquilonalem, iacentem inter
terram que fuit Ricardi filii Martini et terram Johannis filii Matilde
Hanc terram Gunwara post mortem Gilberti iterum dedit fabrice
cuius carta iungitur cum prima

Gunwara, according to Ormerod, was the mother of Geoffrey the
cook who had a grant of the convent kitchen in fee from abbot William
Marmion, between 1226 and 1228 (Orm ii 384), but cf No 609 and
No 633 n   After Gilbert's death Gunwara granted other lands in
the same quarter to Nicholas de Frodsham (No 632)   Ormerod dates
this later grant about 1190, but that is almost certainly too early.

467. Quitclaim by Geva, daughter of Anketil, to Gilbert, son of
Richard (?) of lands lying outside the Northgate and the
land of Bache with a copse and a furlong near the churchyard of St. Thomas

Geua filia Anketilli quietum clamauit Gilberto filio Ricardi
terras iacentes extra portam aquilonalem inter terram R[icardi]
filii Martini et R[oberti] filii Matilde, et terram de Bache cum
virgulto et cultura iuxta cimiterium sancti Thome.

See note on No. 465

468. Grant by Robert de Waley (Wallasey), son of Alan de
Waley, of an oxgang of land in Kirkby in Waley (Wallasey)
with messuages and croft, etc.

Robertus de Waleya filius Alani de Waleya dedit vnam [f 25 (22
bouatam terre in Kirkebi in Waleya cum mesuagiis et crofto, cum
omnibus pertinenciis

An Alan de Waley, perhaps the father of the grantor, witnesses
charters between 1184 and 1217 (Orm i 36, 54)   The relation of
this Alan to William, son of Richard de Waley, who gave half the
advowson of the church of Kirkby in Waley to Chester Abbey between
1162 and 1182 (No 595) cannot be clearly determined, but they were
of the same family (Orm ii 472, 476). [See Addenda]

469. Grant by Gilbert de Barnston of an oxgang of land in
Bainston (in Wirral).

Gilbertus de Berleston dedit vnam bouatam terre in Berleston
cum omnibus pertinenciis, liberam ab omni seruicio

The tithes of Barnston had been given to the abbey at or shortly after its foundation by Ralph, son of Ermewine (p 19)   Ormerod (ii. 529), does not mention the grantor of the present entry in his account of the Barnston family

470. Grant in fee farm by abbot Thomas (II) and the convent to H[ugh] de Brickhill and M[   ] his wife, of certain land of theirs in Fleshmonger Lane for 4s. yearly   c. 1293–1320

Thomas abbas et conuentus ad perpetuam firmam tradiderunt H[ugoni] de Bricch[ill] et M[   ] vxori sue quandam terram suam in Flesmongerlone pro iiii solidis annuis ad festum natiuitatis sancti Johannis Baptiste et ad festum sancti Martini per equales porciones soluendis, et ad horum solucionem predicti H[ugo] et M[   ] obligauerunt terram illam et omnes suas extra portam aquilonalem districcioni abbatis

Hugh de Brickhill was many times mayor of Chester between 1272 and 1312 (Orm i 207–8)   The family doubtless came from Brickhill in Buckinghamshire, which had belonged to the earls of Chester from the Conquest (D B , i. 147)   Fleshmonger Lane seems to have been the old name of Newgate Street (Orm i 187).

471. Grant by abbot Roger and the convent to Hugh de Helsby and M[   ] his wife, of land with houses in Bridge Street which Richard de Kingsley bequeathed to them, paying 18s yearly.   1240–49

Rogerus abbas et conuentus dederunt Hugoni de Helysbi et M[   ] vxori sue quandam terram cum edificiis in Brugestrete quam Ricardus de Kyngesleye eis legauit, iacentem inter terram Roberti filii Thurstani et terram [   ] [1] filii Gilberti filii Petri, reddendo annuatim xviii solidos ad Anunciacionem beate Marie et ad Natiuitatem sancti Johannis Baptiste et ad festum sancti Michaelis per equales porciones

Richard de Kingsley, from whom the abbey derived the property (No 472), may have been Sir Richard de Kingsley, the last of the direct line of that family, who died between 1241 and 1244 (Orm ii 88–90).   Robert, son of Thurstan, occurs in Chester deeds of the second quarter of the 13th century (Journ Chester Arch Soc , N S x 20, 26) and perhaps earlier if he is the Robert, son of Thurstan Duc of another deed (ib 18).

[1] Christian name omitted in MS

472. Bequest by Richard de Kingsley of the land conveyed in No 471   ? 1240–44

Ricardus de Kyngesleya dedit cum corpore suo totam terram suam in Bruggestrete, iacentem inter terram Roberti filii Thurstani et terram que fuit Ranulphi rotarii

473. Grant by John Blunt of Chester of land lying between the land of H Waterman and the churchyard of St Werburgh in width, descending from the churchyard towards the Eastgate as far as the land of Fulk de Orreby in length, paying to him 3s yearly by the hand of the master of the fabric of the church

Johannes Blund de Cestre dedit terram iacentem inter terram H. Aquarii et cimiterium sancte Werburge in latitudine, descendentem de predicto cimiterio uersus portam orientalem vsque ad terram Fulconis de Orreby in longitudine, reddendo annuatim sibi iii solidos per magistrum fabrice ecclesie

A John Blound was sheriff of Chester in 1310 and mayor in 1314 and 1317, in which latter year he died during his term of office (Orm i 208)   But if the Fulk de Orreby referred to was the justice who gave his name to Fulk Stapleford and died in 1261 (*Ann Cestr* 78) and if he must be supposed to have been living at the date of the grant, the identification of the grantor with the mayor becomes unlikely. A John Blund witnessed a deed *c* 1244 (*Journ Chester Arch Soc*, N S x p 26)   Earlier, Master John Blund was official of Chester (*ib* xiii 97)

474. Release by Alice, daughter and heir of John Blunt, of the rent of 3s paid by the abbot and convent for the land given to them by her father.

Alicia filia et heres Johannis Blund dedit iii solidos annuos quos abbas et conuentus sibi soluere tenebantur de terra quam pater eius eis dedit.

A Mariot, daughter of John Blond, occurs 1279–80 (*Journ Chester Arch Soc*, N.S x p 38)

475. Grant by Roald, son of Odo, of half his land in Fulchard's Lane, next the land which Ranulf de Frodsham held

Roaldus filius Odonis dedit medietatem terre sue in Fulchardeslone, proxime (*sic*) terre quam Ranulphus de Frodesham tenuit.

If Roald's son Alan (No 477) is the Alan, son of Roald, of a deed which is probably earlier than the date (c 1225) assigned to it in *Journ Chester Arch Soc*, N S x p 18, this grant cannot be much later than 1200

476. Grant by Roald, son of Odo, of his land lying between the land of Hawise de Hoole and the land which was Roger de Warwick's

Roaldus filius Odonis dedit terram suam iacentem inter terram Hawisie de Hole et terram que fuit Rogeri de Warewic'

477. Confirmation by Alan, son of Roald, of his father's grants to the abbey (Nos 475–6)

Alanus filius Roaldi dedit et confirmauit donaciones terrarum quas pater suus ante dedit monachis, scilicet teriam que iacet inter terram Hawisie de Hole et terram que fuit Rogeri de Warewic', et terram que iacet in Fulchardeslone proximam terre quam Radulphus [1] de Frodesham tenuit

478. Grant by Guy, bishop of Bangor, that if goods stolen from the lands or tenants of St Werburgh be found in the parishes of his diocese and the detainers do not restore them to the messengers of the abbey at the instance of the clergy of the said diocese, they shall be excommunicated and their church placed under interdict pending full restitution   1177–c 1190

Wido Bangorensis episcopus concessit et carta sua confirmauit quod si quando bona ecclesie sancte Werburge furto ablata a terris uel ab hominibus suis in parochiis sue diocesis inueniantur nec ad instanciam clericorum dicte diocesis eorum detentores nuncus dicte ecclesie ea non restituerint, anathematizentur, et ecclesia cuius ipsi parochiam fuerint interdicatur donec omnia fuerint restituta

A similar concession was obtained from Reinei, bishop of St Asaph (No 93)

479. Grant by Norreys, son of Hugh de Preston of all his land in Chester by the churchyard of St Werburgh, which land abbot Roger (1240–49) assigned to the altar of St Mary by the choir   (No 415)

Norreys filius Hugonis de Preston dedit et quiete clamauit totam terram [2] suam in Cestria iuxta cimiterium sancte Werburge

[1] Ranulphus in No 475
[2] Mesuagium altaris S Marie in the heading

Hanc teriam abbas Rogerus altari sancte Marie iuxta chorum assignauit   Quere de hoc inter cartas caritatum, abbas Thomas, etc [1]

480. Quitclaim by abbot Thomas (I) and the convent to the abbot of Rocester of 5s a year which they received for the demesne tithes of Rocester (No 119), in exchange for the land which the abbey of Rocester held in Fleshmonger Lane (*i e* Newgate Street), Chester, paying yearly 2s to Sir W[illiam] de Boydell   1249–65

Abbas Thomas et conuentus quiete clamauerunt abbati Roucestrie in perpetuum v solidos annuos quos perceperunt pro decimis dominicis manerii de Roucestria, vnde abbas de Roucestria et conuentus eiusdem eis dederunt totam terram suam quam habuerunt de dono Johannis vicarii de Roucestria in Flesmonger-lane, iacentem inter terram que fuit Hugonis filii Osberni et terram que fuit Matilde vxoris Willelmi Lombc, reddendo annuatim domino W[illelmo] de Boydel ii solidos   Si uero abbas Roucestrie terram illam non warentizauerit, liceat abbati Cestrie edificia a se uel a suis imposita penitus asportare et v predictos solidos redibere

The demesne tithes of Rocester in Staffordshire were among those given to the abbey at its foundation by earl Hugh I (above, p 17)

481. Quitclaim by Sir John Boydell, kt , of the rent reserved in the preceding charter.   1270–1309

Dominus Johannes Boydel miles dedit et quiete clamauit ii solidos annuos quos ante percepit de quadam terra sua in Fles-mongerlone, iacentem inter terram Matilde Lombe et terram que fuit Hugonis filii Osberti.

482. Confirmation by earl Hugh (II.) of a gift of half a mark yearly by Randulf de Kingsley.   1154–81

H[ugo] comes Cestrie confirmauit donacionem Randulf[i] de Chingesleye de dimidia marca annuatim soluenda ad festum sancti Marci (April 25) et inde plegius fuit et balliuis suis precepit vt eum si necesse esset ad solucionem compellerent

483. Grant by the lady Mabel de Beck' of ½ mark yearly from the mill of " Wodinton," etc , and confirmation by Roger, earl of Clare   1152–73.

[1] No 393

Domina Mabilia de Beck' dedit dimidiam marcam annuatim persoluendam, scilicet in octauis Pasche iiii solidos de molendino de Wodinton, et xxii denarios de censa Willelmi de Pohenhale et x denarios de censa Azi   Rogerus comes de Clare donacionem hanc confirmauit

The grantor was probably the Mabel de Bec who held a small Norfolk estate in 1166 and whose heir was married to Robert Fitz-Humphrey (*Red Book of Exchequer*, i 402 , cf Pipe R Soc., No 12, p 21, No 18, p 31, and No 35, p 48)   The Norfolk land was held of the crown and so cannot have been " Wodinton," which has so far defied identification   It was probably in the east of England, and the abbey doubtless owed the gift to the influence of its over-lord, who was a nephew of earl Ranulf II , and himself a benefactor (p 140)   The half-mark was assigned before 1194 to the upkeep of the fabric of the abbey (No 487)

484. Grant by Robert de Coudray and Matilda his wife of the tithe of all the multure of the mill of Worleston (cf No 496) *c.* 1216–50.

Robertus de Coudrey et Matildis vxor eius dederunt decimam tocius moliture molendini de Werleston

Matilda, who was heiress of Worleston, survived her husband and afterwards married Hugh de Longford   Ormerod (iii 354) strangely ascribes the above gift to " her first widowhood "   Robert was one of the witnesses of Ranulf III 's charter to his barons in 1215–1216 (p 106)

485. Confirmation by earl H[ugh] (II.) of the gift by Robert Sauvage of an oxgang of land in Storeton, which Wulfric used to hold   [1154–81]

H[ugo] comes Cestrie confirmauit donacionem Roberti Sauvage de vna bouata terre in Stortone, quam Wlfricus tenebat

This brief abstract, in conjunction with that which follows, may possibly clear up a difficulty which has greatly exercised Cheshire genealogists. Storeton was granted with Puddington and (according to the plea mentioned below, though not expressly conveyed in the charter) the bailliwick of the forest of Wirral by earl Ranulf II.[1] to Alan Sauvage (Salvagius or Sylvester)   In a plea to a *quo warranto* in 1362 Sir William Stanley in claiming the privileges of the master forestership of Wirral stated his descent from Alan Sauvage, to whom he assigns a son Ralph (Radulphus) and a grandson Alexander, son

[1] Harl MS 2079 f 7*d* (old 15)   The Stanley plea and Ormerod (ii 445) ascribe it to Ranulf I , but the witnesses show that it was granted by his son.

and heir of Ralph, who left no male issue   One of his two daughters dying without issue, the other carried the inheritance to her husband, Sir Thomas de Baumville, whose grand-daughter and co-heiress married John de Stanley (Orm ii 355)   The third step of this pedigree is, however, contradicted by a charter of earl Hugh II , issued between 1170 and 1181, in which he bestows upon Alexander, the tutor (*magister*) of his son, afterwards earl Ranulf III (*b* 1170, *Ann. Cestr* 26), Annabella " filiam filii Alani Salvagii," with her whole inheritance, viz Storeton and Pudington (*ib* ii 446)   Ormerod's attempt to reconcile this contradiction by the assumption that the " Alexander filius et heres ipsius Radulphi " of the plea is merely a loose way of describing the son-in-law of Ralph, is not altogether satisfactory   If, as the abstract before us seems to suggest, the real name of Alan's son was not Ralph but Robert, a more plausible explanation of the error in the plea is possible   The next charter implies that Alexander the tutor was sometimes described as Alexander, son of Ralph, and at a distance of two centuries this may easily have caused a confusion between his father and the father of his wife with whom he obtained the estate   See also *Chesh Sheaf*, 3rd ser., No 4529

A further difficulty, of which no satisfactory solution at present offers itself, is the association of Puddington with Storeton in the grant to Alan Sauvage and in earl Hugh's charter to Alexander the tutor   Puddington was held by Hamon de Massy in 1086, and the barons of Dunham were practically always regarded as chief lords of the manor   There are, however, several inquisitions of the 15th and 16th centuries in which it is said to be held of the manor of Storeton (Orm. ii. 558)   As the grant to Alan Sauvage was made by earl Ranulf II., it may have been one of his high-handed interferences with the rights of the weaker in the time of the anarchy

486. Grant by abbot Hugh and the convent to Alexander, son of Ralph, of an oxgang of land in Storeton which Robert Sauvage gave to them, paying yearly to the fabric of the church 12*d*   1208–26

Abbas Hugo et conuentus dederunt Alexandro filio Radulphi vnam bouatam terre in Stortona quam Robertus Sauuage eis dedit, reddendo annuatim fabrice ecclesie xii denarios ad festum sancti Martini

See note to No 485   Alexander, son of Ralph, witnessed a charter of earl Ranulf III , between 1208 and 1211 (Orm i 38)

487. Assignment by abbot Robert and the convent to the fabric of the abbey of the demesne tithes of Rocester, Leek, Macclesfield, Weaverham, Frodsham, Overpool, Over,

Hawarden, Eaton, Eastham, half the tithe of the demesne
of Dutton and two-thirds of that of Preston (by Dutton,
see No 494), the demesne tithes of Worleston (?), " Woder-
stone," Bebington, Bromhall (p 20), Weston (upon Trent),
and Maltby in Lindsey, and a croft in " Wentala," and
others which Edwin, son of Outred, and Andrew Catchpoll
gave, and 8d. from a shop before the abbey gate, and two-
thirds of the tithe of Clotton Mill (p 19), and the church of
Bebington, and half the church of Wallasey, and 10s yearly
from (Chipping) Campden, and whatever can be obtained
from its church (p 138), and half a mark from " Wodynton "
(No 483), and the demesne tithe of Sotterley (co Suffolk,
cf. No 888) and half a mark from Kingsley, and oxgangs
in Bainston and Storeton.   1157–94

Abbas Robertus et conuentus dederunt operi ecclesie decimam
de dominio de Roucestria, et decimam de dominio de Leec, et de
dominio de Macclisfelda, et de dominio de Weuerham, et de
2) d] dominio de Frodesham, de Pulla, de Ovnera, de dominio de Hawrdyn, de dominio de Etona, de dominio de Estham, et medietatem
decime de dominio de Dottona, et duas partes decime de dominio
de Prestona, et decimam de dominio de Werrestona, et de Woders-
tona, et de Bebyntona, et de Biomhale, et de Westona, et de
Malteby in Lyndeshay, et quamdam croftam in Wentala, et vnam
croftam quam Edwinus filius Outredi dedit operi ecclesie, et aliam
quam Andreas Kachepol dedit, et octo denarios de quadam scoppa
ante portam monasterii, et duas partes decime de molendino de
Clottona, et ecclesiam de Bebyntona, et medietatem ecclesie de
Waleya, et decem solidos annuos de Campedena et quicquid de
ecclesia de Campedena poterit adquirere, et dimidiam marcam de
Wodynton, et decimam de dominio de Sotreleya, et dimidiam
marcam de Kyngesleya, et quamdam bouatam in Berlestona, et
aliam in Stortona

As the Duttons of Dutton had given two-thirds of the tithes of
Preston to the abbey before 1194, its acquisition by them is slightly
post-dated by Leycester (Orm i 739, cf 644)

488. Confirmation by abbot H[ugh] of all tithes and revenues
given to the fabric of the church and especially those which
his predecessors have alienated, when they shall fall in
1208–26

Abbas H[ugo] confirmauit omnes decimas et redditus ante
datas operi ecclesie et maxime redditus et decimas, cum redierint,
quos predecessores sui alienauerunt in detrimentum operis ecclesie

489. Grant by abbot Roger to the fabric of the abbey of all their tithes from the demesnes of both Caldys, Leighton, Meolse, Noctorum, Landican, Arrow, Barnston, and Great and Little Storeton in Wirral, with all the demesne tithes formerly conferred by the earl's charter in the parish of Prestbury 1240–49

Abbas Rogerus et conuentus dederunt operi ecclesie omnes decimas ad eos spectantes de dominicis de utraque Caldera, Leychtona,[1] Moeles, Knoctyrum, Landekan, Arwe, Berlestona, Stortona et de alia Stortona in Wirhale, et omnes decimas de dominicis per cart[as ?] com[itum] prius collatas in parochia de Prestbury

With the exception of those of Leighton, Meolse, Landican, and Arrow, the grant of the Wirral tithes here mentioned can be traced to the time of earls Hugh I. and Richard.

490. Assignment by Edward I to the abbey of 6 marks annually from the exchequer at Chester until lands or rent of the same yearly value shall be given to it in return for the demesne tithes of Frodsham, which at the king's request the monks quitclaimed to the abbey of Vale Royal. March 23, 1284

Edwardus rex, filius Henrici regis, dedit sex marcas annuatim percipiendas de scacario suo Cestrie ad Pascha et ad festum sancti Michaelis Maioris per equales porciones quousque monachis in terris vel redditibus ad ualenciam sex marcarum per annum alibi per se vel heredes suos fuerit prouisum in recompensacione decimarum de dominicis de Frodesham quas ad regis instanciam quietas clamauerunt abbathie de Valli Regali [2]

491. Quitclaim by Hervey, rector of the church of Weaverham to the abbey of the tithes of the colts of the earl's demesnes in the parish of Weaverham

Herueus rector ecclesie de Weuerham quiete clamauit ecclesie sancte Werburge decimas pullorum equinorum [3] de dominicis comitis de parochia de Weuerham

For the original grant of these and other tithes to the abbey by earl Hugh I see p 17

492. Agreement whereby the abbot and convent of Vale Royal undertook to pay 6 marks yearly to Chester Abbey in

[1] Leighton, Hail MS 2062   [2] C P R 1281–92, 117
[3] Not " pullorum et equarum," as in Orm ii 118

recompense for the tithes of the demesnes in the parish of Weaverham   After 1277

Abbas et conuentus de Valle Regali soluent annuatim sex marcas sterlingorum, scilicet infra triduum post festum Annunciacionis Dominice et ad festum sancti Michaelis per equales porciones in recompensacione decimarum de dominicis in parochia de Weuerham in ecclesia sancte Werburge, et ad hanc solucionem faciendam obligauerunt se et successores suos et omnia bona sua districcioni dyocesani per quamcunque censuram ecclesiasticam fiende,[1] quod si aliqua indulgencia vel potestate confisi districcioni episcopi non paruerint, licebit Cestrensibus monachis post duas menses a tempore quo de contemptu eorum constiterit possessionem dictarum decimarum ingredi sine alicuius contradiccione.

493. Grant in fee farm to the abbot and convent of Dieulacres of all tithes of the earl's demesnes in the parish of Leek (Staffs) from the abbot of Chester, at a yearly rent of half a mark, payable at Chester on the feast of St Werburgh in summer (June 21)   After 1214

Abbas et conuentus de Dulacres acceperunt ad perpetuam firmam de abbate Cestrie omnes decimas de dominicis comitis in parochia de Leech   Soluendo annuatim dimidiam marcam monachis Cestrie ad festum sancte Werburge in estate apud Cestriam

The tithes of the demesnes of Leek were given to Chester Abbey by earl Hugh I. (p. 17)   The monks of Pulton were removed to Leek and their new house named Dieulacres by earl Ranulf III in 1214 (Orm ii 862)

494. Grant in fee farm to the prior and convent of Norton of two-thirds of the tithes of the demesne of Preston and half of the tithes of the demesne of Dutton, at a yearly rent of 36s. payable in three equal instalments

Prior et conuentus de Nortona acceperunt a monachis Cestrie ad perpetuam firmam duas partes decimarum de dominico de Prestona et medietatem decimarum de dominico Duttone.   Reddendo inde annuatim triginta sex solidos ad Annunciacionem beate Marie et ad Natiuitatem sancti Johannis Baptiste et ad festum sancti Michaelis per equales porciones predictis monachis

These tithes were assigned to the fabric of the abbey by one of the abbots named Robert (No 487), i e between 1157 and 1194 The lease to Norton Priory was presumably later

[1] feriende, Harl MS 2062, f 19

495. Grant for ever by the abbot and convent of Combermere
to the monks of Chester of all their tithes in the vill of Worleston, as well of land held in villenage as of land in
demesne and of tithe of hay, saving to the vicar (of Acton)
his portion of the said hay and whatever he was used to
take there, for the tithes which they received in Austerson
and Badington (?) (and) Bromhall which they demised
wholly to the mother church of Acton, the monks of Chester
not to be bound to serve the (? a) chapel at Worleston but
to be preserved uninjured in this point by the monks of
Combermere, and not to erect a chapel there without the
consent of the latter   ? After 1266

Abbas et conuentus de Combermere concesserunt et resigna-
uerunt monachis Cestrie imperpetuum omnimodas decimas suas
in villa de Werlestona, tam de villenagio quam de dominico et de
decima feni, salua vicario porcione sua de dicto feno et quicquid
ibi percipere consueuit, pro decimis quas acceperunt in Alstones-
tona et Catyntona [et] Bromhala, quas matrici ecclesie de Actona
integre dimiserunt , nec monachi Cestrie obligantur capelle de
Werlestona deseruire, set in hoc monachi de Combermere eos conseruabunt indempnes, nec capellam ibi erigent sine consensu
monachorum de Combeimere.

The date of this exchange of tithes between the two abbeys is
uncertain, but apparently subsequent to the ordination of the vicarage
of Acton in 1266 by Roger de Meulan, bishop of Coventry and Lichfield, in which the share assigned to the vicar included half the tithe
of hay (Orm iii 347, where it is dated a year too early)   License
for the appropriation of the rectory of Acton had been given to Combeimere by bishop Richard (1162–1182)   Chester Abbey received a
giant of the tithes of Bromhall from Scirard at or shortly after the
foundation (above, p 20), but we do not know when it obtained those
of Austerson and Badington (the obvious conjecture for the non-
existent " Catyntona ")   The tithes of Worleston had been given
to St Werburgh's in the time of the founder by Ralph, son of Ermewine (pp 19, 34), but its rights must have been disputed by the local
Combermere abbey (founded 1133)

496. Grant (by the abbot and convent of Combermere ?) to the
abbot and convent of Chester of a moiety of the tithe of the
whole multure of Worleston mill, the vicar of Acton to have
the other moiety   Cf No 484   After 1266

Abbas et conuentus Cestrie percipient medietatem decime

tocius multure molendini de Werlestona et vicarius de Acton alteram eius medietatem

497. Mandate by H[ugh],[1] bishop of Coventry, to the archdeacon and his officials in the archdeaconry of Chester to protect the possessions, tithes, and offerings of the abbey, and to constrain those withholding what was due to it, especially for the fabric of the church, by ecclesiastical censure. 1188–98 or 1240–41

26 (23)]   H[ugo] Conuentrensis episcopus mandauit archidiacono et omnibus officiariis suis per archidiaconatum Cestrie constitutis quatenus ecclesie sancte Werburge possessiones protegant et eius decimarum et oblacionum, et debitorum detentores, et maxime que pertinent operi ecclesie, ad satisfaccionem ecclesiastica censura compellant

498. Grant by R. Bishop of Coventry to R abbot (of Chester) and his successors and the whole convent of power to coerce those who do ill to the monastery and withhold rents and debts, and after a third admonition to publish a sentence approved by the bishop   1162–82 or 1246–49

R Conuentrensis episcopus dedit R abbati et suis successoribus et toti conuentui potestatem cohercendi malefactores monasterii, et reddituum et debitorum detentores, et post trinam admonicionem in eos sentenciam promulgandi, quam episcopus confirmauit

The grantor is bishop Richard Peche or Roger de Weseham and the abbot in the one alternative Robert I or II and in the other Roger Frend

499. Grant by earl Ranulf (II) to the abbey, of the church of St Mary on the Hill (formerly " of the Castle "), Chester, in pure alms   1141–53

Ranulphus comes Cestrie dedit ecclesie [ecclesiam] sancte Marie de Castro Cestrie in puram elemosinam.

See No 8, p 59, and Orm. 1 333

500. Surrender by Robert (de Mold) the Steward (of the earl) to God and St Werburgh of the church of St Mary of Bruera which he and his father before him held under the monks at a yearly rent of 7s , in consideration of which

[1] Hugh de Nonant or Hugh de Pateshull

surrender abbot Ralph and the convent quitclaimed to the
said Robert the vill of Lea (cum Newbold) to which they
had often laid claim as a gift of William de Mold   1141–57

Robertus dapifer reddidit Deo et sancte Werburge ecclesiam
sancte Marie de Bruera solutam et quietam, quam ipse et pater
suus prius ad firmam tenuerunt sub monachis pro septem solidis
annuis, et Radulphus abbas et conuentus villam de Leey propter
hanc eidem Roberto quieta[m] clamauerunt, quam ipsi [1] sepius de
dono Willelmi de Monte Alto vendicauerunt.

This interesting deed was overlooked by Ormerod and Helsby
(ii 762, 764), who therefore missed its proof of the existence of the
chapel of Bruera in the first half of the 12th century and the light it
throws upon the early history of Lea cum Newbold and of the family
of Mold   The gift of Le Lay or Lea to the abbey by William de Moalt
in the time of earl Ranulf I (died c 1129) was confirmed by Ranulf
II. (No. 8, p 58), apparently between 1141 and 1154.   This William
was son of Hugh Fitz Norman, a Domesday tenant of the earl of
Chester in Suffolk and Yorkshire as well as in Cheshire, and an early
benefactor of the abbey [2]   In the Pipe Roll of 1130, p 96, under
Suffolk William appears as owing a considerable sum of money to
the king for his father's land which Ralph, steward of earl Hugh,
held, and to have right in respect to the inheritance of his mother
Ralph the Steward, who was apparently his uncle, was succeeded in
his office before 1136 by his son Robert, the grantor of the charter
under consideration (Orm i 15 · in a charter witnessed by Richard
Fitz Gilbert (de Clare) who was killed in 1136)   Robert also inherited
the estate of his cousin William, and, as here stated, refused to recog-
nise his gift of Lea to the abbey   This evidence that he was in possession of William's lands before 1157 is important, because it confirms
Sir George Sitwell's contention (*Barons of Pulford*, 63) that the Simon
Fitz William who was part farmer of the honour of Chester in 1160
was not a son of William de Mold, as Helsby thought (Orm i 57–8),
but a Lincolnshire baron, father of Philip de Kyme.

On the restoration of order under Henry II , the stewards, though
retaining Lea as tenants of the abbey, found it prudent to make some
reparation for the evil they had done to the house, especially in the
matter of Lea   Ralph, son of Robert, mentions this as his reason
for granting the church of Neston to the monastery (No. 527)

Ormerod's ignorance of this exchange between the abbey and
Robert the Steward leads him into much confusion in his account
of Lea (ii 764), where he identifies the William de Moalt of earl Ranulf
II 's charter with the William de Mold, rector of Neston, who con-
sented to his brother Ralph's grant of that church between 1162 and

[1] ipse MS   [2] He gave *inter alia* the tithes of Lea (p 19)

1182, and makes confusion worse confounded by describing this composite William as brother of *Robert* de Mold   Yet even with the documents that he had before him Ormerod might have seen that the donor of Lea before 1130 could not have been (as he states) rector of Neston in the time of Richard I

Another result of his oversight is that he postdates by half a century the subinfeudation of the Molds in Lea by the abbey, describing it as part of the price paid by the monks for the restitution of Neston church when it was forcibly re-entered upon by Roger de Mold, as he thought, in the reign of John, but really about 1258 (*loc cit*) The actual cessions made on that occasion (No 532) are quoted by him elsewhere (II 535), and they do not include Lea, for the very good reason that the stewards were already in possession of the manor as tenants of the abbey

501. Quitclaim by Robert de Pulford of the church of Bruera with the adjacent croft, lying between the garden of the said church and the highway going from his house towards the vill of Lea (cum Newbold)

Dominus Robertus de Pulford quietam clamauit ecclesiam de Bruera cum crofto adiacente inter gardinum dicte ecclesie et magnam viam tendentem de domo sua versus uillam de Lee.

The first recorded Robert de Pulford lived in the early part of the 13th century   He may possibly be the grantor of this quitclaim, and he and his son of the subsequent renunciation of the croft contained in No 836, but the Pulford pedigree is much too imperfect to allow of certainty (Orm II 857)   Important corrections are supplied by Sitwell (*Barons of Pulford*, 83, 85-6, 103)   The Pulford interest in Bruera seems to have escaped notice hitherto   For the church garden see No 78   [See Addenda]

502. Grant by Simon Fitz Osbern (of Pulford (in Cheshire) and Ormesby (in Lincolnshire)) to the abbey of the church of St. Peter in Chester   c 1153–84

Symon filius Osberni dedit ecclesiam sancti Petri in Cestria

The church of St Peter of the Market-place (*de Foro*), as it was then called, was given at the Conquest to Robert of Rhuddlan, who bestowed it with West Kirby, etc , on the abbey of St. Evroult in Normandy Robert's tenure of it is casually mentioned in Domesday Book (I 262b) without any reference to this gift, though, if we may trust a charter of confirmation by William I given by Orderic Vitalis (ed Le Prévost, III 19, v 186), it was made at least five years before the date of the survey   The gift was confirmed by earl Ranulf I [1] (1121–

[1] Round, *C D F* , 223

1129) and by Henry I between 1123 and 1128,[1] but afterwards, in some unexplained way, the church passed into the possession of Simon Fitz Osbern, who here gives it to Chester Abbey   See note on No. 504.   Simon Fitz Osbern was the grandson of Hugh Fitz Osbern, the first baron of Pulford (Sitwell, *Barons of Pulford*, 88) He was one of the witnesses of duke Henry's Devizes charter to earl Ranulf II in 1153 (Farrer, *Lancashire Pipe Rolls*, 371), and died in 1184 (*Ann Cestr* 32)

503. Surrender of the church of St. Peter in Chester by Alexander its rector to the monks of Chester, on condition of their paying him 3 marks yearly for his life   ? c 1153–84

Alexander rector ecclesie sancti Petri in Cestria commendauit eandem ecclesiam monachis Cestrie vt singulis annis vite sue tres marcas de eis reciperet

It may be conjectured that Alexander was rector of St Peter's when Simon Fitz Osbern gave it to the abbey (No. 502) and by this arrangement enabled it to exercise its new right of presentation at once

504. Quitclaim by the abbot and convent of St Evroult to St. Werburgh's of the vill and church of (West) Kirby and the chapel of Hilbre, and the church of St Peter in Chester, on the sole condition of the payment of 30s yearly.

Abbas et conuentus sancti Ebrulfi dederunt et quiete clamaue-runt sancte Werburge totum ius et clamium quod habuerunt in villa et ecclesia de Kirkeby et capella de Hildeburgheye, et ecclesia sancti Petri in Cestria, nichil imperpetuum exigentes preter triginta solidos annuos

Unluckily this document is not among those extracted from the cartulary of St Evroult by Mr Round, but a second charter (No 505) and earl Hugh's confirmation (No 509) mention only (West) Kirby and its appurtenances (which included the dependent chapel of Hilbre), saying nothing of the church of St Peter, which had been given with it to the Norman abbey by Robert de Rhuddlan (Round, *C D F*, 623   This omission seems to be justified by the existence of a separate grant of St Peter's to the abbey by Simon Fitz Osbern (No 502). Simon might indeed have been only the tenant of St Evroult; but while this supposition would account for the inclusion of the church in the quitclaim by that house, it would leave its omission in the earl's confirmation a difficulty   Sir George Sitwell explains St. Evroult's loss of the church by a weakness in Robert de Rhuddlan's

---

[1] *Gallia Christiana*, xi , Instrumenta, p 207

D

claim to it, referring to the dispute recorded in Domesday Book
whether its site was thegnland belonging to a manor outside the
city, or belonged to the borough and paid dues to the king and
earl like the land of other burgesses (*D B* 1 262*b*)   "No doubt,"
he says, "the case was still undecided at the date of Simon Fitz
Osbern's charter, who, we may conjecture, was heir to the claim put
forward in 1086 that it was within the city's jurisdiction, while the
monks of St Evroult inherited Robert de Rhuddlan's pretended
rights"[1] (*Barons of Pulford*, 64)   Unfortunately for this hypothesis,
(1) Robert's claim was disallowed by the county court before 1086,
as the passage in Domesday expressly states   (2) The dispute had
reference to the status of the land, not to its tenure, and the decision
accordingly did not prevent the confirmation of the church to St
Evroult by earl Ranulf I

If the manor outside Chester to which Robert of Rhuddlan wished
to attach the site of St Peter's was West Kirby, the church might
conceivably have been silently included in earl Hugh's confirmation
of the transference of that vill to St Werburgh's, but this supposition is in itself unlikely, and it finds no support in the wording of
the various charters

505. Grant by the abbot and convent of St Evroult to the abbey,
of the vill of (West) Kirby with the advowson of the church,
which, as they said, they had of the gift of Richard (*rectius*
Robert) de Rhuddlan, and for which 30s are to be paid to
them yearly in the manor of Peatling (Magna), to be conveyed there at the expense of the monks of Chester   1137–
1140

Abbas et conuentus sancti Ebrulfi dederunt villam de Kirkeby
cum aduocacione[2] ecclesie, quas, vt ipsi dixerunt, de dono Ricardi
de Rothelento habuerunt, et pro hiis reddentur eis annuatim
triginta solidi in Natiuitate sancti Johannis Baptiste in manerio de
Pethelynga sumptibus monachorum Cestrie deferendi

See note to No 504, and for the date No 509*a*   Ormerod (ii
485) by an unlucky slip makes the payment £30 per annum   Peatling
Magna near Lutterworth in Leicestershire was a manor of the priory
of Ware in Hertfordshire, the only English cell of St. Evroult (Tanner,
Notitia Monastica)   Cf also No 392

506. Grant to the abbey by Richard, monk of St Evroult, with
the consent of the abbot and convent thereof, of the vill of

---

[1] Sir George seems to imply later that the loss of West Kirby by St Evroult
was due to the same weakness of claim, but of course there is not an atom of
evidence for this
[2] evocacione, MS

(West) Kirby with the advowson of the church, " for which are to be paid," etc (as in No 505) 1137–40

Ricardus monachus sancti Ebrulfi, cum consensu abbatis et conuentus eiusdem, dedit villam de Kyrkeby cum aduocacione ecclesie, pro quibus reddentur, etc.

Ormerod (ii 488) confuses the agent of St Evroult in the 12th century with Richard de Kirkby, the head of a local family, who made a quitclaim of the advowson in the 13th. For the date see No 509a

507. Ratification of No 506 by the abbot (Richard) and convent of St Evroult 1137–40

Abbas et conuentus sancti Ebrulfi ratificauerunt factum Ricardi sui monachi de donacione ville de Kirkeby et aduocacione ecclesie

508. Agreement between the abbeys of St. Werburgh and St Evroult for the performance of the condition of the grant made in No 505 1137–40.

Conuenit inter monachos sancte Werburge et monachos sancti Ebrulfi quod monachi sancte Werburge Cestrie deferent annuatim triginta solidos sumptibus propiis in manerium de Pethelynga in Natiuitate sancti Johannis Baptiste pro villa et ecclesia de Kirkeby.

509. Confirmation of No 505 by earl Hugh (II.) 1154–81.

P R O Transcripts, Series II , 140B f 281, No 99

Notum sit tam presentibus quam futuris quod ego Hugo comes Cestrie concessi et presenti carta mea confirmavi conventionem inter ecclesiam sancti Werburge de Cestria et ecclesiam de sancto Ebrulfo, videlicet quod ecclesia sancte Werburge de Cestria reddet annuatim xxxª solidos argenti ecclesie de sancto Ebrulfo pro villa de Kircheby et monasterio et pro omni rectitudine quam abbas et monachi de sancto Ebrulfo habuerunt in prefata possessione Testibus Radulfo de Meinegar[ino], Conano, Ricardo de Liveto, Ricardo de Cumbray, Radulfo filio Warin, Alveredo de Cumbray, Rogero de Liveto, et aliis.

(Seal broken)

The church of West Kirby is here described as a minster For the application of the word to ordinary parish churches see Stenton, *Danelaw Charters* (Brit Acad), lxxiii *n*

The long interval between the date of the bargain between the
two abbeys and its confirmation by the earl is accounted for by the
high-handed action of Ranulf II , who seems to have ignored the
rights of both houses and to have transferred West Kirby to his
new foundation at Basingwerk (No 513 *n*)

509a. Notification by abbot Simon of a regrant by abbot
Nicholas (II.) of St. Evroult to St Werburgh's abbey of
the vill and church of West Kirby on the terms of No 505.
November 20, 1271

P R O Transcripts, Series II , 140B, p 233, No 37

Omnibus Christi fidelibus ad quos presens scriptum pervenerit
S[imon] miseratione divina abbas Cestriensis et eiusdem loci conventus humilis salutem in Domino sempiternam   Noverit universitas vestra quod licet frater Nicholas Dei gratia humilis abbas
sancti Ebrulfi et eiusdem loci conventus nobis et successoribus
nostris scriptum quoddam de villa de Kyrkeby in Wirhall' cum
ecclesia in eadem sita, cum eius advocatione in forma que de verbo
ad verbum subsequenter inseritur concesserunt, quaquidem forma
talis est   Omnibus Christi fidelibus presens scriptum visuris vel
audituris, frater Nicholas Dei gratia humilis abbas sancti Ebrulfi
et eiusdem loci conventus salutem in Domino sempiternam
Noveritis nos unanimi assensu et concordia [et] voluntate totius
capituli nostri dedisse, concessisse et hac presenti carta nostra
confirmasse Deo et ecclesie sancte Werburge de Cestria ac
monachis ibidem Deo seruientibus eorumque successoribus in
perpetuum villam de Kyrkeby in Wyrhale cum ecclesia in eadem
sita et eius advocatione, omnibusque iuribus et pertinentiis suis
que Ricardus (*sic*) de Rulento quondam dedit sancto Ebrulfo et
que Ricardus monachus noster postea ecclesie sancte Werburge
de Cestria, etc , ex consensu et consilio Ricardi abbatis et totius
capituli concessit, sicut carta confirmationis Hugonis comitis
Cestrie super concessione predicti Ricardi monachi nostri facta
plenius testatur, habendas et tenendas de sancto Ebrulfo et nobis
dicti abbatis (*sic*)[1] et monachis in dicta ecclesia sancte Werburge
Deo militantibus eorumque successoribus vel assignatis, cum omni
iure et rectitudine que sanctus Ebrulfus et nos in prefato possessione de Kyrkeby habuimus, cum omnibus libertatibus, pertinentiis suis et cum incrementis, escaetis et approvamentis que
ecclesie sancte Ebrulfi et nobis, aliquo casu contingente, de dictis
villa et ecclesia cum pert evenire vel accrescere possent, reddendo
inde annuatim nobis et successoribus nostris triginta solidos

[1] For dicto abbati

sterlingorum ad festum sancti Johannis Baptiste in manerio nostro de Petling' sumptibus suis et periculo ipsorum abbatis et conventus ibidem deferendos pro omni servitio et exactione quacunque   In cuius rei testimonium presenti scripto sigilla nostra apposuimus Teste Deo et omnibus sanctis eius totoque capitulo nostro

Nos tamen volumus et concedimus quod nec dicti abbas et conventus de sancto Ebrulfo nec successores eorum nobis vel successoribus nostris dictam villam, ecclesiam seu advocationem in toto vel in parte aliquo casu perdere (*sic*). Volumus tamen quod nominus (*sic*) nos et successores nostros ad solutionem redditus predictorum triginta solidorum annuatim persolvendi memoratis abbati, etc , de sancto Ebrulfo eorumque successoribus obligari in posterum. Insuper, si accidat nos vel successores nostros per breve domini regis vel per aliquid aliud breve vel sine brevi occasione dictarum ville et ecclesie cum eiusdem advocatione coram quibuscumque iudicibus implacitari, nolumus tamen quod dicti abbas, etc , de sancto Ebrulfo seu successores eorum nobis seu successoribus nostris ad aliquam warantiam, defensionem seu adquietanciam pro dictis villa et ecclesia vel aliquibus earum pert aliquatenus teneantur   In cuius rei testimonium nos et capitulum nostrum unanimi consensu huic scripto sigilla nostra apposuimus. Teste Deo et omnibus sanctis eius totoque capitulo nostro   Datum apud Cestriam die sancti Edmundi regis et martyris anno gratie MCC septuagesimo primo

Drawing of remaining half of seal (seated figure of king (?) with sceptre and orb, Leg PARTITUR PROPRIUM .   ) *and counter seal (Si Werburgh with crook and book, Leg.* . . SANCIE WERBURGE CESTR .), *which are of 13th century execution.* (Cf. No 665a)

The regiant was probably obtained from abbot Nicholas II (1269–1274) of St Evroult in preparation for proceedings taken by Basingwerk abbey, which claimed the advowson and held the manor (Nos 513–4).

The document is important as giving the early date of the first grant to Chester Abbey. Richard of Leicester was abbot of St. Evroult 1137–40.

510. Acknowledgement by Richard de Kirkby in the full county court of Chester that 4 oxgangs of land in (West) Kirby, with the advowson of the church, were the right and inheritance of St Werburgh of Chester, and quitclaim of them for ever   May 15, 1263

Ricardus de Kirkeby recognouit in pleno comitatu Cestrie quatuor bouatas terre in villa de Kirkeby cum aduocacione ecclesie esse ius et hereditatem sancte Werburge Cestrie, quas ipse R[icar-dus] imperpetuum quietas clamauit [1] [See Addenda]

Orm *Domesday*, p 16, No 42 This acknowledgement preceded by more than twenty years that of the abbot of Basingwerk (No 513), of whom the Kirkbys held the manor of West Kirby (Orm ii 488)

5 I I. Quitclaim of the church of (West) Kirby by Richard de Kirkby. May 15, 1263

Ricardus de Kirkeby quietam clamauit ecclesiam de Kirkeby cum omnibus ad eandem pertinentibus imperpetuum

5 I 2. Letter of Richard de Kirkby to the bishop of Coventry and Lichfield informing him of his quitclaim of the advowson of the church of (West) Kirby (No 511), and revoking the presentation of a rector which he had made to the bishop. 1263

Ricardus de Kirkeby ad episcopum Conuentrensem et Liche-feldensem scripsit se quiete clamasse totum ius et clamium quod habuit in aduocacione ecclesie de Kirkeby monachis sancte Wer-burge et presentacionem rectoris quam episcopo [2] fecit reuocauit

5 I 3. Acknowledgement by Hugh, abbot of Basingwerk, in full county court of Chester, before Reginald de Grey, then justice, that the advowson of the church of (West) Kirby was the right and inheritance of St Werburgh of Chester, and quitclaim thereof by him 1287

Abbas de Basinwerk' in pleno comitatu Cestrie coram Regi-naldo de Gray tunc Iusticiario recognouit aduocacionem ecclesie de Kirkeby esse ius et hereditatem sancte Werburge Cestrensis et eam quietam clamauit imperpetuum.

The fine of which the above is a brief abstract is copied in the Shakerley MSS at Somerford Park (No 4, f 95*d*) Its substance is represented in the quitclaim which followed (No 514), but the consideration included a palfrey as well as 9 marks The date given is 15 Edward I (1286–87), " before Reginald de Grey justice, barons, freeholders, suitors and judgers (see p 104, § 7) of the county," but Harl MS 2072, f 21, misleading Ormerod, puts it a year earlier

The abbey of Basingwerk in Flintshire claimed to have received the advowson of (West) Kirby, annexed to the manor of (Great)

---

[1] There is a long gap in Harl MS 2062 from the end of f 19*b*, and the next charter given is No 693 below

[2] The MS seems to read Eps , but the dative is required

Caldey, from its founder, earl Ranulf II , and to have been unjustly deprived of it by Ranulf III (Orm ii 485) Needless doubt has been thrown upon the first part of their contention by an entry in the *Annales Cestrienses* (p 22), copied by Higden in the Polychronicon (viii 40, R S), that the abbey was founded in 1157 during Henry II 's first expedition into Wales Leland describes Henry as its original founder (*Collectanea*, i 101) Henry's own charter, granted between 1154 and 1162, in all probability in 1157, but unknown to Leland, ought to have set matters right, for while himself giving Glossop to the abbey, he confirms the gifts of earl Ranulf, among which Caldey appears, though the advowson of West Kirby is not expressly mentioned [1] (Dugdale, *Mon* v 263) This charter was, however, absurdly transferred to Henry III by bishop Fleetwood of St Asaph (*Life and Miracles of St Wenefrede*, 1713, p 24), who was blindly followed by bishop Tanner (or his editor Nasmyth) and by the editors of the Monasticon [2] Although no charter of foundation by earl Ranulf is extant, his grant of Fulbrook and that of Holywell by Robert de Pierrepont with his consent were inspected in 1285 (*C Ch R* i 289–90)

The advowson of West Kirby may have been included in the confirmation of Caldey, and, indeed, the monks of Chester do not seem to have disputed the Basingwerk claim to have presented to the rectory down to about 1215 If that was so, the transaction between the abbeys of St Evroult and St Werburgh, although confirmed by earl Hugh (Nos 504–9), must have remained a dead letter until earl Ranulf III was induced to put the Chester monks in possession of the advowson, which they retained down to the time of the suit of 1286–87 The decision was then given in their favour on the finding of the jury that the last presentation before the Barons' War had been made by them [See Addenda]

Basingwerk retained Caldey (though Ranulf III was said to have seized that also with the manor of (West) Kirby), and it is curious that in 1535 Caldey seems to be included in their "dominium de Westkyrby " (Dugdale, *Mon* v 261, 263) The Kirkbys continued to hold the manor of (West) Kirby under Basingwerk

514. Quitclaim by (Hugh) abbot of Basingwerk and the convent of their right and claim in the advowson of the church of (West) Kirby, for which they sued the monks of Chester. 1287.

> Peter Shakerley's Vernon MSS No 4, f 98b, Somerford Park, Congleton

---

[1] It was not of course Ranulf's to give, being the property of St Evroult, but that would not have deterred him (cf Nos 349, 354)

[2] There is now independent proof of the existence of Basingwerk before 1157 (*Eng Hist Rev* viii 669) It was one of the houses of the order of Savigny which became Cistercian in 1148

Omnibus, etc , Hugo abbas ecclesie sancte Marie de Basing-
werke, etc , salutem   Noueritis nos remisisse Deo et ecclesie
sancte Werburge Cestrie et domino Symoni abbati, etc , et eorum
successoribus totum ius, etc , in aduocatione seu iure patronatus
ecclesie sancte Brigitte [de] WestKuby [1] in Wyrhale cum omnibus
iuribus et pertinentiis suis, de qua aduocatione predictum abbatem
et conuentum Cestrie per breue quare impedit in comitatu Cestrie
implacitauimus [2]   Pro hac re dederunt nobis 9 marcas argenti
Huis testibus domino Reginaldo de Gray tunc iusticiario Cestrie,
Willelmo de Venables, Petro de Ardern, Hamone de Mascy,
Radulpho de Vernon, Hugone de Dutton, Ricardo de Mascy,
Patricio de Hasilwall, Rogero de Dumvyle, militibus, Roberto
Grosvenatore tunc vicecomite, Alexandro de Banvyle, Jacobo de
Pulle, Willelmo de Brexin, Willelmo de Bonebure, Willelmo de
Stanlega, Patricio de Bartun, Hugone de Berliston, et multis aliis

To the abstract in the chartulary is appended the note   " et hec
irrotulatur in Domisday "   This of course is the lost Domesday Book
of the palatinate

515. Quitclaim by William, rector of (West) Kirby, with the
consent of the bishop (of Coventry), of Hilbre Island with
its chapel, etc , retaining nothing but the offerings on the
feast of the Assumption B V M. (August 15).   Saving the
rights of burial, etc , of the mother church of (West) Kirby.
? 1287

Willelmus rector ecclesie de Kirkeby cum consensu dyocesani
episcopi quiete clamauit insulam de Hildeburghey cum sua capella
et omnibus pertinenciis, nichil sibi retinens preter obuenciones
Assumpcionis beate Marie.   Saluo eciam tam in sepultura quam
in omnibus aliis iure matricis ecclesie de Kyrkeby

A William was presented to the rectory by St Werburgh's on the
successful termination of the suit with Basingwerk in 1286-87, and
it is conceivable that the opportunity was taken to obtain from him
a renunciation of certain rights in Hilbre Island, where the abbey
had long had a cell   But Ormerod in his account of this cell (ii
501) prefers to identify the grantor with William FitzRichard, who
is said to have been rector in the time of Richard I   This is open
to the objection that the earlier William was presented by Basingwerk (ib ii 486) and therefore unlikely to have made such a concession to the rival house at that date   [See however Addenda]

Kirkeby, Chart   [2] implacitauerunt, MS.

516. Grant by Bertram, son of Richard, son of Herbert, to St. Werburgh and the monks dwelling at Hilbre, of a selion, with meadow adjacent, in Great Meolse, lying between the land of Bertram, son of Henry and lord (of the manor), and the land of Fulk de Meolse. *c.* 1280–1320.

Bertrammus filius Ricardi filii Herberti dedit sancte Werburge et monachis apud Hildeburweye commorantibus vnam sellionem tendentem ad pratum quod dicitur Iagowesmedwe cum prato adiacente, que quidem sellio iacet inter terram Bertrammi filii Henrici et domini et terram Fulconis de Meles in villa de Magna Meles [1]

It is impossible to fit the Bertram, son of Henry of this charter, into the pedigree of Meoles of Meoles as given by Ormerod (ii 494), the only Bertram, son of Henry, in which did not obtain the manor until after 1353, while an earlier Bertram is said to have been son of John de Meoles. [See Addenda.]

517. Grant by Robert Lancelyn, kt., of 3s yearly from the whole of his demesne in Little Meolse, with the homage of the said demesne and right to distrain for them [Also confirmation of this grant by William Lancelyn III] *c* 1200–1245

Robertus Lancelyn miles dedit tres solidos de toto dominico [f 26 suo de Parua Moeles annuatim percipiendos in Natiuitate sancti Johannis Baptiste et in festo sancti Martini per equales porciones cum homagio dicti dominici, ita quod liceat abbati in toto dicto dominico distringere pro dictis redditu et homagio
[In the margin [2]] Hunc redditum iii solidorum Willelmus Lancelyn 3us confirmauit et concessit, nonobstante qualibet quieta clamacione antecessoribus suis uel sibi super hoc concessa, vt patet in sua carta.

Although the grantor is clearly identified in No 692 with Robert Lancelyn II, who was alive as late as 1241 (No 688 *n*), Ormerod (ii 498) dates the gift about the time of Richard I, which might refer it to the first Robert, father of the donor But cf ii 444.
The Lancelyns (of Poulton Lancelyn) held Little Meolse of the holders of the hundred of Caldey The grant is not stated to be made for the cell of Hilbre Island as asserted by Ormerod, who converts the 3s into £3 (ii 501), but it is a fair inference from the fact that it comes in a series of charters relating to Hilbre. Abbot Simon resigned

[1] This abstract is entered in the bottom margin
[2] In darker ink

the rent in his agreement with William Lancelyn I , but it was re-granted by William Lancelyn III , according to the note in the margin here

518. Quitclaim by William Lancelyn, kt , of the lake of Hilbre which is called the Heypool   *c* 1245–83

Willelmus Lancelyn, miles, quiete clamauit lacum de Hilde-burghey que uocatur le Heypol imperpetuum

The grantor of this, as of the next, charter was doubtless William Lancelyn I , who died in 1283   He was succeeded by his grandson and namesake, the William Lancelyn of the marginal note to No. 517 (cf No 689 *n*)

519. Grant by William Lancelyn (I), kt , of a messuage with curtilage in Little Meolse as the site of a house for 40 sheep and 3 cows and 2 draught horses, with their young, and for the reception of the turf and hay of the monks of Hilbre, with pasture for the said animals and the liberties of the said vill   *c* 1270–83

Willelmus Lancelyn, miles, dedit quoddam mesuagium cum curtilagio in Parua Moeles ad situm domus ad quadraginta oues et tres vaccas et duos afros, cum exitibus eorum, et ad turbas et ad fenum monachorum de Hildeburghey recipienda, cum pastura dictorum animalium et libertatibus dicte ville.

[In the margin] Hec omnia Willelmus Lancelyn nepos dicti Willelmi militis quiete clamauit

520. Confirmation of the preceding grant by Robert Grosvenor and Margery his wife, chief lords of Little Meolse   *c* 1270–1283

Robertus Grouenour et Margeria vxoi eius, capitales domini de Parua Moeles, confirmauerunt donacionem mesuagii factam monachis Hildeburgheye a domino W[illelmo] Lancelyn milite

The grantors were Robert Grosvenor of Hulme in Allostock and his wife, who are supposed to have had a grant from the earl of the hundred of Caldey in the jurisdiction of which Little Meolse was comprised (Orm iii. 145, 151, ii 516, 518)   Grosvenor lived until 1292–93, but he had ceased to be lord of Little Meolse by 1285, when it was regranted to Ranulf Merton (*ib* ii 179)   The original was until recently among the Baskerville deeds at Old Withington

521. Grant by John (le Scot) earl of Chester to the chapel of

Hilbre and the monks living there, for the light of St Mary, of 10s from the exchequer of Chester, by the hand of the chamberlain of the Castle 1232–37

Johannes comes Cestrie dedit capelle de Hildeburghey et monachis ibi degentibus ad luminaria sancte Marie decem solidos argenti de scacario Cestrie per manum camerarii Castri ad festum sancti Martini percipiendos

In the Fine Roll of 2 Edw III (m 2), where this endowment is said to issue " de castro Cestrie," the cell is called a hermitage (Tanner, *Notitia Monastica*, Chesh No xi)

522. Agreement between the abbot of Chester and the brethren of the hospital of St John (without the Northgate) that all the servants of the hospital wearing secular garb shall pay their tithes and offerings to the mother church of St Werburgh except the gardener, the butler,[1] the prior's groom, and the woman in attendance on the sick, but that any of these engaging in trade shall pay tithes and offerings from his trade (gains) to the mother church Strangers and wayfarers, however, to receive the sacraments and make offerings in the church of the hospital, provided it be not to the prejudice of the parishioners of the mother church. All staying there, not as servants, in secular garb to pay tithes and offerings to the mother church

Omnes seruientes Hospitalis sancti Johannis habitum secularem gestantes decimas suas et oblaciones matrici ecclesie sancte Werburge persoluent, preter quatuor, videlicet gardinarium, clauigerum, garcionem prioris, et ancillam infirmorum. Set si quis istorum negocietur, matrici ecclesie decimas et oblaciones de sua negociacione conferet, peregrini vero et transeuntes in ecclesia Hospitalis sacramenta possunt recipere et ibi offerre, dum tamen non fiet preiudicium in proprios parochianos matrici[s] ecclesie

Item, omnes ibi moram trahentes, vt non seruientes,[2] in habitu seculari decimas et oblaciones matrici ecclesie persoluent

This agreement and the next are not noticed in Ormerod's account of the Hospital (i 350 *sqq*)

523. Agreement between the abbot and convent (of St Werburgh) and the dean of St John's on the one part, and the brethren of the hospital of St John on the other, in a synod

---

[1] Ducange, *Glossarium* s v claviger
[2] vt non seruientes is interlined in the MS

in the presence of G[eoffrey] bishop of Coventry, that the said brethren shall be allowed to have a graveyard and rights of burial for the poor only who die in the said house, and for its brethren and sisters who have worn its habit while in good health, and for at least eight days, its privilege of burial to be forfeited if this agreement is violated 1198–1208.

Abbas et conuentus et Decanus sancti Johannis ex vna parte et fratres Hospitalis sancti Johannis ex alia inuicem in sinodo coram G[alfrido] Conuentrensi episcopo composuerunt quod liceat eisdem fratribus cimiterium et sepultuiam habere pro pauperibus tantum in eadem domo mortuis, et fratribus et sororibus eiusdem domus qui in prosperitate habitum suum, et ad minus per octo dies, portauerunt Et si illi fratres contra hanc formam venerint et tertio commoniti non se emendauerint, de cetero priuilegio sepeliendi apud ipsos careant, et ad hoc tenendum omnes fratres iurauerunt, et omnes futuri fratres antequam habitum recipient iurabunt

By this agreement the two great churches hoped to prevent the evasion of their profitable burial rights by the Hospital in the reception of well-to-do persons on their death-beds to the fraternity of the house

It is clear from Nos 523–6 that St Werburgh's and St John's were the original parish churches of the city and its suburbs.

524. Agreement between the monks of St Werburgh's and the canons of St John's to preserve inviolate the ancient customs observed between them with regard to burial in the city, which is common to both, and to resist any infringement of their right

Monachi sancte Werburge et canonici sancti Johannis Baptiste antiquas consuetudines inter ecclesias eorum conseruatas super sepultura ciuitatis, que vtriusque communis est, inuiolabiliter conseruabunt Si vero aliquis alius super re aliqua predictas ecclesias contingente eos iniuste vexare voluerit, monachi et canonici pro defensione sui iuris pariter pro posse ei resistent

525. Agreement between the monks of St. Werburgh's and the canons of St. John's on the one part, and the nuns (of St Mary's) on the other, allowing the nuns to bury in their own precincts persons dying in Chester who shall choose to be buried there, provided that the chaplains of the said

churches shall perform the obsequies in the houses of the
defunct and the nuns' church and in attending the funeral
and in the burial office, the churches taking two-thirds of
the offerings and wax (each party, however, to hold freely
whatever shall be bequeathed to it), but that the nuns shall
not invite any resident in Chester to be buried among them.
Strangers, however, not belonging to Chester who choose
to be so buried they may freely inter and take all the
offerings therefrom.

Monachi sancti Werburge et canonici sancti Johannis con[ces-
s]erunt monialibus licenciam sepeliendi apud ipsas corpora defunctorum in ciuitate Cestrie qui ibi sepulturam elegerint, ita quod
capellani dictarum ecclesiarum faciant exequias in domibus defunctorum et in ecclesia monialium et in secucione funeris et officio
sepeliendi, et quod dicte ecclesie duas partes obuencionum habeant,
tam in oblacionibus quam in cera, set cui cum aliquid legatum
fuerit hoc libere habeat ; set moniales vel capellani earum neminem
in ciuitate ad eligendum apud ipsas sepulturam inuitabunt, ex-
traneos vero qui de ciuitate non sunt et ibi sepeliri elegerint
possunt libere sepelire, et exinde omnes obuenciones possidere.
Vt hec composicio firme teneatur, dicte partes se iuramento con-
strinxerunt et sub pena viginti librarum se obligauerunt

The Benedictine nunnery of St Mary, founded by earl Ranulf
II between 1147 and 1153, stood close to the castle on the north-
east (Orm 1 346).

526. Similar agreement with the friars preachers of St Nicholas
After 1221

Monachi sancte Werburge et canonici sancti Johannis concesserunt fratribus predicatoribus sancti Nicholai quod cum contigerit quemquam de Cestria vel de villis adiacentibus, qui de
iure communi deberet sepeliri in cimiterio sancti Johannis vel
sancte Werburge, eligere sibi sepulturam apud dictos fratres,
liceat eis fratribus illum apud ipsos sepelire, ita quod due partes
omnium obuencionum tam in cera quam in oblacionibus diuidan-
tur inter monachos et canonicos et tercia pars fratribus remaneat
saluo fratribus dictis integraliter legato principali, salua eciam
dictis ecclesiis sancti [1] Johannis et sancte Werburge debi[ta] [2]
consuetudine legatorum , extranei vero possunt ibi sepeliri cum
omnibus obuencionibus. Sed fratres nullum de ciuitate vel de
villis predictis ut apud ipsos sepeliatur inducent

[1] sancte, MS.   [2] The reading is not quite certain

The dedication of the Dominican friary at Chester to St Nicholas has not been hitherto noticed (Orm 1 349) It evidently gave its name to Nicholas Street, close to which it stood, in Watergate Street. See p [xix]

527. Grant by Ralph de Mold, steward of earl of Chester, to the abbey, in atonement for injuries done to it by himself and his father, etc , especially in the case of Lea, of the church of Neston, with the counsel and consent of his mother Leucha, on whose dower land the church was founded, and of his brother William (who resigned the rectory , see No 79) 1177–82

Harl MS. 2071, f 106 (old 100)   Pd in Orm ii 554

(24)]   Notum sit omnibus quod ego Radulfus de Montealto, dapifer comitis Cestrie, dedi ecclesie sancte Werburge ecclesiam de Neston, pro anima Roberti patris mei et Leuche matris mee [et pro animabus] [1] omnium heredum et parentum meorum   Hec autem omnia feci consensu et consilio Leuche matris mee, in cuius dote ipsa ecclesia quam donaui fundata est, et W[illelm]i de Montealto fiatris mei et aliorum amicorum meorum   Hanc autem eleemo-synam feci pro excessibus meis et patris mei et antecessorum meorum in prefatam ecclesiam sancte Werburge, et maxime de Lay [2] et aliis rebus, illatis   Hiis testibus   Ada de Dumvile, Haytropo filio Hugonis, Stephano Mallanel, Radulfo filio Rogeri, Ricardo abbate de Hage[mond], Gilberto de Malopassu, etc

The attestation of Richard, abbot of Haughmond, helps to fix the date of Ralph's gift   Aelfric was abbot in 1170 (Eyton, *Itin of Hen II* 136), and as the confirmation of the grant by archbishop Richard (No 81) was made after 1177 and before the death in 1182 of Richard, bishop of Lichfield, who had previously confirmed it, its date seems to fall between these two years

528. Confirmation of the gift made in No 527, by Robert de Mold, steward of the earl of Chester, brother of the donor *c.* 1208–11

Harl MS 2071, f 106 (old 100)

Universis, etc Robertus de Montealto, dapifer comitis Cestrie salutem   Noueritis me concessisse et confirmasse et omnino quiete clamasse in puram elemosinam ecclesie sancte Werburge ius patronatus ecclesie de Neston, sicut carta Radulphi de Montealto,

---

[1] Omitted by the transcriber
[2] Lea cum Newbold   Ormerod (ii 746) identifies its donor, William de Mold, with the rector , but see note to No 500

fratris mei, testatur, etc   Testibus   Philippo de Orreby, ius-
t[iciario] de Cestria, Thoma de Orreby, Rannulfo de Montealto,
Brito [1] Pantul', Matheo de Robi (*sic*), Radulpho Corbia, etc

Ormerod (ii 535), overlooking the description of Philip de Orreby,
invented a Philip de Orreby the elder, and so dated the charter before
1209 (*rectius* 1208)   In the Mold pedigree it is definitely assigned
to 1209 [1]   The pedigree omits Robert's stewardship

529. Renunciation by Richard de Neston, clerk, of all his right
and claim in the church of Neston

Ricardus de Nestona clericus renunciauit omni iuri et clamio
quod habuit in ecclesia de Nestona, et ad hoc fideliter tenendum,
tactis sacrosanctis, iurauit

In agreement with the date which he assigns to No 531, Ormerod
(ii 535-6) dates this *c* 1210   But that date is much too early   He
was doubtless the Ricardus clericus, farmer of a portion of the church
from the abbey, who died shortly before 1258 (No 531)   In any
case, he was not rector as described by Ormerod, for St Werburgh's
acquired the rectory before 1182 (No 79)

530. Similar quitclaim by Patrick, son of Richard de Neston.
1249–65.

Harl MS 2071, f 38 (old 24)

Omnibus Christi fidelibus presens scriptum uisuris uel audituris
Patricius filius Ricardi de Neston [2] salutem   Sciatis me concessisse, quiete clamasse, et hac presenti carta mea confirmasse, pro
me et heredibus meis, Thome abbati sancte Werburge Cestrie et
monachis ibidem Deo seruientibus et eorum successoribus in
perpetuum totum ius et clamium quod habui uel aliquo iure habere
potui in aduocacione ecclesie de Nestona cum iure patronatus
eiusdem et cum omnibus pertinentiis ad eandem spectantibus ,
habendum et tenendum dictis abbati et monachis et eorum successoribus in perpetuum in liberam puram et perpetuam elemosinam, ita quod nec ego nec heredes mei nec aliquis per nos in
aduocatione dicte ecclesie nec in iure patronatus eiusdem cum
pertinenciis ad eandem spectantibus de cetero exigemus uel exigere
poterimus   In huius rei testimonium presenti scripto sigillum
meum apposui.   His testibus   Patricio de Haselwall', Willelmo

[1] For Bricio   He was son of Ivo de Pantulf of Wem (*d c* 1176)   Another
form of the name was Panton   Brice's brother Norman, a Staffordshire landholder, witnessed earl Ranulf's charter to his barons (No 60)
[2] Chart adds clerici, which seems to identify him with the grantor of
No. 529

de Hoton', Bertramo de Meles, Ricardo Bernard', Roberto de Bulkeleg', Willelmo de Riddeleg', Ricardo de Coudray, Ricardo de Orrebi, et aliis

The abbot Thomas of this charter was evidently Thomas de Capenhurst (1249–65), for an *inq p m* was held in 1275–76 on the decease of Richard de Orreby, one of the witnesses, so that abbot Thomas de Burchells (1291–1324) is excluded The renunciation may have been executed at the time of the agreement between the monks and Roger de Mold in 1258 (No 532) Patrick who makes it is said to occur in 1260 (Orm 1. 538)

531. Intimation by the monks of Chester to the Court of Canterbury that despite their uncontested possession of the appropriation of Neston church for upwards of forty years, Roger de Mold on the death of Richard, a clerk who held a portion of the church from the monks at a rent, has forcibly entered on the church and has presented Ralph de Mold, clerk, to the bishop for institution to the church, and request for judgement. *c* 1258

Monachi Cestrie intimauerunt curie Cantuariensi quod, cum ipsi ecclesiam de Nestona in proprios usus per quadraginta annos et amplius pacifice possiderunt, dominus Rogerus de Monte alto, cuius predecessores ius patronatus in ipsa ecclesia olim optinebant, occasione mortis Ricardi clerici, nuper in fata decedentis, qui ab ipsis quandam porcionem prefate ecclesie tenebat ad firmam, ipsos super dicta ecclesia graui inquietacione molestauit, armata manu laicali prefatam ecclesiam inuadendo , insuper Radulphum de Monte alto clericum, sub ymagine porcionis quam supra dictus Ricardus defunctus in ipsa ecclesia optinuerat, ad dictam ecclesiam dyocesano presentauit, cum nec eadem ecclesia vacaret nec ipsa porcio quam defunctus in ipsa prius optinuerat   Vnde super hiis curie Cantuariensis postulabant iudicium.

Ormerod and Helsby have fallen into great confusion with regard to the chronology of this invasion of the rights of the abbey in Neston church   Under Neston (ii 535) Ormerod identifies the invader with the first Roger de Mold, younger brother of the grantors of Nos. 527 and 528, who died in 1232, but in the lives of the abbots of Chester (i 251) he more correctly attributes the proceeding to his son Roger, the justice (*d* 1260)   Here he follows the narrative of the Chester annalist who dates in 1258 the one-sided exchange (No 532) which closed the dispute (*Ann Cestr* 76)   The provision made for the clerk Ralph de Mold in the latter disposes of any possible suggestion that the complaint before us had reference to an earlier attack in the time of Roger I

Quite consistently with his better mind Ormerod made Ralph de Mold a son of Roger II , though on what evidence does not appear; but Helsby, adopting the false alternative he offered, inserts Ralph higher in the pedigree as brother of Roger I (Orm 1 58) He asserts that a charter (for which he gives no reference) calls him Ranulphus frater Ranulfi (*i e* , he says, of Ralph, elder brother of Roger I., and original grantor of the church) The practical certainty that Ralph the clerk did not die until about 1285 (see on No 532) is enough to disprove this affiliation

532. Exchange between Chester Abbey and Sir Roger de Mold whereby Roger gave to the abbey two oxgangs of land in (Great) Neston and all his right and claim in the advowson of the church of Neston, and also confirmed all the gifts and confirmations of his ancestors to the monks, while the abbot and convent granted to the said Roger the manor of Broughton (?) with the chapel and the tenement (called) del Sponne, and quitclaimed to him one mark yearly for the tenement of Bechene with homage, etc , and to the rector of Hawarden all the demesne tithes thereof, and further granted to Ralph de Mold 5 marks yearly from their chamber until he should be better provided for by them 1258.

In quadam periculosa conuencione dominus Rogerus de Monte alto dedit duas bouatas terre in Nestona cum suis libertatibus, et totum ius et clamium quod aliquo modo habuit vel habere potuit in aduocacione ecclesie de Nestona

Item concessit et confirmauit omnes donaciones et confirmaciones antecessorum suorum in omnibus tenementis et aduocationibus ecclesiarum datis monachis

Preterea abbas et conuentus dederunt dicto Rogero manerium de Brocton [1] cum capella et tenemento del Sponne,[2] et quiete clamauerunt et remiserunt eidem Rogero vnam marcam annuam pro tenemento de Bechene cum homagio et seruicio quod inde habere consueuerant, et rectori ecclesie de Hawrdyn omnes decimas de dominico de eadem

Item, dederunt Radulpho de Monte alto quinque marcas annuas de camera sua percipiendas quousque vberius per eos prouisus fuerit

Roger de Mold's concessions (and perhaps those made by the

---

[1] de Brocton interlined   [2] See Addenda

E

abbey) were apparently embodied in more specific grants   In Nos. 534 and 535 he assigns an actual couple of oxgangs in Neston and confirms by name the manors and advowsons which his ancestors had given to the abbey, the list of which is reproduced by its chronicler (*Ann Cestr* 76)   It is not necessary to suppose with Ormerod (1. 251) that Roger had actually sought restitution of all these, or indeed of more than the advowson of Neston, and the suggestion that Lea cum Newbold, though not named, was one of the losses of the abbey on this occasion has been shown elsewhere to be ill founded (note on No 500)   The Brocton which was lost (Brotton in *Ann Cestr* 76), doubtless Brochetuna in which Ralph the Hunter gave 3 carucates to the abbey shortly after its foundation (above, p 19), and his son seems to have given the rest of the vill (No 536), was probably Broughton, near Hawarden, rather than the neighbouring Bretton with which Ormerod identified it.   The demesne tithes of Hawarden which were surrendered to the rector had been given to St Werburgh's by earl Hugh I before Hawarden was granted out to the Molds (p 17)   .

The richer provision which the abbey undertook to find for Ralph de Mold to compensate him for his disappointment of the living of Neston seems to have been found in the rectory of West Kirby, for there can be no real doubt that the Ralph de Mold who held that benefice from "the time of the (barons') war" until shortly before 1287 (Orm II 485) was the same person   It may seem strange that Helsby should have accepted their identity, and yet antedated Ralph by more than a century (*ib* 1 58), but this was the unhappy result of Ormerod's transferring events which really happened in 1258 to a date nearly fifty years' earlier (note on No 531) in his account of Neston where he makes Ralph rector *c* 1210 (II 536)

533. Grant by Roger de Mold to the abbey of certain lands in (Great) Neston which he had formerly given to the church of Neston in exchange for certain lands enclosed within his park at Neston, which lands belonged to the said church *c* 1258 (?)

Rogerus de Monte alto dedit quasdam terras in Nestona quas quondam dedit ecclesie de Neston in escambium quarundam terrarum infra parcum suum de Nestona inclusarum, que quidem terre fuerunt ecclesie de Nestona

534. Grant by Sir Roger de Mold of 2 oxgangs in (Great) Neston which William, son of Henry, held   1258

Dominus Rogerus de Monte alto dedit duas bouatas terre in Nestona, cum suis pertinenciis, quas Willelmus filius Henrici tenuit.

535. Grant by Sir Roger de Mold of 2 oxgangs in (Great) Neston (as in No 534), with his right and claim in the advowson of the church of Neston, etc (saving his approvements in his waste and saving his whole park, Chart) ; also confirmation of the vills of Goostrey and Lawton under Lyme (Church Lawton) with its chapel, and of the church of Coddington, all of the gift of Hugh Fitz Norman, and of the chapel of Bruera (with a note in Chart , marked for deletion, that in reality Roger gave nothing save the 2 oxgangs, but on the contrary robbed the abbey) 1258.

Harl MS 2071, f 106 (old 100)

Uniuersis, etc. Rogerus de Montealto, senescallus Cestrie, salutem Sciatis me pro salute anime, etc , confirmasse Deo et sancte Werburge Cestrie et Thome abbati et monachis ibidem Deo seruientibus duas bouatas terre in uilla de Neston, illas scilicet quas W[s] filius Henrici de Neston de me ten[et], una [1] cum toto iure patronatus [1] ecclesie predicte uille de Neston in Wyrhal [2] Conc[essi] insuper eisdem totam uillam de Goostre [3] quam habent de dono Hugonis filii Normanni, et uillam de Lauton subtus Lymam quam habent de dono ipsius Hugonis,[4] et ecclesiam de Codington quam habent de dono dicti Hugonis Normani filii, et capellam de Bruera quam habent de dono Roberti de Montealto aui mei [5] Et ego Rogerus et heredes mei omnia predicta, prout in cartis antecessorum meorum quas de donis suis inspexi plenius continetur, dictis abbati et conuentui imperpetuum warr[antizabimus]. Testibus domino Rogero de Venables, domino Thoma de Maingarin, domino Hamone de Massy, domino Fulcone de Orreby, domino W° de Boydel, domino Henrico de Torbock, domino Thoma de Orreby, militibus, et aliis.

See the notes on Nos 531 and 532 The chronicler of the abbey gives the names of the manors and advowsons confirmed, but Bruera owing to an imperfection of the MS appears in the form Bii (*Ann Cestr* , 76) In the spirit of the note which the indignant com-

---

[1] cum iure et clamio in aduocacione, Chart
[2] cum omnibus ad eam spectantibus, saluo approueamentis suis in vasto suo et saluo parco suo integro, Chart
[3] Gosetie, Chart
[4] una cum aduocacione capelle de eadem, Chart
[5] Instead of habent mei the Chart has antea iuste possederunt The scribe goes on Set sciendum quod Rogerus de Monte alto nihil dedit set pocius iaput, preter duas bouatas ultimo prescriptas , unde de eo potest dici illud Ysaie propheticum " Ve qui predaris nonne et ipse predaberis, cum consummaueris depredacionem depredaberis '' (Isaiah xxxiii 1) The passage has been subsequently crossed through with the pen and dotted underneath.

piler has appended to this charter, the chronicler rejoices over the misfortunes which soon after befell the depredator of the house. For Hugh Fitz Norman's gifts to St. Werburgh's see above, pp. 19, 40, and for Bruera No. 500.

536. Grant by Serlo the Hunter to the abbey, of all his land in Broughton (?) free of all service in free alms, as they already possessed the rest of that vill by the gift of his father. ? *t.* Stephen.

Serlo venator dedit monachis totam terram suam in Broctona solutam et liberam ab omni seruicio, ita quod illa pars ville in pura elemosina ex dono suo semper maneat quemadmodum reliquam partem ville ex dono patris sui prius possederunt.

Serlo was doubtless son of Ralph the Hunter, who had given the abbey 3 carucates in Brochetuna at, or shortly after, its foundation (pp. 19, 34). Serlo witnesses several of the extant charters of Ranulf II.

537. Grant by Meyler, son of Osbert, to abbot Roger etc. of a moiety of all his land in Broughton which he held of them, with a messuage, etc., for which he received five marks from them. See No. 835. 1240–49.

Meyler filius Osberti dedit abbati Rogero et conuentui medietatem tocius terre sue in Broctona quam de eis tenuit cum mesuagio et pertinenciis, vnde quinque marcas ab eis percepit.

538. Quitclaim by Richard, son of Griffin, to abbot Walter etc. of all his land in Cheveley, which he held of them, for 2 oxgangs of land in Broughton. Paying to them yearly 12*d.* for the said oxgangs. 1228–40.

Ricardus filius Gryffini quiete clamauit abbati Waltero et conuentui totam terram suam in Cheueleye quam de eis tenuit pro duabus bouatis terre in Broctona. Reddendo eis annuatim duodecim denarios de dictis bouatis.

539. Exchange between abbot Walter etc. and Sir Roger de Mold, the former granting to the latter an oxgang in Hawarden and a yearly rent of 3*s.* 4*d.* from 2 oxgangs there, for which Roger is to pay 12*d.* yearly and do fealty, and Roger quitclaiming to them 2½ oxgangs in Cheveley which he obtained by exchange from Wenthilian, daughter of Robert the Priest. 1228–40.

Abbas Walterus et conuentus dederunt domino Rogero de [f 2
Monte alto vnam bouatam terre in Hawrdyn et redditum de
duabus bouatis in eadem que illi percipere consueuerunt, scilicet
quadraginta denarios annuos, vnde predictus Rogerus annuatim
reddet duodecim denarios dictis monachis ad festum sancti Martini
et faciet inde eis fidelitatem , dictus vero Rogerus quiete clamauit
duas bouatas terre et dimidiam in Cheueley, quas dictus Rogerus
perquisiuit per escambium de Wenthilian filia Roberti presbiteri

540. Quitclaims (c 1240–80) by Ranulf, son of William, and
William, son of Adam de Lawton, and by William, son of
William de Lawton, priest, to the abbey, of the advowson
of the church of Lawton , institution of Edward the clerk
(to the rectory of Lawton) by Richard, bishop of Coventry
(1162–82), on the presentation of abbot Robert, and consecration of a graveyard by the same bishop, subject to a
payment of 12*d* a year to the mother church of Astbury,
also institution by bishop William (1214–23) on the presentation of abbot H[ugh] of W[illiam de Massey] clerk of
Rostherne

Ranulphus filius Willelmi et Willelmus filius Ade de Lautona
quiete clamauerunt monachis aduocacionem ecclesie de Lautona
Hanc eciam Willelmus filius Willelmi de Lautona presbiteri quiete
clamauit in hanc ecclesiam

Ricardus Conuentrensis episcopus ad presentacionem Roberti
abbatis Cestrie Edwardum clericum instituit, et ad peticionem
dicti abbatis eius cimiterium ad sepulturam consecrauit Soluendo
annuatim matrici ecclesie de Astbury duodecim denarios   Item
in hanc W[illelmus] Conuentrensis episcopus ad presentacionem
H[ugonis] abbatis W[illelmum] clericum de Rouestorn instituit

For the grantors of the quitclaim of the advowson of Lawton
church, which was still often called a chapel, see below, Nos 788 ff
The identification of " W clericum de Rouestorn " with William de
Massey, rector of Rostherne, is Ormerod's (iii 18, 1 437)

541. Confirmation by Robert, lord of Mold, steward of the earl
of Chester, to the abbey of the whole vill of Goostrey with
all its appurtenances in pure alms for ever   1192–1208

Harl MS 2071, f 39*d* (old 24)   The witnesses in brackets are taken
from another copy in Harl MS 2074, f 192

Sciant omnes tam presentes quam futuri quod ego Robertus,
dominus Moaldie et senescaldus comitis Cestrie concessi et pre-

senti carta confirmaui domui beate Werburge uirginis in Cestria et monachis ibidem Deo seruientibus totam uillam de Gorestre plene et integre cum omnibus pertinenciis suis in puram et perpetuam elemosinam, pro salute anime mee et animarum omnium predecessorum meorum, liberam, quietam et solutam ab omni seculari seruicio et omni seculari exaccione, ita quod in eadem uilla de Gorestre nichil ad opus meum uel heredum meorum retinui preter elemosinam et orationes ; et tantam libertatem in ipsa eadem uilla predicte domui et predictis monachis concessi quod imposterum nullus heredum meorum quicquam libertatis possit superaddere   Et ut hec mea concessio rata et inconuulsa permaneat in perpetuum eam sigilli mei apposicione roboraui   Hiis testibus   Radulfo de Menilw[arin] tunc iusticiario, Hamo[ne] de Masci, Gwarino de Vernun, Radulfo filio Simonis [Philippo de Orreby, Simone de Tuschet, Rogero de Mesnilwarin, Willelmo de Venables, Toma dispensatore, Roberto filio Pigot, Petro clerico comitis, Ricardo de Vernun, Roberto de Menilwarin, Brito'[1] Pantun', Patricio de Mobburley, Liulfo de Twamlow, Petro de Suet[enha]m, Ranulfo de Praers, Ricardo de Kingsley, Johanne de Sancta Maria] et multis aliis

A moiety of Goostrey had been given to the abbey by Hugh Fitz Norman, the Domesday ancestor of the grantor (above, p 40)   The other moiety then formed part of the Constable's fee   Ormerod (iii 131) does not trace its history, but both moieties, constituting the township of Barnshaw cum Goostrey, were afterwards in possession of the abbey, in virtue of the present or some earlier charter

The limits of date are fixed by the appearance of Ralph, the grantor's brother and predecessor, in a charter not earlier than 1192 (Morris, *Chester*, 482–3), and by the fact that Mainwaring's justiciarship was before October 1208

542. Quitclaim by Robert le Brun to the abbey of all his right and claim in the vill of Goostrey.   1208–26

Harl MS 2071, f 39d (old 24)

Uniuersis sancte matris ecclesie filiis presentibus et futuris Robertus Brunus salutem in Domino   Sciatis me remisisse et quietum clamasse de me et de meis heredibus imperpetuum Deo et domui sancte Werburge Cestrie et domino H[ugoni] abbati et monachis ibidem Deo seruientibus totum ius et clamium quod ego habui uel aliquis antecessorum meorum in uilla de Gorestre et in eius pertinenciis, ita quod nec ego nec aliquis heredum meorum in dicta uilla de Gorestre uel eius pertinenciis quicquam iuris de

[1] Bricro   Cf No 528

cetero contra sanctam domum predictam uendicare poterimus. Sed eciam si aliquis moueat contencionem uersus dictam domum sancte Werburge de prenominata uilla uel eius pertinenciis ego et heredes mei stabimus pro toto posse nostro cum domino abbate et monachis supradictis ad defendendam uillam memoratam cum omnibus pertinenciis suis ad opus sancte Werburge Cestrie   Et ut hec mea remissio et quieta clamancia firme sint et stabiles imperpetuum eas hac carta mea et sigilli mei munimine roboraui. Testibus   domino P[hilippo] de Orrebi tunc iusticiario Cestrie, R[   ] de Montealto senescallo Cestrie, Willelmo de Venabl', Warino de Vernun, Hamo[ne] de Massci et multis aliis

The family of Le Brun is said to have descended from Randle, brother of Liulf de Twemlow, and Croxton, sheriff of Cheshire in the latter part of the reign of John, but its interest in Goostrey is not otherwise indicated (Orm iii 135, 210)   The Croxtons certainly had lands there which they gave to the abbey (*ib.* iii 131). [Add]

543. Quitclaim by Thomas le Palmer and Cecilia his wife to abbot S[imon] of an oxgang of land in Goostrey which Cecilia's father, Thomas, son of [Reginald] Brun, gave them   1283–88

Harl MS 2074, f 89 (old 192) *d*

Omnibus, etc., Thomas le Palmer de Gorstre[1] et Cecilia uxor eius, filia Thome de Tuamlowe, salutem, etc   [Sciatis] nos concessisse Deo et ecclesie sancte Werburge Cestrie et capitalibus dominis nostris domino S[ymoni] abbati et conuentui eiusdem loci unam bouatam terre in Gortre cum pertinenciis, illam, scilicet, quam Thomas filius Brun de Tuamlowe nobis dedit, tenendam de eisdem abbate et conuentu per homagium et seruitium unius libri cumini annuatim soluendi ; habendam et tenendam, etc.   Pro hac concessione dicti abbas et conuentus centum solidos argenti nobis pre manibus pacauerunt   Testibus · domino Reginaldo de Gray tunc iusticiario Cestrie, dominis Willelmo de Venables, Roberto Grosso Venatore tunc uicecomite Cestri[shiri]e, Johanne de Wetenhale, Radulfo de Brereton, Ricardo de Suetenham, Thoma de Gorstree, Ricardo de Crawlach, Henrico de eadem, Thoma de Tuamlowe, et aliis

Thomas son of Reginald's confirmation was given between 1286 and 1288 (No 776), and the gift may have been made just before

544. Agreement by which William Jokel recognised that the

[1] Gosetre, Ch

common pasture of Goostrey was the right and inheritance of the monks of Chester, for which they granted to him and his tenants in Cepmondswich, for his homage and service and 12*d* yearly on the day of the Translation of St Werburgh (June 21), common of herbage in the whole pasture for their draught beasts and cattle, it being understood that the monks and their men of Goostrey and Barnshaw should make essarts and enclosures, etc, without opposition from William and his tenants, saving to them free passage to and from the remaining pasture at all seasons after the removal of the corn and hay, except in the season of mast, when they were to go by the usual way to the heath ? 1249–65

In quadam puplica concordia   Willelmus Jokel recognouit et concessit communem pasturam de Gosetre esse ius et hereditatem monachorum Cestrie, ita quod nichil in ea possit vendicare, vnde monachi concesserunt ei et suis tenentibus in Schappemonneswicho,[1] pro homagio et seruicio suo et duodecim denariis annuatim die Translacionis sancte Werburge monachis soluendis, comunam herbagii tocius pasture ad aueria sua et catalla, nec aliquid aliud poterit dictus Willelmus vel sui tenentes preter dictum herbagium exigere   Preterea monachi et homines sui de Gosetre et de Bernuleshawe assartabunt et includent et omnia commoda sua inde facient sine aliqua contradictione dicti Willelmi vel suorum tenencium   Saluis eis libero introitu et exitu ad pasturam remanentem omni tempore anni, bladis et fenis asportatis, excepto tempore pessone, et tunc per viam vsitatam ad bruariam eant.

Cepmondswich or Cepmondwich was formerly a hamlet in the neighbouring vill of Over Peover (Orm 1 478)   The facts of the agreement seem to point to one of those cases of intercommoning between adjoining vills which were not infrequent while boundaries were still imperfectly drawn (Maitland, *Hist. of Eng Law*, 1 619) For the date cf No 768*b*

545. Grant by William Patrick (of Malpas) of the dwelling house of Patemon

Willelmus Patric dedit masuram Patemon liberam et solutam.

There is nothing to show which of the two or three barons of Malpas of this Christian name was the grantor

546. Grant by Hugh, son of Robert of the Castle, of 8

[1] Scapimonneswic in the heading

oxgangs of land in Barrow which earl H[ugh II] gave to his father

Hugo filius Roberti de Castello dedit octo bouatas terre in Barwe quas H[ugo] comes dedit patri suo

547. Grant by Brice Coterel of 2 oxgangs of land in Gayton and a fishery called Carrow.

Bricius Coterel dedit duas bouatas terre in Gaytone et vnam piscariam que uocabatur Cairowe

548. Grant by John de Panton to Brice, his son, and Leuke, daughter of Richard, son of Robert, of a fourth part of the mill of Tilstone (Fearnall) and all his demesne land there, with the wood of Northwood, etc., paying to him yearly two white gloves and to the abbot of Chester (as chief lord) 15*d* Before 1208

Johannes de Pantona [1] dedit Briccio filio suo et Leuke filie Ricardi filii Roberti quartam partem totius molendini de Tidelstona cum omnibus pertinenciis, et totam terram suam de dominico suo in Tidulstona cum bosco de Northwode, et cum omnibus dominico suo pertinentibus, reddendo sibi annuatim duas albas cirotecas et faciendo seruicium domino abbati Cestrie, quindecim denarios annuos ei reddendo

The vill of Tilstone Fearnall had been given to the abbey by Robert de Tremons in the time of earl Hugh I (p 20)

548a. Quitclaim by John, son of Brice de Paunton, to the abbey of the fourth part of Tilstone (Fearnall), which he held of them, reserving only their prayers.

Johannes filius Briccii de Pauntona dedit et quiete clamauit monachis Cestrie totam quartam partem ville de Tydulstona quam de eis tenuit, nichil sibi retinens preter oraciones

549. Quitclaim by Andrew Batail to abbot William of any right or claim he had in the vill of Tilstone (Fearnall) 1121–40 or 1226–28.

Andreas Batail [2] quiete clamauit quicquid iuris vel clamii habuit in villa de Tudelstona, cum omnibus pertinenciis, Willelmo abbati

---

[1] Paunton in heading The Pantons were probably related to the Pantons or Pantulfs of Wem (No 528 *n*) [2] Batayle in heading

550. Quitclaim by Richard, son of Simon de Tilstone, of all his land in Tilstone (Fearnall)

Ricardus filius Symonis de Tudelston quiete clamauit totam terram suam in Tidulstan

551. Quitclaim by William Hall (de Aula) of Tilstone of all his land in Tilstone (Fearnall)

Willelmus de Aula de Tidelstona quiete clamauit totam terram suam de Tidulstona

552. Grant by William de Burmingham of all his land in Tilstone (Fearnall) for the support of a chaplain in the monastery of St Werburgh, Chester, to celebrate divine service for ever for his soul and that of Margery his wife and the souls of their heirs, etc

Willelmus de Burmyngham dedit totam terram suam in Tidulstona pro sustentacione vnius capellani in monasterio sancte Werburge Cestrie pro anima sua, et Margerie vxoris sue, et animabus heredum suorum, et animabus omnium fidelium defunctorum divina celebrantis imperpetuum.

552a.[1] Grant by abbot Simon, etc, to William de Bunbury of a moiety of a close in Tilstone (Fearnall) called Le Bruches, etc.   1265–84

Shakerley (Vernon) MS 3, f 272 at Somerford Park, Congleton " Penes Hen Bunburie a° 1640 "

Simo abbas sancte Werburge Cestrie et conuentus dederunt Willelmo de Boneburie et heredibus suis, pro homagio et seruicio suo, medietatem cuiusdam clausure in Tydleston vocate Le Bruches ubi via de Bunburie et [via de] Tildeston simul conueniunt, etc , et clausur[am ?] J Bernard, etc.   Saluo approuiam[ento]. Habend' predicto Willelmo, heredibus et assignatis suis de nobis et successoribus [nostris], Reddendo 3s ad festum sancti Martini pro omnibus seruiciis   Testibus, Roberto de Huxlegh, W° de Brex, W° de Ridlegh, W° de Bulkley, Hugone[2] de Torperlegh, Hugone de Hatton, W° de Bruer[a], Patricio de Barton, Roberto le Brun, Roberto de Ynes, et aliis

Hugh de Hatton died 1284 (*Cal Inq* ii 523)   For other Tilstone charters see Nos 344–344*a*

---

[1] This deed is not inserted in the Chartulary
[2] Henrico in a copy in Harl MS 2131, f 88 (old 91)*d*

553. Grant by William Boydell to Liulf de Twemlow of a moiety
of the vill of Winnington, to hold by the service of a sixth
part of a knight's fee   *c* 1199–1216

Harl MS 2074, f 68*d* (old 171*d*)   Pd (in part) in Orm ii 200

Ego Willelmus de Boidele concessi, etc , Lidulpho de Twam- [f 28
lawe,[1] pro homagio et seruicio suo, medietatem de Wynington,[2]
illam, scilicet, que est de feodo meo, illi et heredibus suis, habendum
de me et heredibus meis in feodo et hereditate, libere et quiete,
cum omnibus pertinentiis suis in bosco, in plano, in pratis, in
pascuis, in aquis, in viis, in semitis, et in omnibus locis et libertatibus, faciendo mihi seruicium quod ante fieri consueuit pro
omnibus seruiciis et exactionibus quibuscunque, videlicet sextam
partem unius feodi militis, etc   Testibus   Adamo de Dutton,
Hugone fratre suo, Willelmo de Tabelle, Thoma filio Willelmi,
Adamo de Aistun, Ricardo de Vernune, Hamone clerico, Henrico
de Aistun, Ricardo de Rodestorn, clerico, et aliis.

For William, youngest son of Heute Boydell of Dodleston, see
above, p 92 (on p 91 Hente should be Heute)   The moiety of Winnington (near Northwich) here granted by him had belonged to his maternal
ancestor Osbern Fitz Tesson in 1086   Liulf de Twemlow was sheriff
of Cheshire in the time of king John, and survived into the reign of
Henry III   From him several Cheshire families descended (Orm
ii 200, iii 210)

554. Grant by Liulf de Twemlow to his (second) son Robert of
the moiety of Winnington acquired by No 553, rendering
two barbed arrows yearly, in addition to external service
c. 1210–20

Harl MS 2119, f 156*d*   Pd (rather incorrectly) in Orm ii 200

Sciant, etc , [quod] ego Liulfus, dominus de Thamlowe,[3] dedi,
etc , Roberto filio meo et sponse mee totam terram meam quam
habui in villa de Wynintona, scilicet medietatem de Wynentona,
tenendam, etc , de me et heredibus meis, reddendo mihi annuatim,
etc , duas sagittas barbatas pro omnibus seruiciis, saluo forinseco
seruicio, etc   Testibus, Ricardo de Sonbach, Petro de Swetenham,
Thoma, persona de Sonbach, Johanne fratre suo, Johanne de
Aculuiston, Henrico de Craunach, Ricardo fratre suo.

The grantee is identified by Ormerod (ii 200) with the Robert de
Winnington who acquired the other moiety of Winnington with its
heiress Margery, daughter of Robert, son of William de Winnington,

---
[1] Tomlowe, Chart   [2] Wininton, Chart
[3] Lidulphus de Thomlowe, Chart

and who, after surviving a second wife, Matilda de Wilbraham, died late in 1294 (*Cal Inq P M* iii 244) This is to attribute an incredible length of life to Liulf's son   As he witnessed a chaiter befoie 1214 (No 753 *n*), he would have been at least ninety years old at his death, and yet we are asked to believe that Robert, his elder son and heir (by Margery), was born as late as 1265, and his second son, Richard (by Matilda), in 1273   It is quite evident that, owing to the identity of Christian name, a generation has been omitted by Ormerod, and that the Robert who died in 1294 was grandson and not son of Liulf   This conclusion is supported by the fact that we have two charters (Nos 753 and 753*a*) granted by Robert "son of Liulf the sheriff," [1] with his wife *Mabel* (Mabilla)   The attempt to explain this as an error in both cases was obviously unsatisfactory   The two Roberts are perhaps distinguished in No 755

From the first of the chaiters just mentioned it seems almost certain that Robert, son of Liulf, was still living in 1244–45   The first charter of Robert de Winnington and his wife Margeiy which can be dated with some precision falls between 1267 and 1270 (Orm i 487)

555. Grant by Sir John Boydell to Sir Richard de Massey, kt. (of Tatton), of the homage and services belonging to him from the moiety of Winnington which William de Boydell gave to Liulf de Twemlow (No 553)   *c* 1272–1300

Johannes Boydel, miles, dedit Ricardo de Mascy, militi, homagium et omnimoda seruicia sibi pertinencia de medietate de Winintone quam W[illelmus] de Boydel dedit Lidulpho de Tomlowe

See note on No 556   Leycester was mistaken in thinking that Massey was knighted about 1286 (Orm i 441)   He was a knight already in 1279 (above, p 205)

556. Quitclaim by Sir Richard de Massey, kt , to abbot Thomas (II) of the homage, etc , due to him from a moiety of Winnington, and the service of a sixth part of a knight's fee   1291–1300.

Ricardus de Mascy, miles, quiete clamauit Thome abbati Cestrie homagium et omnimodum seruicium sibi debitum pro medietate de Weninton, et seruicium sexte partis feodi vnius militis

From a brief note of this charter in Harl. MS 2074, f 70 (old 172) we learn the name of the first witness, William de Piaers, sheriff of Cheshire   His last term of office ended in 1300.   The years 1293–95 are excluded fiom the possible dates, as he was not then sheiiff

[1] There does not seem evidence that he called himself Robert de Winnington

557. Grant by Richard de Wybunbury (? I) to abbot Thomas (I) of the homage and service of Robert de Winnington for a moiety of Winnington. 1249–65.

Ricardus de Wibbenbur[ia] dedit Thome abbati Cestrie homagium et totum seruicium Roberti de Wininton sibi quondam debita pro medietate de Wininton cum omnibus pertinenciis. [Test magistro Ricardo de Kegworth, Ricardo Coudrey, Ricardo Toft, et aliis Harl MS 2074, f 68 (171)]

This was the (Mainwaring) moiety which Robert acquired by marriage (Nos 554 n , 558 n) The relation of this grant to that of Richard de Wynbunbury (II) to abbot Simon is obscure. There are two dots over " Thome," which may mean that the scribe had his doubts, but the witnesses are not those of the grant of 1270–71

558. Grant by Robert de Lees to Richard de Wybunbury (I , cf No 559) of the homage and service of Robert de Winnington, etc., and a rent of 10s from a moiety of Winnington, paying to him yearly two white gloves and doing external service ? *temp* abbot Roger or Thomas (I).

Robertus de Leghes dedit Ricardo de Wibbenbury homagium et totum seruicium Roberti de Winintona cum omnibus pertinenciis et redditum x solidorum de medietate de Winintona ad Natiuitatem sancti Johannis Bapt et ad festum sancti Martini per equales porciones soluendorum, reddendo sibi annuatim duas albas cirothecas et faciendo forinsecum seruicium.

From Nos 752–5 it would appear that the grantor of this charter was tenant of Lees under Robert, son of Liulf the sheriff, who held of the Rundchamps of Lostock. Comparison of dates might suggest (but cf. 559) that Robert de Winnington is not the son of Robert, son of Liulf, whose father gave him the other (Boydell) moiety of Winnington (No 554), but this son's father-in-law, Robert, son of William de Winnington. In a charter recorded by Randle Holme, Richard de Wybunbury gives a moiety of Winnington to this Robert, son of William (Harl MS 2074, f 68 (171) , cf Orm. ii 200, who has *Robert* de Wybunbury) This is not easily reconciled with the present charter, and with the fact that the first Winnington family seem to have inherited here and in Warford from the Warfords, who were tenants of the Mainwarings in both (Orm i 424, 487, ii. 200, iii 584). Perhaps Wybunbury on acquiring a mesne interest in the moiety merely confirmed the tenancy of the Winningtons

It is curious that in the *Inq P M* in 1295 of Robert de Winnington, son-in-law of the Robert of this charter (*Cal* iii 244), this interest which had passed to the abbey is ignored, and Robert is said to have

held after his first wife's death by the courtesy of England and of
the heirs of Sir Warin de Mainwaring (d 1288–89).

559. Grant by Richard de Wybunbury (II) to abbot S[imon] of
the homage and service of Robert de Winnington for a
moiety of Winnington, which Robert de Lees gave to
Richard's father (No 558)   1270–71

Harl MS 2074, f 171d (new 68d)

Ricardus de Wybunbury salutem. Sciatis me pro salute
anime mee et antecessorum et successorum meorum dedisse Deo
et ecclesie sancte Werburge Cestrie et domino S abbati et conuentui eiusdem loci [et] eorum successoribus homagium et totum
seruicium Roberti de Wyninton [pro medietate de Winintona]
cum pertinenciis quam Robertus de Leghes dedit Ricardo patri
meo, quam prefatus Robertus post[ea] de me tenuit, una cum
annuo redditu 10s quos mihi ad duos anni terminos soluere consueuit , habendum predictis abbati et conuentui [et] eorum successoribus uel quibuscumque assignatis quiete et integre, cum
wardis, releuiis, escaetis, approviamentis et omnibus aliis pertinenciis sine ullo retenemento, in liberam, puram et perpetuam
elemosinam et ab omni seculari seruicio et exaccione quacunque
solutam et quietam , quod nec ego nec heredes mei nec aliquis
nomine meo uel per nos aliquid iuris uel clamii in predicta medietate ville de Wininton et homagio et seruicio dictorum Roberti uel
heredum suorum aliquo modo exigere uel uendicare poterimus
preter oraciones tantum   Predicti tam[en] Robertus et heredes
sui faciant forinsecum [seruicium] quod inde prius facere consueuerunt, etc   Hiis testibus . domino Reg[inaldo] de Gray tunc
iusticiario Cestrie, Thoma Maingerin, Thoma de Orreby, Ricardo
de Wilbraham tunc vicecomite Cestrie, Roberto de Huxleg',
Johanne de Wetenham,[1] Ricardo de Orreby, Willelmo [de]
Bonebur', Willelmo Bernard, et aliis

By this grant, with which cf No 557, the abbey acquired a mesne
superiority of the second moiety of Winnington, which was the inheritance of Margery, wife of Robert de Winnington (Orm ii 200)
Ormerod does not seem to distinguish between the grantor of this
charter and his father and namesake, who doubtless was the sheriff
of 1233, 1236, 1239, and 1244   See No 755 and Addenda

By Richard's precept Robert duly did homage to the abbot, etc
(Harl MS 2074, f 172 (69))

560. Grant by Robert, son of Robert de Winnington, to the abbey

[1] *Rectius* Wetenhale

of 6d of yearly rent which Richard de Wybunbury was bound to pay to him for certain lands in Nantwich, along with the lordship of all the said lands. *c.* 1295–1320

Robertus filius Roberti de Winintona dedit monachis Cestrie vi denarios annui redditus quas Ricardus de Wibinbury sibi soluere tenebatur pio quibusdam terris in Wico Mauban, vna cum dominio omnium dictaium terraium

561. Grant by Robert Picot (Pigot) to Robert de Worth, of the whole vill of Chelford, with the lordship and rent of Astle and (Old) Withington, paying to him and his heirs 7s yearly and a pair of spurs (gloves ?) for all secular service, saving entertainment for the serjeants of the peace, and that part of the duty of enclosing the hays of the forest (of Macclesfield) which falls to Chelford   1245–50

Harl MS 2074, f 185d (new 82d)

Sciant, etc., ego Robertus Picot dedi, etc , Roberto de Worth pro homagio et servitio suo totam villam de Cholleford,[1] cum dominio et redditu de Asthull et de Whithinton,[2] cum pertinentiis suis, infra dictas villas et extra , tenendum et habendum, etc , ieddendo inde annuatim 7s argenti et unum par calcaiium[3] in festo Omnium Sanctorum pro omni servitio,[4] etc , salvo pouturo[5] servientium pacis et clausura hayarum[6] de foresta de Macclesf[eld] quantum pertinet ad terram de Cheleford faciend[a], sicut de iure debet et solet, etc   His testibus   domino Johanne de Gray tunc iusticiario Cestrensi, domino Radulfo de Vernon, domino Roberto de Mascy, Benedicto de Coudray tunc ballivo de Macclesfeld, Viviano de Davenport, Thoma de Orreby, Sewall de Tidderington, Adam de Sutton, Ricardo de Mottram, Adam de Aldridell[ea], Adam de Brishell, Rogero de Aldridell[ea] clerico, et aliis.

The grantor is presumed to have been of the family of Pigot of Waverton, Butley, etc   The grantee was son of Jordan de Worth (Orm iii 687, 711)

The attestation of John de Gray supplies the date   Most of the witnesses belonged to Macclesfield hundred   Thomas de Orreby was of Gawsworth

562. Grant by Robert Pigot to Robert de Worth, foi his homage

---

[1] Chelleford, Ch (*rectius*)   [2] Wiyinton, Ch
[3] cirothecarum, Ch   This is proved to be wiong by No 564.
[4] seculari added, Ch   [5] salua putura, Ch
[6] claustuia hidarum, Ch

and service, of the mill of Chelford and (Old) Withington, with all its suits and appurtenances and a supply of water and a site for the mill anywhere within the bounds of Chelford and Withington, paying to him yearly therefor one barbed arrow for all secular service, the grantee being entitled to distrain upon the lord and the suitors to the mill for the repair of the pool, the making of sluices and millstones, the rebuilding of the mill, when necessary, and the carriage of timber and millstones thereto by the suitors in accordance with previous custom   ? 1245–50

Robertus Pigot dedit Roberto de Worth pro homagio et seruicio suo molendinum de Chelleford et de Withington,[1] cum omnibus sectis suis et pertinenciis, et agistiamento aque et attachiamento molendini vbicunque voluerit infra diuisas de Chelleford et de Withington,[1] cum piscaria aque, reddendo inde annuatim sibi vnam sagittam barbatam in festo Omnium Sanctorum pro omni seruicio seculari , ita quod predictus Robertus de Worth et heredes sui possint [2] distringere se et heredes suos cum secta dicti molendini per terras et possessiones et catalla sua ad stagnum reparandum, exclusas et molas faciendas, et ad molendinum reficiendum cum necesse fuerit, et ad meremium et molas cariandas ad predictum molendinum, sicut aliquando dicta secta facere consueuit

563. Grant by Robert de Worth to the abbey, with his body to be buried there, of the whole vill of Chelford, with its mill, the lordship and rent of Astle and (Old) Withington, and land called Longfordcroft formerly held by Jordan de Bromley, the monks to find a competent chaplain to celebrate the office of the dead for the souls of Robert and his ancestors and successors either continually in the chapel of Chelford, or if they please, thrice a week there and on the other days at the altar of St Nicholas in the mother church of Prestbury, where his ancestors lie buried , the monks are also to perform the services due to the chief lords   1267

Charter Roll, No 73, 13 Edw I , m 15, No 46, collated with Harl MS 2074, f 198d, and Shakerley MS 1 f 181

Omnibus Christi fidelibus presentem cartam uisuris uel audituris Robertus filius Jordani de Worth salutem in domino sempiternam   Nouitur (sic) vniuersitas vestra me pro salute anime mee et antecessorum et successorum meorum concessisse,

¹ Wiynton (for Wipinton) MS   Itself corrected from Wininton, due to the Winnington entries above (see old index, p 5 above)
² possunt, MS

dedisse, et hac presenti carta mea confirmasse, et eciam pro me et heredibus meis imperpetuum quietum clamasse Deo et beate Marie et monasterio sancte Werburge Cestrie et domino S[imoni] abbati et conuentui eorumque successoribus, in liberam puram et perpetuam elemosinam, totam villam de Cholleford [1] cum molendino et omnibus aliis pertinenciis, et cum dominio et redditu de Asthull et de Wythinton cum omnibus pertinenciis suis infra predictas villas et extra, ac eciam quandam terram que vocatur Longefordecroft cum omnibus pertinenciis suis quam Iordanus de Bromlegh [2] aliquo tempore tenuit, cum corpore meo in monasterio predicto sepeliendo cum humanitas de me contigerit, tenendam et habendam dictis abbati et conuentui eorumque successoribus vel assignatis quibuscunque adeo libere et quiete sicut ego Robertus vel aliquis feoffatorum meorum aliquando liberius et quietius dictas terras cum pertinenciis tenuimus vel tenere debuimus in homagio,[3] releuiis, reddittibus, custodiis, escaetis, villenagiis, libertatibus et liberis consuetudinibus in aquis, in stagnis, in molendinis factis et faciendis, in piscariis, in viuariis, in moris, in maris, in mariscis, in viis, in semitis, [in turbariis,][4] in bosco, in plano, in pratis, in pascuis, et in pasturis, et in omnibus aliis aisiamentis et commoditatibus que in dictis terris aliquando fieri solent vel possunt, nichil iuris vel clamii michi vel heredibus meis in terris prenotatis retinendo preter orationes et elemosinas [5] tantum Ita, scilicet, quod predicti abbas et conuentus eorumque successores inuenient [6] sumptibus eorum unum capellanum idoneum imperpetuum qui sciat et velit et possit officium defunctorum prout decet [7] plene adimplere pro anima mea et animabus antecessorum et successorum meorum et omnium fidelium defunctorum, vel in capella de Cholleford continue celebrantem vel, si dictis abbati et conuentui vel successoribus suis visum fuerit expedire, singulis diebus Dominicis et aliis duobus in septimana, quibus ministranti placuerit, in eadem capella, reliquis vero quatuor diebus ad altare sancti Nicholai quod constructum est in matri [8] ecclesia de Prestebury, ubi ossa predecessorum meorum humata quiescunt, faciendo inde [9] capitalibus dominis dicti feodi seruicia que ego facere consueui et debui, prout in cartis Roberti Picot feoffatoris mei michi factis, quas eisdem tradidi in [10] testimonium, plenius continetur Et ego vero [11] dictus Robertus et heredes mei predictas terras cum molendino et omnibus aliis pertinenciis suis, sicut predictum est,

---

[1] Chelleford, Ch (*rectius*) [2] Bromeleg', H. [3] homagiis, Ch.
[4] Supplied from Ch [5] elemosinam, H [6] inuenerint, H.
[7] debet, H [8] *Sic* also in H , matrici, Ch , S
[9] insuper, H, S [10] om H [11] verus, MS

prefatis abbati et conuentui eorumque successoribus vel quibuscunque assignatis imperpetuum contra omnes homines war-
rantizabimus.   In cuius rei testimonium presenti carte mee sigillum meum apposui.   Hiis testibus : domino Iacobo de Audithleg' tunc iusticiario Cestrie, domino R[oberto] de Stokeport tunc
constabulario castri Cestrie, domino Thoma de Orreby, Iordano
de Peulesdon' tunc vicecomite Cestres[irie], Roberto de Dunes,
Benedicto de Coudrey, Ricardo de Orreby, Henrico de Birchel,
Johanne de Werenh',[1] Roberto de Huxelegh, Willelmo Meingarin,
Michaele de Gorstre, Ricardo Bonetable, Warino de Crokeston,
Roberto fratre eius, Rogero de Toft, Ada de Bothes, Thoma fratre
eius, Rogero de Ber[n]ulfsh[aw] et aliis.

The date seems fixed to the early months of 1267 by No. 563a
and by the fact that this seems to have been the year of Puleston's
sheriffdom (Orm. i. 70).   It is strange that the gift is placed in 1270
by the *Annales Cestrienses* (100).

563a. Appointment by Robert de Worth of Ralph de Wich as
his attorney or proctor to give seisin of Chelford, etc., to
abbot S[imon] and the convent.   March 15, 1266-67.

Harl. MS. 2074, f. 185d (new 82d).

Universis Christi fidelibus, etc., Robertus filius Iordani de
Worth salutem.   Noveritis me concessisse et ordinasse Radulfum
de Wico valetum meum verum et legitimum attornatum meum
seu procuratorem meum ad faciendum et tradendum domino
S. abbati Cestrensi et eiusdem loci conventui nomine meo plenam
seseinam ville de Chelleford, cum molendino et omnibus aliis
pertinentiis, et dominio et redditu de Asthull et de Whithinton.
In cuius rei testimonium has literas patentes sigillo meo signatas
eidem Radulfo fieri feci.   Dat(as) apud Cestriam die Martis
proximo post festum beati Gregorii pape anno Domini 1266.

The grantor seems to have died early in 1268, when his heirs were
found to be William de Stretton, *aet.* 32, Henry de Coudre, *aet.* 28,
and Jordan de Tyderington, *aet.* 26 (*Cal. Inq.* i. 674).

563b. Injunction by Robert de Worth to John de Astle and the
guardian of the land and heir of Gilbert Pigot to render to
the abbot and convent (to whom he has quitclaimed
Chelford, etc.) the homage and service which they had
been accustomed to render to him.   June 20, 1267.

Harl. MS. 2074, f. 186 (new 83).

---

[1] Wetenhall, H. correctly ; Wrenbury, Shakerley MS.

Robertus filius Jordani de Worth dilectis sibi in Christo Johanni de Asthull et custodi terre et heredis Gilberti Pigot salutem in Domino Quia villam de Chelleford cum dominio de Asthull et de Whythinton cum omnibus suis pertinentiis dedi et in perpetuum per cartam meam quietam clamavi, in liberam, puram et perpetuam elemosinam, domino S abbati sancte Werburge Cestrensis et eiusdem loci conventui eorumque successoribus in perpetuum, ideo vobis mando quatinus [1] homagia et servitia que mihi facere consuevistis et debuistis eisdem abbati et conventui facietis In cuius rei testimonium has literas sigillo meo signatas vobis mitto patentes coalt (*sic*) Dat[as] apud Macclesfeld die lune proximo ante festum Nativitatis sancti Johannis Baptiste anno Domini 1267

Randle Holme notes that he copied this and the two preceding charters from a book (ff 235–6) belonging to Peter Daniell (of Over Tabley, 1584–1652), into which they had been transcribed from the evidences of Henry Mainwaring of Kermincham Daniell's mother was of this family Nos 563*a* and *b* are not entered in the Chartulary

564. Confirmation by William, son of Robert Pigot, of the grant of Chelford to the abbey (No 563) 1271–74

Mainwaring Charter 54 (John Rylands Library)

Omnibus Christi fidelibus presens scriptum visuris uel audituris Willelmus filius Roberti Pigot salutem in Domino sempiternam Nouerit vniuersitas vestra me pro salute anime mee et antecessorum et successorum meorum concessisse, confirmasse et presenti carta mea pro me et heredibus meis inperpetuum quiete clamasse Deo et ecclesie beate Werburge Cestrie et domino Symoni abbati et conuentui eiusdem loci eorumque successoribus uel assignatis totam villam de Chelleford' cum molendino et cum dominio et redditibus de Asthull' et cum omnibus aliis pertinenciis infra dictas villas et extra Habendam et tenendam de me et heredibus meis dictis abbati, etc, adeo libere et quiete, plene, pacifice et integre sicut carta quam Robertus Pigot pater meus Roberto filio Iordani de Worth inde fecit plenius testatur, que dictos abbatem et conuentum de dicta villa de Chelleford' cum pertinenciis feofauit, saluis mihi et heredibus meis dominio et homagio de Wythintona. Reddendo inde annuatim mihi, etc, vnum par calcarium alborum et vnam sagittam barbatam et soluendo pro me, etc, tamquam attornati nostri, heredibus domini Hugonis Dispensatoris tres solidos et heredibus domini Hugonis de Wauertona quatuor solidos

[1] Quotius, MS

argenti in festo Omnium Sanctorum de illis septem solidis quos
(25)d] mihi et heredibus meis de predictis villis reddere tenebantur, pro
omni seruicio seculari, consuetudine, exaccione et demanda, saluo
forinseco [seruicio] domino Cestresir' debito, sicut in predicta carta
patris mei plenius continetur   Remisi eciam dictis dominis abbati,
etc , et hac presenti carta mea pro me, etc , inperpetuum quiete
clamaui homagium quod prefatus Robertus filius Iordani de Worth
et heredes sui uel sui assignati de predictis villis, Chelleford' et
Asthull' mihi, etc , facere deberent vna cum wardis, releuiis,
escaetis et omnibus aliis commoditatibus et approuiamentis qui
mihi vel, etc , aliquo casu contingente de dictis terris accidere uel
accrescere possent   Et ego, etc (warranty clause). Testibus,
Dominis Reginaldo de Grey tunc iusticiario Cestrie, Thoma de
Meyngarin, Petro de Ardena, Roberto de Stokeport, Hugone de
Hattona tunc vicecomite Cestresir', Roberto de Hux[leg'] tunc
constabulario castri Cestrie, Iohanne de Wetenhale, Ricardo de
Orreby, Rogero de Daueneport, Henrico de Birchel', Iohanne
fratre eius, Rogero de Vernona, Willelmo de Baggeleg', Ricardo de
Craulache, Ricardo Bonetable, Thoma de Gorstre, Rogero de
Bernulf[shawe], Willelmo de Wythintona, et aliis

Slits for seal (missing).

Helsby erroneously identified the grantor with William, son of
Robert de Mugebroc (Orm. iii 711)   See note to No 565a   William
Pigot in 1268 renounced in favour of the abbey any right he might
have to the advowson of Prestbury (No 575 , *Ann Cestr* 98)   He
died 1287–8 (Orm iii 667)

It will be noticed that the lordship and rent of Withington, which
were included in his father's grant to Robert de Worth and in Worth's
gift to the abbey, are by this deed reserved for the Pigots   The
barbed arrow in the service is not mentioned in the preceding charters.

565. Perpetual licence by Robert de Mugebroc to the abbot
and convent to dig and remove turf and to take heath and
earth anywhere in his waste of (Old) Withington, outside
his arable land, for the upkeep of the mill and (mill) pool
of Chelford, saving a green plot in front of his house and
his other approvements (from the waste).

Robertus de Mugebroc dedit monachis Cestrie, uel suis assignatis villam uel molendinum de Chelleford tenentibus, perpetuam
licenciam fodiendi et asportandi turbas et capiendi brueram et
terram vbique in vasto suo de Withington [1] extra terram suam

[1] Corrected in MS from Wininton

arabilem ad sustentacionem molendini et stagni de Chelleford. Salua tamen sibi quadam placea viridi ante domum suam et aliis approuiamentis suis, ita racionabiliter habendis quod nec monachi nec homines eorum de Chelleford a predicta libertate et communis et aysiamentis suis pristinis ibi impediantur.

But for the name of the grantor, this might be an abstract of the charter which follows (No. 565a), and as the latter is not entered in the Chartulary and does not profess to be a confirmation, it is possible, indeed probable, that the scribe has assigned the son's deed to the father.

565a. Similar licence by William, son and heir of Robert de Mugebrooke (see the note to No. 565). 1283–88.

Harl. MS. 2074, f. 199 (new 96).

Omnibus Christi fidelibus, etc. Willelmus filius et heres Roberti de Magebrooke (*sic*) salutem, etc. [Sciatis] me dedisse, etc., Deo et ecclesie Sancte Werburge Cestrensis et domino S. abbati et conventui eiusdem loci, dominis ville de Chelford, et eorum successoribus uel assignatis quibuscumque villam vel molendinum de Chelford de eis tenentibus, licentiam meam et perpetuam libertatem fodiendi et asportandi turbas et capiendi brueram et terram ubicumque sibi melius viderunt expedire in toto vasto meo de Whythinton, scilicet extra sepes camporum meorum arrabilium, ad sustentacionem et reparacionem predicti molendini sui de Chelford et stagni, pro libitu suo quotiescumque volueri[n]t sine impedimento vel reclamacione mei vel heredum meorum seu quorumcumque assignat(orum) ; saluis tantum mihi et heredibus meis uel assignatis quadam viridi placea ante domum meam in Whythinton iacente et alijs approviamentis meis in eadem ita rationabiliter factis et faciendis quod nec ipsi abbas et conventus nec eorum successores vel assignati a predicta libertate et licencia presenti scripto eis concessis nec homines eorum de Chelford a liberis communis et aysiamentis predictis consuetis et rationabiliter usitatis minime impediantur. In cuius rei testimonium presens carta mea inter me ex una parte et dictos abbatem et conventum ex altera est cyrografata et sigilla nostra alternatim eidem sunt appensa. Testibus : domino Reginaldo de Gray tunc iusticiario Cestrie, dominis Petro de Ardena, Ricardo de Sondbach militibus, Roberto Grosso-venatore tunc vicecomite Cestrie, Thoma clerico tunc balliuo de Macclesfeld, Willelmo Pigot, Henrico de Byrchells, Ricardo de Swettenham, Rogero de Vernon, Ricardo de Mottram, Ricardo filio eius, et multis alijs.

The grantor was a grand-nephew of Robert Pigot (Nos 566–7), not his son as supposed by Ormerod's editor Helsby (iii 711), who also was in error in regarding this grant as one of the lordship of Chelford

566. Quitclaim by William, son and heir of Robert de Mugebroc, to the monks of all his land in Chelford, viz a croft outside the field of Crakemers, called Puttes, formerly given to Roger Hurne, his grandfather, by Robert Pigot   Late 13th century

Willelmus filius et heres Roberti de Mugebroc dedit et quiete clamauit monachis Cestrie totam terram suam in Chelleford, videlicet vnum croftum extra campum de Crakemers quod uocatur Puttes, datam quondam Rogero Hurne auo suo a Roberto Pigot.

According to the Latin heading, the land was bought by the abbey.

567. Grant by Robert Pigot to Roger Hurne (Roger de Molendino in the Lat heading) in free marriage with his sister Isabel of a croft on his demesne at Chelford, outside the field of Crakemers, surrounded by an ancient ditch, with all the liberties of the vill   c. 1230–50

R[obertus] Pigot dedit Rogeio Huine in libeio maiitagio cum Ysabella sorore sua vnum croftum de dominico suo de Chelleford extra campum de Crakemers, veteri quadam fossa circumdatum, cum omnibus libertatibus uille

568. Grant by William, son of Robert Pigot, to St Werburgh of the homage and service owed to him by Hugh de Waverton for his whole tenement in Waverton and Hatton. 1249–65

Willelmus filius Roberti Pigot dedit beate Werburge homagium et totum seruicium sibi debitum ab Hugone de Wauerton de toto tenemento suo de Wauerton et de Hatton, cum omnibus pertinenciis

The consequent instruction to Hugh de Waverton to render his homage, etc , to abbot Thomas (I)—No 841—fixes the date within narrow limits
Hugh de Waverton seems to have died before 1274 (No 564). William, son of Robert Pigot, also quitclaimed (in 1268) his rights in the vill and advowson of Prestbury and gave land at Butley, etc (*Ann. Cestr* 98 , Nos 575, 587)

569. Grant by Warin de Croxton (Croston) of the homage and service which the heirs of Richard de(l) Ermitage owed him for the whole tenement which they held of him in Cranage   After 1260

Warinus de Croston dedit beate Werburge homagium et totum seruicium quod heredes Ricardi de Ermitage sibi debuerunt de toto tenemento cum pertinenciis quod de eo tenuerunt in Croulache

Richard del Hermitage or Ermitage is said to have been a cousin of the grantor, being son of Henry de Cranage and grandson of Randle, younger brother of Liulf de Croxton (or Twemlow, No 553), Warin's grandfather (Orm iii 127–9, 211, 213) °He was living in 1260

570. Recognition by William, lord of Snelson, and Ralph de Mobberley, parcener of the said vill, of the true course of the boundaries between Snelson and the abbey's vill of Chelford   1271–74

Mainwaring Charter 59 (John Rylands Library)

Omnibus Christi fidelibus presens scriptum visuris uel audituris Willelmus dominus de Snelleston' et Radulphus de Mobburleg' parceonarius eiusdem ville salutem in Domino Sciatis quod cum mota esset contencio inter dominum Symonem abbatem et conuentum sancte Werburge Cestrie ex vna parte et nos ex altera super quibusdam diuisis terrarum suarum de Chelleford et nostrarum de Snelleston' nos spontanea voluntate nostra pro nobis et heredibus nostris concesserunt et presenti scripto nostro recognouimus quod recte diuise inter predictas villas de Chelleford et Snelleston' incipiunt ad vadum aqueductus subtus molendinum de Chelleford, et ascendunt per quandam vallem que vocatur le Merecloh usque ad dupplicem hesam [1] que solet fieri inter campos dictarum villarum, et ab illa hesa per quendam sichetum extra sepem de Snelleston' usque in profundam mossam, et sic sequendo illum sichetum per dictam profundam mossam uersus Faudon' usque ad Leylache ubi diuise de Chelleford et de Faudon' et de Veteri Werford sibi inuicem obuiant. Vnde nos omnimode vendicacioni ultra prefatas diuisas penitus renunciauimus, et omnia ad dictam villam de Chelleford pertinencia prefatis abbati, etc , inperpetuum totaliter quiete clamauimus [2] ita quod nec nos nec heredes nostri nec aliquis per nos aut nomine nostro quicquam iuris aut clamii in omnibus et singulis uel aliqua

[1] So also Chart , hayam, Harl 2074, f 198, the ordinary form of the word
[2] End of Chart abstract

sua porcione ultra predictas diuisas uersus Chelleford aliquo modo
de cetero poterimus exigere uel vendicare   Pro hac autem recognicione, concessione et quieta clamancia predicti abbas, etc ,
dederunt nobis viginti solidos argenti pre manibus   In cuius rei
testimonium presenti scripto sigilla nostra fecimus apponi et
ipsum in pleno comitatu Cestr' recitatum in rotulo qui vocatur
Domesday procurauimus inrotulari.   Testibus, Dominis Reginaldo de Grey tunc iusticiario Cestrie, Thoma de Mayngar', Roberto de Stokeport, Roberto de Hux[eleg'] tunc constabulario
castri Cestrie, Hugone de Hatton' tunc vicecomite Cestresir',
Iohanne de Heyham'[1] tunc balliuo de Maclesfeld, Ricardo de
Orrebi, Iohanne de Wetenhal', Rogero de Daneport, Willelmo de
Maygar' (sic), Rogero de Vernon, Roberto de Wyninton', Henrico
de Birchel', Iohanne de Asthul, et aliis

Two seals in greenish-grey wax, l conventional plant, leg s' WILL
DE S   . , *r. (broken) similar design, leg* s' RADVLF D.
The name of the lost hamlet of Faudon is perhaps preserved in
Foden Lane in Great Warford, and the " profunda mossa " may be
Soss Moss   A family called Fowden perhaps took their name from
the place (Orm iii 632, cf 584)   For Fodon or Fawdon in Over
Peovei see Orm i 478 and Harl MS 2074, f 19 (old 130)

571. Duplicate abstract of the confirmation (No 25) by earl
Ranulf III to the abbey of his father's gift of the church
of Prestbury (No 24)

572. Confirmation by Richard, bishop of Coventry, of the
grant of the church of Prestbury to the abbey by earl
Hugh II.   1170–82

Ricardus Couentrensis episcopus ecclesiam de Prestebur[ia]
cum omnibus pertinenciis suis quam vir nobilis Hugo, comes
Cestrie, dedit cum corpore suo sancte Werburge, sicut carta
eiusdem comitis quam prefatus episcopus inspexit protestatur,
confirmauit et sigillo suo communiuit, ita quod qui hanc confirmacionem temere perturbauerit indignacionem Dei et suam nouerit
incursurum

573. Confirmation by Hugh, cardinal-deacon of St Angelo and
legate of the apostolic see, of the churches, possessions,
and dignities of the monks of Chester   1175–76.

Hugo Dei gracia sancti Angeli diaconus Cardinalis, apostolice

---

[1] Elsewhere spelt Hegham

sedis legatus, ecclesias et possessiones et dignitates quas canonice monachi Cestrie in presenciarum habuerunt autoritate apostoloium Petri et Pauli et sua confirmauit, ita quod si quis hanc confirmacionem infregerit indignacionem Dei et sancte Romane ecclesie se nouerit incursurum

Hugh, cardinal-deacon of St Angelo, came to England as legate in October 1175 and left in June 1176 (Eyton, *Itin of Hen II.*, 196, 205)

574. Quitclaim by Sir Richard de Stockport, kt , to the abbey of his right and claim in the vill of Prestbury and the advowson of its church, which quitclaim was enrolled in Domesday on February 24, 1289   ? 1281–3

Peter Shakerley's Vernon MSS , No 4, f 96*h*, Somerford Park, Congleton

Omnibus, etc , Ricardus de Stockport, miles, salutem No-veritis me remisisse, etc , ecclesie sancte Werburge Cestrie et domino Symoni abbati et conventui eiusdem loci corundemque successoribus totum ius, etc , quod habui, etc., in villa de Prestbury et advocacione ecclesie que in eadem villa de Prestbury sita est, cum omnibus iuribus et libertatibus tam predicte ville quam ecclesie ubique pertinentibus, ita quod nec ego nec heredes mei nec aliquis pro me seu nomine nostro aliquod iuris, possessionis vel clamii in eadem villa de Prestbury aut in advocacione ecclesie in eadem site, etc   Pro hac remissione et quieta clamatione predictus abbas, etc , me et Johannam consortem meam ad beneficia que in dicto monasterio decetero fient caritate fratris admiserunt, etc.   In cuius iei testimonium presenti scripto sigillum meum apposui   His testibus, domino Reginaldo de Gray tunc iusticiario Cestrie, domino Johanne filio eius, dominis Hamone de Mascy, Willelmo de Venables, Petro de Ardern, Galfrido de Chedle, Ricardo de Mascy, Willelmo de Baggele, Rogero de Dumvyle, militibus, Willelmo de Spurstowe tunc vicecomite Cestriscire, magistro Johanne de Stanlegh, Johanne de Wetenhale, Thoma clerico tunc ballivo de Macclesfeld, Ricardo de Worth, Ricardo de Mottram, Johanne filio eius, Willelmo Pigod, et aliis.[1]

Sir Richard de Stockport succeeded his father Robert before 1278 and died in 1291–2 (Earwaker, *East Cheshire*, 1 338)   He claimed Prestbury in right of his manor of Poynton, and about 1275 he had joined with his stepfather, John de Mold (Montalt), steward of the earl of Chester, whose wife had dower in Poynton, in presenting Walter de Kent to the rectory of Prestbury (*ib* ii 180, 206)

[1] The Chart abstract adds   ista quieta clamacia fuit irrotulata in Domesday in festo sancti Mathei anno regni regis Edwardi filii Henrici septimo decimo

575. Grant by William, son of Robert Pigot, to the abbey of an acre of his demesne in Butley, adjoining the river Bollin, between the monks' land of Prestbury and Birtles, with power to attach their pool and mill to the grantor's land and with water and other easements   William also quit-claimed any right which his ancestors were thought to have in the vill and church of Prestbury   1268

Willelmus filius Roberti Pigot dedit sancte Werburge vnam acram dominice terre sue in Butteleg[a], iacentem iuxta aquam de Bolni inter terram sancte Werburge de Prestebur[ia] et Birchelis, 29 (26)] vna cum attachiamento stagni et molendini eorum ad terram pre-dicti Willelmi de Butteleg[a] ascendendo per aquam, cum refluxu et agistiamento aque et omnibus aliis aysiamentis ad dictum molendinum pertinentibus   Insuper idem Willelmus recognouit villam de Prestebur[ia] et aduocacionem ecclesie de eadem esse ius sancte Werburge, et si aliquando antecessores sui hec puta-bantur habuisse, illud penitus sancte Werburge quiete clamauit

See No 568 *n* for the date.

576. Quitclaim by Arnewey le Brun to Serlo, his brother, of all the land which he held of the church of Prestbury

Arnewey Brunus quiete clamauit totam terram suam in villa de Prestebur[ia] Serloni fratri suo quam tenuit de ecclesia de Prestebur[ia]

577. Quitclaim by Serlo de Prestbury to the abbey of all the land in Prestbury which he held of the church of that vill

Serlo de Prestebur[ia] quiete clamauit sancte Werburge Cestrie totam terram suam in Prestebur[ia] quam tenuit de ecclesia de Prestebur[ia]

578. Quitclaim by Richard, son of William, son of Orm, to the abbey of all his land (in Prestbury, heading), ratified later by his son Reginald (No 592)

Ricardus filius Willelmi filii [1] Ormi quiete clamauit totam terram suam sancte Werburge Cestrie, quam quietam claman-ciam Reginaldus filius eius postea ratificauit

579. Quitclaim by Thomas de Tudalee to the abbey of all his right in the land which William, son of Richard Skinner,

[1] Willelmi filii is interlined

held of him in Prestbury between the bounds of Frewins-
lache as far as William son of Orme's field

Thomas de Tudalee quiete clamauit sancte Werburge Cestrie
ius suum de terra quam Willelmus filius Ricardi Pelliparii de se
tenuit in Prestebur[ia] inter diuisas de Frewineslache vsque
campum Willelmi filii Ormi

580. Grant by Robert, son of William le Paker, to St Werburgh
and the church of Prestbury of all his land which his father
held of that church.

Robertus filius Willelmi le Paker dedit sancte Werburge et
ecclesie de Prestebur[ia] totam terram suam quam pater suus
tenuit de ecclesia de Prestebur[ia]

581. Definitive decision of the official of the archdeacon of
Chester, after much disputing, that the parishioners of the
church of Prestbury shall repair the nave of the said church
and find vestments and other ecclesiastical ornaments for
it, except a worthy pyx for the eucharist and corporals
(*i e.* fine cloths to cover it), for which the vicar shall answer

Sentencia diffinitiua post magnam altercacionem constitutum
fuit ab officiali Archidiaconi Cestrie quod parochiani ecclesie de
Prestebur[ia] nauem dicte ecclesie reparabunt, et vestimenta et
libros et alia ornamenta ecclesiastica ei inuenient, excepta honesta
pixide pro eucaristia et corporalibus, de quibus vicarius qui pro
tempore fuerit respondebit

582. Letter patent of Edward I. decreeing that the chapel of
Macclesfield, with all its rights and those ministering
therein, should be subject to the mother church of Prestbury, notwithstanding that the said chapel with its churchyard was dedicated [by bishop Anian of St. Asaph acting
for the bishop of Coventry and Lichfield] at the instance
of Eleanor, his wife and queen   January 25, 1279

Edwardus filius Henrici, rex Anglie, statuit ut capella de
Maclesfeld cum omnibus iuribus suis et in eadem ministrantibus
matrici ecclesie de Prestebur[ia] sit subiecta, non obstante quod
dicta capella cum atrio Alianore uxor[i] sue et regine (*sic*) ad
instanciam predicte regine fuerit dedicata

The scribe copied the royal letter unintelligently   See *C.P R*,
1272–81, p 300.

583. Similar grant by Queen Eleanor   February 4, 1279

Alienora regina Anglie quantum in se fuit concessit quatenus *
capella de Maclesfeld matrici ecclesie de Prestebur[ia] sit subiecta,
non obstante, etc.

See Earwaker, *East Cheshire*, ii 487

584. Similar grant by Roger (de Meulan), bishop of Coventry
    ? 1279

Rogerus Couentrensis episcopus statuit ut capella de Maclesfeld cum omnibus iuribus suis et in eadem ministrantibus matrici
ecclesie de Prestebur[ia] sit subiecta, non obstante quod dicta
capella cum atrio Alionore, etc

585. Quitclaim by the rector of Leek (Staffs) of the tithes of
    the vaccaries of H[ugh] le Despenser and of the countess
    (of Chester) in the parish of Prestbury   1214–23

Rector ecclesie de Leec quiete clamauit decimas de vaccariis
domini H[ugonis] dispensatoris et de vaccariis domine Comitisse
in parochia de Presteb[uria]

This was before the appropriation of the church of Leek to Dieulacres Abbey by William, bishop of Coventry and Lichfield (1214–23),
when the rector was replaced by a vicar (Sleigh, *Hist. of Leek*, 41),
and apparently after the foundation of Dieulacres Abbey (No 586)

586. Similar quitclaim by the monks of Dieulacres.   1214–23

Monachi de Deulacres quiete clamauerunt decimas de vaccariis
H[ugonis] dispensatoris et domine Comitisse quanta sunt in
parochia de Prestebur[ia] ultra Dauen' (i e the Dane)

Dieulacres Abbey, near Leek, was founded in 1214 (Dugd *Mon*
v 627)   The countess in question was either Clemence, wife of Ranulf
III , or his mother Bertrade, who survived until 1227

587. Grant by William, son of Robert Pigot, to the abbey of
    his whole land of Heybirches, bounded by Titherington,
    the Bollin, Nouthereuese and a ditch, with rights of
    enclosure, etc , grant also of two " eyes " near the Bollin
    on the Mottram (St Andrew) side, paying 10s a year
    c 1250–88.

Willelmus filius Roberti Pigot dedit sancte Werburge Cestrie
totam terram suam de Heyebirches infra diuisas, scilicet a ductu
aque currentis inter Tiderton et Heyebirches, qui ductus descendit

in Bolyn, et sic descendendo in Bolyn usque ad riuulum iuxta pontem de Tiderton, et sic per illum riuulum ascendendo inter metas de Nouthereuese et Heyebuches usque fossatum quod se extendit usque ad dictum ductum aque currentis inter Tudirton et Heyeleyes (*sic*), ad includendum et omne commodum faciendum Preterea dedit totas illas insulas iuxta Bolyn uersus Mottrom, cum omnibus pertinenciis, reddendo x solidos annuos ad festum' Omnium Sanctorum

For the grantor see No 564 " *Two* islands " from Lat. heading.

588. Grant by Richard de Mottram to the abbey of his homage and that of his heirs and 6*d.* a year at Martinmas, and one oak a year from his wood at Mottram (St Andrew) outside Hawkshert (unless there is none sufficient outside), and enough dead wood for the use of their demesne house at Prestbury, and the usual common of herbage for themselves and the men of Prestbury out of mast-time, except in the fields, and mast for all their tithed pigs in the said tenement, except the tithe of their pannage and the food of the aforesaid tithed pigs Before 1288.

Ricardus de Mottrom dedit monachis Cestrie homagium suum et heredum suorum et vi denarios annuos ad festum sancti Martini percipiendos, et vnam quercum annuam de bosco suo de Mottrom vbicunque eis placuerit extra Haukeshert, quamdiu extra inueniri poterit, quod si extra non sufficiat, infra capiatur et ab eis ammoueatur Item, dedit mortuum boscum ad dominicam domum suam de Prestebury sufficiens, et communam herbagii ipsis et hominibus de Prestebur[ia] extia tempus pessone consuetam, exceptis campis, et pessonam omnibus porcis suis infra dictum [f. 29 (tenementum decimatis, exceptis decima panagii sui et excepto nutrimento de predictis porcis decimatis

For the date see Nos 565*a* and 589, also Orm iii 692–3

589. Agreement that Richard de Mottram and John, his son and heir, shall have only 10½ acres assorted from the wood within the manor of Mottram (St Andrew) where the monks have common, paying to the abbot 18*d* yearly, saving to the abbot and his men of Prestbury free common in the said acres when the hay and corn are carried away, as in the whole manor of Mottram, the first chartei (No 588) of the aforesaid Richard remaining in full force. *c* 1283–88

In quadam publica concordia ordinatum fuit quod Ricardus de Mottrom et Johannes filius eius et heres habebunt x acras et dimidiam assartatas de bosco infra manerium de Mottrom tantum vbi monachi communam habuerunt, reddendo abbati xviii denarios annuos in festo apostolorum Petri et Pauli, salua abbati et hominibus suis de Prestebur[ia] libera communa in dictis acris, fenis et bladis asportatis, sicut in toto manerio de Mottrom, prima carta predicti Ricardi in suo robore permanente

John de Mottram had succeeded his father by 16 Edward I (1287–1288) (Oim iii 693)

590. Obligation of Roger de Stockport to pay yearly one pound of wax to the church of Prestbury for licence to have a chantry in the oratory in his manor of Woodford during the pleasure of the monks of Chester, on condition that the chaplain ministering there shall yearly take an oath of fidelity to them or their proctor at Prestbury and pay the whole of the offerings of the said oratory to the parish church of Prestbury   c 1274–92

Rogerus de Stokeport bona fide promisit et scripto se obligauit quod singulis annis soluet vnam libram cere ecclesie de Prestebur[ia] pro licencia habendi cantariam in oratorio in manerio suo de Wideford, quamdiu monachis Cestrie placuerit, ita quod capellanus ibi ministrans, prestito eis uel procuratori suo de Prestebur[ia] singulis annis fidelitatis iuramento, omnes obuenciones dicti oratorii parochiali ecclesie de Prestebur[ia] integraliter soluet.

Woodford was a member of the manor of Poynton, which was part of the barony of Stockport, and in the reign of Edward I, after his father's death (cf. No 777), Sir Richard de Stockport, the last baron of his line, enfeoffed his younger brother Roger with certain lands in this subordinate manor (Oim iii 688, 795)   Roger was dead by 1292 (ib)

591. Grant by Richard de Fallybroom to the abbey of a certain portion of his land in Hurdsfield, 80 feet long and 60 feet wide, with the grange built on it and all buildings to be erected on it, with free exit and entry for all vehicles, on condition that an anniversary day for the souls of his father and mother, etc , should be solemnly celebrated every year on December 1

Ricardus de Falingbrom dedit monachis Cestrie quamdam partem terre sue in Hirdelesfeld continentem octoginta pedes in

longitudine et lx pedes in latitudine, cum grangia in ea edificata
et omnibus in ea edificandis, cum libero exitu et introitu ex
utraque parte grangie cum omnibus vehiculis, ita quod singulis
annis in crastino sancti Andree apostoli dies anniuersarius pro
animabus patris sui et matris et antecessorum et successorum
suorum in ecclesia de Prestebur[ia] sollempniter celebretur.

592. Confirmation by Reginald, son of Richard, of the lands in
Prestbury which his father gave to the abbey (No 578)

Reginaldus filius Ricardi ratificauit et quiete clamauit terras
quas pater suus dedit sancte Werburge in Presteb[uria] cum
omnibus pertinenciis

593. Grant by Richard, son of Richard de Wynbunbury, of
three plots of land, one in the town of Macclesfield next his
garden, another at Ollers, and the third at Hope, with free
entry and exit with every kind of vehicle, paying to him
yearly 2s 6d

Ricardus filius Ricardi de Wibbinbur[ia] dedit monachis
Cestrie tres placeas terre, quarum vna iacet in villa de Maclesfeld
iuxta gardinum suum, continens octoginta pedes in longitudine et
totidem in latitudine, et alia apud Olres continens cxl pedes in
longitudine et c in latitudine, et tercia apud Hope continens cxl
pedes in longitudine et c in latitudine, cum libero introitu et exitu
cum omni genere vehiculi, reddendo sibi annuatim ii solidos et vi
denarios in festo Pentecostes et in festo sancti Martini per equales
porciones

The father of the grantor was possibly the sheriff of 1233 and 1244
(Orm i 70, ii 75)

594. Confirmation by Baldwin, archbishop of Canterbury, of all
gifts to the abbey, and especially of the moiety of the
church of Wallesey given by William de Waley (No 595),
the rent of 8s given by Heute de Boydell from the church
of Handley (No 40), the church of Astbury given by
William de Venables (No 329), and the church of Prestbury given by Hugh, earl of Chester (No 24). 1185–89.

B[aldwinus] Cantuariensis archiepiscopus sub proteccione
Cantuariensis ecclesie recepit omnia sancte Werburge collata,
inter que precipue suscepit et confirmauit videlicet medietatem
ecclesie de Waleya quam Willelmus de eadem dedit, et redditum
viii solidorum quos Helto de Boydel dedit de ecclesia de Hanleye

percipiendos, et ecclesiam de Estebur[ia] quam Willelmus de Venables dedit, et ecclesiam de Prestebur[ia], cum omnibus pertinenciis, quam H[ugo] comes Cestrie cum corpore suo dedit, sicut carta sua protestatur [1]

595. Grant by William, son of Richard de Waley (Wallasey), of a moiety of the church of Wallesey, the grantor with his wife and heirs being received into the fraternity of the abbey and to be buried in its cemetery with their ancestors Before 1182

Chester Plea Roll, 125, m 42 (9 Hen V)

Notum sit tam presentibus quam futuris quod ego Willelmus filius Ricardi de Waley, pro anima mea et pro anima patris mei et matris mei et heredum meorum et omnium parentum meorum, dedi et hac presenti carta confirmaui Deo et ecclesie sancte Werburge Cestrie et monachis ibidem Deo seruientibus medietatem ecclesie de Waley cum omnibus pertinentiis suis, liberam, solutam et quietam, nichil in ea retinens preter orationes et beneficia predicte ecclesie, nec etiam ius aduocationis   Et ego vero predictus Willelmus filius Ricardi et sponsa mea et heredes mei suscepti sumus in fraternitate sepedicte ecclesie, ita quod post obitum nostrum corpora nostra in cimiterio sancte Werburge sepelientur ubi corpora antecessorum nostrorum sepulta sunt   Hiis testibus, Roberto archidiacono Cestrie, Andrea, Philippo, canonicis sancti Johannis, Willelmo capellano, Andrea capellano, Radulfo filio Buchard, Willelmo filio Giliend, Roberto Sarazin, Willelmo fratre eius, Widone de Abacia, Hugone fratre eius, Ascchetillo, et multis aliis

The other moiety of the church was probably already appropriated to Birkenhead priory   There was, however, no division of the advowson or the parochial duty, the priory apparently contenting itself with a separate chapel for its own men (Orm ii 458, 476)   In 1330 the abbey obtained a licence to alienate its moiety to the priory (C P R, 1327-30, p 512).   But this was not acted upon   The abbey's right of presentation was disputed in the 15th century by the Litherlands, who seem to have held the moiety of the manor formerly belonging to the Waleys (ib ii 476)   For the names Waley and Wallasey see ib 472   [See Addenda]

596. Confirmation by Richard, bishop of Coventry, to the abbey, of Robert Lancelyn's gift of the church of Bebing-

[1] pertestatur, MS

ton with four oxgangs of land, the gift of a moiety of Wallasey church by William de Waley (Wallesey), and the rent of 8s given by Heute de Boydell from the church of Handley 1161–82

Ricardus Couentrensis episcopus confirmauit donacionem quam Robertus Lancelyn fecit sancte Werburge super ecclesia de Bebinton et iiii bouatis terre cum omnibus pertinenciis, in quibus predictus Robertus nichil retinuit preter oraciones, et donacionem W[illelmi] de Waleya super medietate ecclesie de eadem cum pertinenciis, et redditum octo solidorum quos Holte (*sic*) de Boydel dedit de ecclesia de Hanleye percipiendos.

Robert Lancelyn's gift of Bebington church was really only a confirmation of that of his ancestor Scirard which is recorded in the "foundation" charter (above, p 20) As Robert's grandson was living after 1270, the date of his charter must have been nearer the lower limit of the bishop's confirmation than the upper one (Orm ii. 436, 444)

597. Obligation of William Gerard of Kingsley, who had been enfeoffed with Cattenhall by the monks, to pay them 30s yearly, and to maintain two chaplains for ever in the chapel of Cattenhall to celebrate the divine offices for the souls of Richard de Kingsley, etc If William should fail in his homage or in the aforesaid services, the abbot may distrain upon his goods in Kingsley and Cattenhall *c.* 1250–1316

Willelmus Gerard de Kengesl[ie] soluet annuatim de tota terra sua de Catenhale, de qua a monachis Cestrie fuit feoffatus, triginta solidos ad Nativitatem sancti Johannis Baptiste et ad festum sancti Martini per equales porciones, et pro eadem terra sustentabit imperpetuum duos capellanos in capella de Catenhale, pro anima Ricardi de Kengesl[ie] et animabus omnium fidelium defunctorum diuina celebrantes Quod si ab homagio suo et predictis seruiciis contingat eundem Willelmum deficere, liceat abbati per omnia bona sua mobilia et immobilia in Catenhale et Keng[eslie] eum ad plenam satisfaccionem distringere

For Cattenhall chapel see No 47 The William Gerard of this deed was probably the first of the name established in Kingsley and Cattenhall, having married one of the four co-heiresses of Richard de Kingsley who died between 1241 and 1244 (Orm ii 90, 96, 98) Richard had given Cattenhall to the abbey on condition of its finding the two chaplains (39 *D K Rep*, 139)

At the Dissolution the monks were drawing a pension of 3s from Cattenhall chapel in addition to the above 30s (Dugd Mon ii 392)

598. Grant by earl Ranulf (III) to the abbey for its own uses of all the demesne tithes of Rhuddlan, with the tithes of its fishery and of all his mills of Englefield Also of a tenement in Rhuddlan and pannage and common for its demesne pigs in his forests of Englefield and Cheshire Restoration also of all its rights in Englefield granted by his predecessors or their men. *c.* 1208–11

Charter Roll 73, 13 Edward I, m 15, No 46 (4)

Ranulphus comes Cestrie, filius Hugonis comitis, constabulario, dapifero, iusticiariis, baronibus, et militibus, vicecomitibus et balliuis suis, et omnibus hominibus suis de Cestresire, et omnibus presentibus et futuris presentem cartam inspecturis vel audituris, salutem Noueritis me pro salute anime mee et antecessorum meorum concessisse et dedisse et hac mea carta confirmasse Deo et sancte Wereburge Cestrie et monachis ibidem Deo seruientibus omnes decimas dominii mei de Ruelent ad proprios usus suos, tam in blado quam in aliis rebus uniuersis, vnde decima dari debet, et decimas piscarie de Ruelent, et decimas omnium molendinorum meorum de Englefeld [1] Dedi eciam unum mansum in villa de Ruelent, habens in latitudine sexaginta pedes et in longitudine quater viginti in via que vadit a castello usque ad piscariam apud aquilonem Concessi eciam et dedi dictis monachis quod habeant pessonam et communam in forestis meis de Englefeld et de Cestresira porcis suis dominicis Insuper reddidi eisdem monachis omnia iura sua in Englefeld tam in terris quam in ecclesiis et decimis, et in omnibus aliis rebus que antecessores mei aut illorum homines eis dederunt, habenda et tenenda libere et quiete, pacifice et honorifice, in puram et perpetuam elemosinam Testibus, Rogero de Lascy constabulario Cestrie, Philippo de Orreby tunc iusticiario Cestrie, Rogero dapifero de Montealto, Warino de Vernoun, Willelmo de Venables, Henrico de Aldidel', Rogero de Mainewarin', Roberto Patrik, Petro clerico domini comitis, Waltero Dariull, Aluredo de Suligni', Normanno Pantof', Roberto de Coudrey, Henrico dispensatore, Bertramo de Verdun, Stephano de Segraue, Roberto de Ardreshill, Henrico de Longo campo, Willelmo de Haselwel', Dauid de Malopassu, Willelmo filio suo, Leoff' vicecomite, magistro Alano, Ricardo vicecomite Cestrie, Ricardo de Kingesle, Hugone de Pascy.

[1] The northern half of the present Flintshire. Welsh, Tegeingl

ISTE CARTE SUBSEQUENTES SUNT DE CAMERA ABBATIS
CARTE CESTRIE

599. Grant by Ranulf de Daresbury and his wife Margery to
St Werburgh and T[homas] (II ?), abbot of Chester, of a
certain yearly rent of two pounds of wax at the two feasts
of St Werburgh,[1] to be paid from the houses which formerly
belonged to Walter Livet in Pepper Street by Wulfhad's
Gate, for which gift the abbot remitted to the donors a
yearly rent of 4s from the said houses   ? 1291–1323.

Rannulphus de Derisbur[ia] et Marg[eria] vxor sua dederunt
sancte Werburge et T[home] abbati Cestrie quemdam annuum
redditum, scilicet duas libras cere ad duo festa sancte Werburge
per equales porciones soluendas de domibus que quondam fuerunt
Walteri Liuet in Pepperstrete iuxta portam Wlfadi, vt liceat
abbati Cestrie pro dicto redditu in dictis domibus distringere, pro
hac donacione dictus abbas dictis Rannulfo et Margerie quatuor
solidos annuos de dictis domibus ante perceptas remisit

Ranulf de Daresbury was mayor of Chester 1277–80 (Orm 1 207)
and was living in 1294–95 (*Journ Chester Arch Soc* N S x p 52).
Margeria uxor Radulphi de Deresbury occurs on the Plea Rolls in
1288–89, but if she is correctly identified with the Margery de Dares-
bury in whose right Henry le Norreys was lord of Daresbury in 1291
(Orm 1 731), her first husband cannot have been the citizen of Chester.
Wulfhad's Gate, which Ormerod (1 358) calls Wolfeldgate or
Wolf's Gate, erroneously deriving the name from " the badge of Hugh
Lupus hung over it," was at the eastern end of Pepper Street, and
from its rebuilding in 1608 was known as Newgate   It is mentioned
as the gate of Wolfeld in a deed of 1282–83 (*Journ Chester Arch Soc*
N S x p 39) [See Addenda]

600. Grant by abbot S[imon] to Sir John de Orreby that he and
his men dwelling in his house by the abbey churchyard may
have a postern 4 feet wide for access to the church, saving
the rights of the ordinaries and parishioners, and on the
understanding that no animals shall be allowed to enter,
and no wood or stone be laid there   1265–91

S[ymon] abbas Cestrie concessit domino Johanni de Orrebi
militi quod ipse et homines sui domum suam iuxta cimiterium
sancte Werburge inhabitantes habeant vnam poternam in latitudine iiii pedum ad gressum [2] ad ecclesiam, saluo tamen iure ordi-

---

[1] 3 Feb and 21 June. See above, p. xiii, *n* 1
[2] *Sic* ? for ingressum

nariorum et parochianorum, et honestate ecclesie uel per ingressum alicuius animalis uel posicione lapidum uel lignorum nequaquam dehonestata

Sir John de Orreby of Fulk Stapleford was grandson and son respectively of Philip and Fulk de Orreby, who were both justices of Chester (Orm ii 803, iii 548)

601. Grant by Sir John de Orreby to the abbot of 4s yearly rent from a burgage in Eastgate Street, Chester, lying between the land of Richard the clerk (or Clerk) and that of William de Bromborough. *c.* 1261–1311. [See Addenda.]

J[ohannes] de Orreby, miles, dedit abbati Cestrie 4 solidos annui redditus quos dictus abbas percipere debet et solet de quodam burgagio in Estgatestrete, iacente inter terram Ricardi clerici et terram Willelmi de Brombur[gh], ad festum sancti Johannis Baptiste et ad festum sancti Martini per equales porciones, pro quibus in dicto burgagio dictus abbas distringere potest.

602. Quitclaim by John, son of Hugh Tardif, citizen of Chester, to abbot S[imon] of his shop lying in Bridge Street between the shop which Robert the Mercer held of the said abbot and the stone shop, with appurtenances and $\frac{1}{2}d$ to be taken yearly of John Arneway and his heirs   1265–78.

Johannes filius Hugonis Tardif ciuis Cestrie quiete clamauit S[ymoni] abbati Cestrie totam seldam suam iacentem in Brugestrete inter seldam quam Robertus le Mercer de dicto abbate tenuit et seldam lapideam, cum pertinenciis et uno obolo de Johanne Arnewey et heredibus suis annuatim percipiendo.

Hugh and John "Cardi" (possibly for Tardi[f]) appear as witnesses to Chester charters *c* 1255–71 (*Journ Chester Arch Soc* N S x pp 25, 27, 31–32)

For John Arneway see p 462

603. Grant in fee farm by abbot S[imon] to Robert, son of William, waterman, of all that land lying between the land of William, son of Hugh, tailor, and the land in Bridge Street which belonged to Hugh de Boughton, paying 10s 6d. yearly, the abbot may distrain on those or any other lands of Robert and his heirs, and if necessary re-enter on the lands   1265–91

S[ymon] abbas Cestrie tradidit ad perpetuam firmam Roberto filio Willelmi aquarii totam terram illam iacentem inter terram

Willelmi filii Hugonis cissoris et terram que fuit Hugonis de
Bothton in Brugestrete, reddendo inde annuatim dicto abbati
xs. et vid , videlicet ad Pascha iis et vid et ad Natiuitatem sancti
Johannis Baptiste iiis et ad festum sancti Michaelis iis. et vid
et ad Natiuitatem Domini iis et vid , ita quod liceat abbati in illis
terris et in aliis dicto Roberto et heredibus suis uel assignatis pertinentibus pro dicto redditu distringere, et si ibi nec alibi distringere possit, liceat ei dictas terras ad firmam traditas sine
alicuius contradiccione ingredi et eas quiete possidere

The grantee witnessed a Chester charter c 1282–83 (*Journ Chester
Arch Soc* N S x p 39) William le Sysors appears a little earlier
(*ib* p 35)

604. Grant in fee farm by abbot S[imon] to David the miller,
citizen of Chester, of all his land in Bridge Street, with all
buildings, paying yearly therefor 20s. at the Nativity of
John the Baptist and 20s. at Martinmas, and 2d to the
lord of Chester for Landgable, and finding a doomsman
in the portmoot of Chester , in which lands the abbot may
distrain for the rent   1265–91.

S[ymon] abbas Cestrie ad perpetuam firmam tradidit David
molendinario, ciui Cestrie, totam terram suam in Brugestrete
cum omnibus edificiis, reddendo inde annuatim xx solidos ad
Natiuitatem sancti Johannis Baptiste et xx solidos ad festum
sancti Martini, et ii denarios domino Cestrie ad Longable, et in-
ueniendo vnum iudicatorem in portmoto Cestrie , in quibus terris
licet abbati distringere pro predicto redditu

The grantee witnessed Chester charters c 1282–92 (*Journ Chester
Arch. Soc.* N S x pp 38, 43–44, 46) From this charter it appears
that the duty of serving as doomsman in the Chester town court
went with the tenement, an arrangement better known in the case
of hundred and shire courts

605. Quitclaim by Eynon the Hooper (cerclator in heading) to
abbot S[imon] of all his right and claim in certain land in
Fleshmonger Lane (Newgate Street) in Chester, lying
between the land which belonged to Cecilia Gamel Girgin
and the land of Matilda Lonb, 30 feet wide and extending
to the town wall, which he before held of the abbot for
12d yearly. This land was also quitclaimed to the abbot
by John, son of the aforesaid Eynon, and by Ralph, son of
Guy, and his wife Christiana William de Peck, citizen of

Chester, took this land in fee farm from abbot Thomas
(II) (1291–1323) for 5s per annum   1265–91

Heynon de (*sic*) Hopere quiete clamauit S[ymoni] abbati
Cestrie totum ius et clamium suum in quadam terra in Flesmongerlone in Cestria, iacente inter terram que fuit Cecilie Gamel Girgin
et terram Matilde Lonb, latitudine xxx pedum et extenditur ad
murum vrbis, quam prius de dicto abbate tenuit pro seruicio xii
denariorum annuorum   Hanc terram Johannes filius predicti
Eynon dicto abbati quiete clamauit, prout in suo scripto patet.
Hanc eciam Radulphus filius Wydonis et Christiana vxor eius
dicto abbati quiete clamauerunt   Item hanc terram cum edificiis suis Willelmus de Pecke, ciuis Cestrie, a Thoma abbate Cestrie
ad perpetuam firmam cepit pro seruicio v solidorum annuorum ad
Natiuitatem sancti Johannis Baptiste et ad Natiuitatem Domini
per equales porciones soluendorum   Necnon dictus Willelmus
tenementa sua adiacentia districcioni abbatis pro dicto redditu
deficiente obligauit, prout in suo scripto patet

The mention of Cecilia (daughter of ?) Gamel (son of) Girgin seems
to show that the date conjecturally assigned to Nos 372–3 is too early

606. Quitclaim by Robert, son of Thurstan, son of Leca, to
Thurstan, son of Ivo de Stanlaw, of certain land lying in
Trinity Street between land which belonged to Philip Gill-
more and the land of the church of Holy Trinity, rendering
yearly to the abbey 10d as Robert had done   This land
J , son of Thurstan, quitclaimed to abbot S[imon], who let
it in fee farm at 3s a year to Robert de Hoole, citizen of
Chester

Robertus filius T[hurstani] [1] filii Lece dedit et quiete clamauit
Thurstano filio Yvonis de Stanlowe quamdam terram iacentem
in vico Trinitatis Cestrie inter terram que fuit Philippi Gilemore
et terram ecclesie sancte Trinitatis, reddendo inde annuatim
domui sancte Werburge x denarios in festo apostolorum Petri et
Pauli, sicut dictus Robertus prius faciebat   Hanc terram J filius
Thurstani quiete clamauit S[ymoni] abbati Cestrie   Hanc eciam
terram Robertus de Hole, ciuis Cestrie, a dicto abbate ad perpetuam firmam cepit pro seruicio trium solidorum annuorum ad
Natiuitatem sancti Johannis Baptiste et ad festum sancti Martini
per equales porciones soluendorum, et dictus Robertus omnes
terras suas districcioni abbatis obligauit pro dicto redditu, si
defecerit, prout in scripto suo habetur.

[1] Extended from heading

Robert, son of Thurstan, son of Lece, lived in the first half of the 13th century (*Journ Chester Arch. Soc* N S. x pp 24, 29) Robert de Hoole witnesses charters from *c* 1260 or earlier (*ib* pp 27, 32), and was sheriff *c* 1280 (*ib* p. 38) and 1282–83 (*ib* pp 38–39).

607. Grant by Richard de Warwick, citizen of Chester, to God and abbot S[imon] of 4s yearly rent from land in St Werbuigh Street lying between the land which was Matthew the goldsmith's and that of Henry de Rhuddlan, two shillings to cover the old rent and the other two in augmentation of his alms 1265–91.

R[icardus] [1] de Warewic, ciuis Cestrie, dedit Deo et S[ymoni] abbati Cestrie iiii solidos annui redditus in festo apostolorum Petri et Pauli et ad Natiuitatem Domini per equales porciones soluendos de quadam terra in vico sancte Werburge, iacente inter terram que fuit Mathei aurifabri et terram Henrici de Rothelan, ita quod duo solidi cedant in antiquuum redditum et alii duo in elemosine sue incrementum

608. Quitclaim by Roger le Duck to abbot S[imon] of 1d annual rent which he used to receive from certain land [in North-gate Street] [2] lying between the land of Robert Moule and the land of John Mainwaring. From this land too John, son of the said Roger, quitclaimed to abbot Thomas (II) 12d of annual rent 1265–1323

R[oger] le Ducke de Cestria quiete clamauit S[ymoni] abbati Cestrie vnum denarium annui redditus quem percipere consueuit de quadam terra iacente inter terram Roberti Moule et terram Iohannis Manwar[ing] De hac eciam terra Iohannes filius dicti Rogeri quiete clamauit T[home] abbati Cestrie xii denarios annui [f 30 (2 redditus, prout patet in sua carta

609. Quitclaim by Geoffrey the cook, son of Robert the cook, to abbot William (II) of all his right and claim in the land [3] between the wall of the city of Chester towards the north and the land which the convent of the monks of Chester bought from Thomas the chamberlain (No. 617) ; Geoffrey also quitclaimed any right he had in 2 oxgangs of land in Bromborough. 1226–28

Galfridus cocus, filius Roberti coci, quiete clamauit Willelmo

---

[1] Extended from the heading   [2] Supplied from the heading
[3] In the heading the land is described as in Northgate Street

abbatı Cestrıe totum ıus et clamıum suum ın terra que est ınter murum cıuıtatıs Cestrıe uersus septentrıonalem et terram quam conuentus monachorum Cestrıe emıt de Thoma camerarıo   Item, ıdem Galfrıdus quıete clamauıt ıus et clamıum suum, sı quıd habuıt, ın duabus bouatıs terre ın Brumbur[gh].

See No. 633 *n*.

610. Grant by Bertram, son of John Norman, to God and abbot Sımon of 12*d* yearly rent from land ın Parson's Lane,[1] lyıng between the land whıch was Geoffrey the cook's and that whıch was Phılıp the sergeant's   1265–91

B[ertram][2] fılıus J[ohannıs][2] Norman de Cestrıa dedıt Deo et S[ymonı] abbatı Cestrıe xıı denarıos annuı reddıtus ın festo sanctı Martını percıpıendos de quadam terra ın Person[es]lone, ıacente ınter terram que fuıt Galfrıdı cocı et terram que fuıt Phılıppi seruıentıs et dıctam terram dıstrıccıonı abbatıs Cestrıe oblıgauıt sı reddıtus dıctus non fuerıt solutus

611. Quıtclaım by Alına, daughter of Gılbert Bloy, to abbot S[ımon] of all her land ın Parson's Lane   1265–91

Alına fılıa Gılbertı Bloy Cestrensıs quıete clamauıt S[ymonı] abbatı Cestrıe totum ıus suum et clamıum ın tota terra sua ın Personeslone

See Nos. 676–86.

612. Quıtclaım by Robert Collan and hıs wıfe Amarıa, daughter of Gılbert Bloy, to abbot S[ımon] of all theır land ın Parson's Lane   1265–91

Robertus Collan et Amarıa, fılıa Gılbertı Bloy, vxor eıus, quıete clamauerunt S[ymonı] abbatı Cestrıe totum ıus et clamıum suum ın tota terra sua ın Personeslone.

613. Grant ın fee farm by abbot S[ımon] to John of the Infırmary of all that land formerly belongıng to Gılbert Bloy and lyıng between the land of Roger de Copston and the land of the aforesaıd John ın Parson's Lane, payıng 3*s* yearly to the abbot   Thıs land Lucy, relıct of the saıd John, who had ıt by gıft of Master Rıchard her son, gave to St Werburgh by the medıatıon of Master Wıllıam de

---

[1] The headıng says ın Northgate Street
[2] Extended from the headıng.

Bruera and the lord Walter, rector of the church of St
Peter, Chester   [This land the said Walter, after the said
Master William [de Bruera]'s death, quitclaimed to the
abbey]   1265–91

S[ymon] abbas Cestrie ad perpetuam firmam dimisit Johanni
de Infirmaria totam terram illam que iacet inter terram Rogeri de
Copston et terram prefati Johannis in Personeslone, que terra fuit
quondam Gilberti Bloy, longitudine lxx pedum, latitudine xxxvi,
reddendo inde annuatim abbati Cestrie iii solidos in festo apostolorum Petri et Pauli   Hanc eciam terram Lucia relicta dicti
Johannis, quam ex dono Magistri Ricardi filii sui habuit, dedit
sancte Werburge, Magistro W[illelmo] de Bruer[a] et domino
Waltero, rectore ecclesie sancti Petri in Cestria, mediantibus,
prout patet in sua carta   [Hanc terram dictus Walterus post
mortem dicti Magistri Willelmi sancte Werburge quiete clamauit][1]

Apparently William and Walter acted as trustees for the abbey
in regard to this land

614. Quitclaim by William de Mudle, carpenter, to abbot
T[homas] of all the land which he held of the said abbot in
Parson's Lane   1249–65 or 1291–1323

Willelmus de Mudle carpentarius quiete clamauit T[home]
abbati Cestrie totam terram suam quam de dicto abbate tenuit
cum omnibus pertinencus in Personeslone.

Some evidence in favour of the earlier date suggested is found in
two Aston deeds (*Journ Chester Arch Soc.* N S x. pp 50–51)

615. Grant by Ralph Saracen to his nephew Richard of all his
land adjoining the churchyard of St 'Werburgh, paying
yearly to Robert Saracen, the said Richard's brother, 4s.,
and to the earl for Landgable 3¾d   Before 1232 ?

Radulphus Saracenus dedit Ricardo Saraceno nepoti suo
terram suam in (*sic*) cimiterio sancte Werburge confinem,[2] reddendo annuatim Roberto Saraceno, fratri dicti Ricardi, iiii solidos
et domino comiti ad longable iii denarios et iii quadrantes

616. Grant by Alexander called Saracen to God and abbot
S[imon] of the homage and 4s. service which he and his
heirs ought to receive from certain land adjoining the
churchyard of St Werburgh which Richard Saracen
obtained from Ralph Saracen (No. 615)   1265–91.

---

[1] In the margin   [2] The heading adds   contra hostium ecclesie

Alexander dictus Saracenus dedit Deo et S[ymoni] abbati Cestrie homagium et seruicium iiii solidorum quos ipse et heredes sui recipere debuerunt de quadam terra cimiterio sancte Werburge adiacente quam Ricardus Saracenus de Radulpho Saraceno optinuit cum omnibus pertinenciis, et ad hanc donacionem warantizandum et defendendum se et heredes suos obligauit.

617. Quitclaim by Thomas Hereward, son of Robert Hereward, to abbot Thomas (I) of a yearly rent of 14s for which Matilda, daughter of Richard, son of Hugh Cademon, gave in fee farm to abbot H[ugh] (1208–1226) all her land by Lonewalth[o]n,[1] extending lengthways from the city wall westwards to the land of the Hospital (of St John) towards Northgate, and in width from the city wall northwards to the land of Thomas the chamberlain and the land of G[eoffrey], son of Robert the cook (No 609)   Thomas Hereward reserved a payment of 2s yearly to the lord of Tattenhall   [This land Robert, son of Hereward, husband of the said Matilda, with whom he had received it, gave in fee farm in the form aforesaid]   1249–65

Matilda filia Ricardi filii Hugonis Cademon ad perpetuam firmam dimisit H[ugoni] abbati Cestrie totam terram suam iuxta Lonewalth[o]n, reddendo sibi annuatim xiiii solidos in vigilia sancte Werburge in estate et in Natiuitate Domini per equales porciones   Extenditur terra hec in longitudine a muro ciuitatis uersus occidentem vsque ad terram Hospitalis uersus portam aquilonalem, in latitudine uero a muro ciuitatis versus aquilonem usque ad terram Thome camerarii et ad terram G[alfridi] filii Roberti coci , predictos autem xiiii solidos Thomas Hereward filius Roberti Hereward Thome abbati Cestrie quiete clamauit. Saluis tamen duobus solidis domino de Tatenhale annuatim in Natiuitate sancti Johannis Baptiste soluendis, prout in carta dicti Thome patet   [Hanc terram Robertus filius Herward maritus dicte Matilde sub formam predictam ad firmam tradidit, quam cum ea accepit][2]

The Touchets were lords of Tattenhall at this date   For the grantor cf Nos. 357–9

618. Grant by Marg[aret], daughter of Thomas de Burgh, to the abbey of a plot of land in Barn Lane, between the land of the abbey and that of Richard de Tuddenham, paying

[1] Described in the heading as " grangia in Croftis "   [2] In margin

to her yearly $\frac{1}{2}d$. of silver. This land was quitclaimed to abbot S[imon] by Hubei t de Hodresham, son and heir of Sara, daughter of Thomas de Burgh The said Margaret gave pledge of warranty or restoration of the 5 marks which the abbot gave her for this land. 1265–91.

Marg[aret] filia Thome de Burgo dedit ecclesie sancte Werburge vnam placeam terre iacentem in Bernelone inter terram ecclesie et terram Ricardi de Tudinham, reddendo sibi annuatim vnum obolum argenti in festo sancti Martini Hanc terram Hubertus de Hodresham filius et heres Sare filie Thome de Burgo S[ymoni] abbati Cestrie quiete clamauit cum omnibus pertinenciis, prout in carta sua patet Item ad hanc terram warantizandum dicta Marg[aret] se et omnia tenementa sua in Cestria et heredes suos, vel ad restituendum v marcas, quas de abbate Cestrie pro dicta terra recepit, obligauit, prout in quadam obligacione patet.

619. Grant by John de Stanlaw and Lucy his wife to God and abbot S[imon] of certain land[1] on the Crofts, lying between the land of Robert de Hoole and that of Agnes Arneway, saving to the lord of the land 1d of Landgable   1265–91.

Johannes de Stanlowe et Lucia vxor eius dederunt Deo et S[ymoni] abbati Cestrie quandam terram super le Croftes, iacentem inter terram Roberti de Hole et terram Agnete Arnewey , saluo domino terre vno denario Longable

The Crofts lay beyond the Northgate (No. 617)

620. Grant by William, son of Hugh le Mercer, to abbot S[imon] of all his land lying on Le Croftes in Chester between the land of the said abbot and the land which was Geoffrey Mazelyn's, paying yearly to Thomas, son of Thomas the chamberlain, 4s   1265–91

Willelmus filius Hugonis le Mercer dedit S[ymoni] abbati Cestrie totam terram[2] suam iacentem super Le Croftes in Cestria inter terram dicti abbatis et terram que fuit Galfridi Mazelyn, reddendo inde annuatim Thome filio Thome Camerarii iiii solidos in Annunciacione Domini et in Natiuitate sancti Johannis Baptiste per equales porciones

Geoffrey Mazelin occurs c 1240 (*Journ Chester Arch Soc* N.S x p 23).

[1] " De duabus domibus " in the heading
[2] " terra empta " in heading

621. Grant by Thomas, son of Robert the chamberlain, to St Mary and St Werburgh of a moiety of the land held by him of the earl on the Crofts in Chester, lying between the land of the abbot of Chester and the land which Hugh Le Mercer held of the said Thomas (see No 620).

Thomas filius Roberti camerarii dedit sancte Marie et sancte Werburge medietatem illius terre quam de domino comite tenuit in Cestria super Le Croftes, iacentem inter terram abbatis Cestrie et terram quam Hugo Le Mercer de dicto Thoma tenuit

This is clearly earlier than No 620

622. Quitclaim by Robert, son of John the chamberlain, citizen of Chester, to abbot S[imon] of all his right, etc , in a croft on Le Croftes in Chester which the abbot held by gift of William, son of Hugh Le Mercer (No 620), and also of the 4s yearly which he received from the said tenement, Robert pledging himself and his heirs to acquit the land of 2d of Landgable due to the earl and for that purpose subjecting his lands in Christleton to distraint by the abbot. 1265–1291

(28)] Robertus filius Johannis Camerarii, ciuis Cestrie, quiete clamauit S[ymoni] abbati Cestrie totum ius et clamium in quodam crofto [1] super le Croftes in Cestria quod dictus abbas tenuit de dono Willelmi filii Hugonis Le Mercer, necnon quiete clamauit illos iiii solidos annuos quos de tenemento dicto annuatim percepit , item dictus Robertus obligauit se et heredes suos ad adquietandum dictam terram a ii denariis de Longable inde domino comiti debitis, et ad hoc tenendum terras suas de Cristelton districcioni abbatis subiecit

623. Quitclaim by Alina and Amaria, daughters of Gilbert Bloy, to abbot S[imon] of all their right, etc , in all land in Bagge Lane outside the Northgate of Chester. 1265–91

Alina et Amaria filie Gilberti Bloy quiete clamauerunt S[ymoni] abbati Cestrie totum ius et clamium suum in tota terra in Baggelone extra portam aquilonalem Cestrie

623a. Grant by Alice, widow of Gilbert Blay, to the abbey of a workshop and garden at the corner of Bagge Lane and at right angles to the Hospital of St John, which William the smith once held of her 1270–71

[1] " Carta de croftis iuxta grangiam " in the heading (cf No 617)

Hail MS 2071, f 47 (old 33), copied by Randle Holme in June 1652 from the original deed "in the round white box in the great chest in the tresury of Chester " Not in Chart

Omnibus, etc , Alicia relicta quondam Gilberti Blae (?) salutem, etc   Sciatis me pro salute anime mee et antecessorum et successorum meorum in legia viduitate mea et libera [1] potestate dedisse, concessisse, et hac presenti carta mea confirmasse, necnon pro me et heredibus meis imperpetuum quietam donasse Deo et ecclesie sancte Werburge Cestrie et capitalibus dominis meis, S[ymoni] abbati et eiusdem loci conuentui, eorumque successoribus, totam illam fabricam cum gardino adiacente extra portam aquilonalem ciuitatis Cestrie que sita est super cornerum [2] de Baggelone ex transuerso hospitalis sancti Johannis, quam Willelmus faber quondam de me tenuit , habendam, etc , in puram et perpetuam elemosinam cum suis pertinenciis et libertatibus adeo libere et quiete sicut aliqua elemosina liberius et quietius dari poterit uel concedi, ita quod nec ego nec heredes, etc , preter oraciones, etc   In cuius rei, etc , apposui.   Testibus domino Reginaldo [3] de Grey tunc iusticiario Cestrie, Ricardo de Wilburham tunc vicecomite Cestresire, Roberto de Nevyle, Ricardo de Oreby, Johanne de Wetenhale, Gilberto de Poimton (?), Roberto de Hokenhul, Roberto de Traford, Alexandro de Limme, Philippo clerico, Roberto de Ynes, Rogero Hole, et aliis.

Oval seal, non-armorial , leg S[IGILLUM] ALICIE BLA[Y]

Holme notes   " Endorsed Cart Alic Bloy de quadam placea ter in Bagelone extra portam aquilon , now Tho Eaton's howse " Alice Blay or Bloye inherited a third part of Little Saughall which was held of the abbey   She and her husband gave two oxgangs there to Richard de Toft, which ultimately came to the abbey (No 676). In her widowhood she quitclaimed various plots to abbot Simon, and finally her whole third part (Nos 678–686)   She was doubtless the mother of Alina and Amaria, daughters of Gilbert Bloy, who singly or together quitclaimed property in Chester to St Werburgh's (Nos. 611–12, 623)   Amaria was married to Robert Collan (No 612)

624. Demise in fee farm by abbot S[imon] to Richard Brown, miller, of three plots of land outside Northgate, Chester, one of which lies between the land which was Alice Barre's and that which was Henry Mainwaring's, the second extends from Alice's land to the corner of Bagge Lane and thence to the land which was Alexander Hurel's, while the third lies between the same land of the said Alexander and

---

[1] libere, MS   [2] cornetum, MS.   [3] Rog , MS

a footpath leading from Bagge Lane to Wallfurlong, paying yearly to the abbot 24s   1265-91.

S[ymon] abbas Cestrie ad perpetuam firmam dimisit Ricardo Brun molendinario, iii placeas terre extra portam aquilonalem Cestrie quarum vna iacet inter terram que fuit Alicie Barre et terram que fuit Henrici Manwar[ing], et alia incipit a terra predicte Alicie et extendit usque ad corneram de Baggelone et a dicta cornera usque ad terram que fuit Alexandri Hurel, tercia uero iacet inter terram eandem predicti Alexandri et quamdam semitam que ducit de Baggelone usque ad Walleforlong, reddendo inde annuatim abbati Cestrie xxiiii solidos argenti in festo apostolorum Petri et Pauli et in festo sancti Martini per equales porciones , ad quorum solucionem dictus Ricardus obligauit se et heredes suos in bonis suis mobilibus et immobilibus vbicunque inuentis districcioni abbatis

625. Quitclaim by Hugh de Lene to abbot S[imon] of all the land which he held of him outside the Northgate.   1265-75

Hugo de Lene quiete clamauit S[ymoni] abbati Cestrie totam terram quam de eo tenuit extra portam aquilonalem Cestrie

Hugh de Lene, who occurs as early as 1244 (*Journ. Chester Arch Soc.* N S x p 26) (misdated), was succeeded by his son Robert before 1275 (*ib* p 31)   [See Addenda]

626. Quitclaim by Hamon, son of Guy, to the abbey of two " lands " outside the Northgate which Osbern Wombe and Alan, son of Aylward, held   Cf No 638

Hamo filius Guydonis quiete clamauit sancte Werburge duas terras extra portam aquilonalem Cestrie, quas Osbernus Wombe et Alanus filius Haylward tenuerunt

627. Quitclaim by John, son of Mayler of Len, to abbot S[imon] of all his right, etc , in all his land lying between the land which John Gamel held and the lane near the Hospital of St John, Chester   1265-91

Johannes filius Mayler de Len quiete clamauit S[ymoni] abbati Cestrie totum ius et clamium suum in tota terra sua iacente inter terram quam Johannes Gamel tenuit et venellum iuxta Hospitale sancti Johannis Cestrie

John Mayler occurs in the Aston deeds *c.* 1274-93 (*Journ Chester Arch Soc.* N S x pp 32, 49)

628. Quitclaim by Alan, son of Richard of Rostherne, to abbot William (II) of half a toft with its croft, lying between the land which Herbert the carter held and the land which Orm Wombe held outside the Northgate 1226–28.

Alanus filius Ricardi de Routhestorn quiete clamauit Willelmo abbati Cestrie dimidiam toftam cum crofto eius, iacentem inter terram quam Herebertus carectarius tenuit et terram quam Orm Wombe tenuit extra portam aquilonalem

See No 390

629. Quitclaim by Alice, widow of John the chamberlain (No 622), to abbot S[imon] of certain land outside the Northgate, lying between the said Alice's land and the land of Henry Manware (Mainwaring), with a garden extending from a house in the said land to a kiln in the garden. 1265–91.

Alicia quondam vxor Iohannis camerarii in viduitate et ligia potestate quiete clamauit S[ymoni] abbati Cestrie quandam terram suam extra portam aquilonalem, inter terram dicte Alicie et terram Henrici Manware (*sic*) iacentem, cum quodam orto dicte terre pertinente extenso a quadam domo in dicta terra posita usque ad quoddam torale in eodem orto

630. Quitclaim by Robert Long to abbot Thomas (? II) of all his land outside the Northgate, lying between the land of Richard de Brunston and the land of Richard the miller, with two butts adjacent. ? 1291–1323

Robertus Longus quiete clamauit Thome abbati Cestrie totam terram suam extra portam aquilonalem Cestrie, iacentem inter terram Ricardi de Brunston et terram Ricardi Molendinarii, cum duabus buttis adiacentibus.

A Richard the miller occurs 1294–95 (*Journ. Chester Arch Soc* N S x p 52)

631. Quitclaim by Alice, daughter and heir of William of Walton (No 405), to the abbot of Chester of all her right, etc , in lands outside the Northgate which her father bought from the said abbot. Cf p 411

Alicia filia et heres Willelmi de Waltona quiete clamauit abbati Cestrie totum ius et clamium suum in terris extra portam aquilonalem, quas dictus Willelmus pater eius de dicto abbate emit

632. Quitclaim by Thomas, brother of Nicholas, son of John of Frodsham, to abbot S[imon] of all the land by the church-yard of St Thomas without the Northgate in the field next the abbot's land which Gunware, widow of Gilbert Gast (Nos 466, 633 *n.*), gave to the said Nicholas, paying her yearly $\frac{1}{2}d$, and the land by the Bache which she also gave him, paying 18*d* yearly to the abbot of Chester, gifts confirmed by her sister Geva   Also a quitclaim by the said Thomas to the same abbot of 12 selions in the fields of Poole, below the road leading to the stone bridge, which he had at first received for life   1265–91.

Gunware relicta Gilberti Gast in ligia potestate dedit Nicholao filio Johannis de Frodesham totam terram suam iacentem iuxta cimiterium sancti Thome extra portam aquilonalem Cestrie in campo iuxta terram abbatis Cestrie, reddendo sibi annuatim vnum obolum ad Natiuitatem sancti Johannis Baptiste   Item eadem Gunware dicto Nicholao dedit totam terram suam iuxta la Bache, reddendo annuatim xviii denarios abbati Cestrie, prout in carta inde facta patet   Geua soror dicte Gunware dictas donaciones concessit et confirmauit, prout in carta sua patet   Dictas terras Thomas frater dicti Nicholai S[ymoni] abbati Cestrie [1] quiete clamauit, prout in carta sua patet   Item dictus Thomas dicto abbati quiete clamauit xii selliones iacentes in territorio de Pulle subtus viam tendentem ad pontem lapideum, quas cepit prius ad terminum vite sue, prout in carta sua patet

Ormerod's date for Gunwara's grant, " about 1190 " (ii 385), seems much too early, in view of the fact that the brother of the grantee did not give the land to the abbey until more than seventy years later   See notes to Nos 466 and 633

The Pulle of this charter was probably not Poole in Wirral   The context and the mention of the stone bridge, which may perhaps be identified with a well-known ancient landmark on the N W side of Chester (Orm i 372, ii 385), suggest an identification with the Port-pool which was near the bridge   [See Addenda]

633. Agreement between the abbot [Thomas (II)] and Richard Coudray, viz that whereas the said abbot in full portmoot at Chester demanded against the said Richard, Ellis (de Chorlton) le Hunte (Venator), and John his son, all tails of salmon and basses, and both heads and tails of codfish, congers, and rays coming to the kitchen of the abbot and

[1] Not to Thomas, as stated by Ormerod (ii 385).

convent, and two pieces of every backbone of oxen and
pigs slaughtered in the abbey, and one loaf and two gallons
of beer to be taken there daily, and the skimming of the fat
of all flesh boiled in the said kitchen, save in the time of
[   ] and except the fat of the said flesh which shall
be necessary for the meat dishes of the abbot and convent
in Chester, all of which things the said abbot claimed as
his right and that of his church, and in which Richard,
Ellis, and John had no right of entry save after the demise
made by the abbot's predecessor William Marmion (1226–
1228) to Geoffrey the cook for a term of years which has
now run out, and which things should after that revert to
the abbot   Richard admitted half of the said things to
be the right of the abbot and his church, and released and
quitclaimed this half for himself and his heirs for ever, in
return for which the abbot and convent [granted] for ever
that Richard and his heirs, etc , instead of the service of
finding a master cook in the kitchen of the abbot and
convent, to which he is bound along with the said Ellis and
John for the said fee and for the lands and tenements which
they hold of the abbot in Chester, Newton, and Lea, shall
hold those lands and tenements of the abbot, etc , for 1d of
rent yearly for all services, etc   [1294]

Matilda, widow of the said Richard, quitclaimed her
dower in the said corrody, and the said John quitclaimed
all his right, etc , in it

Ita conuenit inter abbatem Cestrie et Ricardum Coudrey,
videlicet quod vbi predictus abbas in pleno portmoto Cestrie peciit
uersus predictum Ricardum, Helyam le Hunte et Johannem filium
eius omnes caudas salmonum et barsarum, et tam capita quam
caudas miluellorum, congruorum et radiorum ad coquinam ipsorum abbatis et conuentus veniencium, et duo friusta de singulis
spinis boum et porcorum in ipsa abbacia mactorum, et vnam
micheam et ii galones ceruisie singulis diebus ibidem percipiendas,
et floturam pinguedinis omnium carnium in predicta coquina
elixarum, excepto tempore tuisionis [1] et excepta pinguedine ipsarum carnium que fuerit necessaria pulmento [2] ipsorum abbatis
et conuentus in Cestria, et que omnia idem abbas clamauit vt ius
suum et ecclesie sue et in que idem Ricardus, Elyas et Johannes
non habuerunt ingressum nisi post dimissionem quam Willelmus

[1] *Sic*   See Glossary
[2] Ormerod (*Hist of Chesh* ii 384) misread the contracted form of this word
as " parliamento "

H

Marmion, quondam abbas Cestrie, predecessor ipsius abbatis
(28) d.] inde fecit Galfrido coco ad terminum qui preteriit, et que post
terminum illum ad prefatum abbatem reuerti debent ut ius ecclesie
sue predicte ; predictus Ricardus concessit et recognouit medietatem omnium premissorum in abbacia predicta percipiendam, vt
predictus abbas ea peciit, esse ius ipsius abbatis et ecclesie sue
predicte, et medietatem omnium premissorum prefato abbati
ibidem reddidit ut ius ecclesie sue predicte, et eam sibi remisit et
omnino quietum (sic) clamauit de se et heredibus suis predicto
abbati et successoribus suis imperpetuum ; pro hac autem recognitione, etc., prefati abbas et conuentus pro se et successoribus
suis imperpetuum [concesserunt] quod dictus Ricardus, heredes et
assignati sui in loco seruicii cuiusdam magistri coci quem inuenire
tenebatur simul cum predictis Helya et Johanne in coquina
ipsorum abbatis et conuentus pro dicto feodo et pro terris et
tenementis quas tenent de predicto abbate in Cestria, Neuton et
la Lee habeant et teneant terras et tenementa illa de predictis
abbate et conuentu et successoribus suis pro vna denarrata redditus singulis annis in festo sancti Johannis Baptiste, pro omnibus
seruiciis, auxiliis, consuetudinibus, sectis curiarum et demandis.

Matilda relicta dicti Ricardi de Coudrey dotem suam in predicto corrodio quiete clamauit.   Item dictus Johannes totum ius
suum et clamium in dicto corrodio sub formam dicte conuencionis quiete clamauit, prout in carta sua patet.

Ormerod, who prints this document, not too correctly, devotes
some space (ii. 384–5) to the curious cook's fee of the abbey which it
discloses (the service of course being rendered by deputy), and to the
family which held it.   He assumes that the agreement was made
with abbot Thomas I. (1249–65), and therefore infers that Reginald
de Poole (Netherpool), who joined with his wife Matilda, daughter
of Geoffrey the cook, here described as widow of Richard de Coudray,
and her sister Agnes and her husband Ellis the hunter in a grant of
homage and rent in Lea to abbot Simon (No. 636), was her second
husband.   But this is clearly impossible if the Richard de Coudray
who occurs in Newton deeds with Ellis the hunter, c. 1290–92 (Journ.
Chester Arch. Soc. x. pp. 43–7),[1] was the Richard of this agreement.
That he was the same person seems placed beyond doubt by the fact
quoted elsewhere by Ormerod himself (ii. 383, 772) that Matilda sued
for dower as widow of Coudray in Lea in 1299–1300, and in Newton
in 1305–6.[2]   We need have no hesitation, then, in ascribing the document

[1] Ellis le Hunte appears in these deeds as early as 1280 (p. 36), and John le
Hunte in 1282–83 (p. 38).   John's wife was Alice, daughter of John Norman.
[2] No. 410 shows that they were married before 1291.   From No. 636 it is
clear that her first husband, Poole, died later than 1265.
It is doubtful, too, whether Ormerod is right in identifying Gunwara, mother

before us to the time of abbot Thomas II , and to some date between 1291 and 1300. [31 May 1294—Chester Plea Roll 6, m 11d]

634. Grant by Geoffrey the cook to William, son of Richard de Ness, in free marriage with his sister Agnes, and to the heirs between them begotten, of 2 oxgangs of land in Huntington which Ralph the smith held at farm of his mother Gunwara, paying 5s yearly to him. ? c 1230

G[alfridus] cocus dedit Willelmo filio Ricardi de Nesse in libero maritagio cum Agnete sorore sua et heredibus inter eos procreatis ii bouatas terre in Huntindon, cum pertinenciis, quas Radulphus faber ad firmam tenuit de Gunwara matre sua, reddendo sibi annuatim v solidos

635. Quitclaim by Geoffrey the cook to the abbot of Chester of 8 oxgangs of land in Huntington in exchange for 8 oxgangs in the vills of Newton (by Chester) and Lea (by Backford). ? c. 1230

G[alfridus] cocus quiete clamauit abbati Cestrie viii bouatas terre cum pertinenciis in Huntindun in escambium viii bouatarum in villa de Neuton et villa de Lee.

636. Quitclaim to abbot S[imon] by Ellis de Chorlton, called the hunter, and Agnes his wife, daughter of Geoffrey the cook of the abbot of Chester, and by Reginald de Poole (Netherpool ?), and Matilda his wife, daughter of the said Geoffrey, of the homage of Adam, son of Agnes de Backford (Orm ii 363), and 5s yearly which the said Adam was bound to pay for 2 oxgangs of land in the vill of Lea by Backford 1265–91

Helyas de Churliston,[1] dictus venator, et Agnes uxor eius, filia Galfridi coci abbatis Cestrie, et Reginaldus de Pulle et Matilda vxor eius, filia dicti Galfridi, quiete clamauerunt S[ymoni] abbati Cestrie homagium Ade filii Agnetis de Bacford et v solidos annuos quos idem Adam pro ii bouatis terre in villa de la Lee iuxta Bacford soluere tenebatur ad Natiuitatem sancti Johannis Baptiste et ad festum sancti Martini per equales porciones

---

of Geoffrey the cook, (No 634) with Gunwara who was a benefactor of the abbey both as wife and widow of Gilbert Gast, which he misspells Sast (Nos 466, 632) For this there seems no evidence beyond the name and the juxtaposition of charters If the identification be correct, Gilbert can only have been Geoffrey's stepfather, his own father being Robert the cook (No 609)
[1] Thurliston, MS

Ormerod (ɪɪ 385) was inclined to read Thurliston rather than Churliston, and so missed identifying Geoffrey the cook's son-in-law with a near neighbour of Geoffrey, for Churliston or Cherliston was the old form of the name of the vill of Chorlton in Backford parish (cf No 667)   Helsby, however, identified Ellis with Chorlton, and attempted to affiliate him to the Helsbys who had a holding there (Orm ɪɪ 375 n , below, No 671)

For Reginald de Poole see No 633 n   Ormerod (ɪɪɪ 419, 423) makes him son of Robert de Poole, lord of Netherpool c 1246–79 (Nos 306, 308, 694) and father of James who succeeded to the estate by 1290 and died c 1307   But James was son of Robert, not of Reginald (No 694 n)   The only Reginald de Poole, clearly of this family, who occurs in the 13th century witnesses a document of 1237–1238 (Chest Arch Soc Journ 1897, 201)   He was probably Robert's father, and can hardly be the Reginald of our charter [1]   Unless, therefore, Robert had an elder son Reginald who died without issue, we are driven to suggest that Poole in this charter is not Netherpool but Poole by Chester (No 632 n)   [See Addenda to p 352]

637. Grant by Guy, son of Hamon son of Guy (cf No 452), to the abbey of the homage and service which Hamon Cosin used to do to him for 2 [2] oxgangs of land in Upton (by Chester)   ? c 1240–60

Wido filius Hamonis filii Wydonis dedit sancte Werburge Cestrie homagium et seruicium que Hamo Cosin sibi facere consueuit de ɪɪ bouatis in Uptona

From the confirmation of his gift by his nephew after 1265 (No. 641) we learn that Guy was a son of the Hamon of the next charter, perhaps by another wife than the Agnes mentioned there

638. Grant by Hamon, son of Guy, to Agnes his wife and Philip his son and heir, begotten of the said Hamon (?) and the said Agnes, of a messuage within the Northgate of Chester, lying between the land of Matthew de Thornton and the land of Thurstan le Duc, and 3 oxgangs in Newton (by Chester) with messuage, etc , paying to him yearly 2s 3d   Early 13th century

Hamundus filius Wydonis dedit Agnete vxori sue et Philippo filio suo et heredi de dicto W[ydone] (sic) et dicta Agneta procreato vnum mesuagium infra portam aquilonalem Cestrie, iacens inter terram Mathei de Thornton et terram Thurstani le

[1] A Matilda, daughter of Reginald de Poole, is recorded as a former tenant of land in Wervin between 1265 and 1291 (No 853).
[2] 2¼ oxgangs in the heading , cf No 641

Duc,[1] et iii bouatas in Neuton cum mesuagio et pertinenciis, reddendo sibi annuatim ii solidos et iii denarios ad festum sancti Martini per equales, etc

See note on No 639, and cf No 626

639. Grant by Philip, son of Hamon son of Guy, to abbot Roger of all his furlong in Newton Field above Bache and all the land between Flookersbrook and the North street of Chester, besides 5 selions (strips) of butt-land above the said abbot's furlong called Well Furlong, and 2 selions extending to Flookersbrook Grant by the said abbot to the said Philip of the serjeanty in his lands for his life. 1240–49

Philippus filius Hamonis filii Wydonis dedit abbati Rogero Cestrie totam culturam suam in campo de Neuton super la Bache et totam terram inter Flokersbroc et vicum aquilonalem Cestrie, preter v selliones abuttislandes super culturam dicti abbati que vocatur Welle forlong et ii selliones extendentes se in Floker[s]broc Dictus abbas concessit dicto Philippo seriansiam in terris eius in tota vita sua

In the generation to which the grantor belonged the family took the surname of Newton from the township adjoining Chester on the north, in which most of their land lay Helsby was inclined to see in them a younger branch of the Duttons, original under-tenants of the abbey in Newton (see No 5), or of the Kinnertons, who, he suggests, were probably Duttons by origin (Orm ii 772) But the Kinnertons seem to have been Welsh (ib ii 852) [See Addenda.]

640. Quitclaim by William the chaplain, son of Philip de Newton, to abbot S[imon] of the whole homage and service which his brother, Robert de Newton, owed him for the land held of him in the said vill, doing suit at the abbot's court and the services thence due 1265–91.

Willelmus capellanus filius Philippi de Neuton quiete clamauit S[ymoni] abbati Cestrie homagium et seruicium totum que Robertus de Neuton frater eius sibi facere debuit de tota terra quam tenuit de se in predicta villa, faciendo sectam curie abbatis et debita inde seruicia

William and Robert de Newton attest charters in 1291 and 1292 (*Journ Chester Arch Soc* x pp 46–7)

[1] Robert, son of Thurstan Duc, witnesses a charter not later than 1225 (*Journ Chester Arch Soc* x p 18)

641. Quitclaim by William the chaplain, son of Philip de Newton, to abbot S[imon] of the homage and service of 12*d* yearly rent which Richard Clerk, citizen of Chester, owed him for 2½ oxgangs of land in Upton which William, father of the said Richard, bought of Hamon Cosyn, and confirmation by the said William the chaplain of his uncle Guy's gift (No. 637) of the services of the same Richard for another 2½ oxgangs in Upton similarly acquired 1265–91.

W[illelmus] capellanus, filius Philippi de Neuton, quiete clamauit S[ymoni] abbati Cestrie homagium et seruicium xii denariorum annui redditus, que Ricardus Clericus, ciuis Cestrie, sibi facere debuit de ii bouatis terre et dimidia in Upton, quas Willelmus pater dicti R[icardi] emit de Hamone Cosyn Item dictus W[illelmus] confirmauit donacionem quam Wydo filius Hamonis auunculus suus abbati Cestrie fecit de homagio et seruicio et vno pari calcarium, que predictus Ricardus Clericus eidem Wydoni facere debuit de aliis ii bouatis terre et dimidia in dicta villa de Upton, quas dictus Willelmus de predicto Hamone emit

Both William and Richard Clerk held the office of mayor of Chester.

642. Grant by Philip, son of Hamon, to Richard de Pinchbeck of all the land which he had in the said Richard's croft, lying between the said Richard's land and the land which was Thomas de Newton's, paying 1*d* to him yearly *c* 1250.

Philippus filius Hamonis dedit Ricardo de Pinchebec totam terram cum pertinenciis quam habuit in crofto dicti Ricardi iacentem inter terram dicti Ricardi et terram que fuit Thome de Neuton, reddendo sibi annuatim i denarium ad festum sancti Johannis Baptiste

The grantee bears a Lincolnshire name, and doubtless belonged to a family who were tenants of the Chester fee there

643. Grant by Richard de Pinchbeck to abbot Thomas (I) of all his land in the vill of Newton which he bought from Robert, son of Osbern, and Philip, son of Hamon, paying yearly to the said Robert a pair of white gloves or 1*d* , and to the said Philip 1*d* 1249–65.

Ricardus de Pinchebec dedit T[home] abbati Cestrie totam terram suam in villa de Neuton cum omnibus pertinenciis, quam (29)] emit de Roberto filio Osberni et de Philippo filio Hamonis, red-

dendo annuatim dicto Roberto vnum par albarum cirotecarum
vel 1 denarium in Natiuitate sancti Johannis Baptiste, et vnum
denarium dicto Philippo ad idem festum

644. Quitclaim by Richard, son of Richard Clerk of Chester, to
abbot S[imon] of all his right, etc , in waste lands, heaths,
marshes, moors, and whatsoever he had in the name of soil
in the vill of Upton over and above 5 oxgangs, with 2
messuages, so binding himself not to lay claim, etc , to
land brought or to be brought into cultivation by the abbot,
but reserving to himself the right of free entry and exit
and common of pasture adequate for such an amount of
land, as well in the waste of the vill all the year round as
in the land approved and to be approved by the abbot
after the corn and hay have been carried away therefrom.
" This is enrolled in Domesday " 1265–91.

Ricardus filius Ricardi clerici de Cestria quiete clamauit
S[ymoni] abbati Cestrie totum ius et clamium suum in terris vastis,
bruens, mariscis, moris et quicquid habuit nomine soli in villa de
Upton ultra v bouatas terre cum ii mesuagiis, ita quidem quod de
terris per abbatem in culturam redactis uel redigendis clamium
uel querelam seu impedimentum non apponet, saluis sibi libero
introitu et exitu et sufficiente communa pasture quanta pertinet
ad tantam terram, tam in vasto eiusdem ville per totum annum
quam in terris abbatis approuiatis et approuiandis, blado et feno
inde asportatis.   Hoc irrotulatur in Domesday

645. Grant by Madock, son of Leca de Woodchurch, to Roger,
son of Northman de Woodchurch, of an oxgang of land in
Woodchurch which Matilda, sister of Leca, and Madock
her husband held, paying yearly 2s. to the chief lord, viz
at the feast of St John the Baptist and at the feast of
St Martin   c 1265–1302

Madocus filius Lece de Wodechirche dedit et warantauit Rogero
filio North[manni] de Wodechirche vnam bouatam terre cum
pertinenciis in Wodechirche, quam Matilda soror dicte Lece et
Madocus maritus suus tenuerunt, reddendo domino capitali ii
solidos annuos, viz ad festum sancti Johannis Baptiste et ad
festum sancti Martini per equales porciones.

Roger afterwards gave this holding to abbot Thomas II (No 654).
Ormerod (ii 521) identifies Leca (? Leta) de Woodchurch with the
Leuka, daughter of Hamon de Woodchurch, of No 656 A comparison,

however, of Nos 645–7 and 654 shows that the same oxgang is in
question in all, and thus proves that Leca was Leticia, daughter of
William Other of Woodchurch, who inherited it from her sister Matilda,
wife of Madock of Pensby (No 646) The grantor of No. 648 was
probably their brother The same local name might be borne by two
different families or by two branches of the same family This warning
applies also to Ormerod's suggestion that Norman de Woodchurch was
brother of Hamon

646. Quitclaim by Madock de Pensby and Matilda his wife to
abbot Thomas (I) of all their land in Woodchurch, saving
to them and their heirs an oxgang which they held of the
said abbot 1261–63

Madocus de Penesby et Matilda vxor eius quiete clamauerunt
T[home] abbati Cestrie omnes terras suas in Wodechirche cum
omnibus pertinenciis, salua sibi et heredibus vna bouata quam de
dicto abbate tenuerunt His testibus T[homa] de Orrebi tunc
iusticiario Cestrie,   . .

See note on No 645 The date is fixed within narrow limits by the
scribe of the chartulary for once inadvertently preserving the name of
a single witness With this precise date, the position conjecturally
assigned to Madock by Ormerod in the Pensby pedigree (ii 530), where
he appears as brother of a Roger de Pensby who was alive sixty-three
years later and whose grandfather was living in 1277–78, is obviously
irreconcilable

For earlier abbey holdings in Woodchurch see p 19 and No 648

647. Quitclaim by Leticia, daughter of William Other of Woodchurch, to abbot S[imon] of all the lands in Woodchurch
which the said abbot held by gift of her ancestors, saving
to her and her heirs an oxgang which she inherited on the
death of her sister Matilda, to be held of the said abbot for
her homage and service and 2s paid yearly See Nos
645–6 1265–91

Leticia filia Willelmi Other de Wodechirche quiete clamauit
S[ymoni] abbati Cestrie omnes terras cum pertinenciis in Wodechirche quas dictus abbas tenuit ex dono antecessorum suorum
Salua sibi et heredibus suis vna bouata que sibi accidit hereditarie
per mortem Matilde sororis sue, tenenda de dicto abbate pro
homagio et seruicio suo et ii solidis annuis soluendis ad festum
sancti Johannis Baptiste et ad festum sancti Martini per equales
porciones

648. Quitclaim by William, son of William Other, to abbot Roger of all his right, etc , in 4 oxgangs in Woodchurch which Hugh, son of William, held of him   1240–49

Willelmus filius Willelmi Other quiete clamauit Rogero abbati Cestrie totum ius et clamium suum in iiii⁰ʳ bouatis terre in Wodechirche, quas Hugo filius Willelmi de se tenuit

For Hugh, son of William, see also No 655

649. Quitclaim by Sir Roger de Domville—of Oxton and Brimstage—to abbot S[imon] of a pair of white gloves which he demanded from the said abbot as yearly rent for the vill of Woodchurch, together with all the right, etc , which he had by grant of Hawise, daughter and heir of Thomas de Thingwall, and Roger the clerk, her husband, or on any other ground   1265–91

Rogerus de D[unuile] [1] miles quiete clamauit S[ymoni] abbati Cestrie vnum par albarum cirotecarum, quas exigebat a dicto abbate nomine annui redditus de villa de Wodechirche cum pertinenciis, vna cum toto iure et clamio quod habuit ex donacione Hawisie filie et heredis Thome de Tingewelle et Rogeri clerici mariti sui, uel quacunque alia racione, cum bosco et uasto et omnibus pertinenciis

The ground of Sir Roger de Domville's claim to a rent of gloves from Woodchurch appears in Nos 650–2   He was enfeoffed with the manor of Thingwall by Hawise, whose right it was, and her husband Roger Lymm, as he is called elsewhere (Orm ii 528)

650. Grant by Thomas de Thingwall to Ralph de Barnston (No 652) of 12 oxgangs in Woodchurch in fee and demesne, paying to him yearly a pair of white gloves for all service, saving the external service   Before 1265

Thomas de Tingewalle dedit et warantizauit Radulpho de Binston (sic) xii bouatas terre in Wodechirche in feodo et dominico, cum omnibus pertinenciis, reddendo sibi annuatim vnum par albarum cirotecarum ad festum sancti Johannis Baptiste pro omni seruicio, saluo forinseco seruicio

651. Grant by Emma, daughter of A[dam of Woodchurch [2]], to Adam, son of Hugh, of 2 oxgangs in Woodchurch out of 4 oxgangs which she got from Gerard de Thingwall of his

[1] Extended from the heading   [2] From the heading.

inheritance, with a messuage lying between the houses which were Richard Clerk's and William de Braose's, paying to her yearly 14d   These 4 oxgangs the said Emma and Walter Walsh, her husband, likewise gave to the said Adam, as appears in their charter

Emma filia Ade dedit Ade filio Hugonis ii bouatas terre in Wodechirche de quatuor bouatis quas adepta fuit de Gerard de Tingewella de hereditate sua, cum mesuagio iacente inter domos qui fuerunt Ricardi Clerici et Willelmi de Braosa cum omnibus pertinenciis, reddendo sibi annuatim xiiii denarios ad Natiuitatem sancti Johannis Baptiste et ad festum sancti Martini per equales porciones   Has iiii bouatas dicta Emma et Walterus Wallensis maritus suus dicto Ade similiter dederunt vt in carta sua patet

The mention of the rent in No 658 shows that Emma was the Emma White (*Alba*) of No 659, and the grantee the Adam, son of Hugh the dean of Woodchurch, of the same charter

652. Grant by Ralph de Barnston to abbot T[homas] (I) of all the land in Woodchurch which he bought of Thomas de Thingwall (No. 650), to wit 12 oxgangs as well in demesnes as in fee, paying therefor yearly to him and his heirs a pair of white gloves for all service, saving foreign service, to wit feeding two foresters   1249–65

Radulphus de Berliston dedit et warantizauit domino T[home] abbati Cestrie totam terram in Wodechirche quam emit de Thoma de Tingewella, scilicet xii bouatas, tam in dominicis quam in feodo, cum omnibus pertinenciis, reddendo inde annuatim sibi et heredibus suis vnum par albarum cirotecarum in Natiuitate sancti Johannis Baptiste pro omni seruicio, saluo forinseco seruicio, scilicet pastura ii forestariorum.

The reference to puture of two foresters of the forest of Wirral (disafforested in 1377) here and in No 660 shows that *forinsec* service was not necessarily military, as it is sometimes assumed to have been (Vinogradoff, *English Society in the Eleventh Century*, 39)

653. Quitclaim by Sir William de Wistaston to the abbey of all his right, etc , in the above 12 oxgangs (No 652) and in all other lands which the monks of Chester at any time held of his fee in the said vill, together with all his rights in the advowson of the church of the same vill   ? 1249–65

Willelmus de Wistanston miles quiete clamauit beate Werburge Cestrie totum ius et clamium suum in xii bouatis terre, cum omnibus pertinenciis, in Wodechuiche quas Radulphus de Berliston eidem antea dedit, et in omnibus aliis terris quas monachi Cestrie de feodo suo alico tempore tenuerunt in dicta uilla vna cum toto iure quod habuit uel habere potuit in aduocacione ecclesie eiusdem ville

Woodchuich (as part of Landican) was in the 11th century, like Thingwall, part of the barony of Wich Malbank (Nantwich), and, again like (a moiety of) Thingwall, it seems in the 13th century to have been held of the lords of Wistaston, a Malbank manor near Nantwich, unless, as Ormerod seems to suggest, the Wistastons had only a large holding here (Orm ii 521, 530 , iii 330)   For the grantor cf No 38

654. Grant by Roger, son of Norman de Woodchurch, to his chief lord, abbot Thomas (II), of all his land in Woodchurch which Madock, son of Leca de Woodchurch, gave him   1291-1302

Rogerus filius Norman de Wodechuiche dedit et warantizauit capitali domino suo, Thome, abbati Cestrie, totam terram suam in Wodechirche cum omnibus pertinenciis, quam Madocus filius Lece de Wodechirche sibi dedit

See No. 645   The grantor died before 1302 (Orm i 521)

655. Grant by Hamon de Woodchurch to William, son of Hugh (cf No 648), of 4 oxgangs in Woodchurch, paying to him 2s yearly   Before 1260

Hamon de Wodechirche dedit et warantizauit Willelmo filio Hugonis iiii bouatas terre in Wodechirche cum omnibus pei tinenciis, reddendo sibi annuatim ii solidos ad festum sancti Martini

656. Quitclaim by Leuka, daughter of Hamon de Woodchurch, to abbot Thomas (I) of all her right, etc , in land which was William her brother's in Woodchurch   1249-65

Leuka filia Hamonis de Wodechirche quiete clamauit Thome abbati Cestrie totum ius et clamium suum in terra que [fuit] Willelmi fratris sui cum pertinenciis in Wodechirche.

No 393 records the purchase of 4 oxgangs of land in Woodchurch by abbot Thomas from the daughters of Hamon de Woodchurch

657. Quitclaim by Henry, son of Adam de Latthon and Mar-g[aret] his wife, daughter of Hamon de Woodchurch, to abbot T[homas] (I.) of all their right, etc , in 4 oxgangs in Woodchurch which had belonged to Hamon de Wood-church   This quitclaim he got enrolled in Domesday 1249–65

(29) *d*]   Henricus filius Ade de Latthon et Marg[areta] vxor eius, filia Hamonis de Wodechirche, quiete clamauit T[home] abbati Cestrie totum ius et clamium suum in iiii bouatis terre in Wodechirche cum pertinenciis, que fuerunt Hamonis de Wodechirche et hanc quietam clamanciam procurauit iriotulari in Domesday

Ormerod suggests that Latthon is a corrupt form of Landican, but query   Mr Irvine suggests Leighton

658. Grant by Thomas de Thingwall to William, son of Colbert de Upton (No 359), of 14*d* of yearly rent formerly taken in respect of 2 oxgangs   which Adam, son of [Hugh] the dean of Woodchurch, sold to the aforesaid William (No 659)

Thomas de Tingewella dedit et warantizauit Willelmo filio Colberti de Vpton xiiii denarios annui redditus de duabus bouatis quondam percepto[s]   quas Adam filius Decani de Wode-chirche predicto Willelmo vendidit

659. Grant by Adam, son of Hugh, dean of Woodchurch, to William, son of Colbert de Upton, of 2 oxgangs in Wood-church which his father Hugh bought of Emma White ? 1265–91

Adam filius Hugonis decani de Wodechirche dedit Willelmo filio Colberti de Vpton ii bouatas terre in Wodechirche cum omnibus pertinenciis, quas Hugo pater suus emit de Emma Alba

See note on No 651, where the previous transaction is between Emma and Adam, not his father

660. Quitclaim by William, son of Colbert de Upton (Nos 359, 854), to abbot S[imon] of 2 oxgangs in Woodchurch which he previously held of the said abbot, doing external service, to wit, puture for two foresters thrice a year   1265–91

Willelmus filius Colberti de Vpton quiete clamauit et waran-tizauit S[ymoni] abbati Cestrie ii bouatas terre in Wodechirche cum omnibus pertinenciis, quas de dicto abbate antea tenuit, faciendo forinsecum seruicium, scilicet pulturam duorum fores-tariorum ter per annum

661. Quitclaim by Ranulf, son of Thomas de Praers, lord of Landican, to abbot S[imon] that he should have common of pasture for his beasts of Woodchurch and the beasts of his natives and lease-holders in Woodchurch, of whatsoever kind, in the territory of the vill of Landican, wherever his own beasts and those of his men of Landican are grazed, saving his reasonable approvements in his waste This pasture the abbot recovered after judicial process by the writ called *quod permittat* 1289–91

Rannulphus filius Thome de Preers, dominus de Landecan, quiete clamauit S[ymoni] abbati Cestrie quod habeat communam pasture animalibus suis de Wodechirche et animalibus natiuorum suorum et ad terminum tenencium in Wodechirche, cuiuscunque generis, in territorio ville de Landecan vbicunque animalia sua et hominum de Landecan pascuntur, saluis sibi approuiamentis racionabilibus in vasto suo Hanc pasturam dictus abbas per breue quod dicitur " quod permittat " [1] iudicialiter recuperauit

Thomas de Praers of Barthomley (Nantwich hundred) and Landican—both Malbank manors—d early in 1290 (*Cal Inq.* ii 462, Orm iii 299) It appears from No 662 that the legal decision was given in his lifetime, and that Ranulf is confirming his father's acceptance of it

662. Quitclaim by abbot Simon to Thomas de Barthomley of all his right, etc., in the advowson of the church of Woodchurch and an oxgang in Landican Confirmation by Thomas to the said abbot of common of pasture in the territory of Landican, according to the form of the preceding charter [2] 1265–90

S[ymon] abbas Cestrie quiete clamauit Thome de Bertumlega totum ius suum et clamium in aduocacione ecclesie de Wodechirche et vna bouata terre in Landecan, cum pertinenciis Predictus uero Thomas confirmauit dicto abbati communam pasture secundum formam carte precedentis in territorio de Landecan

663. Agreement between abbot S[imon] and the rector of Woodchurch that the rector should take the tithes of all lands from which the said church was wont to take tithes, and the abbot should have his newly tilled lands free and quit

[1] " The writ *Quod permittat* on a disseisin of common of pasture, directed to the sheriff, *Commands A that justly, etc, he permit B to have common of pasture in, etc, which he ought to have, as is said* " (Jacob, *Law Dict* (1782), s v)
[2] The Latin heading is Finalis concordia inter Simonem abbatem et Thomam de Bertumlega

in the teriitory of Woodchuich, without payment of tithes, accoiding to the tenor of the abbey privileges (No 61, p 110). This agreement is sealed with the seals of each party and with the seal of the officiality of Chester   1265–91

S[ymon] abbas Cestrie concessit quod rector ecclesie de Wodechirche percipiat decimas de omnibus terris de quibus dicta ecclesia decimas percipere consueuit , predictus uero rector concessit dicto abbati quod habeat noualia sua facta et facienda nomine suo et ecclesie sue libeia et quieta in territorio de Wodechirche sine prestacione decimarum, secundum tenorem priuilegiorum suorum   Hec composicio vtriusque partis sigillis et eciam sigillo officialitatis Cestrie signatur

The rector was probably Ralph de Caldwell, who occurs in an assize in 1286 (Orm ii 523)

664. Grant by Richard, son of Leuka de Ledesbera, with the consent of his wife Agnes, to Marg[aret], formerly wife of Ralph de Moston, of all his land in Moston (by Chester) which the said Ralph and Marg[aret] gave him in free marriage with the said Agnes, their daughter, paying to him yearly a robe   Richard, son of the said Richard and Agnes, confiimed this gift, retaining no right, etc , in this land

Ricardus filius Leuke de Ledesbera ex consensu Agnetis vxoris sue dedit Marg[arete], quondam vxori Radulphi de Morston, totam terram suam in Morston quam dicti Radulphus et Marg[aieta] sibi dederunt in libeio maiitagio cum dicta Agnete filia sua, reddendo sibi annuatim i robam ad Natiuitatem sancti Johannis Baptiste   Ricardus filius dictorum Ricardi et Agnetis hanc donacionem confirmauit, nichil sibi in dicta teria iuris uel clamii retinens, vt in carta sua patet

Ormeiod (i 282) turns Ledesbera into Ledsham

665. Grant by Richard de Moston to abbot Thomas (II) of a messuage and 4 oxgangs in Moston, doing therefor the services due to the chief lords   The king's licence was obtained for this acquisition   c 1305.

Ricardus de Morston dedit Thome abbati Cestrie vnum mesuagium et quatuor bouatas terre cum peitinenciis in Moiston, faciendo inde dominis capitalibus debita seruicia, et hanc donacionem dictus Ricardus et heredes sui warantizauerunt   Hec adquisicio fuit licenciata a rege

As this gift was made after the passing of the statute of mortmain (1279), the royal licence was necessary   On an *inq ad quod damnum* in 33 Edw I (1304–5), it was found that the earl could give licence for the transfer " inasmuch as Hugh de Lou, formerly earl of Chester, gave the same tenements to the church of St Werburgh at its foundation, and the predecessors of the then abbot enfeoffed certain persons of the same tenements, to be held of the said abbot and convent by certain yearly services " (Orm ii 818)   Moston is not, however, included by name in the founder's charter   The only gift there which is recorded was in the time of earl Ranulf I , when Richard de Cruce gave either the whole vill or part of it (p 48 above)

665a.[1] Grant by abbot Hugh to Simon, son of William de Spalding, of three oxgangs in Moston and a house in Chester over against St Werburgh's gate. (Cf. No 370)   1208–26

Brit Mus Addit Charter 49974

Uniuersis sancte matris ecclesie filiis ad quos presens scriptum peruenerit Hugo Dei gracia abbas Cestr' et eiusdem loci conuentus salutem in Domino   Nouerit uniuersitas uestra nos dedisse et concessisse et hac presenti carta nostra confirmasse Symoni filio Willelmi de Spaldinges iii bouatas terre in uilla de Morsetun, scilicet ii bouatas quas Orm camerarius tenuit et i bouatam quam Swein tenuit, cum omnibus pertinenciis suis, et unum mesuagium in uilla Cestr' contra portam sancte Werburge, scilicet quod Ricardus de Grendun tenuit   Habendas et tenendas libere et quiete sibi et heredibus suis, reddendo annuatim domui sancte Werburge pro omnibus seruiciis ad eas pertinentibus dimidiam marcam argenti ad duos terminos, scilicet quadraginta denarios ad festum apostolorum Petri et Pauli et quadraginta denarios ad festum sancti Martini   Nos uero hanc predictam donacionem et concessionem predicto Symoni et heredibus suis contra omnes homines warentizabimus   Et ut hec concessio nostra perpetue firmitatis robur optineat eam sigillorum nostrorum munimine roborauimus   His testibus . Hugone suppriore, Willelmo de Walej, Roberto de West[on], Thoma de Chelleia, Rogero Fiend, Philippo de Orreby tunc tempore iusticiario, Petro clerico, Ricardo vicecomite, magistro Alano officiali, magistro Johanne de sancta Maria, magistro Hugone Iuuene, Roberto de Pincebec, Ricardo Portario, Gilberto filio Galfridi, et multis aliis.

[1] Not in Chartulary.

368 CHARTULARY OF CHESTER ABBEY

*Two vesica-shaped seals (1) a figure of St Werburgh in grave-clothes,
leg* SIGILLVM SANTE [WERB]VRGC VIRGINIS , (2) *an Abbot, leg*
SIGILLUM HUGONIS ABBATIS CESTR , *secretum, a classical gem (male head),
leg* ✠ GRACIA DEI SVM ID QUOD SVM Figured in *Journal of Chester
Arch Soc* N S x 16, 20 Cf No 509a

666. Quitclaim by James de (Nether) Poole to God and abbot
[Thomas (II)] of all his right, etc , in the heath between
the vill of Lea (by Backford) and Capenhurst, to wit, from
the vill of Lea to the road extending from Lensethorn to
the cross situate between Sutton and Backford, according
to the boundaries there placed, reserving nothing for himself in the said heath or its turbary, herbage, or any other
common In like manner William, son of Richard de
Capenhurst, quitclaimed the said heath, as did also Thomas
de Capenhurst, son of John de Frodsham and Amaria
[? daughter] of the said Thomas 1292–1308

Iacobus de Pulle quiete clamauit Deo et abbati Cestrie totum
ius et clamium suum in brueria inter villam de Lee et Capenhurst,
scilicet, a villa de Lee usque ad viam extensam a Lensethorn vsque
ad crucem sitam inter Sotton et Bacford, secundum diuisas ibi
positas, nichil sibi retinens in dicto bruerio vel eius turbaria,
herbagio uel aliqua alia communa. Simili modo Willelmus filius
Ricardi de Capenhurst dictum bruerium quiete clamauit, prout in
carta sua patet Necnon Thomas de Capenhurst filius Johannis
de Frodisham, prout in carta sua patet Necnon Amaria [? filia] [1]
dicti Thome, prout in carta sua patet [See Addenda]

The date of this deed lies between 21 Edw I (1292–93), when Hugh
de Barnston gave the homages and services of William de Capenhurst
and other free tenants of his in Capenhurst to James de Poole, and
1307–8, the year of the latter's death (Orm ii 568) See No 636 n

667. Render by abbot Robert de Hastings to William, son of
Warner, of 20 oxgangs in Chorlton (by Backford) and a
croft as his right, and of 8 oxgangs in Backford, to hold
the said lands of St Werburgh, and paying 7s yearly to her
church at Chester on the feast of St Martin, and a pound
of cummin and another of pepper at both the feast days
of St Werburgh 1186–94.

Robertus de Hastings, abbas Cestrie, reddidit Willelmo filio
Warneri xx bouatas terre in Cherliston [2] et vnam croftam sicut

---
[1] A blank space of about this length
[2] Altered in later hand to Chorlton See No 636 n

ius suum, et viii bouatas in Backford, tenendo dictas terras de sancta Werburga et reddendo ecclesie sue Cestrie annuatim vii solidos ad festum sancti Martini, et vnam libram cimini et aliam piperis ad utramque festiuitatem sancte Werburge

Ormerod traces the abbey holding in Chorlton to a gift by Hamon de Massey in the 12th century, but does not state his authority (ii 374) The eight oxgangs in Backford were given by Robert and Simon de Massey in the time of earl Ranulf II (p 59 *supra*) On the ground that no lands were held by the abbey in the *present* township of Backford, Ormerod conjectured that the eight oxgangs afterwards became the adjoining township of Lea (ii 362) Yet Helsby accepts the identification of this Lea with the Wisdeleth given by the founder (ii 383) The suggestion that part of Chorlton was also originally in Backford is even less substantiated (ii 374)

668. Grant by Gilbert de Arderne, rector of the church of Aldford, to his brother T[homas] of all his land in the vill of Chorlton, to him and the legitimate heirs of his body, with the villeins and their offspring, and, if he has no heirs, the land to revert (to the grantor)

Gilbertus de Arderna, rector ecclesie de Aldeford[ia] dedit T[home] fratri suo totam terram suam cum omnibus pertinenciis in villa de Cherlton, sibi et heredibus suis de corpore suo legitime procreatis, cum natiuis et eorum sequela, et si non (*sic*) heredes non habuerit, terra reuertetur

The place of the grantor and his brother in the Arderne pedigree is uncertain Helsby suggests that they were sons of Sir Walkelin de Arderne (Orm ii 79, 85), but if he is right in identifying Gilbert with the grantee of No 673 his suggestion falls to the ground His further identification of Thomas with Thomas de Ardern of Ratley, co Warwick (*not* York), is very doubtful (Orm ii 79, iii 680, 793, 795).

669. Quitclaim by G[ilbert] de Arderne, rector of the church of Aldford, to T[homas] de Arderne his brother of all his right, etc , in all the lands and tenements which he had of his gift in Roodeye (?) and Chorlton, doing therefor the due and wonted services

G[ilbertus] de Ardena, rector ecclesie de Aldef[ordia], quiete clamauit T[home] de Ardena, fratri suo, totum ius et clamium suum in omnibus terris et tenementis cum pertinenciis que habuit de dono suo in Rodey et Cherlton sine alico retenemento, faciendo inde debita seruicia et consueta

I

670. Grant by Thomas de Arderne to Sir Richard de Massey of all the lands, etc , which he had in Frodsham, Bradley (in Frodsham), Helsby, and Chorlton, with his villeins and their offspring and their chattels, doing therefor to the chief lords the services due   1290–1305

(30)]   Thomas de Arderna dedit Ricardo de Masci militi omnes terras et tenementa que habuit in Frodesham, Bradelega, Hellesby et Chorlton cum nativis suis et sequela et eorum catallis, faciendo inde debita seruicia dominis capitalibus.

Sir Richard de Massey was knighted before 1279 (p 205), and died April 20, 1305, but the above grant can be more closely dated. Its terms show that it was made after the passing of the statute of *Quia Emptores* in 1290, and as an *Inq ad quod damnum* was to be held at the time of Massey's death as to whether the earl could give licence, *inter alia* for a grant by Sir Richard to Chester Abbey of one messuage and four oxgangs in Chorlton (Orm ii 374), and his intentions were carried out by his brother Robert (Nos 674–5), this and the following acquisitions (Nos 671–2) from the Helsbys were probably made towards the close of his life.

671. Grant by William de Helsby to Sir Richard de Massey of all lands and tenements which he had in the vill of Chorlton in Wirral, doing therefor to the chief lords the due and wonted services   1290–1305

Willelmus de Hellesbi dedit Ricardo de Masci militi omnes terras et tenementa que habuit in villa de Chorlton in Wirall[ia], faciendo inde dominis capitalibus debita seruicia et consueta

The Helsbys of Helsby, etc , acquired a sixth part of Chorlton about the end of the 12th century by the marriage of Jocerame de Helsby with Agatha, daughter of Hamon de Massey III (Orm ii 72, 374) The present grantor is supposed to have been their great-great-grandson (Sir) William de Helsby (*ib* 65 *n*)

672. Grant by William de Helsby to Sir R[ichard] de Massey of the rent and service of Robert de Sale for his lands and tenements in Backford and Chorlton   *c.* 1290–1305.

Willelmus de Hellesbi dedit R[icardo] de Masci militi redditum et seruicium Roberti de Sale de terris et tenementis suis in Bacford et Chorlton cum pertinenciis suis.

The subsequent conveyance to the abbey (No 675) identifies the tenant with Robert Massey of Sale, head of a branch of the barons of

Dunham, who were chief lords of Backford and Chorlton from the 11th century

673. Grant by Adam de Helsby to his kinsman Gilbert, son of Walter the parson of Frodsham, of 2 oxgangs of land in Chorlton which William, son of Agnes, held of him, with the said William and all his progeny, paying him 1*d* yearly

Adam de Hellesby dedit Gilberto cognato suo, filio Walteri persone de Frodesham, quamdam partem terre sue in Chorlton, scilicet illas ii bouatas quas Willelmus filius Agnetis tenuit de se cum dicto Willelmo et omni sequela sua, reddendo sibi annuatim vnum denarium ad festum sancti Martini

Adam de Helsby was younger brother of the grantor of the two preceding charters (Orm ii 64, 363 , cf No 636) Ormerod's editor, who by an extraordinary misreading of the contracted words of the Chartulary describes the grantee as " fitz Walkelin (?), governor or constable (?) of Frodsham " (*ib* 65 *n*), identifies him with Gilbert de Arderne (Nos 668–9). This would certainly account for the Arderne interest in Chorlton, otherwise unexplained, besides supplying an avenue by which the land here granted came to the abbey

674. Grant by Robert de Massey of Tatton to Henry de Bromborough, clerk, of all his lands and tenements in Chorlton and Backford, doing therefor the due services to the chief lords , and regrant by the said Henry to God and abbot Thomas (II) 1305–23

Robertus de Masci de Tatton dedit Henrico de Brombur[ia], clerico, omnes terras et omnia tenementa sua cum omnibus pertinenciis in Chorltona et in Bacforda vt in mesuagiis, terris dominicis, vastis, pasturis, moris, mariscis, redditibus, homagiis, seruiciis, releuiis, escaetis, natiuis et eorum sequela et catallis, faciendo inde debita seruicia dominis capitalibus. Omnia hec dictus Henricus dedit Deo et T[home] abbati Cestrie, prout in carta sua patet

675. Grant by R[obert] de Massey of Tatton to abbot T[homas] (II) of the homage and all services of Robert de Massey of Sale for all lands and tenements which he held of him in Chorlton and Backford, to hold of the chief lords by the services due therefrom. Cf. No 672. 1305–23

R[obertus] de Masci de Tatton dedit T[home] abbati Cestrie homagium et seruicia omnimoda Roberti de Masci de Sale de

omnibus terris et tenementis que de se tenuit in Cherlton et Bacford, cum omnibus pertinenciis, tenenda de dominis capitalibus
per debita inde seruicia

676. Grant and quitclaim by Gilbert Blay or Bloy and Alice,
his wife, to Richard de Toft and Alina, his wife, of 2 oxgangs
in Little Saughall which Wilym Alñ held, paying to them
yearly a barbed arrow   Before 1271

Gilbertus Blay et Alicia uxor eius concesserunt et quiete clamauerunt Ricardo de Toft et Aline vxori eius duas bouatas terre in
Parua Salighale [1] quas Wilym Alñ [2] tenuit, reddendo eis annuatim
vnam sagittam barbatam ad Natiuitatem sancti Johannis Baptiste

Alice Blay or Bloy and her daughters Alina and Amaria gave land,
etc , in Chester to the abbey (Nos 611–12, 623)   There seems to be
no positive evidence that Alina de Toft was the first-named daughter
This grant is merely a confirmation of the gift of an undertenant by his
immediate lord   No place has been found for Alina's husband in the
pedigree of Toft of Toft   He lived in Chester, occurs in a deed c 1258
(*Journ Chester Arch Soc* x p 32), and died before 1288 (*ib* p 42 , cf
No 380, *supra*).

From Nos. 678 and 686 it appears that the ancestors of Alice de
Bloy had been tenants of a third part of Little Saughall under the abbey.
It is possible that the " third part of Saughall " which earl Hugh I.
confirmed to the abbey (p 16) comprehended that fraction of Little as
well as Great Saughall   In her widowhood Alice quitclaimed to the
abbey, first a number of parcels of land in her estate, and finally the
whole third part (No 686)

677. Grant by Alina, formerly wife of Richard de Toft, to
William de Albo Monasterio of 2 messuages and 2 oxgangs
in Little Saughall, [which] Wilym son of Andrew gave her,
paying to her yearly a barbed arrow   (Before 1290)
Quitclaims of the same to the said William by Richard,
son of the said Alina, and to God and abbot T[homas] (II.
1291–1323), by Roger, rector of the church of Denford
(Northants), brother of the said William.

Alina quondam vxor Ricardi de Toft in ligia viduitate dedit
Willelmo de Albo Monasterio duo mesuagia et ii bouatas terre in
Parua Saligh' quas Wilym filius Andree sibi dedit, reddendo sibi
annuatim vnam sagittam barbatam in Natiuitate sancti Johannis
Baptiste   Has terras Ricardus, filius dicte Aline, dicto Willelmo

_____
[1] Written in full   [2] filius Andree in No 677

quiete clamauit, prout in carta patet   Item has terras Rogerus,
rector ecclesie de Deneford, frater dicti Willelmi, Deo et T[home]
abbati Cestrie quietas clamauit, vt in carta sua patet

William "de Albo Monasterio" and his brother Roger, who held a
living which was in the gift of Chester Abbey (No 126), were perhaps
relatives of abbot Simon de Albo Monasterio (1265–90), who is
generally called by modern writers Simon of Whitchurch, but occasionally, and apparently more correctly, Simon of Blanchminster, being
probably either a native of Oswestry (Album Monasterium) or a
member of a family which derived its name from that town

678. Quitclaim by Alice, widow of Gilbert Blay, to abbot S[imon]
of 1½ oxgangs which John Catel held of her, and her bond
for herself and her heirs to do to the said abbot the whole
service which her ancestors did for a third part of (Little)
Saughall   1265–81

Alicia relicta G[ilberti] Blay in ligia viduitate quiete clamauit
S[ymoni] abbati Cestrie vnam bouatam terre et dimidiam quas
Johannes Catel de se tenuit   Item dicta Alicia obligauit se et
heredes suos ad faciendum totum seruicium dicto abbati quod
antecessores sui fecerunt pro tercia parte de Salhal'.

For the lower limit of date see No. 686

679. Quitclaim by Alice, widow of Gilbert Blay, to abbot
S[imon] of 1½ oxgangs in Saughall which William Bullock
held of her at farm   Also bond as in No 678.   1265–81

Alicia relicta G[ilberti] Blay quiete clamauit S[ymoni] abbati
Cestrie vnam bouatam et dimidiam terre in Salighal', quas
Willelmus Bulloc de se ad firmam tenuit , necnon obligauit se, etc

680. Quitclaim by Alice, widow of Gilbert Blay, to abbot
S[imon] of 8 acres in Saughall, viz 2 in Woodfurlong, and
3 which are called Le Long Acre, and 3 which formerly
belonged to William Schail, with 2 butts in Wildemarelode
1265–81

A[licia], relicta G[ilberti] Blay, quiete clamauit S[ymoni]
abbati Cestrie viii acras terre in Salighal', videlicet ii in Wodeforlong, et iii que vocantur Le Longe Acre, et iii que fuerunt
quondam Willelmi Schail, cum duabus buttis in Wildemarelode ,
necnon obligauit se, etc

681. Quitclaim by Alice, widow of Gilbert Blay, to abbot

S[ımon] of an oxgang ın Saughall ın the field called Renesfeld, whıch Wıllıam de Ireland held   1265–81

A[lıcıa] relıcta G[ılbertı] Blay quıete clamauıt S[ymonı] abbatı
Cestrıe vnam bouatam terre ın Salıgh', ın campo quı vocatur
Renesfeld, quam Wıllelmus de Hybernıa tenuıt ; necnon oblıgauıt
se, etc

682. Quıtclaım by Alıce, wıdow of Gılbert Blay, to abbot
S[ımon] of an oxgang ın Saughall whıch Roger, son of
Wılym, held   1265–81

A[lıcıa] relıcta G[ılbertı] Blay quıete clamauıt S[ymonı] abbatı
Cestrıe vnam bouatam terre ın Salıgh', quam Rogerus filıus Wılym
tenuıt , necnon oblıgauıt se, etc

683. Quıtclaım by Alıce, wıdow of Gılbert Blay, to abbot
S[ımon] of 3 acres lyıng between the wood of Lıttle Saughall
and the vıll of Crabwall, and one between Saughall and
the wood nearer for takıng beasts to pasture, wıth half her
part of the wood, and her part of a certaın croft outsıde
the Northgate at Chester, to wıt, Battlecroft   1265–81

A[lıcıa] relıcta G[ılbertı] Blay quıete clamauıt S[ymonı] abbatı
Cestrıe ııı acras terre ıacentes ınter boscum de Parua Salıgh' et
vıllam de Crabbewalle, et vnam ınter Salıgh' et boscum propın-
quıore[m] fuge auerıorum cum medıetate partıs sue de bosco, et
partem suam cuıusdam croftı extra portam aquılonalem Cestrıe,
scılıcet Bateylcroft , necnon oblıgauıt se, etc

684. Quıtclaım by Alıce, wıdow of Gılbert Blay, to abbot
S[ımon] of an oxgang ın Saughall whıch Rıchard, son of
Pımmere, her vılleın, held, together wıth the same Rıchard
and hıs progeny   1265–81

A[lıcıa], relıcta G[ılbertı] Blay, quıete clamauıt S[ymonı] abbatı
Cestrıe vnam bouatam terre ın Salıgh' quam Rıcardus filıus
Pımmere natıuus suus tenuıt, vna cum eodem Rıcardo et eıus
sequela , necnon oblıgauıt se, etc

685. Quıtclaım by Alıce, wıdow of Gılbert Blay, to abbot
S[ımon] of a whole moıety of all her essarts and lands
newly broken up, wıth appurtenances, whıch have been
made ın Lıttle Saughall sınce the lord Edward, son of Kıng
Henry, first became lord of Cheshıre (ı.e 1254), and to be
made ın future   1265–81

A[licia] relicta G[ilberti] Blay quiete clamauit S[ymoni] abbati
Cestrie totam medietatem omnium assartorum et frussurarum
suarum, cum pertinenciis, que facte sunt in Parua Saligh' a tempore prime dominacionis domini Edwardi, filii regis Henrici, in
Cestrisiria et imposterum sunt faciende , necnon obligauit se, etc.

686. Quitclaim by Alice, widow of Gilbert Blay, to the abbey of
the whole third part of the vill of Little Saughall which she
previously held of it by hereditary right (No 676 *n*), reserving nothing but prayers   1274–81.

A[licia], relicta Gilberti Blay, quiete clamauit ecclesie sancte [f 33
Werburge totam terciam partem ville de Salighale ¹ quam prius
de dicta ecclesia tenuit iure hereditario sine alicuius rei in ea
retenemento, exceptis oracionibus   Hiis testibus   Domino
Guncelino de Badelesmere, tunc iusticiario Cestrie, etc

687. Grant by Sir Hamon de Massey to God and abbot Thomas
( ) of 60 waggon-loads of turf, to be dug and taken yearly
at the will of the abbot in his (Hamon's) mosses of Bidston
and Saughall (Massey) and dried on his land near the pits,
and with free entry and exit to be carried by a suitable
road to the abbot's manors of Irby and Greasby without
impediment

Dominus Hamon de Mascy miles dedit Deo et Thome abbati
Cestrie imperpetuum lx carectatas turbarum in mossis suis de
Bideston et Saligh' ad uoluntatem abbatis Cestrie singulis annis
fodiendarum et capiendarum et in terris suis iuxta fossuras ex-
siccandarum, et cum libero ingressu et egressu per viam competentem ad maneria sua de Irreby et Greuesby cariandarum,
sine ullo impedimento.

There is no notice of this gift in Ormerod's account of Bidston
manor and its member Saughall (ii 466–70)   As the barons of Dunham
were all called Hamon, there seem no means of deciding whether it was
in the time of abbot Thomas de Capenhurst (1249–65), or that of abbot
Thomas de Burchells (1291–1323)   For the St Werburgh manor of
Irby see No 3, p 17, and for Greasby, Nos 22–3   [Cf Addenda]

688. Grant by William, son of Robert Lancelyn, to abbot
S[imon], who gave therefor a horse worth 20 marks, and
his successors, of (the right of making) the abutment of a
certain bridge (its width at their discretion) on his soil of

¹ Written in full.

Poulton (Lancelyn) beyond The Pool (Le Pul) in Poultondale, between Bromborough and Bebington, wherever they
think fit, with liberty and common of taking timber in his
woods of Poulton and Bebington for the entire construction, repair, and maintenance of the said bridge for ever,
with power to choose a new site if the first, or any subsequent one, should prove unsatisfactory; also common of
pasture in all his lands in Poulton and Bebington for the
demesne beasts of the abbey manor of Bromborough, with
free entry, etc , saving in the corn and meadows at reaping-
time and in the woods at mast-time, where, however, the
abbots shall have 50 of their pigs free from payment of
pannage   The grant, which was confirmed for themselves
by Thomas (de Praers) de Barthomley and his wife Avice
de Poulton, and provision for recovery of the consideration,
if its terms were not observed, were witnessed by Guncelin
de Badlesmere when justice of Chester   1274–80.

Willelmus filius Roberti Lancelyn dedit S[ymoni] abbati Cestrie
et successoribus suis attachiamentum cuiusdam pontis latitudine
quam uoluerint in solo suo de Pulton ultra Le Pul in Pultundale
inter Brumbur[gh] et Bebinton, vbicumque melius sibi viderint
expedire, cum libertate et communa capiendi meremium in boscis
suis de Pulton et Bebinton ad ipsum pontem totaliter faciendum,
reficiendum et sustentandum imperpetuum, ita quod si dictus pons
in loco ubi constructus fuerit subsistere uel durare comode non
poterit, liceat eis in alio loco quociens opus fuerit pro uoluntate
sua ipsum attachiare, construere et sustentare, et ad ipsius construc-
tionem et sustentacionem meremium in dictis boscis sufficienter
capere   Item idem concessit dictis abbatibus uel assignatis suis
communem pasturam omnibus dominicis scilicet animalibus de
manerio eorum de Brumbur[gh] cuiuscunque generis in omnibus
dictis terris suis de Pulton et Bebinton, cum libero introitu et
exitu ad eandem pasturam omni tempore anni et vbique, saluis
bladis et pratis tempore messium et dictis boscis tempore pessone,
in quibus tamen dicti abbates l porcos a prestacione pannagii
habebunt liberos et quietos , et hec omnia dictus Willelmus imperpetuum warantizauit, testibus, Guncelino de Badilismere tunc
iusticiario Cestrie, etc   Item hec omnia Thomas de Bertumlega
et Auicia de Pulton vxor sua S[ymoni] abbati Cestrie concesserunt
imperpetuum, prout in carta sua patet   Item pro supradictis
S[ymon] abbas Cestrie dedit Willelmo Lancelyn vnum equum
precii xx marcarum, vt patet in quadam ipsius obligacione vbi
dicitur quod si contingat dictum Willelmum uel heredes suos

contra predictas donaciones venirent, obligauit omnia bona sua et heredum suorum districcioni iusticiarii Cestrie qui pro tempore fuerit, qui possit eos ad solucionem dictarum xx marcarum abbati Cestrie infra xv dies atque (*sic*) talis impedimenti faciendam, cum dampnis et expensis eius, vna cum c solidis ad opus dicti regis, per capcionem et vendicionem bonorum suorum compellere Teste Guncelino de Badelesmere, tunc iusticiario Cestrie, etc

Poulton and Bebington descended to the Lancelyns from their ancestor Scirard or Sherard (above, p 35) For the tenure of Bromborough by the abbey see No 349 The interest of Thomas de Praers, lord of Barthomley and Landican, in Poulton Lancelyn is unnoticed by Ormerod (ii 440 *sqq*) It seems to have been acquired by marriage with an heiress, perhaps of a branch of the Lancelyn family

The grantor occurs in 1244–45 (Orm ii 89), and died 1282–83 (*Cal Inq P M* ii 298) For other grants by him to the abbey see Nos 518–9 His father Robert (II) is mentioned between 1241 and 1245 (*Staffs Hist Coll* ix 326)

689. Grant by W[illiam], son of W[illiam] Lancelyn, to T(homas II), abbot of Chester, of liberty of digging in his land of Poulton (Lancelyn) and Bebington beyond The Pool in Poultondale, and of making ditches and hags (?) to drain away the excess of water coming down to the abbot's mill or mills, built or to be built in his said lands, as often as necessary, also liberty of digging in the said lands stones for the needs of the mills and causeway or causeways, wall or walls, pool or pools, ditch or ditches, bay or bays Bond in £200 to observe this 1291–1323

W[illelmus] filius W[illelmi] Lancelyn dedit T[home] abbati Cestrie libertatem fodiendi in terra sua de Pulton et Bebinton ultra le Pul in Pultondale, et fossata et hayas faciendi ad euacuandum superfluitatem vndarum superuemencium molendino uel molendinis [1] dicti abbatis in dictis terris suis constructis uel construendis, quociens necesse fuerit Item idem dedit dicto abbati libertatem fodiendi in dictis terris lapides, ad necessaria dictorum molendinorum et calceti uel calcetorum, muri uel murorum, stagni uel stagnorum, fossati uel fossatorum, baye uel bayarum, et ad hec tenenda fideliter obligauit se et heredes suos et tenementa siue tenentes in pena cc librarum sterlingorum dicto abbati soluendarum.

The grantor was the grandson and successor of the William, son of Robert, of No 688, his father having died *viuente patre* (*Cal. Inq P M*

[1] de Biombur[gh] in heading

11 298 and No 690)   Ormerod (11 444) causes much confusion by making him *son* of his predecessor and die in the year which was really that of his grandfather's death   He is probably the Willelmus Lancelyn *tertius* of a marginal note to No 517, unless the William who settled Poulton, etc , by fine in 9 Edw. II was not himself but a son and namesake   Ormerod makes him a son of Henry Lancelyn, which cannot be right

690. Inspeximus and confirmation by W[illiam], son of W[illiam] Lancelyn, of the charter of William his grandfather relating to Poulton Bridge, etc (No 688), and grant by himself to the said abbot of liberty of attaching a causeway, wall, or (mill)pool on his soil of Poulton and Bebington wherever necessary beyond The Pool in Poultondale, and of building his mills and changing their sites, and land for them and the pool, etc., on the said William's land, and of taking timber when necessary from his woods of Poulton and Bebington   Bond in £5 yearly, to be paid by his tenants, that these liberties shall be maintained   ? 1291–1323

W[illelmus] filius W[illelmi] Lancelyn testatur se inspexisse cartam W[illelmi] aui sui de ponte de Pulton et communa in terris suis de Pulton et Bebinton, quam quidem cartam de verbo ad verbum transcripsit et confirmauit

Item idem concessit dicto abbati libertatem attachiandi calcetum, murum, uel stagnum in solo suo de Pulton et Bebinton vbicunque necesse fuerit ultra le Pul in Pultondale, et molendina sua cum omnibus necessariis construendi et loca construccionis eorum mutandi, et eis et stagno et calceto et muro terram necessariam de terra dicti W[illelmi] et meremium de boscis suis de Pulton et Bebinton capiendi quociens necesse fuerit, et eas per terras suas cariandi , et ad hec omnia fideliter obseruanda dictus W[illelmus] obligauit se et heredes suos et tenentes suos de Pulton et Bebinton ad penam c solidorum annuatim ad festum sancti Michaelis a dictis tenentibus soluendorum per districcionem dicti abbatis et hec omnia et communia pasture omnibus dominicalibus animalibus manerii de Brumbur[gh] in omnibus dictis terris suis de Pulton et Bebinton dictus W[illelmus] et heredes sui imperpetuum warantizabunt

690a. Lease of part of the waste of Poulton Lancelyn by William, son of William Lancelyn, to abbot Thomas (II) for thirty years   1313
Harl MS 2022, f 13

Universis Christi fidelibus, etc , Willelmus filius Willelmi Lancelyn salutem, etc [Sciatis] me concessisse, etc , domino Thome abbati Cestrie et eiusdem loci conuentui unam placeam vasti mei in Pulton Lancelyn iacentem inter has diuisas, videlicet a molendino dicti abbatis de Bromburgh et sic ascendendo per quandam viam et sequendo eandem usque ad quoddam vetus fossatum et sic sequendo illud fossatum usque Crosdale et de Crosdale descendendo usque in le Pull' et sic sequendo le Pull' usque ad predictum molendinum Habendam et tenendam predictam placeam vasti predicto abbati et eorum (sic) successoribus a festo Purificationis beate Marie anno regni regis Edwardi filii regis Edwardi sexto usque ad terminum triginta annorum proximo sequentium, etc , et post terminum predictum tota predicta placea vasti mihi et heredibus [meis] absque contradictione predictorum abbatis, etc , integre reuertatur Et si continget predictum abbatem et conuentum vel eorum successores per me vel heredes meos vel aliquem alium de predicta placea vasti durante termino predicto inplacitari, inquietari vel expelli quoquomodo extunc obligo me et heredes meos per presentes teneri prefatis abbati, etc , in triginta marcis sterlingorum infra mensem, etc Et volo et concedo pro me et heredibus meis quod istud scriptum quoad triginta marcas dictis abbati, etc , soluendas sit loco scripti obligatorii, si casus contingat in forma prenotata Et ego [warranty clause] Hiis testibus : domino Hugone de Audelegh tunc iusticiario Cestrie, Ricardo de Fouleshurst tunc vicecomite Cestriscir', Rogero Dounvill, Roberto de Bebinton, Folk de Meelys, Will de Stanleghe, Will de Lasselys, et aliis Dat. ap Cestr' die et anno prenominato

The Tithe maps mark Crosdale on the west side of Bromborough Pool, close to the mill dam (W F I) [See Addenda]

691. Final concord in full county court between the abbot of Chester and William, son of Robert Lancelyn, who recognised that the advowson of the church of Bebington was the right of the monks of Chester by the gift of a certain ancestor of his named S(c)irard, who first gave it to them, as the charter of earl Hugh (I) bears witness (p 20), and by grant and gift of Richard Lancelyn, his great-grandfather, who afterwards gave all his right in that advowson to them with his body, and by the confirmations of Robert, son of the said Richard, grandfather of the aforesaid William, and of Robert his father, who confirmed these gifts by their charters, which William admitted that he had seen and handled in their original wording Also quitclaim

by the said William to the abbey of a messuage and toft to
the south of the rector of Bebington's garden, and half an
oxgang there which Adam de Thurstaston once held, and
7 selions in the field called the Bruche on the west, following
an old ditch extending to the lepers' houses as far as Poulton
Millway, and so along it to the corner of the Bruche on the
east, and a fishery in the Mersey once held by Robert, son
of Geoffrey, and a falconry by the lime-pit which Simon de
Bebington at one time held, with all his right, etc , in the
advowson of the church of Bebington, with housebote and
haybote in his wood there, common of wood for the abbot
and his men dwelling there, free pannage for their pigs, etc
Grant also by William that if any previous renunciation of
the abbey's rights be found, it shall be considered null and
void [with warranty]   Also quitclaim, etc , of the above
and of 2 oxgangs in Bebington, with the advowson of the
church by W[illiam], son (? grandson) of the aforesaid
William Lancelyn   Also grant of right of taking turf, rods,
and gorse for the manor of Bromborough, and of 3 butts,
etc , in Poulton   Also quitclaim of his right, etc , in 2
oxgangs in Chorlton which William his grandfather had
held of the abbot and afterwards restored to him.   1270–
1274 or 1281–83

W[illelmus] Lancelyn in pleno comitatu Cesti[ie] coram R[egi-
naldo] de Grey iusticiario Cestrie et militibus aliis recognouit
aduocacionem ecclesie de Bebinton cum pertinenti esse ius monachorum Cestrie ex donacione cuiusdam progenitoris sui Suardi
nomine qui primus eam illis contulit, prout carta H[ugonis] quondam comitis Cestrie testatur, et ex concessione et donacione
Ricaidi Lancelyn proaui sui qui totum ius quod habuit in dicta
aduocacione cum corpore suo postea dedit et concessit eisdem, et
ex confirmacionibus Roberti filii dicti Ricaidi, aui predicti Willelmi, et Roberti patris sui, qui dictas donaciones per certas cartas
suas successiue confirmarunt, quorum cartas dictus Willelmus
Lancelyn recognouit se vidisse, audiuisse et propriis manibus
(31)] tractasse, integras, non cancellatas, viciatas, nec in aliqua sui
parte abolitas uel deletas   Insuper dictus Willelmus dedit et con-
[firmauit] imperpetuum pro se et heredibus suis per cartam suam
quiete clamacionis dictis abbati et conuentui eorumque successoribus in puram et perpetuam elemosinam vnum mesuagium et
toftum cum pertinenciis in Bebinton que iacent iuxta gardinum
persone eiusdem uille ex parte austiali, et vnam dimidiam bouatam terre cum pertinenciis in eadem villa quam Adam de Thui-

stanston tenuit, et vii selliones cum pertinenciis in campo qui
vocatur le Bruche ex parte occidentali, sequendo quoddam uetus
fossatum extendens se uersus domos Leprosorum usque ad quandam uiridem uiam, et sequendo illam uiam que dicitur Pulton
Mulnewey, et sic per illam uiam communem usque ad corneram
predicti campi de Bruche ex parte orientali, et vnam piscariam
super aquam de Merse cum pertinenciis quam Robertus filius
Galfridi aliquando tenuit, et vnum uolatum cum pertinenciis iuxta
le Lym put, quem Symon de Bebinton aliquando tenuit, vna cum
toto iure et clamio, si quod habuit uel ipse seu heredes sui alico
casu in aduocacione ecclesie dicte ville de Bebinton habere possent,
cum housbota et haybota capiendis in bosco suo de Bebinton tam
ad edificacionem et reparacionem domorum suarum in eadem uilla
quam ad piscariam prefatam, et cum bosco sibi et hominibus suis
in dictis terris commorantibus ad comburendum necessario, et
eciam cum adquietancia pannagii dominicorum porcorum, uel
hominum suorum predictas terras tenencium, quo ad tantas terras,
et cum omnibus libertatibus, communis, asyamentis, commoditatibus et approuiamentis in boscis, planis, viis et semitis, aquis,
piscariis, pratis, pascuis, pasturis, moris, mariscis et turbariis
dictis terris et aduocacioni dicte ecclesie infra villam et extra
vbique pertinentibus

Item idem Willelmus, prout in quadam quieta clamacione
patet, in dicto comitatu concessit quod si aliqua finalis concordia
uel carta inter aliquem abbatem Cestrie et se, uel aliquem anteces-
sorem suum confecta super remissione iuris ipsorum in dicta aduocacione inueniatur, pro vacua et irrita habeatur imperpetuum

Item idem Willelmus, ut in alia carta patet, omnia predicta
quiete clamauit uel concessit, et ad hec warantizanda et defen-
denda se et suos heredes obligauit

Item hec omnia W[illelmus] filius [1] predicti Willelmi Lancelyn
concessit et quiete clamauit, prout in carta sua patet, necnon
quiete clamauit ius et clamium suum in ii bouatis terre in villa de
Bebinton cum aduocacione ecclesie eiusdem

Item concessit abbati Cestrie liberam fossuram omnimodarum
turbarum manerio de Brumbur[gh] sufficientem cum sufficienti
i[n]seccione cannarum et gorstarum ad dictum manerium cariandarum, et iii buttas cum edificiis in villa de Pulton

Item quiete clamauit totum ius et clamium suum in ii bouatis
terre in villa de Choilton quas W[illelmus] auus suus de dicto
abbate tenuit et postea ei reddidit

---

[1] Apparently an error for *nepos*, as appears in the last grant of this deed.
William I 's son died in his lifetime

The mention of the justice shows that this settlement with William, son of Robert Lancelyn, for which the abbey had to pay a substantial sum (No 692), must have been effected either between 1270 and 1274 or between 1281 and 1283   The Elizabethan herald Flower in his extracts from the Cheshire Domesday seems to have placed it in the justiceship of Badlesmere (1274–81) along with a confirmation by Ranulf, son of William de (*sic*) Lancelyn (Orm *Domesday*, p 17)   [See Addenda.]

692. Bond by William, son of Robert Lancelyn,[1] for himself and his heirs, in consideration of the fact that abbot S[imon] and the convent, in return for his recognition of their rights in the preceding deed, had paid him £60 and remitted his homage and 10s rent from Bebington and 3s from Little Meolse which his father gave them, not to question their rights until the £60 has been repaid with a like sum for their damages and expenses, and the homage and rents resumed, the monks reserving all their rights , the justice of Chester to have power of distraint for the above sums, etc , and a penalty of £20 to the lord of Cheshire (the king), and the archdeacon of Chester, if temporal penalties fail to secure observance of the premisses, to resort to spiritual ones and exact £10 for the fabric of the church of Lichfield, £10 for that of the church of St John, Chester, and £10 for himself. 1270–74 or 1281–83

Omnibus Christianis, etc , W[illelmus] Lancelyn salutem, etc Quia dominus S[ymon] abbas Cestrie et conuentus pro recognitione iuris sui in aduocacione ecclesie de Bebinton, concessione et quieta clamancia eiusdem, et eciam pro quibusdam terris, vna piscaria, et vno volatu, cum aduocacione ecclesie predicte in villa de Bebington, quas eisdem donaui et per cartam meam confirmaui, mihi dederunt et integraliter pacauerunt lx libras sterlingorum, et eciam remiserunt mihi et heredibus meis homagium quod eis facere debui et consueui et x solidos annui redditus quos eis de manerio meo de Bebinton soluere debui, et iii solidos de Parua Meles quos Robertus pater meus per cartam suam eis dedit, Volo et concedo et presenti scripto me et heredes meos obligo si ego uel heredes, etc , uel aliquis per nos seu nomine nostro dictis abbati et conuentui seu eorum successoribus aliqua temeritate uel presumpcione alico tempore placitum super iure dictarum terrarum, etc , seu super ultima presentacione ad eandem ecclesiam, uel alico alio modo mouerimus, quod nec in aliqua curia coram alico iudice audiamur, nisi prius dictis abbati et conuentui eorumque,

[1] Extended from the heading

etc., dictas lx libras quas mihi premanibus numerauerunt, vna
cum aliis lx libris nomine dampnorum et expensarum suarum,
soluerimus integraliter, et eciam de dictis xiii solidis annuis quos
mihi et heredibus meis remiserunt cum omnibus arreragiis eisdem
fideliter soluendis vna cum dicto homagio eis faciendo plenis-
simam fecerimus securitatem, saluo nichilominus eisdem iure tam
in predictis terris quas eis donaui quam in aduocacione ecclesie
que eis ex recognicione seu donacione mea uel progenitorum
meorum competiit, uel alico alio iure competere poterit   Ad hec
omnia fideliter obseruanda subieci omnia bona mea et heredum
meorum terras, redditus et catalla districcioni Iusticiarii Cestrie
qui pro tempore fuerit, uel cuiuscunque balliui sui quem dicti
abbas et conuentus eligere uoluerint, qui possit leuare de dictis
bonis meis, etc , ad opus dictorum abbatis et conuentus, eorumque
etc , vtramque summam pecunie prenotate, vna cum xx libris
domino Cestrisirie nomine pene soluendis, sine reclamacione uel
contradiccione mei, etc , et nichilominus post solucionem omnium
summarum nos ad plenam warantiam carte quam eis feci de dictis
terris, piscaria, etc , quocunque modo dicti abbas et conuentus
elegerint distringere   Item quia ad obseruacionem omnium predictorum fide mea me et heredes meos obligaui et quod in nullo
contra premissa veniemus, tactis sacris euangeliis, corporale prestiti
iuramentum, subieci me et dictos heredes meos et omnia bona
nostra adquisita et adquirenda iuridiccioni domini archidiaconi
Cestrie et eius officialis qui pro tempore fuerint quod possint uel
eorum alter per suspencionis, excommunicacionis et interdicti
sentencias ad obseruacionem omnium premissorum sub pena x
librarum fabrice ecclesie Lichfeldensis et x librarum ecclesie sancti
Johannis Cestrie et x libras dicto archidiacono soluendarum nos,
si necesse fuerit, de die in diem sine strepitu iudiciali et cause
cognitione compellere, etc

For the date see note to No 691

693. Grant by Richard Walsh of Hooton to his daughter Isoult
of 2 oxgangs in Eastham, which he held of the abbot of
Chester, and a fishery close by the boundaries of Hooton,
paying to him yearly 8d on June 20   Quitclaims of this
land to the said abbot by Isoult and William Walsh her
brother

[1] Ricardus Walensis de Hotona dedit Ysolde filie sue ii bouatas
terre in villa de Estham, quas tenuit de abbate Cestrie, et vnam [f 34

[1] Harl MS 2062 resumes here (f 20)

piscariam iacentem proximam in diuisas de Hotona.   Reddendo
sibi annuatim octo denarios in vigilia sancte Werburge in estate
Hanc terram dicta Yseuda dicto abbati quiete clamauit, vt patet
in sua carta, et Willelmus Walensis frater eius eam quiete clamauit,
vt patet in sua carta

A Richard Walensis received a grant of Hooton from his brother
Thomas between 1208 and 1229 (Orm ii 410), and was probably the
Richard who gave 4 oxgangs there to his son Randulf c 1238 (*Journ
Chester Arch Soc* N S x p 200)   William, who was lord of Hooton
temp Hen III and Edw I , may be the son here mentioned

694. Final concord in the county court of Cheshire between
abbot [Roger] and Robert de Poole (Netherpool), who
granted to the abbot and his men all common rights in
Netherpool for their beasts, except in the wood during
mast-time (September 29–November 11), and received from
them for himself and his men common of pasture, turbary,
and furze in St(h)amladeheth, the monks reserving the
right of cultivating any part of the heath broken up before
the date of the concord, for which Robert gave the abbot
½ mark of silver   1245–49

Robertus de Pulle coram Johanne de Grey, tunc iusticiario
Cestrie, et multis aliis in pleno comitatu recognouit et concessit
imperpetuum abbati et conuentui Cestrie et eorum hominibus
habere comunam omnimodam tam in bosco quam in plano omni
tempore anni in totali terra sua de Pulle ad omnia genera animalium
longe et prope, bladis et fenis asportatis   Saluo tempore pessone
in bosco suo de Pulle a festo sancti Michaelis usque ad festum
sancti Martini   Et predictus abbas et conuentus concesserunt pro
se et successoribus suis Roberto de Pulle et successoribus suis imperpetuum [et] eorum hominibus de Pulle habere comunam tam
pasture quam turbarie et de Iaun in Sthamladeheth longe et
prope, bladis et fenis asportatis   Saluo quod liceat abbati Cestrie
et conuentui et eorum successoribus imperpetuum totam terram
que tempore finalis concordie facte fuscata fuit in Stamladeheth
arare et seminare et ad quamcunque utilitatem voluerint con-
uertere sine impedimento vel vexacione dicti Roberti uel heredum
suorum   Pro hac recognicione et concordia dedit dictus Robertus
dicto abbati dimidiam marcam argenti

Robert de Poole was possibly father of another benefactor of the
abbey, Reginald de Poole, husband of one of the co-heiresses of Geoffrey
the cook of Lea (No 636 n and Orm ii 419), but if so, Reginald probably

predeceased him Robert was living in 1279 (No 308). James de Poole who had succeeded to the estate by about 1290 (*Journ Chester Arch Soc* N S x p 44) was his son, not Reginald's as given in Ormerod's pedigree (ii 423 , cf *J C A S* N S vi. p 20, No 3)

695. Final concord between abbot Simon and Robert de Poole (Netherpool), who was charged with violating the earlier agreement (No 694) by breaking up new land in Poole and preventing the monks and their men from driving their beasts to pasture in that manor Robert and his heirs to have all existing new-tilled lands and approvements in Poole unquestioned, and at their own expense to make a bridge or causeway over the syke called The Wolfpool (le Wlpul) between Stanladeheath and the land of the said Robert, and to allow pasture in Poole to 500 of the beasts of the monks and their men with free passage of the said causeway, but to have a site and earth for half the causeway on the abbot's side and, subject to not putting up any mill or other buildings, to have the benefit of the water, reserving access to the other party for the purpose of watering their beasts, the excess of water to be let off when most convenient for both , Robert and his heirs also to have sufficient access to pasture between the fields of Whitby and Poole to the great heath of Whitby as far as the boundaries of Sutton Heath, saving to the abbey its approvements in the said heath and in a certain plot of land in Stanladeheth, neither party without the consent of the other to bring into cultivation or preserve for game any fresh land in Stanladeheth and Poole respectively July 4, 1272

Cum materia contencionis fuit orta inter dominum Symonem abbatem Cestrie et eiusdem loci conuentum ex vna parte et Robertum de Pulle ex altera parte, pro eo quod idem Robertus quasdam frussuras fecerat infra diuisas ville sue de Pulle contra tenorem finalis concordie inter dominum Rogerum bone memorie quondam abbatem Cestrie et eiusdem loci conuentum et dictum Robertum in comitatu facte, et eciam pro eo quod idem abbas et conuentus non habuerunt fugam aueriis suis et hominum suorum competentem ad comunam pasturam infra diuisas de Pulle, dicta contencio die translacionis sancti Martini anno Domini M°cc°LXX secundo conquieuit in hunc modum, videlicet quod dictus Robertus et heredes sui in pace tenebunt et habebunt omnes frussuras et approuiamenta die presentis conuencionis infra diuisas ville de

K

Pulle factas sine impedimento et contradiccione dictorum abbatis et conuentus et eorum successorum   Et idem Robertus et heredes sui sumptibus suis faciant pontem vel calceam sufficientem ultra sichetum qui uocatur Le Wlpul ubi melius viderint expedire sine incomodo dictorum abbatis et conuentus inter Stanladehet[h] et terram dicti Roberti sicut descendit in mariscum, et imperpetuum sustinebunt V^c animalia dictorum abbatis et conuentus et hominum suorum ad pasturam quam infra diuisas uille de Pulle secundum tenorem dicte finalis concordie habere debent per dictam calceam, et sine impedimento libere possint transire et redire

Idem uero Robertus et heredes sui habebunt atachiamentum super terram dictorum abbatis et conuentus et terram ad faciendum medietatem dicte calcee vbi minus pastura poterit deteriorari et refulsum aque cum calcea facta fuerit, ita tamen quod nullum molendinum vel aliud edificium ibidem construatur , predictus eciam Robertus et heredes sui comoditatem dicte aque habebunt sine factione molendini, saluo dictis abbati et conuentui et eorum hominibus quod animalia sua libere ad dictam aquam accedere possint causa adaquandi et in eadem morari dum voluerint, sine dicti Roberti et heredum suorum impedimento , superabundancia uero dicte aque euacuabitur vbi melius fieri possit ad minus dampnum et maius commodum vtriusque partis   Dicti uero abbas et conuentus concesserunt dicto Roberto et heredibus suis quod habeant fugam sufficientem animalibus suis et hominum suorum inter campos de Witeby et de Pulle ad magnum bruerium de Witeby et de Pulle usque ad diuisas bruerii de Sotton   Saluis dictis abbati et conuentui suis approuiamentis in dicto bruerio. Dicti abbas et conuentus approuiabunt se de quadam placea terre de Stanladehet[h] iuxta campos de Wyteby, scilicet ab inferiori angulo terre arabilis directe sequendo diuisas usque ad superiorem campum de Witeby, ad arandum et faciendum omnimodam com-
(32)] moditatem suam imperpetuum, sine dicti Roberti et heredum suorum impedimento   Neutra uero parcium, scilicet nec abbas et conuentus sine consensu et uoluntate dicti Roberti et heredum suorum in Stanladehet[h], nec idem Robertus nec heredes sui infra diuisas de Pulle sine consensu dictorum abbatis et conuentus uel successorum [suorum] ulterius frussuras facient, uel aliquid in agriculturam conuertent, uel in defensionem ponent   Concessit eciam vtraque pars quod dicta finalis concordia in comitatu Cestrie inter dictum dominum Rogerum quondam abbatem Cestrie et dictum Robertum de Pulle dudum facta, exceptis articulis in presenti instrumento contentis, in suo robore et virtute penitus perseueret.

696. Settlement of boundaries between the manors of Irby and Thurstaston by agreement of abbot Thomas (II.) and William, son of Patrick de Heswall, the boundaries to begin at the head of an old ditch where a leper house formerly stood, proceeding thence in a straight line to a spring, walled in with large stones and called Londymere, and so through the centre of the spring in a straight line to a little hill called Knukyn, each manor to have the use of the spring without hindrance from either, without claim to any soil outside its own boundaries   *c* 1307–23

Vnanimi consensu Thome abbatis Cestrie et Willelmi filii Patricii de Hasiwalle facte fuerunt certe bunde et diuise inter maneria de Irreby et de Thurstanston, incipientes ad capud cuiusdam ueteris fossati vbi quedam domus leprosorum quondam fuit sita ; et ex illo fossato linealiter et directe procedendo usque ad quemdam fontem magnis lapidibus circumuallatum qui vocatur Londymere, et sic per medium illius fontis linealiter procedendo et directe usque ad quemdam monticulum qui vocatur Knukyn, sicut bunde et diuise modo de nouo ibidem facte plenius ostendunt Ita quod vtrumque manerium habeat usum fontis sine impedimento alterius, absque aliqua vendicacione soli extra proprias diuisas   Dicti uero abbas et conuentus remiserunt et quiete clamauerunt imperpetuum dicto Willelmo et heredibus suis totum ius et clamium que habuerunt in proprietate soli uersus Thurstanston ultra bundas ibidem de nouo factas, et dictus Willelmus similiter remisit, etc , totum ius et clamium que habuit in proprietate soli uersus Irreby ultra bundas ibidem de nouo factas

Sir Patrick de Heswall died before 30 Sept 1307 (*Cal. Inq.* v 9).

697. Quitclaims of villeins to the abbey by various landholders

Ricardus Walensis [1] de Hoton dedit libertatem Secherith de Hoton et Nicholao filio suo et Alicie filie sue, reddendo sibi annuatim vi denarios ad festum beati Martini de dicta Secherith et heredibus suis.   Item Philippus de Bamuile [2] quiete clamauit S[ymoni] abbati Cestrie Margaretam filiam Roberti de Pulle de Storton et Walterum filium suum et Margaretam filiam suam Item Robertus filius Roberti de Waleya quiete clamauit Johannem filium Germani de Irreby cum tota sequela et catallis   Item Agnes de Storton vxor quondam Thome de Bamuile quiete cla-

[1] See No 693   [2] Of Storeton, *d* before Feb 12, 1284

mauit Mariam de Sotton ; et W[illelmus ?] Walensis de Hoton [1]
quiete clamauit Hugonem Scoct' cum tota sequela sua et omnibus
natis ex Matilde matre eius. Item Robertus de Waleya quiete
clamauit Aliciam filiam Paulini cum tota sequela eius. Item
Willelmus Lancelyn quiete clamauit Reginaldum Le Mug' et
Seyerith vxorem eius, cum tota sequela eius et parentela. Item
Bertramus de Meles [2] quiete clamauit S[ymoni] abbati Cestrie
Robertum filium Galfridi de Meles, cum tota sequela sua et catallis,
ita quod sint liberi homines dicti abbatis, reddendo dicto abbati
in festo Translationis sancte Werburge (June 21) vi*d.* et in decessu
cuiuslibet eorum suum melius auerium pro omni seruicio seculari,
et ad predictum seruicium dictus Robertus se et heredes suos dicto
abbati obligauit, vt in carta sua patet.

It is probable that in all these cases, as certainly in the first and
last, transference to the abbey involved emancipation.

698. Duplicate of No. 410. In the margin : vacat quia alibi.

699. Quitclaims by Henry de Tabley and his wife and by Gilbert
de Limme (cf. No. 649 *n.*) and his wife Mabel of a third part
of a messuage and two oxgangs in Lower Bebington.

Henricus de Tabelega et vxor eius quiete clamauerunt T[home]
abbati Cestrie totum ius et clamium suum in tercia parte vnius
mesuagii et duarum bouatarum terre in Netherbebinton. Hanc
terram Gilbertus de Limme et Mabilia vxor eius quiete clamauerunt,
prout in carta sua patet.

700. Quitclaim by Robert, son of John de Bromborough, to
abbot T[homas] of two oxgangs in Bromborough which his
father had held. 1249-65 or 1291–1323.

Robertus filius Iohannis de Brombur' quiete clamauit T[home]
abbati Cestrie totum ius et clamium suum in ii bouatis terre in
Brombur' quas Iohannes pater suus aliquando tenuit.

701. Exchange of land in Bromborough between Robert the
clerk of the same and abbot S[imon]. 1265–91.

S[ymon] abbas Cestrie dedit Roberto clerico de Bromb' et
heredibus suis vnam sellionem et vnam buttam eidem proximam
in Ranesfeld' eiusdem ville pro vna sellione iacente in campo qui
vocatur le Chirchecrof[t] subtus ecclesiam, et pro vna sagitta
barbata dicto abbati in festo sancti Martini annuatim reddenda.

---

[1] Cf. No. 693.   [2] Orm. ii. 494.

702. Another exchange of land in Bromborough (heading) by abbot S[imon] 1265–91

S[ymon] abbas Cestrie dedit Henrico Withod et Agneti vxori eius duas dimidias selliones que vocantur Suchacresendes extensas directe ad torellum dicte Agnetis, pro vna sellione et dimidia iacentibus in Le Chirchecroft subtus ecclesiam.

703. Further exchange of land in Bromborough by abbot S[imon] 1265–91

S[ymon] abbas Cestrie dedit Andree filio Dandi de Brombur' vnam dimidiam sellionem in Manislawe feld' de Bromb', pro vna dimidia sellione in le Chirchecroft

704. Grant of land in Bromborough by John of the same to Raven, son of Raven

Iohannes de Bromb' dedit Rauenno filio Rauenni de Bromb' ii bouatas terre in eadem, reddendo sibi annuatim xd ad festum sancti Martini, saluo forinseco seruicio

705. Grant of land in Bromborough by William, son of Reginald de Bromborough, to Henry, son of Raven

Willelmus filius Reginaldi de Brombur' dedit Henrico filio [f 35 (3 Rauenni duas landas terre in territorio de Brombur', reddendo sibi annuatim vnum par albarum cirotecarum, uel vnum obolum in festo sancte Andree.

706. Quitclaim by Henry, son of Raven, to abbot S[imon] of the land granted in No. 704 1265–91

Henricus filius Rauenni de Brombur[gh] quiete clamauit S[ymoni] abbati Cestrie duas bouatas terre in Bromburgh quas Iohannes de Brombur' dedit Rauenno filio Rauenni. Iste eciam Henricus quiete clamauit dicto abbati totam terram suam in Bromb', vt patet in sua carta

707. Quitclaim by Agnes, daughter of Reginald, son of Raban de Bromborough, to abbot S[imon] of land there which her brother Alcok (Alan) gave to the abbot and also to her in free marriage 1265–91

Agnes filia Reginaldi filii Rabani de Bromb' quiete clamauit S[ymoni] abbati Cestrie totum ius et clamium in duabus sellionibus terre in Bromb' quas Alcok frater suus dicto abbati dederat. Hanc terram dictus Alanus dicte Agneti eciam dedit in libero maritagio, vt patet in sua carta

From No 708 it appears that Rabanus = Ravennus

708. Quitclaim by Alan, son of Reginald de Bromborough, to abbot S[imon] of two oxgangs there which his grandfather Raven gave to his father Reginald   1265–91

Alanus filius Reginaldi de Bromb' quiete clamauit S[ymoni] abbati Cestrie duas bouatas terre in Brombur' quas Rauennus auus suus dedit Reginaldo patri suo

709. Grant by Roger de Manley to his son Henry of an assart in Manley (near Frodsham), and regrant of it by Henry to abbot S[imon]   1265–91

Rogerus de Manleye dedit Henrico filio suo vnum assartum in Manleye extensum a quadam quercu que vocatur Siridac iuxta sepem suam, usque ad viam de la Lee, et a dicta via usque ad ripam de La Lee, et a dicta ripa usque ad capud marisci, et a dicto marisco usque Cakebroc, et a Cakebroc usque ad predictam quercum, reddendo sibi annuatim vnum obolum ad festum sancti Johannis Baptiste   Hanc terram dictus Henricus dedit S[ymoni] abbati Cestrie, vt patet in sua carta   Item, dictus Rogerus eius donacionem confirmauit, et dictum obolum annuum quiete clamauit, ut patet in sua carta.

For the Manley pedigree see Ormerod ii 101, 105, where Roger's brother Ralph (Nos 712–15) is called Ranulf, and Roger's son Robert (Nos 717–18) is omitted, or made son of his brother Henry

710. Grant by Roger de Manley to abbot S[imon] of a field which Punne Teyt formerly held of him in Manley   1265–1291.

Rogerus de Manleye dedit S[ymoni] abbati Cestrie totum campum quem Punne Teyt aliquando de se tenuit in Manleg' infra has diuisas, scilicet, de Stokenewalle sequendo le blake lake usque ad sepem communem campi de Manleg', et sic de sepe descendendo usque ad Mosewalle, et de Moswalle sequendo veterem sepem usque ad Stokenewalle, salua alta via prius vsitata

Manley seems only to have had one common village field, which was enclosed by a hedge   See Gray, *English Field Systems* (Harvard Hist Studies xxii), 249 *sqq*   In No 718 Asponesforlong is called *campus*, though a part of Manley Field (No. 714)   .

711. Grant by Roger de Manley to abbot S[imon] of a selion in
Manley called the Hullond   1265–91

Rogerus de Manleye dedit S[ymoni] abbati Cestrie vnam sellionem in Manl', que vocatur le Hullond, terciam a via que vocatur
le Chircheweye, cuius capud abbuttat super pratum

712. Grant by Roger de Manley to abbot S[imon] of 4 selions
in the territory of Manley   1265–91

Rogerus de Manleg' dedit S[ymoni] abbati Cestrie duas selliones in Aspone forlong in territorio de Manl', quarum vna vocatur
Aleynes Haddelond, et alia iacet iuxta sellionem dicti abbatis in
eodem campo, quem habuit ex dono Radulphi de Manleye fratris
sui, et duas selliones in campo de Grenewalle, que vocantur
Lambelachelond et Schadlond

713. Grant by Roger, son of Robert de Manley, to his brother
Ralph of land in Manley, and regrant of this by Ralph to
abbot S[imon]   1265–91

Rogerus filius Roberti de Manl' dedit Radulpho fratri suo
totam terram suam tendentem ab assarto Rogeri Moldeworye[1]
iuxta Cakebroc sequendo[2] usque ad vadum sub Bernullisleg' et
prosequendo idem iter commune extensum uersus Huchenescote
usque ad Leysigesmulnebroc, et sic prosequendo Leysig' usque
ad assartum predicti Rogeri, et prosequendo gardinum eiusdem ex
transuerso ad predictum Cakebroc, reddendo sibi annuatim vid ad
festum sancti Martini   Hanc terram predictus Radulphus dedit
S[ymoni] abbati Cestrie, vt patet in sua carta, et eius donacionem
dictus Rogerus concessit et confirmauit et dictos vid quietos
clamauit, vt patet in sua carta

714. Grant by Ralph, son of Robert de Manley, to abbot S[imon]
of 4 selions in Manley Field.   1265–91

Radulphus filius Roberti de Manl' dedit S[ymoni] abbati
Cestrie iiii selliones in campo de Manleye, scilicet, ii iacentes in
Asponesforlong, quas Edusa vidua aliquando tenuit, et vnam
sellionem iacentem inter terras quas Wilde le Wodeward et Hugo
filius Goduse in Asponeforlong tenuerunt, et vnam sellionem in le
Grenelawe iacentem in le Gosebuttes, reddendo sibi annuatim
vnum obolum in festo sancti Martini.

[1] The original had Moldeworþe = Mouldsworth
[2] Sicut supra fol , in margin

715. Grant by Ralph, son of Robert de Manley, to abbot S[imon] of all lands in Manley within certain bounds   1265–91

Radulphus filius R[oberti] de Manl' dedit S[ymoni] abbati Cestrie omnes terras in Manl', cum omnibus suis edificiis et pertinenciis, infra has diuisas iacentes, scilicet, a Fouleleesheued ascendendo Salterestrete vsque angulum sepis Asponeforlong ad veterem sepem, et sic sequendo situm prefate sepis, saluo dicto situ, descendendo usque ad moram de Cakebroc, salua via sufficiente ad bigam et quadrigam inter dictam moram et sepem dicti Radulphi, sequendo dictam moram usque ad Gerardesweye, et inde descendendo usque ad medium Wetelache, et inde ascendendo usque ad Ynumhoc, et inde ascendendo usque ad Stonhul iuxta Hullesholm tre usque ad Foulesleeheued, saluis viis prius usitatis, cum omnibus suis libertatibus, husbold, etc , et quietacione pannagii sibi et suis tenentibus, reddendo dicto Radulpho annuatim vnum denarium ad Natiuitatem sancti Iohannes Baptiste   Hanc donacionem Rogerus frater dicti Radulphi confirmauit, vt patet in sua carta

716. Grant by Henry, son of Roger de Manley, to abbot S[imon] of a selion in Manley Field, etc   1265–91

Henricus filius Rogeri de Manleg' dedit S[ymoni] abbati Cestrie vnam sellionem in campo de Manl', que vocatur Le Leylond, extensam ad domum dicti abbatis in eadem, et vnam dimidiam sellionem in Asponeforlong iacentem inter selliones dicti abbatis

717. Quitclaim by Robert, son of Roger de Manley, to the abbey of all his uncle Ralph's gifts, and of gifts of his father and brother   ? 1265–91

36 (33)] Robertus filius Rogeri de Manleg' quiete clamauit abbati Cestrie omnes terras illas et assarta cum mesuagiis et omnibus aliis pertinenciis quas Radulphus auunculus suus dicto abbati dedit, vna cum quodam campo qui vocatur Teytesfeld et tribus sellionibus in campo de Manleye quas Rogerus pater suus dicto abbati dedit, et vno assarto quod Henricus frater eius eidem abbati dedit. De quibus terris et earum seruiciis nichil preter oraciones predictus Robertus sibi reseruauit

718. Quitclaim by Robert, son of Roger de Manley, to abbot S[imon] of 2½ selions in Asponesforlong, etc.   1265–91

Robertus filius Rogeri de Manleye quiete clamauit S[ymoni]

abbatı Cestrıe ıı sellıones et dımıdıam ın Asponesforlong quarum vna ıacet ıuxta sellıonem que vocatur Aleynesheuedlond, et alıa ıuxta sellıonem quam Henrıcus frater eıus dedıt dıcto abbatı aule propınquıorem, et dımıdıam sellıonem propınquıorem terre dıctı abbatıs ın eodem campo   Item dıctus Robertus dedıt lıcencıam abbatı extendendı sepem suam uel fossatum leuandı a quodam veterı alueo dırecte ultra campum quı uocatur Asponesforlong vsque ad albam spınam que stat ın sepe alte vıe propınquıorı, et de tota terra ınfra predıctam sepem uel fossatum ıacentem quod-cunque comodum suum facıendı

Professor Gray quotes thıs charter to ıllustrate the consolıdatıon of monastıc holdıngs ın the fields (*Eng Fıeld Systems*, p 256).

719. Quıtclaım by Wıllıam Lancelyn, chıef lord of Manley, to the abbey of all lands whıch Roger, lord of Manley, Ralph hıs brother, and hıs own sons had gıven   *c.* 1250–1315

Wıllelmus Lancelyn, capıtalıs domınus de Manleye, quıete clamauıt abbatı Cestrıe omnes terras quas Rogerus domınus de Manl' et Radulphus frater eıus et filıı suı dıcto abbatı dederunt, vel eorum heredes daturı sunt ımposterum, cum omnıbus per-tınencııs

Ormerod does not notıce the Lancelyn superıorıty, statıng that the local famıly held under the Dones of Crouton, who held from the Dones of Utkınton, as part of the fee of Kıngsley (ıı 101)   [See Addenda]

720. Grant by Wıllıam, son and heır of Henry de Helsby, to abbot S[ımon] of a field, etc , ın Helsby   1265–91.

Wıllelmus filıus et heres Henrıcı de Hellesby dedıt S[ymonı] abbatı Cestrıe quandam terram ın Hellesby que vocatur Ernutıs-feld[1] cum prato adıacente et cum ıı acrıs et dımıdıa more de Hellesbı predıcto prato proxımo adıacentıbus, ad lıbıtum abbatıs Cestrıe de lıcentıa domını Cestrısırıe assartandıs, vel qualıter-cunque approuıandıs, cum omnıbus pertınencııs

Henry de Helsby of Chorlton was a younger son of Sır John de Helsby of Helsby (Orm ıı 72, 374)   Curıously, Ormerod seems to date thıs gıft *c* 1305

721. Exchange by Sır Peter de Arderne, kt , wıth abbot S[ımon] of an assart ın Alvanley called Ichıncote for all the abbot's land ın Aldford and a messuage and selıon ın Elton, pro-

[1] -croft, margın   Ernutısfeld possıbly for Ermıtısfeld

vided that no mill or building should be erected on the assart, a condition afterwards withdrawn by Sir Peter's son, John de Arderne (c 1292–1308), in favour of abbot Thomas II 1265–91

Petrus de Ardene miles dedit S[ymoni] abbati Cestrie totum illud assartum in Aluadeleg', que vocatur Ichincote [1] cum pertinenciis sicut sepes et fossata circumeunt uersus boscum de Aluedeleg' vsque in sichetum qui diuidit inter Aluedel' et Donam in escambium tocius terre dicti abbatis in Aldeford' et illius mesuagii et sellionis iacentis in Elton' que Ricardus de Halton de dicto abbate aliquando tenuit ad firmam, cum omnibus pertinenciis, ita quod in dicto assarto nullum molendinum vel edificium uel stagnum faciet, set ad sepes dicti assarti faciendas et reficiendas cum necesse fuerit de bosco de Alued' sufficienter capiet. Hec conuencio irrotulatur in Domesd[ay] Set sciendum quod Johannes de Arden' filius et heres dicti Petri concessit T[home] abbati Cestrie housbold et haybold et racionabilia estoueria in bosco suo de Alued' ad quoddam mesuagium construendum et reparandum in dicto assarto ad opus vnius tenentis, nonobstante illa clausula superius scripta de non edificando edificia in dicto assarto, vt patet in sua carta

722. Quitclaim by Robert, son of Herbert de Hulse, to abbot Simon of a plot of land in Hulse 1283–91

Mainwaring Charter No 68 (John Rylands Library)

Omnibus Christi fidelibus ad quos presens scriptum peruenerit Robertus filius Herberti de Holis salutem in Domino Noueritis me remisisse et inperpetuum pro me et heredibus meis quiete clamasse domino Symoni abbati sancte Werburge Cestrie et eiusdem loci conuentui, dominis meis capitalibus, quandam placeam terre que iacet inter terram quam Symon de Caldekote [2] tempore confeccionis huius scripti in villa de Holis de me tenuit et terram ipsorum abbatis, etc , in eadem villa sicut per metas distinguitur Tenendam et habendam ipsis abbati, etc , et eorum successoribus in liberam, puram et perpetuam elemosinam nichil inde reddendo nisi oraciones tantum In cuius rei testimonium presenti scripto sigillum meum apposui Hiis testibus, Roberto Grosso Venatore tunc vicecomite Cestresir', Ricardo de Lostok', Willelmo de Thoft, Iohanne de Vernun, Roberto de Wininton', Iohanne de le Redemor, et aliis

Oval seal, arrow head (?), *leg* s' R°   DE HOLIS

[1] Huchenescote in No 713   [2] Caldecote, Chart

723. Grant by Jonas de Hulse to Robert the clerk, eldest son of
Richard le Grouenour, of all his land in Hulse, and regrant
thereof by Robert to abbot S[imon]   1265–91

Yonas de Holys dedit Roberto clerico filio Ricardi Le Grouenour primogenito totam terram suam in villa de Holys, cum
omnibus pertinenciis, faciendo inde debita seruicia capitali domino.
Hanc terram dictus Robertus dedit S[ymoni] abbati Cestrie, prout
in carta sua patet

724. Quitclaim by William de Lawton [1] to abbot S[imon], his
chief lord, of a selion in Hulse   (Cf No 831)   1269–91.

Willelmus de Lauton quiete clamauit S[ymoni] abbati Cestrie,
domino capitali, quandam sellionem in dicta villa de Holis in
campo qui dicitur Pilotescroft, iacentem inter selliones Roberti
filii Hereberti [2] extensam a Bacforlong usque Le Leueth

725. Grant by Ralph Turnevileyn to abbot S[imon] of all the
land held of him in Hulse by his brother Jonas   1265–91

Radulphus Turneuileyn [3] dedit S[ymoni] abbati Cestrie totam
terram in villa de Holys, cum omnibus pertinenciis, quam Yonas
frater suus de se tenuit, reddendo sibi annuatim xii*d* ad festum
sancti Andree apostoli

726. Grant by Ralph Turnevileyn to abbot S[imon] of a moiety
of Sulinesfield in Hulse   1267–70

Mainwaring Charter 48 (John Rylands Library)

Omnibus Christi fidelibus presens scriptum visuris uel audituris
Radulphus Turneuileyn de Holes salutem in domino   Sciatis me
pro salute anime mee et animarum antecessorum et successorum
meorum dedisse et concessisse, et hac presenti carta mea confirmasse, Deo et beate Werburge Cestrie et dominis meis S[ymoni]
abbati et eiusdem loci conuentui eorumque successoribus totam
medietatem meam cuiusdam terre in territorio de Holes que
vocatur Sulinesfeld,[4] cuius terre alteram medietatem Willelmus
filius sororis mee de dictis abbate et conuentu tenuit   Tenendam
et habendam dictis abbati, etc , in liberam, puram, et perpetuam
elemosinam, cum omnibus pertinenciis, libertatibus, asiamentis,
communis et omnimodis approuiamentis dicte terre vbique pertinentibus, ita libere et quiete quod nec ego nec heredes mei nec

---

[1] manentis in villa de Holys, heading   [2] See No 732
[3] See No 726   [4] Sulineffeld, Chart

aliquis per nos vel pro nobis seu nomine nostro quicquid iuris, clamii, uel seruicii inde decetero poterimus exigere uel vendicare, preter oraciones tantum.   Et ego prefatus Radulphus et heredes mei totam predictam medietatem terre cum pert. prefatis abbati, etc., contra omnes homines et feminas imperpetuum warantiza- bimus, etc.   In cuius rei testimonium presenti scripto sigillum meum feci apponi.   Hiis testibus, Th[oma] de Boulton' tunc iusti- ciario Cestrie, Ricardo de Orreby, Roberto de Huxel[ega], Ricardo le Grosvenour, Ricardo de Lostok', Hugone de Coton', et aliis.

Oval seal : figure with arms extended (?)   S. R. . . TVRNVILEIN.

727. Grant by Ralph Turnevileyn to abbot S[imon] of the homage and service of his nephew William, son of Eva, in Hulse.   Before 1270.

Radulphus Turneuileyn dedit S[ymoni] abbati Cestrie homa- gium et seruicium Willelmi filii Eue sororis sue et xii*d.* annuos, quos sibi dictus Willelmus reddere tenebatur ad festum sancti Andree apostoli de terra quam de se tenuit in Holys.

For the date see the reference to William's tenure in No. 726.

728. Grant by William, son of Richard de Pulford, to abbot [Simon] of the land in Hulse which Ralph de Turnevileyn bought from his uncle Ralph and gave to William.   1269– 1270.

Mainwaring Charter 50 (John Rylands Library).

Omnibus Christi fidelibus presens scriptum inspecturis vel audituris Willelmus filius Ricardi de Pulford eternam in Domino salutem.   Nouerit vniuersitas vestra me dedisse, concessisse, et hac presenti carta mea confirmasse Deo et ecclesie sancte Wer- burge Cestrie et abbati et monachis ibidem Deo seruientibus totam terram meam quam habui in villa de Holes, illam scilicet quam Radulphus Turneuileyn de Rannulpho auunculo suo quondam emit et mihi per cartam suam contulit ;[1] habendam et tenendam predictis abbati et conuentui et eorum successoribus in liberam, puram, et perpetuam elemosinam, quiete, plene, et pacifice, in boscis, planis, pratis, pascuis, pasturis, turbariis, viis, semitis, et cum mesuagiis, aesiamentis, libertatibus et pertinenciis vniuersis predicte terre spectantibus, infra villam aut extra.   Reddendo inde annuatim capitalibus eiusdem terre dominis de prefatis abbate, etc., duodecim denarios in festo sancti Martini, quos quidem ego

[1] saluis sibi terris suis de nouis frussuris, Chart.

prius eis reddere solebam. Et ego Willelmus et heredes mei (warranty clause). Et ut hec mea donacio, concessio perpetue firmitatis robur optineat, eam sigilli mei munimine roboraui His testibus, dominis Thoma de Boulton' tunc iusticiario Cestrie, Ricardo de Wyburham' tunc vicecomite Cestresirie, Willelmo de Venables, militibus, Roberto de Huxle tunc constabulario Cestrie, Ricardo le Graunt Venur, Roberto filio eius, Ricardo Bonetable, et multis aliis

Seal of green wax on parchment tag en double queue · floral star . leg
. FIL. RIC. DE VL ORD

There were two Richards in the family of Pulford of Pulford about this time, but neither is recorded to have had a son William (Orm ii 841, 857)
The land was granted by the abbey (No 831) to William, son of William de Lawton, in exchange for his holding in Church Lawton.

729. Quitclaim by William, son of W de Birches, to his chief lord abbot S[imon] of all his land in Hulse formerly held by him of the gift of Ralph Turnevileyn   1265–91

Willelmus filius W de Birches[1] quiete clamauit capitali domino suo S[ymoni] abbati Cestrie totam terram suam in Holis quam aliquando de dono Radulphi Turneuileyn tenuit Habuit sine alicuius rei retenemento

730. Grant by Richard de Lostock (Gralam) to abbot Thomas (I), his lord, of the homage and service which Ralph Turnevileyn owed him for a tenement in Hulse   1249–65

Ricardus de Lostoc filius Gralani de Lostoc dedit Thome abbati [f Cestrie, domino suo, homagium et totum seruicium quod Radulphus Turneuileyn de Holys sibi facere debuit de toto tenemento quod de se tenuit in villa de Holys, cum omnibus pertinenciis

See note to next charter and No 737

731. Quitclaim by Richard, son of Richard de Lostock (Gralam), to abbot [Thomas II] of the waste of Hulse super Rudheath 1291–1316

Ricardus filius Ricardi de Lostoc concessit quod abbas et conuentus Cestrie tenentes villam de Holys super le Rodehet in dominicis et seruic[iis] tam in terra uasta et bruerio quam arabili licite et sine contradiccione eius vel heredum suorum se possint

[1] Birches is near Hulse and Lostock

approuiare de omnibus terris vastis, brueriis et aliis, et eam in cultura redigere, et comodum suum inde facere, scilicet, quod sibi viderint expedire, et terras illas haya et fossato includere, et inclusas omni tempore retinere sine reclamacione eius uel heredum suorum per limites et metas subscriptas, videlicet, a villa de Holys descendendo per altam viam de Maclesfeld vsque ad vadum de Porteford', et sic reuertendo uersus meridiem per viam illam que vocatur Le Wyteweye usque ad diuisas de Birches, et sic ex trans- uerso linealiter usque ad viuam hayam que facit diuisas inter Le Holes et Birches. Remisit eciam et quiete clamauit de se et heredibus suis predicto abbati et conuentui et successoribus suis, scilicet imperpetuum totum ius et clamium quod habuit uel alico more habere potuit in dictis vasto et bruerio infra metas et limites prenotatas contentis.

At a later date Hulse is found to be treated as a part of the abbey's manor of Barnshaw (near Goostrey), but on the strength of No. 730, and of a later quitclaim of the waste of the vill by the daughter of Richard de Lostock and her husband, Ormerod (iii. 167) concluded that Hulse was part of the original estates of the Lostocks (Runchamps), and that it was probably formed out of the adjacent Lostock Gralam. His first piece of evidence is bad, because the abbot was the lord of Richard de Lostock for the particular tenement in question. But the quitclaims give him more support, unless they were merely the result of original intercommoning in the waste between Lostock Gralam, Birches (a Lostock vill) and Hulse. If Ormerod is right (cf. No. 736) Hulse may possibly be the part of Lostock which Hugh fitz Norman and his brother Ralph gave to the abbey at or shortly after its founda- tion (p. 19). The connection with Barnshaw on the other side of Rud- heath may have been one of later convenience, as in the case of Plumley (Orm. i. 669). For the lower limit of date see *Ancestor*, ii. 150.

Hulse Lane, which seems to be the part of the old road to Maccles- field referred to, now crosses the Crow Brook by Portford Bridge.

732. Quitclaim by Robert, son of Herbert de Hulse, to abbot S[imon] of 8 butts in Hulse field and of all right, etc., in the lands granted in Nos. 723–9. 1269–91.

Robertus filius Herebərti de Holys dedit capitali domino suo S[ymoni] abbati Cestrie viii buttas terre in campo de Holys iacentes inter terram que quondam fuit Willelmi de Birches et le Sulinfeld vna cum medietate omnium vastorum ad predictam villam de Holis pertinencium qui tempore huius confeccionis carte fuerunt extra sepes. Item quiete clamauit totum ius et clamium suum quod habuit uel habere potuit in omnibus terris quas dictus

abbas habuit ex dono Radulphi Turneuileyn [1], et Yuone auunculi
sui, et Willelmi de Pulford, et Willelmi de Birches, cum omnibus
pertinenciis sine alicuius rei retenemento preter oraciones   Item
concessit quod ipse Radulphus [2] pro reliquis terris quas de dicto
abbate tempore confeccionis huius carte in dicta villa de Holys
tenuit homagium et seruicium que Radulphus Turneuileyn dicto
abbati facere debuit decetero fideliter faciet   Reddendo annuatim
eidem abbati tres solidos in festo sancti Andree apostoli

733. Quitclaim by William, son of W[ilham] de Lawton, to abbot
S[imon] of 7 selions in Hulse field   (See No 831 *n*)   1269–
1291

Willelmus filius W. de Lauton quiete clamauit capitali domino
suo S[ymoni] abbati Cestrie vii selliones in campo de Holys iacentes
diuisim in campo de Hewesfeld', videlicet, totam terram suam
quam de dicto abbate tenuit in dicto campo

734. Quitclaim by W[ilham], son of W[ilham] de Lawton, to
abbot S[imon] of 3*d* rent in Hulse   1269–91

W[illelmus] filius W de Lauton quiete clamauit S[ymoni]abbati
Cestrie, capitali domino suo, totum ius et clamium suum in tribus
denariis annui redditus de vi sellionibus quas dedit Radulpho filio
Hereberti cum dominio et omnibus pertinenciis

735. Quitclaim by Adam, son of Hawise de Hulse, to abbot
S[imon] of half a headland in Hulse   1265–91.

Adam filius Hawisie de Holys quiete clamauit S[ymoni] abbati
Cestrie medietatem cuiusdam forain iacentis inter terram dicti
abbatis et terram suam uersus villam.

736. Recognition by Richard, son of Richard de Lostock
(Gralam), that a plot of land without the old dyke of Hulse
field [3] was the inheritance of Robert, son of Herbert de
Hulse, who quitclaimed it to abbot S[imon]   1265–91.

Ricardus filius Ricaidi de Lostoc recognouit quandam placeam
terre extra antiquum fossatum campi de Holys uersus meridiem,
iacentem inter dictum fossatum et Le Wyteweye, prout quodam
nouo fossato includitur, esse hereditatem Roberti filii Hereberti de

---

[1] See note to No 725
[2] *Sic*   If Ralph Turnevileyn is meant, this is awkward   Perhaps there is
some omission in the Chartulary transcript
[3] de nouo assarto de Holys, heading

Holys infra diuisas de Holis, quam eidem Roberto penitus quiete clamauit   Hanc terram dictus R[obertus] S[ymoni] abbati Cestrie quiete clamauit, prout in carta sua patet

737. Grant by Richard, son of Gralam de Lostock (Gralam), to abbot Roger of a rent of 5s from Lees, and of all his lordships of Cranage with Hermitage, Lees, Crooked Lache, and Windgates   1245–49

Original charter *penes* J Hatton Wood, Esq , Burnham, Bucks

Omnibus Christi fidelibus presens scriptum visuris uel audituris Ricardus filius Gralami de Lostok salutem   Nouerit uniuersitas vestra me remisisse et quietum clamasse in perpetuum de me et heredibus meis Rogero abbati sancte Werburge Cestrie et monachis eiusdem loci et eorum successoribus in perpetuum totum redditum quem ego et antecessores mei percepimus et recipere solebamus in villa de Leg', scilicet quinque solidos   Insuper, dedi et concessi et hac carta mea confirmaui eisdem abbati, etc , in perpetuum pro me et per me tota dominia de Craulach cum Ermitagio et de Leg' et de Crokedlache et de Windhgates [1] (*sic*) cum omnibus per- tinenciis, habenda et tenenda eisdem abbati, etc , in perpetuum adeo libere et quiete sicut ego et antecessores mei aliquo tempore ea melius, liberius et quietius tenui uel tenuerunt, et quicquid in eisdem habui uel habere potui aliquo iure sine ullo retenemento in homagiis, seruiciis, redditibus, releuiis, wardis, escaetis, exitibus, libertatibus, aesiamentis, et omnimodis commoditatibus que inde aliquo modo peruenient uel inde poterunt peruenire.   [Warranty clause]   Pro hac autem donacione, et concessione, remissione et quieta clamacione dedit mihi predictus Rogerus abbas sancte Werburge Cestrie undecim marcas argenti premanibus.   Et in huius rei testimonium presenti scripto sigillum meum apposui   Testibus   domino Iohanne de Grey tunc iusticiario Cestrie, domino R[ogero] de Montealto senescallo Cestrie, H[enrico] de Turboc tunc constabulario castri Cestrie, Walkelino de Arderne, Fulcone de Orreby, Roberto Lancelin, Hugone de Limme, Rogero de Tofte, Willelmo de Craulach', Roberto de Leg', Iurdano de Stubbs, Ricardo de Ermitagio, et multis aliis

An original charter in the Mainwaring collection (*infra*, No 758) is similarly attested, except that it adds the name of Richard Bernard, sheriff of Cheshire, after that of Robert Lancelin and omits the last three witnesses, but it is a grant of the Lees rent only.   There is a transcript in Harl MS 2074, f 190

[1] Wyngat', Chart.

Ormerod's brief abstract of the Wood original omits the last witness (iii. 139). The abstract in the chartulary, evidently taken from the latter, is duplicated in part under Lees (No. 758). [See Addenda.]

Nothing seems to be otherwise known of a Lostock interest in Cranage proper, but Williamson states that Hermitage had originally belonged to Roger (? Richard, but cf. *Pipe R.* 30 Hen. II. 23) de Runchamp (Orm. iii. 129). For this family see Orm. i. 670.

738. Grant by Warin de Croxton to abbot Thomas (I.) of the homage, etc., of his brother Robert de Croxton for a tenement in Cranage. 1249–61.

Original charter *penes* J. Hatton Wood, Esq., Burnham, Bucks.

Uniuersis Christi fidelibus ad quos presens scriptum peruenerit Warinus de Crocston' salutem in Domino. Nouerit uniuersitas vestra me dedisse, concessisse, et hac presenti carta mea confirmasse dominis Thome abbati ecclesie sancte Werburge Cestrie et eiusdem loci conuentui homagium et totum seruicium cum pertinenciis que Robertus de Crocston' frater meus et heredes sui mihi fecerunt uel facere debuerunt de toto tenemento cum pertinenciis quod de me tenuerunt uel tenere debuerunt pro villa de Croulache cum pertinenciis. Habenda et tenenda ipsis et successoribus suis in perpetuum in liberam, puram et perpetuam elemosynam, libere et quiete in wardis, releuiis et eschaetis et in omnibus aliis rebus et commoditatibus inde prouenientibus, sine aliquo retenemento. Ita uidelicet quod nec ego nec heredes mei aliquid iuris uel clamii inde de cetero exigemus uel exigere poterimus. Et ego Warinus et heredes mei [warranty clause]. In cuius rei testimonium presenti scripto sigillum meum apposui. Hiis testibus : dominis Rogero de Venables, Thoma de Meinwaring', Ricardo de le Hoke(?), Rogero de Daneport', Benedicto de Coudr[ay], Ricardo de Coudr[ay] clerico, Willelmo Pigot, Michael[e] de Gosetre, Ricardo Benfre(?), Rogero et Roberto de Bernuluess'.

Parchment tag for seal (missing).

Warin's grant to his brother gave him all the land he (Warin) had in Cranage in demesne with a messuage appurtenant, saving the lands which Thomas de Cranage (Craulache) formerly held of him, and all his right in Rudheath mine. It was witnessed by Richard de Sandbach, Richard de Wybunbury then sheriff, Henry de Cranage (Craulach), Henry de Hulm, William de Ketin, William de Vernon, John de Occleston (Accleston) and others (Harl. MS. 2074, f. 87 (old 190). The date was 1233–44.

L

740.[1] Grant by Robert de Croxton to his chief lord abbot S[imon] of all his land in Cranage called Stanilands except 4 selions, and of a selion in Serlecroft with two houses. Also quitclaim of all his right, etc., in Rudheath mine. 1270–71.

Original charter *penes* J. Hatton Wood, Esq., Burnham, Bucks.

Omnibus Christi fidelibus presens scriptum visuris uel audituris Robertus de Croxton' salutem in domino.	Sciatis me pro salute anime mee et antecessorum meorum dedisse, concessisse, et hac presenti carta mea confirmasse Deo et ecclesie sancte Werburge Cestrie, et capitalibus dominis meis S[ymoni] abbati et conuentui eiusdem loci, totam terram meam in Craulach' que vocatur Stani-landes,[2] tam cultam quam incultam, cum bosco in eadem crescente, exceptis quatuor sellionibus iacentibus propinquioribus ville de Craulach'.	Dedi eciam eisdem vnam sellionem iacentem in Serle-croft cum duabus domibus in eadem edificatis, habendas et tenendas dictis abbati et conuentui eorumque successoribus uel assignatis in liberam, puram et perpetuam elemosynam, cum omnibus pertinenciis in terra arrabili et non arrabili, in bosco et plano, in pratis et pascuis, pasturis, viis et semitis, cum libero introitu et exitu et omnibus libertatibus, asiamentis, liberis com-munis et approuiamentis dicte terre infra villam et extra vbique pertinentibus.	Dedi insuper et concessi eisdem abbati et con-uentui eorumque successoribus uel assignatis totum ius meum et clamium quod habui vel aliquo iure habere potui in tota minera de Ruddheth infra meras de Craulach' ita integre sicut Warinus frater meus illam mihi dedit cum omnibus commoditatibus et incrementis que mihi aut heredibus meis inde poterunt acrescere sine ullo retenemento.	Ita libere et quiete sicut aliqua elemosyna liberius aut quietius dari poterit uel concedi.	Et ego predictus Robertus et heredes mei totam predictam terram cum dicta minera et omnibus pertinenciis, libertatibus et asyamentis ad predictam terram et mineram vbique spectantibus et omnibus approuia-mentis que mihi aut heredibus meis aliquo modo euenire uel acrescere possent prefatis abbati, etc., contra omnes homines et feminas imperpetuum warantizabimus et sicut liberam elemo-synam nostram adquietabimus et defendemus.	In cuius rei testi-monium presenti scripto sigillum meum apposui.	Hiis testibus : dominis Reginaldo de Grey tunc iusticiario Cestrie, Ricardo de

[1] The transcriber accidentally gave two numbers (738 and 739) to the preced-ing entry, and the mistake could not be corrected because references had been made in Part I. to subsequent charters before it was noticed.
[2] Stanlands, Ch.

Wılburh[am] tunc vıcecomıte Cestrısır', Roberto de Huxel[ey],
Rıcardo de Orreby, Iohanne de Wetenh[ale], Rıcardo Bonetable,
Rıcardo de Craulach', Henrıco de Craulach', Thoma de Gorstre,
Rogero de Bernuls[haw], et alııs

Parchment tag for seal (missing)

740a. Richard, son of Robert de Croxton, confirms hıs father's
grant of Stanılands ın Cranage to abbot Sımon (No 740),
but reserves hıs rıght ın Rudheath mıne accordıng to an
agreement wıth the abbot *c* 1277

Orıgınal charter *penes* J Hatton Wood, Esq , Burnham, Bucks

Omnıbus Chrıstı fidelıbus ad quos presens scrıptum peruenerıt
Rıcardus filıus Robertı de Croxton' salutem ın Domıno sempıter-
nam Nouerıt unıuersıtas vestra me dedısse et pro me et heredıbus
meıs ınperpetuum quıete clamasse Deo et ecclesıe sancte Werburge
Cestrıe, et capıtalıbus domınıs meıs Symonı abbatı et conuentuı
eıusdem locı eorumque successorıbus uel assıgnatıs, totam terram
ın Craulache cum pertınencııs que vocatur Stanılandes quam dıctus
Robertus pater meus eısdem dedıt et per cartam suam confirmauıt.
Ita quod nec ego nec heredes meı nec alıquıs per nos seu nomine
nostro quıcquıd ıurıs uel clamıı ın dıcta terra cum pertınencııs de
cetero exıgere uel vendıcare poterımus preter medıetatem mınere
de Ruddehet ad vıllam de Craulache pertınente, prout ın cyrographo ınter dıctos abbatem et conuentum et me confecto plenıus
contınetur In cuıus reı testımonıum presentı scrıpto sıgıllum
meum apposuı Hııs testıbus domınıs Guncelıno de Bade-
lesmer', tunc ıustıcıarıo Cestrıe, Patrıcıo de Haselwall', tunc vıcecomıte Cestsır' (*sıc*), magıstro Iohanne de Stanleg', Iohanne de
Wetenh[ale], Roberto de Hux[ley], Rogero de Dauenport, Rıcardo
de Craulache, Henrıco de eadem, Rıcardo Bonetabl', Thoma de
Gorst[re], Rogero de Bernul[shaw], et alııs

Parchment tag for seal (missing).

Rıchard had wıthdrawn half hıs father's concessıon of the Rudheath mıne wıthın the boundarıes of Cranage (Nos 740, 750)

741. Quıtclaım by Robert de Croxton to abbot Sımon, hıs chıef
lord, of the whole servıce whıch Rıchard hıs son was bound
to do to hım for all the land whıch he gave hım ın Cranage
c 1271–75

Orıgınal charter *penes* J Hatton Wood, Esq , Burnham, Bucks

Omnıbus Chrıstı fidelıbus presens scrıptum vısurıs uel audıturıs

Robertus de Croxton' salutem in Domino   Sciatis me concessisse et hac presenti carta mea confirmasse necnon inperpetuum quiete clamasse Deo et ecclesie sancte Werburge Cestrie et capitalibus dominis meis Symoni abbati et conuentui eiusdem loci totum seruitium quod Ricardus filius meus mihi facere debuit et consueuit de tota terra quam ei dedi in Craunach cum pertinenciis, una cum dominio, toto iure et clamio quod ego in eadem terra cum pertinenciis habui uel aliquo casu contingente habere potero, sine ullo retenemento, habenda et tenenda predictis abbati et conuentui eorumque successoribus uel assignatis in liberam, puram et perpetuam elemosynam libere et quiete, plene et pacifice quod nec ego nec heredes mei nec aliquis per nos uel pro nobis seu nomine nostro quicquid iuris aut clamii in seruicio predicti Ricardi uel dominio eiusdem terre cum pert seu aliquibus escaetis uel approuiamentis aliquo casu contingente de dicta terra prouenientibus uel accidentibus exigere poteiimus uel vendicare preter oraciones tantum   Et ad maiorem securitatem faciendam tradidi prefatis abbati et conuentui quoddam scriptum obligatorium quod prefatus Ricardus filius meus mihi fecit de predicta teira nullo tempore alienanda   In cuius rei testimonuim, etc   Hiis testibus dominis Thoma de Meyngar[in] et Willelmo de Venables, militibus, Roberto de Hux[le] tunc constabulario castri Cestrie, Hugone de Hatton tunc vicecomite Cestris[irie], Roberto de Wynninton, Willelmo de Bostok, Hugone de eadem, Warino Grosso Venatoie, Alexandro Craket, Hugone de Coton', Ricardo de Craunach', Ricardo de Bonetable. Thoma de Gorstre, et aliis

Seal missing

742. Grant by Gralam de Runchamp of all the land which Wulfric held in Windgates (cf No 737)   1185–1240

Gralanus de Runchamp' dedit monachis Cestrie totam terram quam Wlfricus tenuit in Winegat', cum omnibus pertinenciis

The grantor was the Grelein de Rundchamp who paid his relief in 1185 (*Receipt Roll of Exchequer*, ed H Hall, p 22)

743. Grant by Yon, son of Richard, to the abbey of a furlong next to Windgates, remaining to Wulfric, man of St. Werburgh

Yon filius Ricardi filii Madoci dedit sancte Werburge vnam culturam terre que propinquior est apud Wyntgat', remanentem Wlfrico homini sancte Werburge, cum omnibus pertinenciis

744. Quitclaim by Matilda de Tarporley to the abbot of all her
land at Windgates which William Blobbe held of her

Matilda de Torperleye quiete clamauit abbati Cestrie totam
terram suam apud Wintgat' quam Willelmus Blobbe de se tenuit, [f 37 (3
cuius duas partes abbas Cestrie tenuit

745. Grant by Warin de Croxton to Adam the clerk of Cranage
of a third part of a moiety of the Netherwood of Cranage,
and regrant of it by Adam to abbot S[imon] in 1265–91

Warinus de Croxton dedit Ade clerico de Craunach' totam
terciam partem de tota medietate tocius bosci qui vocatur le
Netherwode de Craunac' cum omnibus pertinenciis, videlicet, vi
partem de toto bosco cum suo solo in longitudine, scilicet, a bosco
qui vocatur Ouerwode de Craunach' usque ad metas dc Leyes, in
latitudine uero a bruerio usque ad sepes de Craunache, reddendo
sibi annuatim ii albas cirotecas ad festum sancti Michaelis in
nundinis de Medio Wyco.[1]   Hunc boscum dictus Adam S[ymoni]
abbati Cestrie, capitali domino suo, dedit, prout patet in sua carta
et in alia quieta clamancia

746. Grant by Warin de Croxton to abbot T[homas] (I ?) of the
homage, etc , which Henry, son of Thomas de Cranage, and
others owed to him for tenements in Cranage. ? 1249–65

Warinus de Croxton dedit T[home] abbati Cestrie homagium
et totum seruicium quod Henricus filius Thome de Cranache [2] sibi
facere debuit et que Marg' filia Willelmi de Ermitagio sibi facere
debuit de tenementis que de se tenuerunt in Craunac', cum omnibus
pertinenciis. Item, vt in alia carta patet, idem Warinus dedit
homagium et seruicium quod Thomas de Craunache sibi facere
debuit de toto tenemento quod de se tenuit in Craunache

747. Quitclaim by Richard and Henry de Cranage and Felice,
widow of Nicholas de Vernon, to abbot S[imon] of 90 acres of
pasture in Cranage, the abbot granting them leave to bring
into cultivation 270 acres in Cranage heath   c 1287–91.

Ricardus de Cranach',[2] Henricus de eadem, et Felicia relicta
Nicholai de Vernon quieta clamauerunt S[ymoni] abbati Cestrie
totum ius et clamium suum in nonaginta acris pasture cum pertinenciis in Cranach' iacentibus extra assartam dicti abbatis in
Le Leyes prius factam, incipiendo ab angulo fossati inter Crounach'

¹ Middlewich Fair   ² Craunache in heading   See Addenda

et Leyes facti, et sic sequendo fossatum dicti abbatis usque ad metas de Biueleg',[1] et sic descendendo per fossatum de Biueleg' usque in le Witesiche, et sic ascendendo per le Witesiche usque ad predictum fossatum inter Crounach' et Leyes factum, ad includendum et ad comodum suum inde faciendum, salua eis et hominibus suis de C[raunache] et de Leyes communam pasture in tempore aperto. Dictus uero abbas concessit dicto Ricardo, etc., quod possint in culturam redigere tredecies viginti x acras pasture in bruerio de Crounach' vbicunque et quandocunque uoluerint in dicta villa, et eas includere, et omne comodum suum inde facere, saluis dicto abbati et hominibus suis de C[raunach'] et Leyes libero et largo introitu et exitu ad omnimoda animalia sua ad pasturam super bruerium et communa pasture in omnibus dictis acris tempore aperto ; ita tamen quod predicti R. et H. et F. nullum fossiculum in quo prius minera extitit inuenta infra dictas acras pasture includant uel sibi approprient. Set sciendum quod dicta Felicia habuit a dicto abbate specialem cartam includendi dictos fossiculos in porcione sua, quam alii non habuerunt. [Cf. Orm. i. 260.]

748. Agreement between the abbots of Chester and Vale Royal in regard to lands and tenements in Lache Dennis (Maubanc) and Crooked Lache.[2]   1288.

Anno Domini M°cc°Lxxxviii' abbas Cestrie quiete clamauit abbati de Valle regali homagium et seruicium de terris et tenementis de Lache Maubanc et de Crokede Lache, et totum ius et clamium suum in quadam cultura de nouo approuiata in Crokede Lache iacente ex opposito manerii (*sic*) abbatis de Valle regali uersus meridiem, et totum ius et clamium suum in vno mesuagio de nouo sito iuxta sichetum descendens de bruerio uersus Crokedelac' cum terra culta et inculta versus partem borialem per metas subscriptas : videlicet, ab angulo fossati circa dictum mesuagium leuati viciniore antique culture de Wingates vnde dictum fossatum mundari et reparari possit, cum necesse fuerit, et sic directe progrediendo ab illo angulo usque ad paruam spinam crescentem in via regia versus nouam culturam abbatis de Valle regali in Crokede Lache, et sic sequendo viam illam regiam descendendo uersus Chippebroc usque Ammerlache.

Abbas uero de Valle regali quiete clamauit abbati Cestrie totum ius et clamium suum in terris et tenementis ex alia parte diuisarum predictarum uersus meridiem iacentibus, salua tamen

---

[1] Byley.   [2] De terra in Rodeheth, heading.

utrıque abbatı communa pasture ın solo alterıus ın Wyngat' et Crokedlache ın tempore aperto et ın vastıs ıncultıs

The Vale Royal manor ın what was then called Lache Maubanc (Orm ııı 168) was the gıft of John dc Cotton, son of Matılda de Lache, daughter of Gralam de Lostock (*ıb* ıı 169, *Ledger Bk of V R* 130)

749. Quıtclaım by Henry, son of Hugh de Cotton (Lache ın headıng), to the abbey of all rıght, etc , ın the waste and heath of Lache Dennıs (Maubanc)

Henrıcus fılıus Hugonıs de Coton' quıcte clamauıt abbatı Cestrıe totum ıus et clamıum suum ın toto vasto et bruerıo de Lache Maubanc

750. Fınal concord between abbot S[ımon] and Rıchard, son of Robert de Croxton, each takıng half of the Rudheath mıne (cf No 740) *c* 1277

Conuentıo [1] ınter S[ymonem] abbatem Cestrıe et Rıcardum fılıum Robertı de Croxton quod dıctus abbas medıetatem cuıusdam mınere super [Rudeheth] [2] ınuente ac denarıorum pro ipsa recıpıendorum plenarıe percıpıet sıne alıco dıctı Rıcardı ımpedımento Sımılı modo dıctus Rıcardus alteram dıcte mınere medıetatem possıdebıt

751. License by Rıchard de Cranage to abbot S[ımon] to take wıllows and soıl on hıs land to maıntaın the mıll-pool of Lees, the abbot gıvıng hım a plot of land ın hıs wood at Cranage 1265-91

Rıcardus de Craulache dedıt S[ymonı] abbatı Cestrıe, quocıens necesse fuerıt, lıcencıam capıendı salices et terram ın terrıs suıs ad sustentacıonem stagnı molendını de Leyes, salua tamen cultura terrarum suarum Vnde dıctus abbas dedıt dıcto Rıcardo quandam placeam terre ın bosco suo de Craul' super le Bradeclıf ınter slaccum ascendendo usque ad quoddam uetus fossatum, et ab ıllo fossato dırecte usque ad sepem eıusdem Rıcardı ıuxta vastum dıctı abbatıs ın eodem bosco ex parte vna et terram eıusdem Rıcardı ex altera

752. Grant by Gralam, son of Rıchard de Runchamp, to Lıulf de Twemlow of all Lees, payıng yearly to hım 5s. and a sore (reddish) hawk 1208-29.

Harl MS 2074, f 190*d* (new 87)

---

[1] Fınalıs concordıa, headıng   [2] Supplıed from the headıng

Sciant, etc , quod ego Gralanus filius Ricardi de Runchamp
(34) *d*] dedi, etc Lidulfo de Twamlowe pro homagio et servicio suo
totam terram de Leyes cum omnibus pertinentiis, etc , reddendo
annuatim mihi et heredibus meis unum nisum ¹ sorum et 5*s* pro
omnibus serviciis, scilicet nisum sorum ad Nativitatem sancti
Johannis Baptiste et 5*s*. ad festum sancti Martini, etc. Hiis
testibus Philippo de Orreby tunc iusticiario Cestrie, Petro clerico
comitis Cestrie, Warino de Vernon, Willelmo de Venables,
Roberto . . . ., Ada de Dutton, Hugone de Dutton, Roberto de
Maynwarham (*sic*), Hamone clerico, et aliis.

Seal, showing a lion passant

753. Grant by Robert, son of Liulf (de Twemlow) the sheriff,
to the abbey, of all his land of Lees, and all the land called
Dernelehe-greue   ? 1244

Original charter *penes* J Hatton Wood, Esq , Burnham, Bucks

Sciant presentes et futuri quod ego Robertus filius Lidulphi
vicecomitis dedi et concessi et hac presenti carta confirmaui,
assensu Mabilie vxoris mee, pro animabus nostris et pro animabus
antecessorum et successorum nostrorum Deo et beate Marie, et
domui sancte Werburge Cestrie et abbati et conuentui ibidem Deo
seruientibus, totam terram meam de Leghes,² in dominicis, vilena-
giis,³ et homagiis, seruiciis, et omnibus pertinenciis, et omnibus
eschaetis et commoditatibus que ad dictam terram de Leghes
pertinent vel poterunt peitinere, et totam terram que vocatur
Dernelehe-greue cum pert , dictis abbati et conuentui, habendas et
tenendas predictas terras cum omnibus pert. in liberam, puram
et perpetuam elemosynam sine aliquo retenemento, liberas, quietas
et solutas de me et de omnibus meis in perpetuum [Warranty
clause follows] Et quia volo quod hec mea donacio et concessio
rata et stabilis permaneat presenti scripto sigillum meum apposui
Hiis testibus dominis Nicholao de Wylileg' tunc constabulario
castri Cestrie, Hugone de Chelmundeleg', Ricardo de Wybenbur'
tunc vicecomite Cestrisirie, Ricardo de Kingeleg', Ada de Hellesby,
Ricardo Bernard, Roberto de Chelmundeleg', Roberto de Tabeleg',
Iohanne Teck, Ricardo de Coudray, Galfrido clerico et aliis

Tag of parchment and cord for seal (missing)

Dernelehe greue (Randle Holme made this " greene," Harl MS
2074, f 87 (190) *d*) was granted to the donor's father by R [?ichard] abbot
of Pulton between 1208 and 1214 (*ib* , No 756) Its boundaries as
perambulated by the earl's justice, Philip de Orreby, and others, were ·

¹ nisi, Harl MS   ² Lehges, MS (*bis*)   ³ vilucagiis, MS

" ab illa quercu duplici que est iuxta sepem prefati Liulfi, [tendendo] per duas quercus usque ad angulum sepis de la Bruch, et per eandem sepem usque ad biueram, et per fossatum usque Perde iuxta Ruhelawe (Rohelawe, Ch), et inde deorsum usque ad predictam quercum duplicem " The rent was 1 lb of incense, and the witnesses besides Orreby were Peter the clerk of Chester, Roger de Mold the seneschal of Chester, William de Venables, Warin de Vernon, Hamon de Massey, Roger de Menilwarin, Richard, son of Liulf, and Robert his brother, Richard sheriff of Chester, Richard de Sandbach, John de Occleston (Acculveston), Richard de Kegworth, Richard de Rodest[orn] clerk, and many others

For Robert's wife Mabel, see No 554a

The date of our charter seems fixed by the witnesses of No 753a, though Richard de Wibbenbury was also sheriff in 1233, etc

753a.[1] Quitclaim by Richard, son of Henry de Lees, to abbot R[oger] of all the land in Lees which he held of Robert de Lees, for which the abbot gave him 35s and 4d September 16, 1244

Mainwaring Charter 15 (John Rylands Library)

Omnibus Christi fidelibus ad quos presens scriptum peruenerit Ricardus filius Henrici de Leyg' salutem Sciatis me concessisse et quiete clamasse R[ogero] abbati Cestrie et successoribus suis, de me et heredibus meis inperpetuum totam terram cum domibus et croftis et cum omnibus pertinenciis quam tenui et habui ad terminum de Roberto de Leyg' in villa de Leys et extra et totum ius et clamium quod habui uel habere potui in dicta terra cum pertinenciis Ita quod nec ego nec heredes mei in dicta terra cum pertinenciis aliquid de cetero exigere poterimus uel exigemus Et pro hac clamatione quieta et concessione dedit mihi abbas Cestrie xxxtav sol ' et iiiior den' pre manibus In huius rei testimonium presenti scripto sigillum meum apposui. Hiis testibus, domino Nicholao de Willeleg' tunc constabulario castri Cestrie, Walkelino de Ardena, Ricardo de Wibbinbur' tunc vicecomite Cestrisir', Roberto de Leys, Radulpho le Turneuilen, Brun de Craunach', Philippo de Neutona, Ricardo de Coudray, et multis aliis Datum die Veneris post exaltacionem sancte Crucis, anno domini M°C°C°X°LIIII°, apud Cestriam

Parchment tag en double queue for (missing) seal.

753b. Renunciation by Robert, son of Liulf the sheriff, and his

[1] Not in chartulary

wife Mabel of all claim upon the abbey beyond the express contents of the charter which they have from it ? 1244

Harl MS 2074, f 190d (new 87d)

Omnibus Christi fidelibus, etc Robertus filius Lidulfi vice-comitis et Mabilla uxor eius salutem Sciatis quod gratis renun-tiavimus et quietum clamavimus domui sancte Werburge et domino abbati et conventui Cestrensi quod non exigemus vel exigere poterimus ex debito nisi ea que expresse continentur in carta quam de ipsis habemus cuius transcriptum penes eos habent Et in cuius rei testimonium ego Robertus pro me et Matilda (sic) uxore mea presenti scripto sigillum meum apposui Hiis testibus · domino Hugone de Chelmundeleg', Roberto filio [suo], Johanne Thēcē, Ricardo de Caudray, Galfrido clerico et aliis.

This deed is not in the chartulary nor is the charter to which it refers

754. Quitclaim by Warin de Croxton to Robert de Lees of the wood of Lees   Before 1244 ?

Warinus de Croxton quiete clamauit Roberto de Leyes omne clamium suum in nemore de Leyes quod vendicauit in comitatu Cestrie per breue mortis antecessoris

755. Quitclaim by William, son of Jordan de Stubbs and Agnes his wife, daughter of Robert de Lees, to abbot Simon, etc., of all the gifts of Robert, son of Liulf de Twemlow in Lees on Rudheath, and the homages, etc , of Richard de Wybun-bury and Robert de Winnington for a moiety of the vill of Winnington (No 557)   1271–74

Harl MS 2074, f 191 (new 88)

Omnibus, etc , Willelmus filius Jordani de Stobbes et Agnes uxor eius, filia Roberti de Leghes, salutem   Sciatis nos pro salute animarum nostrarum et antecessorum nostrorum et successorum nostrorum concessisse, etc   Deo et ecclesie sancte Werburge Cestrie et capitalibus dominis nostris Symoni abbati et conventui eiusdem loci eorumque successoribus vel assignatis omnes dona-tiones et concessiones quas Robertus filius Lidulfi de Twamlowe concessit prefate ecclesie, etc [tam] de villa de Leghes super Ruddehet cum dominiis, homagiis et serviciis, etc , quam etiam de homagiis et serviciis Ricardi de Wybenbury et Roberti de Wininton de tota medietate eiusdem ville de Wininton iuxta Northwych cum wardis, relevis, escaetis, serviciis debitis et consuetis et omnimodis approviamentis que de dicta medietate de Wyninton

aliquo accidere, evenire vel accressere (*sic*) poterint, sine ullo
retenemento, Habendum, etc   In cuius rei testimonium presenti
scripto sigilla nostra fecimus apponi et hanc nostram concessionem,
confirmacionem et quietam clamacionem in rotulo qui vocatur
Domesday irrotulari   Testibus   dominis Reginaldo de Gray tunc
iust[iciario] Cestrie, Thoma de Meingarin, Roberto de Stockport,
Hugone de Hatton tunc vicecomite Cestr[isir'], Roberto de Huxley,
Johanne de Wetenhal', Ricardo de Orreby, Warino de Croxton,
Ricardo de Lostok, Henrico de Craunach, Ricardo de eadem,
Ricardo Bonetable, Thoma de Goostre, Rogero de Beinulf',
Willelmo de Wythinton et aliis

The chartulary adds   " Saluis terris propriis quas in villa de
Leyes tempore confectionis huius scripti per homagium et serui-
cium de dicto abbate tenuerunt," and notes that "Hec omnia
Willelmus de Walton et Marg[eria ?] vxor eius, filia altera dicti
Roberti quiete clamauerunt, ut patet in sua carta "

For Robert de Lees' gift of half Winnington to Richard de Wybunbury, who gave it to the abbey, see No 559   Cf Addenda

756. Grant by Pulton [1] abbey to Liulf de Twemlow of Derneley-
greue in Lees   See No 753 *n.*

757. Quitclaim by Warin de Croxton to abbot Roger of all
his rights in Lees   ? 1247–48

Original charter *penes* J Hatton Wood, Esq , Burnham, Bucks

Omnibus Christi fidelibus presens scriptum visuris uel audituris Warinus de Crokeston' salutem   Nouerit uniuersitas vestra
me pro salute anime mee et animarum antecessorum et heredum
meorum dedisse et concessisse et pei cartam meam confirmasse et
in perpetuum de me et heredibus meis quietum clamasse domino
Rogero abbati sancte Werburge Cestrie et monachis eiusdem loci
totum ius et clamium quod habui uel aliquo iure habere potui in
villa de Leg', cum omnibus pertinenciis, habendum et tenendum
eisdem abbati et monachis et eorum successoribus, in pace, libere
et quiete in bosco et plano, in pratis et in pascuis, in viis, in semitis,
in aquis et molendinis et omnibus aliis libertatibus et aesiamentis
predicte ville de Leg' pertinentibus   Ita quidem quod nec ego
Warinus nec heredes mei nec aliquis pro me uel per me aliquod
ius uel clamium in tota villa de Leg' cum omnibus pert , ut dictum
est, aliquo tempore habere poterimus.   Et in huius rei maiorem
securitatem huic scripto sigillum meum apposui   Testibus

[1] Dieulacres in heading

domimis Henrico de Toiboc tunc constabulario castri Cestrie, Walkelino de Arderne, Willelmo de Boydele, Galfrido de Cliftun, Fulcone de Orreby, Hugone Wauertun, Ricardo Bernard tunc vicecomite Cestrisir', Rogero de Toft, Radulfo Turnevilain, et multis aliis.

Seal (damaged) on parchment tag
A fleur de lys (?) Legend illegible.

758. Quitclaim by Richard, son of Gralam de Lostock (Gralam), to abbot Roger of a rent of 5s from Lees (cf No 737) 1245–49

Mainwaring Charter 17 (John Rylands Library)

Omnibus Christi fidelibus presens scriptum visuris uel audituris Ricardus filius Gralami de Lostoc salutem   Nouerit vniuersitas vestra me remisisse et quietum clamasse in perpetuum de me et heredibus meis Rogero abbati sancte Wereburge Cestrie et monachis eiusdem loci et eorum successoribus totum redditum quem ego et antecessores mei percepimus et recipere solebamus de villa de Leg' cum pertinenciis, scilicet annuatim quinque solidos argenti   Ita quidem quod ego Ricardus uel heredes mihi nichil de toto predicto redditu de Leg' aliquo tempore exigemus uel exigere poterimus   Et in huius rei testimonium huic scripto sigillum meum apposui   Hiis testibus, dominis Iohanne de Grey iusticiario Cestrie, Rogero de Monte alto senescallo Cestrie, Henrico de Turbock' tunc constabulario castri Cestrie, Walkelino de Arderna, Fulcone de Orreby, Roberto Lancelin, Ricardo Bern[ard] tunc vicecomite Cestrisirie, Hugone de Limme, Rogero de Toft', Willelmo de Craulach', et multis aliis

Non-armorial seal en double queue leg [SIGILLUM R]ICARD' DE LO[STOC].

759. Grant by Thomas, son of Reginald de Twemlow, to the abbey of all the land in Lees which he formerly held of the monks, in return for which they gave him an oxgang in Goostrey 1266–67

Original charter *penes* J Hatton Wood, Esq , Burnham, Bucks

Omnibus Christi fidelibus ad quos presens scriptum peruenerit Thomas filius Reginaldi de Twomlowe [1] salutem   Noueritis me dedisse, concessisse, remisisse et pro me et heredibus meis imperpetuum quiete clamasse Deo et ecclesie sancte Werburge Cestrie

[1] Tamlawe, Chart

[et] abbati et conuentui eiusdem loci, et eorum successoribus ibidem Deo seruientibus, totam terram cum pertinenciis quam habui in villa de Leyes uel, aliquo casu contingente, habere potui, illam scilicet quam de eisdem abbate et conuentu per homagium et seruicium in dicta villa quondam tenui, adeo libere, solute et quiete quod ego dictus Thomas uel heredes mei uel aliquis per nos uel nomine nostro uel aliquo iure nostro nichil iuris uel clamii in dicta terra cum pert exigere uel vendicare de cetero poterimus Pro hac autem donacione, concessione, remissione et quieta clamacione predicti abbas et conuentus dederunt mihi et heredibus meis unam bouatam terre cum pert in villa de Gorstre,[1] et per cartam suam confirmauerunt Ita tamen quod ego prefatus Thomas et heredes mei piedictam terram de Leyes cum pert dictis abbati, etc, contra omnes gentes imperpetuum warantizabimus, acquietabimus et defendemus Hiis testibus dominis I[acobo] de Audeth[ley] tunc iusticiario Cestrie, R[oberto] de Stokeport tunc constabulario castri Cestrie, Iordano de Peulesdon tunc vicecomite Cestri[sirie], Ricardo de Orreby, Roberto de Huxeleg', Hugone de Cotes, Rogero de Toft, Ricardo Bonetable, Michaele de Gorstre, Rogero de Bernulsh[aw], et multis aliis

Parchment tag for (missing) seal

The father of the grantor is identified by Ormerod (iii 127, 135) with Reginald de Cranage *alias* le Brun, son of Ranulf brother of Liulf de Twemlow, and himself progenitor of the Twemlows of Twemlow Elsewhere he suggests that Thomas is an error for Robert, but gives no reason (*ib* 139) See No. 543

760. Exchange of lands in Lees between William, son of Jordan de Stubbs (No 755), and abbot S[imon] 1271–74
Mainwaring Charter 60 (John Rylands Library)

Omnibus Christi fidelibus presens scriptum visuris uel audituris Willelmus filius Iordani de Stobbes salutem in Domino Sciatis me dedisse, concessisse, et hac presenti carta mea confirmasse, necnon et in perpetuum de me et heredibus meis quiete clamasse Deo et ecclesie sancte Werburge Cestrie et capitalibus dominis meis S[ymoni] abbati et conuentui eiusdem loci quasdam terras meas in villa de Leghes subscriptas, videlicet mesuagia mea et omnia edificia cum tofto et crofto et gardinis dictis mesuagiis adiacentibus que Rannulphus de Sprouston' aliquando tenuit ad terminum de Iordano patre meo, et totum le Claycroft cum pertinenciis quod Henricus Malger tenuit ad terminum, et vnum mesua-

___
[1] Gostre, Chart

gium cum crofto quod Henricus Louecok' aliquando tenuit ad
terminum, et septem landas in le Hethfeld', cum pertinenciis, quas
predictus Rannulphus de Sprouston' tenuit ad terminum, et totam
terram que vocatur Littlecroft, cum pertinenciis, cum duabus
landis et duabus buttis in le Hethfeld, quas dictus Henricus
Louecok' tenuit ad terminum, Habenda et tenenda prefatis abbati,
etc , eorumque successoribus vel assignatis inperpetuum ita libere
et quiete, bene, pacifice et integre quod nec ego nec heredes mei,
nec aliquis per nos seu nomine nostro quicquid iuris aut clamni
exactionis vel seruicii de dictis terris cum omnibus pertinenciis
de cetero poterimus exigere vel vendicare Pro hac autem
donacione mea, concessione et quieta clamancia predicti domini
mei abbas, etc , dederunt mihi et heredibus meis in escambium
predictarum terrarum per cartam suam in villa predicta de Leghes
decem landas in le Hethfeld continentes tres acras et vnam rodam
iacentes inter sex landas meas, et vnam assartum continens
quinque acras et vnam rodam, faciendo inde eisdem de me, etc ,
homagium et seruicium vnius libre cymini quod prius eisdem facere
consuevi Et ego predictus Willelmus, etc (warranty clause)
In cuius rei testimonium presenti scripto sigillum meum apposui
Testibus, Dominis Reginaldo de Grey tunc iusticiario Cestrie,
Thoma de Meyngar', Roberto de Stokeport, Hugone de Hatton'
tunc vicecomite Cestresir', Roberto de Hux[leg'], Iohanne de
Wetenh[ale], Ricardo de Oireby, Ricardo de Lostok', Warino de
Croxton', Henrico de Craulach', Ricardo de eadem, Ricardo
Bonetable, Thoma de Gorstre, Rogero de Bernulf[schawe],
Willelmo de Wythinton', et aliis

Parchment tag for seal (missing)

For the hamlet of Stubbs which gave its name to the family of the
grantor see Stublach in Orm iii 208

761. Grant by William, son of Jordan de Stubbs, to abbot Simon,
etc , of three sellions of land in the territory of Lees, in
Heathfield   1281–83

Harl MS 2074, i 191 (new 88)

Sciant, etc , quod ego Willelmus filius Jordani de la Stobbes
remisi pro me et heredibus meis imperpetuum [et] quietos clamaui
capitalibus dominis meis domino Symoni abbati et conuentui
sancte Werburge Cestrie tres selliones[1] terre in territorio de Leghes
acentis in campo vocato le Hethfeild[2] etc , tenendum, etc Huis

---

[1] Ch , solidos, H
[2] Hedfeld, Ch , which adds inter terras dicti abbatis et dicti Willelmi.

testibus   domino Reginaldo de Gray tunc iusticiario Cestrie, Willelmo de Sporstow tunc vicecomite comitatus Cestrie, Ricardo de Craulache, Henrico de eadem, Roberto le Grosvenour, Willelmo de Toft, Warino de Croxton, et aliis

762. Grant and confirmation by Henry, son of William, son of Jordan de Stubbs, to abbot Simon, etc., of 3 selions and 2 half selions in Hetfield in the territory of Lees, and of all the lands which his father William gave to them   1287–91

Harl MS 2074, f 191 (new 88)

Omnibus, etc , Henricus filius Willelmi filii Jordani de Stobbes salutem, etc   [Sciatis] me concessisse et confirmasse pro me et heredibus meis imperpetuum domino Symoni abbati et conventui sancte Werburge Cestrie, capitalibus dominis meis, tres seliones et duas dimidias seliones in territorio de Leyes iacentes in campo vocato le Hetfeld,[1] et etiam omnes terras quas predictus Willelmus pater meus per cartam suam easdem dedit , tenendas et habendas, etc   His testibus   domino Reginaldo de Gray tunc iusticiario Cestrie, dominis Ricardo de Mascy et Rogero de Domville militibus, Willelmo de Praers tunc vic(ecomite) com(itatus) Cestrie, Roberto Grosso-venatore, Willelmo de Thoft, Thoma de Weloc, Ricardo de Craunach, Henrico de eadem, Thoma de Goostre, Rogero de Bernulfsh' et aliis

Holme notes that this was among Henry Mainwaring's deeds (at Kermincham) transcribed by Peter Daniell

763. Agreement between the abbot and Hugh de Sproston for the erection and maintenance of a joint mill (or mills) on the Sproston bank of the Dane opposite Lees

Conuenit inter eos [2] ita quod dictus Hugo concessit et dedit dicto abbati imperpetuum totam partem suam aque de Dauene et attachiamenta vnius molendini et stagni vel duorum si voluerit, ad terras suas de Sproust'[3] cum piscaiiis inter terras dicti abbatis de Leyes et terras dicti Hugonis de Sproust' super aquam de Dauene vbicunque placuerit, et licenciam ripas dicte aque ex- altandi et turbas et terram in solo suo et meremium in bosco suo de Sproust' sufficientia capiendi ad medietatis construccionem dictorum molendinorum et stagnorum et piscariarum, et eorum reparacionem et sustentacionem, et viam sufficientem ad omnes homines venientes et redeuntes et equos honustos et bigas per

[1] Hedfeld, Ch , which adds   propinquiores terre dominice dicti abbatis
[2] Referring to heading   [3] Sproustowe, heading

mediam villam de Sproust', et ab ea usque ad dicta molendina Dictus uero abbas simili modo faciet pro altera parte dictorum molendinorum, stagnorum, etc., in solo suo de Leyes tam in bosco quam in terra et in via, et sic vtraque pars ea communibus sumptibus sustentabit, et equales prouentus inde habebit , et si vna pars medietatem suam non sustentauerit, post trinam admonicionem liceat alteri defectum illius suplere et prouentus omnes dicti molendini percipere quousque exinde omnes sumptus suos deduxit secundum visum legalium virorum

Ormerod (iii 204) notes that a family bearing the local name probably held land at Sproston under the Venables, but he gives no name before the 15th century For a Ranulf de Sproston before 1274 see No 760

764. Quitclaim by Henry de Cranage and William de Hermitage to Richard, son of Liulf de Croxton, of the wood of Crewe (in Cranage ?) with Saxiruding. Early 13th century

Henricus de Craunache et Willelmus de Heremitorio quiete clamauerunt Ricardo filio Lidulphi de Croxton totum nemus de 5) l Cruwe situm super fossatum in bruerio, et sic per diuisas quercuum ad Saxirudingesclow, et ita descendens per prefatum Clow ad Elif, et de Elif ad sepem de Saxiruding sicut divise quercuum protestantur et ita per sepem de Saxiruding in aquam de Dauene Et dicta sepes de Saxiruding nunquam sit remota quia in diuisa et meta nominatur de diuisis quercuum in aqua de Dauene Et eciam cum dicto nemore quiete clamauerunt dicto Ricardo Saxiruding, scilicet de metis et diuisis predictis predicti nemoris usque ad Leyes

As Richard, son of Liulf, was living in the time of Philip de Orreby as justice of Chester, this Henry de Cranage is no doubt his cousin, the first of his Christian name, who occurs c 1230 (Orm iii 127) But as his son Richard was the first of the later family of Hermitage, the William de Heremitorio of this deed must be the William Fitz Roger who held the Hermitage from the Hospitallers before Richard de Orreby gave it to Henry de Cranage (ib 129, 130) .

765. Grant of a chantry at Barnshaw by W[?illiam], abbot of Dieulacres, to abbot Thomas (? I), saving the rights of the mother church of Sandbach and its chapels. ? 1249–65.

Harl MS 2074, f 89 (old 192) d

Uniuersis Christi fidelibus, etc W[?illelmus] Dei gracia abbas de Deulacresse et humilis conuentus eiusdem loci salutem, etc.

[Sciatis] nos pro nobis et successoribus nostris concessisse Thome Dei gracia abbati sancte Werburge Cestrie et eiusdem loci conuentui et successoribus eorum licenciam in perpetuum quod possint audire et selebrare (sic) diuina in capella sua de Bernulfeshah ; salua indempnitate parochialis ecclesie nostre de Sandbach et capellaium eiusdem secundum formam obligacionis quam [de] dictis abbate et conuentu Cestrie inde habemus, saluis eis in omnibus priuilegiis suis a sede apostolica eis indultis, prout in dicta obligacione plenius continetur. In cuius rei testimonium presenti scripto sigillum nostium fecimus apponi.

Dugd *Mon* v 626 quotes Harl MS 280, f 78b, for William, abbot of Dieulacres, t Tho Abb Cestr Sleigh gives an abbot William, August 1240, without reference (*Leek*, 63)

766. Grant by Roger de Barnshaw to abbot Thomas (II), in exchange for land in Bystousnabbe and Rogeresway, etc , of a moiety of Barnshaw which Liulf and Gilbert de Twemlow gave to Roger, son of Ralph Palmer, Rogei's giandfather (No. 766a), with the liberty of the vill of Goostrey, quittance of pannage in all the woods of Goostrey and housebote and haybote, paying 2s yearly 1291–1305

Mainwaring Charter 20 (John Rylands Library)

Nouerint vniuersi quod Rogerus de Bernesschawe dedit, concessit, et hac presenti carta sua confirmauit Thome abbati sancte Werbuige Cestrie et eiusdem loci conuentui et eorum successoribus totam terram suam cum pertinenciis in Bernesschawe que est de feodo de Gostre, quam quidem terram Lidulphus de Twomlowe et Gilbertus de eadem dederunt Rogero filio Radulphi le Palmer auo suo per metas et diuisas, prout in carta de feoffamento eorum plenius continetur, nichil sibi vel heredibus suis commoditatis dominii vel feodi in predictis tenementis nec in eorum pertinenciis retinendo Tenenda et habenda Deo et ecclesie sancte Werburge et monachis ibidem Deo seruientibus libere, quiete, bene et in pace imperpetuum in boscis, planis, pascuis, pasturis, viis, semitis, moris, moscis, mariscis, turbariis, vastis, liberis communis et in omnibus aliis locis, et cum omnibus libertatibus et eysiamentis, prout in carta de feoffamento predictorum Radulphi et Gilberti continetur. Pro hac autem donacione, concessione predictus Thomas abbas Cestrie assensu et voluntate tocius capituli sui dedit et concessit predicto Rogero et heredibus suis nomine escambii pro predictis tenementis totam illam terram quam Iohannes Dedishay et Robertus filius predicti Rogeri quondam de

M

predicto abbate tenuerunt in quodam loco qui vocatur Bystousnabbe et Rogereswey cum edificiis in predicta terra constructis,
cum duabus insulis quas Thomas filius Michaelis de Gostre quondam tenuit cum housbote et heybote ad vnum solum astrum per
visum balliuorum predictorum abbatis et conuentus qui pro
tempore fuerint et cum libero pannagio tempore pessone cum
propriis porcis in bosco del Ewode, cum communa pasture propriis
animalibus suis et cum aysiamentis in bruera de Gostre et in Gostreschawe versus metas de Craunache, prout homines dominici dicti
abbatis communicant, faciendo inde homagium et reddendo inde
annuatim predictis abbati, etc., duos solidos argenti videlicet
medietatem ad festum sancti Martini et aliam medietatem in
festo sancti Johannis Baptiste.   Preterea idem abbas assensu
tocius capituli sui concessit eidem Rogero ad terminum vite sue
quod libere possit turbam in moscis de Gostre quantum sufficit ad
aliud solum astrum pro voluntate sua capere fodiendo et predictus Rogerus et heredes sui et predicti abbas, etc., predicta
tenementa alternatim warantizabunt, acquietabunt et contra
omnes homines imperpetuum defendent.   In cuius rei testimonium utraque pars sigilla sua huic scripto in modum cyrographi indentato vna cum sigillo conuentus apposuerunt.   Hiis
testibus, dominis Hamone de Mascy, Ricardo de Mascy,[1] militibus,
Willelmo de Meynwaring', Ricardo de Lostok', Iohanne de Holt,
Rogero de Daneport, Thoma filio eius, et aliis.

Seal (illegible) on parchment tag.

766a. Charter of Liulf and Gilbert de Twemlow referred to in
No. 766.   *c.* 1190–1220.
Mainwaring Charter 38 (John Rylands Library).

Sciant omnes presentes et futuri presentem cartam inspecturi
et audituri quod ego Lydulfus de Twamelowe et ego Gilbertus de
Twamelawe dedimus et concessimus et hac presenti carta nostra
confirmauimus Rogero filio Radulfi Palmeri de Gostre, pro
homagio et seruicio suo, totam dimidietatem tocius terre de
Bernulisah' cum omnibus pertinenciis, que continetur infra has
diuisas incipiendo, scilicet, ad tres quercus stantes inter capitale
mesuagium predicti Rogeri et Wulfrici de Lache, et sic descendendo doetum et sicut sepes et fossa circuit in longitudine, et in
latitudine usque ad predictas tres quercus, et totam dimidietatem
tocius terre que vocatur Bernulisah' croft cum pertinenciis, scilicet
in duas partes, quatuor landas et dimidiam in medio campo, in
longitudine et latitudine, et superiorem partem predicti campi cum

[1] Sir Richard de Massey died 1305.

pertinenciis sicut sepes et fossa includit in longitudine et latitudine ex vna parte, et vnum croftum cum pertinenciis quod vocatur
Syddenale in longitudine et latitudine sicut sepis et fossa circuunt
et includunt, et totam dimidietatem vnius campi cum pertinenciis
quod vocatur Sercroft, scilicet superiorem paitem in longitudine
et latitudine sicut sepis dictum campum includit.   Tenenda et
habenda de nobis et heredibus nostris illi et heredibus suis uel suis
assignatis in feodo et hereditate inperpetuum, libere, quiete, bene
et pacifice, in bosco, in plano, in pratis, in pascuis, in viis, in
semitis, in aquis, in moscis et turbariis et marleris, et in omnibus
aliis locis, esiamentis, et libens communis vbique teiie predicte
et ville de Gostre pertinentibus, et cum acquietancia de pannagio
omnibus poicis eorum in omnibus boscis de Gostre et husbold et
haybold in omnibus boscis de Gostre.   Reddendo inde annuatim
nobis et heredibus nostris de illo et heredibus suis uel de suis assign'
duos solidos argenti ad duos terminos scilicet ad Natiuitatem sancti
Iohannis Baptiste xii den et ad festum sancti Martini xii den pro
omnibus seruitiis et demandis secularibus vniuersis, saluo foiinseco
seruicio   Pro hac autem nostra donacione et concessione dedit
nobis predictus Rogerus tres marcas et duas bacones de precio octo
solidorum   Et nos et heredes nostri totam teiram predictam cum
omnibus pertinenciis predicto Rogero et heredibus suis uel suis
assingnatis (sic) contra omnes homines et feminas warantizabimus
inperpetuum   Et vt hec carta nostra perpetue firmitatis robur
semper optineat eam sigillorum nostroium apposicione confirmauimus   Hiis testibus, Roberto capellano de Gostre, Alexandio persona de Esteburi, Ran[ulfo] fratre suo, Ricardo clerico de Esteburi,
Willelmo domino de Somerford, Petro de Suetenham, Willelmo
de Ermitage, Iohanne filio Hugonis, Deai' fratre eius, Simone
clerico, et multis aliis

Liulf's seal missing, Gilbert's bears a rose (?), *leg* SIGILL GILBERTI
D[E CR]OXTVM (*sic*)

767. Quitclaim by Warin de Croxton to abbot Walter, etc , of
the moiety of Goostrey formerly held by (his grandfather)
Liulf the sheriff   1233–39
Mainwaring Charter 13 (John Rylands Library)

Sciant presentes et futuri quod ego Warinus de Croxton' filius
Ricardi de Croxton' concessi et remisi et quietum clamaui de me
et heredibus meis Deo et sancte Werburge et domino Waltero
abbati Cestrie et monachis ibidem Deo ministrantibus, in puram
et perpetuam elemosinam, pro salute animarum antecessorum

meorum, et pro participatione orationum monachorum, totum ius
et clamium quod habui uel habere potui in medietate ville de
Goristre cum pertinenciis quam Lidulphus vicecomes aliquando
tenuit, tam in homagiis et releuiis quam in omnibus aliis seruiciis
et exaccionibus.   Ita quidem quod nec ego nec heredes mei nec
aliquis occasione mei vel heredum meorum in dicta medietate de
Goristre cum pertinenciis aliquid iuris aut clamii habere poterimus
de cetero uel exigere.   In cuius rei testimonium presenti scripto
sigillum meum apposui.   Hiis testibus, domino Willelmo de Malo
Passu, Ricardo de Wybenbury tunc vicecomite Cestrisyr', Ricardo
de Kingesleg', Ada de Hellesby, Simone de Neutona, Ricardo
Walensi, Ricardo de Calueleg', Ricardo Bernard' et aliis.

Parchment tag en double queue for (missing) seal.

768. Licence by Michael de Goostrey to abbot T[homas] (I.) to
raise a pool and make a fish-pond on Barnshaw Brook, in
exchange for two assarts near Rogersway ; quitclaim by
Richard Bonetable and similar licence from Rose, widow of
Gilbert de Mooresbarrow.   1249–65.

Michael de Gostre dedit domino suo T[home] abbati Cestrie
licenciam leuandi stagnum et faciendi viuarium super aquam de
Bernulschawe vbi melius viderit expedire, cum eysiamentis et
pertinenciis, et totam terram que est a vado que se extendit uersus
Maclesfeld per quoddam nouum fossatum usque ad vetus fossatum
prope domos Roberti Brun de Berneshawe, quantum ad ipsum
pertinet, pro escambio duorum assartorum iuxta Rogerisweye.
Dictum eciam stagnum Ricardus Bonetable T[home] abbati
Cestrie quiete clamauit, cum omnibus pert., prout in carta sua
patet.   Item, Roysia vxor quondam Gilberti de Morisbarwe dedit
licenciam leuandi dictum stagnum, et faciendi viuarium, cum
omnibus pert. et eysiam., excepta construccione molendini ad
bladum.

Rose's licence seems to be lost ; she gave her share of Goostrey Mill
in a charter (No. 768*b*), which is overlooked in the Chartulary.

768a. Quitclaim by Richard de Bonetable to abbot Thomas (I.)
of the " stagnum " licensed in No. 768.   1249–65.

Mainwaring Charter No. 71 (John Rylands Library).

Omnibus Christi fidelibus ad quos presens scriptum peruenerit
Ricardus de Bonetable, filius Willelmi de Bonetable, salutem in
Domino.   Nouerit vniuersitas vestra me dedisse, concessisse et

quiete clamasse et presenti carta mea confirmasse dominis meis
Thome abbati ecclesie sancte Werburge Cestrie, et eiusdem loci
conuentui et eorum successoribus, totum ius et clamium quod
habui uel aliquo tempore habere potui in toto stangno de Bernol-
schaue cum longitudine, latitudine, refulso, et in tota terra cum
pertinenciis, prout circumclauditui fossato et pallacio, in liberam,
puram et perpetuam elemosinam, ita, videlicet, quod nec ego nec
heredes mei nec aliquis ex parte nostra aliquid iuris, etc , in predictis cum pert de cetero exigere vel vendicare poterimus In
cuius iei testimonium huic scripto sigillum meum apposui Hiis
testibus Rogero de Daueneport', Willelmo de Meynwaring',
magistro Hugone vicario de Piestbui', Ricardo de Coudrey,
Iohanne de Birchlis, Henrico de Birchlis, Michaele de Goristre,
et aliis.

Seal missing

768b. Grant at a rent for her life by Rose, widow of Gilbeit
de Mooresbarrow, to abbot Thomas (I) of her share (in
dower) of Goostrey Mill 1249–65

Mainwaring Charter 19 (John Rylands Library)

Omnibus Christi fidelibus presens scriptum visuris uel audituris
Roesia quondam vxor Gilberti de Moresbarewe salutem Sciatis
me concessisse et tradidisse ad firmam dominis meis Thome abbati
Cestrie et eiusdem loci conuentui totam partem meam molendini
de Gorestre quam habui in eadem villa nomine dotis, tenendam et
habendam predictis abbati et conuentui, et eorum successoribus,
uel cui assignare voluerint, quoad uixero, libere, quiete, bene et
pacifice, cum omnibus sectis et libertatibus et aisiamentis dicto
molendino infra villam et extra peitinentibus Reddendo inde
annuatim mihi uel assignatis meis, de dictis abbate et conuentu
uel eorum assignatis, quinque solidos aigenti, et pro viuario de
Bernuls[hawe] sex denarios annuos ad duos terminos, scilicet in
translatione sancte Werburge xxxiiid et in festo Omnium Sanctorum xxxiiid pro omni seiuicio, exaccione et demanda Ego
vero Roesia predicta predictis abbati et conuentui et eorum, etc ,
predictam partem meam molendini cum omnibus pertinenciis
contra omnes homines quamdiu vixero warantizabo In cuius
rei testimonium presenti scripto sigillum meum apposui Hiis
testibus, Michaele de Gorestre, Ricardo de Coudray, Radulpho
Turneuileyn, Roberto Brun de Bernulues', Willelmo Iukel, et aliis.

Parchment tag en double queue for (missing) seal

769. Grant by Thomas de Goostrey to abbot Simon of a fourth part of Goostrey Mill in fee farm for 42*d*. yearly, reserving to Thomas or other occupant of his chief house at Goostrey priority in grinding the corn for his household over all but the monks, and provision for feeding his draught cattle in Goostrey Wood in hard years, when forage is scarce.   1271.

Mainwaring Charter 51 (John Rylands Library).

Anno gratie M° CC° septuagesimo primo infra octauas Ascensionis Domini, ita conuenit inter dominum Symonem abbatem et conuentum Cestrie ex vna parte et Thomam filium Michaelis de Gorstre ex altera, videlicet quod idem Thomas concessit, dimisit et tradidit ad feodalem firmam predictis dominis suis abbati, etc., totam quartam partem sui molendini de Gorstre vna cum stagno et eius attachiamentis, aqueductu et agistiamento viuarii, refulsu,[1] et quarta parte piscacionis eiusdem aque, scilicet a situ quo predictum molendinum tempore huius conuencionis positum fuit usque ad vadum chymini quod ducit a Gorstre usque ad Bernulfsh[awe].   Habendam et tenendam de dicto Thoma et heredibus suis prefatis abbati, etc., imperpetuum, libere et quiete cum viis et semitis ad dictum molendinum ducentibus, cum bosco et terra ad sustentacionem dictorum molendini et stagni necessariis, cum omnibus aliis pertinenciis, libertatibus, commoditatibus et asyamentis predictis molendino, etc., infra villam et extra pertinentibus.   Et si contingat dictum molendinum vel stagnum per inundacionem aque uel aliud casum contingentem non posse stare competenter in locis vbi sita fuerunt tempore huius conuencionis facte, liceat predictis abbati, etc., ipsum molendinum vel stagnum facere vbicunque sibi melius viderint expedire inter situm illum vbi dictum molendinum cum stagno tempore huius conuencionis facta fuerunt et predictum vadum, ita tamen quod per nimium aque refulsum via pupplica non obstruatur.   Reddendo inde annuatim de predictis abbate, etc., prefato Thome et heredibus suis quadraginta duos denarios argenti ad duos anni terminos, scilicet infra Octauas sancti Iohannis Baptiste viginti vnum den., et infra octauas sancti Martini viginti vnum den., pro omni seruicio, exaccione et demanda.   Ita quidem quod si dicta firma infra predictos terminos aliquando non fuerit soluta, liceat prefatis Thome, etc., homines dictorum abbatis, etc., tenentes illam bouatam terre quam Matheus aliquando tenuit in Gorstre racionabiliter distringere donec predicta firma sua plenarie persoluatur.   Predicti eciam abbas, etc., concesserunt predicto

[1] refluxu, Ch.

Thome, etc, quod quicunque illorum habitauerit in domo capitali eiusdem Thome in Gorstre habeat libertatem molendi totum bladum ad sustentacionem familie eiusdem domus necessariuum post illud bladum quod in tremio molendini inuenerint pro racionabili tolneto quod alii dederint, nisi forte dominicum bladum dictorum abbatis, etc, superuenerit molendino Concesserunt insuper iidem abbas, etc, predicto Thome, etc, quod quando annus ita durus venerit quod pro defectu foragii de necessitate oporteat eos auena sua propria de bosco de Gorstre iuuare, seruiens dictorum abbatis, etc, ipsum manerium custodiens, ab eisdem Thoma, etc, coram testibus racionabiliter monitus, sine contradiccione uel impedimento dictorum abbatis, etc., assignabit eis certum locum in dicto bosco ubi propria auena sua tantum racionabiliter pascere poterunt, sine vendicione, donacione, uel ullo vasto faciendo Predictus autem Thomas, etc, predictis abbati, etc, totam predictam partem dictorum molendini, etc (warranty clause) In cuius rei testimonium partes alternatim huic scripto in modum cyrographi confecto sigilla sua fecerunt apponi Testibus dominis Reginaldo de Grey tunc iusticiario Cestrie, Petro de Ardern', Ricardo de Wilburham' tunc vicecomite Cestrisir', Roberto de Hux[leg'], Iohanne de Wetenh[ale], Ricardo de Croxtona, Warino fratre eius, Willelmo de Bonebur', Ricardo de Swetenham', Ada de Craulache clerico, Ricardo de Craulache, Ricardo Bonetable, Thoma de Twamlawe, Rogero de Bernulfsh', et aliis

Seal of green wax, leaf star of eight rays, leg s' TH'E DE GOSTRE

770. Agreement between abbot [Simon] and Thomas de Goostrey, his tenant in a fourth part of Goostrey, for a partition between them of the waste of the vill, with right to enclose and assart, etc, but not, in Thomas's case, to make a mill, and saving Roger de Barnshaw's right of common The abbot saved to Thomas two "eyes" near Roger's way and the rent, etc, reserved in No 769, and gave him an alder grove opposite his house August 1, 1287

Mainwaring Charter No 70 (John Rylands Library)

Pateat omnibus quod cum abbas monasterii sancte Wereburge [f 38 (3. Cestrie et eiusdem loci conuentus, capitales domini ville de Gorstre, tres partes terre arabilis eiusdem ville, cum omnibus pertinenciis, in dominico suo tenuissent, et Thomas filius Mychaelis de eadem quartam partem eiusdem per homagium et seruicium de eisdem

teneret, nemoribus, vastis, moris, mariscis, brueris vsque ad
confeccionem presentis scripti inter eos pro indiuiso iacentibus
anno gracie M°cc octogesimo septimo et domini regis Edwardi
quintodecimo in festo sancti Petri ad Vincula ita conuenit inter
eosdem et vtrique parti placuit pro bono pacis, quietis, concordie
et vtriusque status certitudine quod predictus Thomas et heredes
sui pro quarta parte dictorum nemorum, morarum, mariscorum,
bruerarum, et omnium vastorum ipsos contingente habeant et
teneant separatim de dictis abbate, etc , eorumque successori-
busque uel assignatis sibi et heredibus suis uel assignatis inperpetuum omnia nemora, bruera, moras, mariscos, mineras, et vasta
infra diuisas subscriptas contenta, videlicet a diuisis de Wythinton'
incipiendo a le Longesthayecloch, et sic ascendendo linealiter
vsque ad chiminum quod dicitur Salteriswey, et sic sequendo viam
illam vsque ad diuisas ville de Twamlowe, et sic descendendo per
diuisas factas vsque ad sepem campi de Gorstre, et sic sequendo et
circuiendo hayam illius campi vsque ad alteram viam infra villam
de Gorstre, et sic sequendo viam illam inter capellam et domum
dicti Thome vsque ad campum qui vocatur Bromicroft, et sic a
campo illo de Bromicroft vsque ad aluam in sicheto per metas et
diuisas ibidem situatas, et sic sequendo riuulum vsque ad metas
de Wythinton', ad includendum, assartandum et omnimode commodum suum inde faciendum quod, salua communa Rogeri de
Bernulschawe et heredum suorum, in eisdem de iure facere poterit
Ita tamen quod idem Thomas et heredes sui ac assignati exclusi
sint omnino virtute concordie et pacis presentis a potestate
leuandi, faciendi aut quoquo modo construendi inposterum per se
uel per alios molendinum uel stagnum infra diuisas suas predictas
super aqueductum que vocatur Blakedenebroc   Si autem idem
Thomas aut aliquis heredum suorum dictam terram aut aliquam
porcionem ipsius vendere aut aliquo modo a liberis eorum alienare
voluerint, predicti abbas, etc , ipsam pro racionabili precio quod
alii fideliter et sine fraude optulerint et dare voluerint pre ceteris
habebunt   Predicti vero abbas, etc , habebunt in suo separali
totum residuum omnium nemorum, etc (as above), dicte ville,
necnon et terram extra Brerehey cultam quam Robertus filius
Rogeri de Bernulschawe tenuit, cum stagnis et molendinis infra
predictas diuisas suas factis et pro libitu suo faciendis pro tribus
partibus ipsos contingentibus ad includendum, frussandum,
assartandum, et pro libitu suo approuandum, sine ullo impedimento uel contradiccione dicti Thome, etc , saluis eisdem Thome,
etc., duabus insulis suis iuxta Rogeriswey iacentibus cum competenti chimino ad easdem et quarta parte vastorum iacencium

infra sepes campi de Gorstre, et tribus solidis et sex denariis pro
sua porcione molendini et stagni de Gorstre annuatim percipiendis,
et libera multura bladi sui proprii in dicto molendino secundum
tenorem scripti inter ipsos abbatem, etc , ex vna parte et Mychaelem
patrem predicti Thome ex altera inde prius confecti. Concesserunt autem iidem abbas, etc , eidem Thome et heredibus suis[1]
quamdam placeam cuiusdam alneti in Gorstre ex opposito domus
dicti Thome crescentis, saluo eis refulsu aque ductus et stagni
eorundem pro porcione cuiusdam insule infra diuisas ipsorum
abbatis, etc , iacente et ipsum Thomam prius contingente Concessit eciam vtraque pars quod neutri parti earum de cetero liceat
alteri in separali parte alterius communicare sine alterius licencia
speciali Et ad hec omnia et singula prescripta inter partes
fideliter, sine fraude et dolo obseruanda huis scriptis ad modum
cyrographi confectis et inperpetuum duraturis partes alternatim
sigilla sua fecerunt apponi Testibus, Dominis Reginaldo de
Grey tunc iusticiario Cestrie, Willelmo de Venablis, Petro de
Arden', Radulpho de Vernon', Hamone de Masci, Warno de May-
waring', Ricardo de Masci, Patricio de Heselewell', Rogero de
Domuill', militibus, magistro Iohanne de Stanleg', domino Rogero
rectore ecclesie de Deneford', Roberto Grosso Venatore, vicecomite Cestres', Alexandro de Bamuill', Willelmo de Bonebur',
Willelmo de Meynwaring', Ricardo de Lostok', Ricardo de Crowe-
lach', Henrico de eadem, Rogero de Bernulsch', et aliis

Portion of the seal of Thomas de Goostrey

771. Grant by Richard Bonetable to his son Henry and Felicia,
his wife, of an oxgang with a messuage in Goostrey, which
Simon, son of Badok (Batecock in No 771*a*), formerly held
of him, and the land and meadow which he exchanged with
Michael de Goostrey Henry and Felicia quitclaimed this
gift to abbot S[imon].(No 771*a*), and Felicia, when a widow,
to abbot Thomas (No 771*b*) 1265–91.

Harl MS 2074, f 89 (old 192) *d*

Sciant, etc , [quod] ego Ricardus Bonetable in legia potestate
et prospera sanitate mea dedi [et] concessi Henrico filio meo et
Felicie uxori sue unam bouatam terre cum messuagio et pertinenciis in uilla de Goustree, illam scilicet quam Simon filius
Badok [2] quondam de me tenuit, et terram cum prato quam escam-
biaui cum Michaele de Goostre , habendam et tenendam, etc ,
reddendo inde annuatim mihi Ricardo uel heredibus meis idem

---

[1] et heredibus suis, after placeam in MS   [2] Badek, Ch

Henricus uel heredes sui de predicta Felicia procreati [1] unum par ciroticaŕum albarum die Natiuitatis sancti Johannis Baptiste pro omnibus que possunt exigi nomine tenentis uel tenementi, saluo forinseco seruicio, etc.[2] Hiis testibus : Thoma de Venables, Rogero de Dauenport, Radulfo de Moreton, Willelmo de Brereton, Ricardo de Craunache, Henrico de eadem, Ada Manualātt clerico compositore huius carte, et aliis.

771 a. Grant by Henry and Felicia Bonetable to abbot S[imon] mentioned in No. 771 *n.* 1265–91.

Mainwaring Charter 46 (John Rylands Library).

Omnibus Christi fidelibus presens scriptum visuris uel audituris Henricus filius Ricardi Bonetable et Felicia vxor sua salutem in domino. Noueritis nos vnanimi assensu et pari voluntate dedisse, concessisse, et hac presenti carta nostra confirmasse, Deo et sancte Werburge Cestrie et domino S[ymoni] abbati et conuentui eiusdem loci vnam bouatam terre in Gorstre cum mesuagio et omnibus pertinenciis suis, illam, scilicet, quam Symon filius Batecok' de dicto Ricardo ad terminum quondam tenuit in eadem, ac eciam quandam terram, cum prato adiacente, quam dictus Ricardus recepit in excambio quondam de Michaele de Gorstre pro quadam terra in eadem, quas per cartam suam nobis dedit. Habenda et tenenda eisdem abbati et conuentui eorumque successoribus et assignatis in perpetuum, cum husbote et haybote in boscis de Gorstre capiendis, et acquietancia pannagii omnium porcorum in dicto tenemento nutritorum et nutriendorum, et cum omnibus asiamentis et libertatibus dictis terris infra villam et extra vbique pertinentibus. Reddendo inde annuatim dicto Ricardo et heredibus suis vnum par albarum cyrothecarum in festo Natiuitatis beati Iohannis Baptiste pro omnibus seruiciis, exaccionibus, et demandis que de dictis terris aliquo modo poterunt exigi uel vendicari. Pro hac autem donacione nostra predicti abbas et conuentus dederunt nobis sex marcas et dimidiam argenti pre manibus. Nos, vero, predicti Henricus et Felicia et heredes nostri dictis abbati, etc., predictas terras, etc., pro predictis sex marcis et dimidia ab eisdem receptis et cirothecis annuatim dicto Ricardo et heredibus suis soluendis contra omnes homines et feminas inperpetuum warantizabimus, adquietabimus et defen-

---

[1] The Chartulary makes this more emphatic : et si obierint sine heredibus inter se procreatis, dicta terra sibi (*i.e.* Ricardo) vel heredibus suis revertetur.

[2] The Chartulary adds : Hanc terram dicti Henricus et Felicia S[ymoni] abbati Cestrie coniunctim dederunt, vt patet in sua carta, et eadem Felicia post decessum Henrici per se quiete clamauit, vt patet, etc.

demus. In cuius rei testimonium presenti scripto sigilla nostra
fecimus apponi Testibus, magistro Iohanne de Stanleg' tunc
rectore ecclesie de Astbury, Radulpho de Thighnes, Henrico
fratre eius, Stephano de Derby, Ada filio Iuliani, Radulpho de
Morton', Galfrido de Lostok', Ada de Lautona, Ricardo de Craulache, Henrico de eadem, Th[oma] de Gorstre, Rogero de Hole,
et aliis

*Seal of Henry (broken) a large and a smaller star-shaped ornament,
that of Felicia (perfect) a bird   For legg see Addenda*

771 b. Quitclaim by Felicia, widow of Henry Bonetable, to abbot
T[homas] (II) of the land given in No 771a   June 21,
1305

Mainwaring Charter No 77 (John Rylands Library)

Omnibus Christi fidelibus ad quos presens scriptum peruenerit
Felicia que fuit vxor Henrici filii Ricardi Bonetable salutem.
Sciatis me remisisse et omnino pro me et heredibus meis imperpetuum quietum clamasse domino Th[ome] abbati sancte Werburge Cestrie et eiusdem loci conuentui et eorum successoribus
totum ius et clamium quod habui vel aliquo modo habere potui in
vno mesuagio et vna bouata terre cum pertinenciis in Gosetre, et
in omnibus aliis terris et tenementis cum pert que fuerunt predicti
Henrici quondam viri mei et predicti Ricardi patris sui in villa
predicta   Ita quod nec ego Felicia nec heredes mei nec aliquis
nomine nostro in pred tenementis seu eorum pert aliquid iuris
vel clamii decetero poterimus vendicare vel exigere, set exclusi
simus ad pred tenementa petenda imperpetuum   In cuius rei
testimonium presenti scripto sigillum meum apposui   Hiis
testibus, domino Willelmo Trussell tunc iusticiario Cestrie, Roberto
de Brescy tunc vicecomite Cestrisir', Ricardo de Foulishurst,
Willelmo de Praers, Willelmo Geraid', Alexandro de Baunuile,
Willelmo de Trofford', et aliis   Dat[um] apud Cestriam die
lune in festo sancte Werburge virginis, anno domini M°CCC° quinto.

Parchment tag for seal (missing)

772. Grant and quitclaim by Richard Bonetable of Twemlow
to abbot Simon, etc , of a fourth part of the vill of Goostrey
and Barnshaw, in free alms   1277

Mainwaring Charter No 64 (John Rylands Library)

Omnibus Christi fidelibus ad quos presens scriptum peruenerit
Ricardus Bonetable de Twamlag' salutem in Domino sempiternam.

Nouentis me dedisse, concessisse, et presenti carta mea con-firmasse, ac eciam pro me et heredibus meis inperpetuum quiete clamasse Deo et ecclesie sancte Werburge Cestrie et capitalibus dominis meis Symoni abbati et conuentui eiusdem loci totam quartam partem ville de Gorstre et de Bernulfesh', cum pertinencus, sine ullo retenemento, Habendam et tenendam dictis abbati, et conuentui eorumque successoribus uel assignatis, in liberam, puram, et perpetuam elemosinam, in boscis, planis, paschuis, pratis, aquis, viis, semitis, moris, mariscis, vastis, stagnis, viuariis, molendinis, waidis, releuiis, homagiis, escaetis, et omnibus aliis commoditatibus, asyementis, et approuiamentis dicte quarte parte mee de Gorstre et de Bernulf' vbique pertinentibus   Ita libere et quiete quod nec ego, nec heredes mei, nec aliquis per nos uel nomine nostro quicquid iuris aut clamii in dicta quarta parte mea predicte ville de Gorstre et Bernulfesh', cum pert , de cetero exigere uel vendicaie poterimus, preter oraciones tantum   Ego vero pre-dictus Ricardus, etc (warranty clause)   In cuius rei testimonium presenti scripto sigillum meum apposui   Hiis testibus, Dominis Guncelino de Badelesmar' tunc iusticiario Cestrie, Thoma de Meyngarin, Warino filio suo, Radulpho de Vernon, Willelmo de Mayngaiin, I[ohanne] de Stanil[eg'], Iohanne de Wetenh[ale], Rogero de Daueneport, Henrico de Birchel', Iohanne de Asthul, Ricardo de Craunach', Henrico de Craunach', Ricardo de Sweten-ham, et aliis

Oval seal, on white cords, figure holding child (?), *leg* s' ric' bone-table

For the date see No 772a

772a. Mandate from Richard Bonetable to his tenant Roger de Barnshaw to render his homage and service henceforth to the abbot of Chestei (in consequence of his gift, No 772). December 27, 1277

Mainwaring Charter No 65 (John Rylands Library)

Ricaidus Bonetable Rogero de Beinulfesh[awe] salutem in Domino.   Quia attornaui domino abbati Cestrie homagium et seruicium que michi facere solebatis, vobis mando quatinus ipsa dicto abbati et eius successoribus de cetero faciatis, et eisdem tamquam dominis vestris sitis attendentes   In cuius iei testi-monium has literas vobis transmitto patentes   Dat' apud Gorstre die sancti Iohannis Apostoli anno regni regis E[dwardi] sexto

The order is on a small piece of parchment about 4 inches long by 1½ broad, the bottom margin of which has been cut away from the right to within an inch of the left margin, leaving a strip depending which has again been cut into a wider and narrower strip, the former may originally have borne a seal (*en simple queue*), but both are now fastened into the cords of No 772

773. Grant by Thomas de Goostrey to abbot T[homas] (II) of two " eyes " in Goostrey (No. 770) and the lordship of the whole tenement which Roger de Barnshaw formerly held of him in Barnshaw, for which he gave the grantor 6 acres nearer Twemlow, and renunciation of common for Roger's tenements. 1291–1323

T[homas] filius Michaelis de Gostre dedit T[home] abbati Cestrie duas insulas in territorio de Gostre iacentes iuxta boscum de Breiehay ex vtraque parte Rogerisweye cum omnibus pertinenciis suis, et totum dominium tocius tenementi quod Rogerus de Bernulfschawe quondam de se tenuit in Bernulfschawe, cum seruicio xii den de eodem tenemento percipiendorum ; dictus uero abbas dedit dicto T[home] vi acras terre propinquiores terre de Twaml' in illo angulo vbi mete de Craunach', Gostre et Twaml' concurrunt, nec dictus abbas vendicabit communam in Bernulschawe in terris dicti T[home] pro tenementis que habet de Rogero de Bern'

774. Quitclaim by Roger de Barnshaw to abbot Thomas (II) of an acre in Goostrey for half an acre in the waste there, nearer his own land 1291–1305

Mainwaring Charter No 79 (John Rylands Library)

Pateat vniuersis per presentes quod ego Rogerus de Bernuleschawe concessi, remisi et omnino quietum clamaui fratri Thome abbati Cestrie et eiusdem loci conuentui totum ius et clamium quod habui et aliquo modo habere potui in vna acra terre cum pertinenciis in Gosetre iacente iuxta ductum molendini de Gosetre, in longitudine incipiente ad paruum ductum campi mei, durante vsque ad capud noui fossati predicti abbatis in eadem villa in latitudine, pro vna dimidia acra vasti in eadem villa iacente in vna cultura que vocatur Bystouwesnabbe iuxta terram meam et extendit se a nouo fossato pred abbatis vsque ad capud grangie mee in eadem villa Ita tamen quod nec ego nec heredes mei nec aliquis nomine nostro aliquid iuris, etc , in predicta acra terre cum suis pert exigere vel clamare poterimus, set ab omni accione simus exclusi inperpetuum In cuius rei testimonium huic presenti scripto quieteclamacionis sigillum meum apposui His testibus, domino Hamone de Macy, Radulpho de Vernun, Ricardo

de Macy milite, Philippo de Egerton', Willelmo de Mengwaryr
Ricardo de Crauenache, Thoma de Gostre, et aliis

Parchment tag for seal (missing)

The date was probably between 1294 and 1296 (see 774a)

774a. Similar quitclaim by Robert, son of Roger de Barnshaw
1291–1305

Harl MS 2074, f 90 (old 193)

Robertus filius Rogeri de Berleschawe salutem, etc   [Sciatis]
me concessisse pro me et heredibus meis dominis Thome abbati et
conuentui sancte Weiburge Cestrensis eorumque successoribus
totum ius et clameum quod habui in tota illa terra quam Rogerus
pater meus in territorio de Gorestre in loco qui dicitur Beileschawe
dedit eisdem abbati et conuentui in escambium pro quadam placea
terre in territorio eiusdem uille de Gorestree inter Bistouisnabbe et
Rog[ers]Way, prout instrumenta inter predictos religiosos et
prefatum Rogeium patrem meum super eodem escambio confecta
plenius testatui *(sic)* , habendum, etc   Testibus dominis Ricardo
de Mascy, Edmundo Phittun militibus, Johanne de Egerton uicecomite Cestrie, Willelmo de Meynwaring, Thoma filio Michaelis,
Ricaido de Craunache, Thoma de eadem, et multis aliis

If, as is probable, *John* de Egerton should be *Philip* de Egerton,
the date can be narrowed to 1294–96

775. Quitclaim by Rose, widow of Thomas de Aston, to the abbot,
etc , of Chester (abbot Thomas in Chart) of all right within
their new dyke of Barnshaw, for which they gave her 10s.
ͻ 1249–65

Mainwaring Charter 18 (John Rylands Library)

Omnibus presens scriptum visuris uel audituris Roysia quondam vxor Thome de Astona salutem   Sciatis me in ligia viduitate
et potestate mea remisisse in tota vita mea et quietum clamasse
dominis meis abbati Cestrie et eiusdem loci conuentui et eorum
successoribus totum ius et clamium quod habui uel aliqua ratione
habere potui infra nouum fossatum suum de Beinulshawe   Ita
quod nec ego nec aliquis pro me uel nomine meo quicquam iuris
aut clamii infra dictum fossatum de cetero exigere uel vendicare
poterimus   Pro hac autem iemissione et quieta clamancia
dederunt mihi piefati abbas et conuentus decem solidos argenti
pre manibus   In cuius rei testimonium presenti scripto sigillum
meum apposui   Hiis testibus, Michaele de Gorestre, Ricardo de

Coudrey, Radulpho Turneuileyn, Roberto Brun de Bernulues', Willelmo Iukel, et aliis

Parchment tag en double queue for (missing) seal

776. Confirmation by Thomas, son of Reginald Brun (Broun, Ch) of Twemlow, of the gift of an oxgang in Goostrey to the abbey by Thomas, son of Robert Paumer (le Palmer, Ch), and Cecilia, Brun's daughter and wife of Palmer (No 543). 1283–88

Harl MS 2074, f 89 (old 192) *d*

Thomas filius Reginaldi Brun de Tuamlowe salutem, etc. [Sciatis] me ratam habere et firmam remissionem et quietam clamanciam unius bouate terre in Gorstree [1] quam Thomas filius Roberti Paumer et Cecilia uxor sua et filia mea domino Symoni abbati et conuentui sancte Werburge Cestrie fecerunt, quam quidem bouatam terre cum pertinenciis eisdem abbati et conuentui eorumque successoribus presenti scripto confirmaui et de me et heredibus meis imperpetuum quietam clamaui, etc Testibus dominis Willelmo de Venables et Ricardo de Mascy militibus, Roberto Grosso Venatore tunc uicecomite Cestrie, Rogero de Stockford, Johanne de Mottrum, Thoma de Gorstre, Ricardo de Crawlach, Henrico de eadem, Rogero de Bernulfeshah, et aliis

The brief entry in the Chartulary here seems to be an abstract of Brown's original grant of the oxgang to his son-in-law and daughter, and does not mention his confirmation of their gift to the abbey

777. Final concord by which Agnes, daughter of Walthew (Waltheof) of Plumley, recognised an eighth part of Plumley as the right and inheritance of Thomas Smith and his son William, also of Plumley, who gave her a mark of silver and to the abbey 4s. rent, and at the death of them and their heirs, etc , their second best beast, as recognition of its chief lordship (No 778) July 3, 1274.

Mainwaring Charters 61 and 62, duplicates (John Rylands Library)

Hec est finalis concordia facta in curia domini regis apud Cestriam die Martis proxima post octauas Nat sancti Iohannis Bapt anno regni regis Edwardi secundo, coram dominis Reginaldo de Grey tunc iusticiario Cestrie, Thoma de Meyngarin, Petro de Arderne, Roberto de Monte alto, Henrico de Audithleg', Uriano de

[1] Gosetre, Chart

sancto Petro, Roberto de Stokeport, Patricio de Haselwalle, militibus, Roberto de Huxeleg' tunc constabulario castri Cestrie, Hugone de Hatton' tunc vicecomite Cestresir', et aliis domini regis fidelibus tunc ibidem presentibus, inter Agnetem filiam Walthew de Plumleya, per Henricum filium suum attornatum positum ad luciandum et perdendum, petentem octauam partem ville de Plumleya, cum pertinenciis, per breue mortis antecessoris ex vna parte et Thomam fabrum de Plumleya et Willelmum filium suum tenentes ex altera parte, videlicet quod predicta Agnes recognouit et concessit pro se et heredibus suis dictam octauam partem de Plumleya, cum pert., esse ius et hereditatem ante-dictorum Thome et Willelmi, Ita quidem quod nec ipsa nec heredes sui nec aliquis per eos uel nomine eorum quicquid iuris uel clamii in prefata terra, cum pert , aut aliqua sui porcione de cetero poterunt exigere vel vendicare Pro hac autem recognicione et concessione predicti Th et W dederunt predicte Agneti vnam marcam argenti premanibus, et insuper pro se, etc., dederunt et concesserunt domino S[ymoni] abbati et conuentui Cestrie eorumque successoribus in liberam, puram et perpetuam ele-mosinam quatuor solidos annuatim inde percipiendos ad duos anni terminos, videlicet in festo Nat S Iohannis Bapt. duos solidos et in festo S Martini duos solidos, et in obitu ipsorum Th et W et singulorum heredum suorum vel successorum secun-dum melius auerium suum nomine recognicionis dominii capitalis eorum   Et si forte nullum omnino habuerint auerium, pro dicto auerio aliam racionabilem faciant recognicionem se et heredes suos uel successores dominacioni et districcioni dictorum abbatis, etc., subicientes quod possint illos ad plenam omnium premissorum solucionem pro libitu suo compellere sine aliquo placito uel con-tradiccione, secundum tenorem carte quam dicti Th et W. pre-dictis abbati, etc , inde fecerunt   In cuius rei testimonium huic cyrographo partes sigilla sua alternatim apponi fecerunt, et hanc finalem concordiam in rotulo qui dicitur Domesday irrotulari coram testibus suprascriptis, et multis aliis

Oval seal, star of (8) *leaves, leg* s' ANGNET' FIL' WALTHEF *Round seal, same bearing, leg.* s' HENR' F' . ANGNETIS DE PLVML' In No. 62 Agnes's seal is missing, Henry's is recognisable. This deed (with others included in this volume) was formerly in the possession of the Mainwarings of Kerminchiam, as the successors of the abbey as lords of Barnshaw, from whom it passed (c 1755) to the Mainwarings of Peover (Orm 1 669, 111 132)

778. Grant by Thomas Smith of Plumley and his son William to abbot S[imon], etc , of 4s. rent and a heriot from the land in Plumley they obtained by No 777. 1274

Mainwaring Charter 53 (John Rylands Library)

Omnibus Christi fidelibus presens scriptum visuris uel audituris Thomas faber de Plumleg' et Willelmus filius eius salutem in Domino Sciatis nos pro salute animarum nostrarum [et] antecessorum et successorum nostrorum dedisse, concessisse, et hac presenti carta nostra confirmasse Deo et ecclesie sancte Werburge Cestrie, et dominis S[ymoni] abbati et conuentui eiusdem loci eorumque successoribus, in liberam, puram et perpetuam elemosinam quatuor solidos annui redditus de octaua parte nostra ville de [f 39 (Plumleg' ad duos anni terminos annuatim percipiendos, scilicet in festo sancti Iohannis Baptiste duos solidos, et in festo sancti Martini duos sol , et in obitu nostro et singulorum heredum nostrorum uel successorum dictam terram de Plumleg' qualitercunque tenencium secundum melius auerium nostrum nomine recognicionis domini capitalis, vel, si forte nullum omnino habuerimus auerium, aliam racionabilem pro dicto auerio faciemus recognicionem, nos et heredes nostros uel successores dictam terram uel alias quascunque infra Cestresir' tenentes presenti scripto imperpetuum obligantes, et dominacioni atque districcioni dictorum abbatis, etc , qui pro tempore fuerint subicientes, quod possint nos tam per predictam terram de Plumleg' quam per omnes alias terras nostras quas infra Cestresir' habemus, uel habere poterimus in posterum, ac omnia bona nostra mobilia et immobilia, vbicunque inuenta, sine aliquo placito uel contradiccione aut reclamacione nostri uel heredum nostrorum aut successorum, et sine impedimento cuiuscunque domini dictorum feodorum uel suorum balliuorum, pro libitu suo distringere ad plenam solucionem dicti annui redditus et antedicte recognicionis quocienscunque terminis statutis ab eisdem uel eorum aliqua porcione cessatum fuerit, et ad racionabiles emendas huiusmodi retencionis faciendas. Et nos predicti Thomas, etc (warranty clause). In cuius rei testimonium presenti scripto sigilla nostra fecimus apponi et hanc concessionem et donacionem nostram in rotulo qui vocatur Domesday irrotulari Testibus, Domino Reginaldo de Grey tunc iusticiario Cestrie, Magistro A[da] de Staunford tunc archidiacono Cestrie, dominis Thoma de Mayngar[in], Petro de Arden', Roberto de Stokeport, Patricio de Haselwall', militibus, Roberto de Huxeleg' tunc constabulario castri Cestrie, Hugone de Hatton' tunc vicecomite Cestresir', Iohanne de Wetenhal, Ricardo de Orreby, Roberto de Wyninton, Ricardo Starky, Galfrido de Morton',

N

Thoma de Lostok', Roberto de Trohford', Rogero de Hole, Roberto de Ynes et aliis multis.

Two parchment tags en double queue for (missing) seals.[1]

779. Final concord of identical date and effect to No. 777 between Agnes, daughter of Walthew de Plumley, plaintiff, and Richard de Plumley (de Sladehurst in No. 780) and Leticia his wife, tenants of an eighth part of the vill of Plumley.   July 3, 1274.

> Shakerley (Vernon) MSS., No. 4, f. 89b (Somerford Park, Congleton).

Leticia, as appears from her seal on No. 780, was daughter of William de Plumley, presumably the William of Nos. 777–8.

780. Grant by Richard de Sladehurst and Leticia his wife to abbot Simon, etc., in the same words, *mutatis mutandis,* as No. 778, and with the same witnesses.   1274.

> Mainwaring Charter 55 (John Rylands Library).

Two seals in green wax : (1) *l., conventional plant (?), leg.* S' RIC. DE PLVMLEG ; (2) *r., leaf star, leg.* S' LETICIE F' WILL'I DE PLOML'.

781. Quitclaim by John de Iddinshall to the abbey of the land in Iddinshall which his brother Robert, son of Richard, gave him.   After 1270.

Robertus filius Ricardi de Idinchale dedit Johanni fratri suo totam terram suam cum pertinenciis quam Ricardus filius Roberti le Bor de se tenuit ad firmam in Idinchale, et quandam placeam que vocatur Morichbuttes cum vi landis in campis de Idinchale, scilicet cum magna landa in le Holefeld, et alia in le Tounstede *uersus le Saweheued, et alia extensa uersus le Gatebrugg', et alia iuxta le Hallecroftislond, et extrema landa in crofto, cum capitali butta et cum le Cokschutehauedlond in le Tounstede et cum le Bradesunderlond in Colemon leye, et totam terciam partem suam vaste terre infra sepes de Idinchale, et medietatem partis sue tocius vaste terre extra sepes de Idinchale, cum pertinenciis et acquietacione pannagii et housbold et hayb', reddendo sibi annuatim iis. viz. ad festum sancti Johannis Baptiste et ad festum sancti Martini per equales porciones.   Hanc terram dictus Johannes abbati Cestrie sine ullo retenemento quiete clamauit, vt patet in sua carta.

---

[1] The legend on William's, according to Leycester, was " Willielmus filius Ceciliae de Plumley " (Orm. i. 669).   * et [? alia].

782. Quitclaim by Robert, son of Richard, to the abbey of a third part of Iddinshall, all his land there, with a rent of 2s from his brother John (No 781) This land Richard had resigned to abbot [Thomas I.], and abbot S[imon] re-enfeoffed Robert with it (No 782a) After 1270

Robertus filius Ricardi de Idinchale quiete clamauit abbati Cestrie sine ullo retenemento totam terram suam quam habuit uel habere potuit in Idinchale vna cum iis annuis de Johanne fratre suo percipiendis Hanc terram, scilicet terciam partem de Idinchale dictus Robertus ab S[ymone] abbate Cestrie recepit de nouo feoffatus, quam dictus Ricaidus in manu abbatis resignauit, pro seruiciis in suo scripto contentis

See *supra*, p 29, where the " probably " in line 16 may be omitted in view of the " seruicia " mentioned in No 782a

782a.[1] Grant of a third part of Iddinshall by abbot Simon to Robert, son of Richard, after the death of Richard, son of Robert, who had resigned it to abbot Thomas (I), being unwilling to render the services due therefor 1270–71

Shakerley (Vernon) MSS , No 4, f 92f (Somerford Park, Congleton)

Vniversis Symon abbas Cestrie et eiusdem loci conventus salutem Cum Ricardus filius Roberti, nolens facere debita seruicia pro tertia parte de Ydinghall, eandem terram in manu domini Thome abbatis, predecessoris [nostri], resignauit, nos post decessum ipsius Ricardi dedimus Roberto filio Ricardi totam tertiam partem ville de Ydinghall, etc , reddendo dimidiam marcam annuatim, etc. Testibus, domino Reginaldo de Gray tunc iusticiario Cestrie, Thoma de Mayngarin, Ricardo de Wilburham tunc vicecomite Cestrisirie, Roberto de Huxlegh tunc constabulario Cestrie, Johanne de Wetenhall, Willelmo de Brichull tunc camerario Cestrie, Roberto le Brun, Ricardo le Bruer, Roberto le Grovenour clerico.

783. Recognition by Richard de Done, lord of Tarporley, of the correct bounds between Tarporley and Iddinshall, which were also recognised by Hugh (de Tarporley), lord of a moiety of Tarporley Before 1293

Ricardus de Doun, dominus de Torperley, recognouit quod recte diuise inter Torperley et Ydinchale incipiunt ad altam viam que ducit a Torperley uersus Cestriam, extendunt se a dicta via

[1] Not in the Chartulary

uersus meridiem per le Witokestonel' vsque ad superiorem partem de Netstallis, et sic a superiore parte de Netstallis versus Torperley, et sic directe sequendo usque ad superiorem partem de Geylmare- siche, et sic directe a Geylmaresiche usque le Derneforde, et sic descendendo aqueductum cum medietate eiusdem cursus aque usque viam que ducit ab Heremitorio ultra predictum ductum uersus Ydinchale, et sic a dicta via que ducit ultra ductum iuxta superiorem partem de Flaxyord uersus Torperley usque ad Boteok weye, et sic sequendo Boteokweye usque ad diuisas de Teuerton. Et istas diuisas dictus Ricardus confirmauit, extra quas nichil vendicabit.   Eandem recognicionem et confirmacionem fecit Hugo dominus medietatis ville de Torperley, vt patet in sua carta.

Despite Ormerod's doubts, the Dones seem to have held a mesne lordship of Tarporley, as of Utkinton, under the Venables (Orm. ii. 226, 236, 248, and No. 382).   The date of the recognition is before the transference of Hugh de Tarporley's moiety to Reginald de Grey (Orm. ii. 226).

For the Hermitage or Free Chapel at Tarporley see Orm. ii. 236.

784. Quitclaim by Gilbert Salomon to abbot S[imon] of Pever- lishurst and Fildingeshurst, etc., as the ancient metes between Tiverton and Iddinshall Woods were made. 1265-91.

Gilbertus Salomon quiete clamauit S[ymoni] abbati Cestrie totum ius et clamium suum in Peuerlishurst[1] et Fildingeshurst, cum omnibus pertinenciis et eciam ultra le Blakesiche, sicut veteres mete inter boscos de Teuerton et Idinchale facte fuerunt.

For the Salomons of Tiverton and Lower Withington see Orm. ii. 277 and iii. 720.

785. Grant by Roger de Venables to the abbot of a bondman with his whole issue.   ? 1240-61.

Rogerus de Venables dedit abbati Cestrie Willelmum filium Reginaldi de Ecclistona, natiuum suum, cum tota sequela sua.

The grantor was probably Sir Roger de Venables of Kinderton, who died in or about 1261 (Orm. iii. 198).

786. Confirmation by Ralph Mansel, rector of Prestbury, to Abraham the clerk and his heirs of all Booths in which he found him vested.   Before 1223 ?

[1] Penerlishurst, MS.

Radulphus Mansel, rector ecclesie de Presteburia confirmauit Abrahe clerico et heredibus suis totam terram de Bothes in qua inuenit eum vestitum, scilicet a Freisteslache usque ad Cokemonscloht, sicut semita tendit ad brueram, et a Presteslache per latus de Harebarwe per torrentem qui vadit usque ad Spelenford, reddendo annuatim altaii sancti Petri duos solidos ad festum sancti Martini.

Licence for the appropriation of Prestbury church was given to the abbey between 1215 and 1223, and the stipend of a vicar fixed (No 98) Presumably, then, Mansel's date as rector is earlier than the latter year   The ordination of the vicar's portion after 1257 (No 99) may have been only a rearrangement   A vicar is said to be mentioned c 1230 (Earwaker, ii. 206)

The mention of Harbarrow seems to fix the position of Booths to the south-west of Prestbury village

787. Agreement between abbot S[imon] and John de Birtles, rector of the chapel of Gawsworth, that the latter should receive for life the corn tithes of land newly ploughed in his parish (which Simon had claimed for the (mother) church of Prestbury), for which he paid the abbot 50s   1265–91.

S[ymon] abbas Cestrie concessit quod dominus Johannes de Birchel', rector capelle de Gouseworth decimas garbarum de frussuiis quibusdam per Henricum de Danne . . factis prouenientibus, quas dictus abbas pro iure ecclesie de Prestebur' prius vendicauit, et omnes decimas de frussuris ceteiis infra limites parochie sue de Gousworth prius et tempore dicti Johannis [f 39 faciendis piouenientes in tota vita sua sibi percipiet. Salua tamen vtriusque ecclesie accione post mortem dicti Johannis. Pro hac concessione predictus Johannes dedit dicto abbati l solidos argenti

John (de Birtles), rector of Gawsworth, occuis in 1262 and 1273 (Earwaker, ii 587 ; Orm iii 554)

788. Quitclaim by Adam de Lawton to his son and heir William of all his land in (Church) Lawton, of which abbot Walter, as lord of the fee, gave him seisin   1236.

Adam de Lautona tradidit et quiete clamauit Willelmo, filio suo et heredi, totam terram suam, cum pertinenciis, in villa de Lautona, coram domino Waltero abbate Cestrie, anno domini M°CC°XXX°VI°   Ita quod ad instanciam suam dictus abbas cepit homagium predicti Willelmi de toto dicto tenemento, et seysinam commisit eidem vt dominus feodi.

The Lawtons held a moiety of the township (Orm. iii. 16) under the abbey, whose lordship went back to the early years of the 12th century (p. 40).

Ormerod's pedigree of the early Lawtons (*op. cit.* iii. 11, 16), constructed mainly from this and the following 43 deeds, is not altogether satisfactory. He may be right in referring all grants ascribed to " William de Lawton " to the William son of Adam who was placed in possession in 1236, but as this makes him live to 1266 at least (No. 802), there is some difficulty in accepting Ranulf, son of William, who made a grant before 1249 (No. 821) as his younger son. The William son of Adam who joined him in that grant and in a quitclaim of the advowson probably as early (No. 540) seems more likely to have been the William of 1236 himself than his nephew. In both cases Ranulf and William appear to be acting as joint lords. But in a grant made by William, son of William, presumed to be eldest son of the William son of Adam of 1236, his father is described as " quondam dominus medietatis de L." (No. 790). This second William also raises difficulties. Ormerod identifies him with the William son of William the priest (or chaplain) who quitclaimed his right to the church (No. 540), and between 1269 and 1291 exchanged all his land in Church Lawton for land, etc., in Hulse (831). In his Hulse deeds (Nos. 724, 733–4) and in two Lawton ones (830–1) he certainly describes himself simply as William, son of William de Lawton, but the note made by Randle Holme of the charter by which " Willelmus fil' Willelmi de Lauton, dominus medietatis de Lauton remississe, etc., totum ius in dicta medietate villa (*sic*) de Lauton dicto abbati et conventui pro homagio, ward', relev', etc., circa anno 1281, 9 Edw. I." (Harl. MS. 2074, f. 90*d* (old 193)) can hardly refer to the original of No. 831.

Ormerod carelessly transfers the priesthood from the father to the son. If his identification is correct the father must have taken orders late in life. If he is wrong the William of No. 831 was perhaps son of a rector of Lawton.

789. Bond by William, son of Adam de Lawton, not to alienate any of his land in (Church) Lawton without the abbot's consent. ? 1236.

Willelmus filius Ade de Lautona obligauit se domino suo, abbati Cestrie, quod nichil de terra sua de Lautona vendet uel inuadiabit, aut alio modo alienabit, nisi per gratum consensum dicti abbatis ; quod si fecerit, totum residuum dicto abbati quietum remaneat imperpetuum.

790. Quitclaim by William, son of W[illiam] formerly lord of a moiety of (Church) Lawton, to abbot S[imon] of an oxgang which Richard the smith rented from him, etc   1265-91

Willelmus filius W ,[1] quondam domini medietatis de Lautona, quiete clamauit capitali domino suo S[ymoni] abbati Cestrie totum ius suum et clamium in vna bouata terie quam Ricardus faber de se tenuit ad firmam in Lautona, et vnam dimidiam sellionem iacentem in campo qui dicitur Barwehedys

791. Quitclaim by W[illiam] de Lawton to abbot S[imon] of 2 half lands in the territory of (Church) Lawton and the homage, etc , of John Harding.   1265-91

W[illelmus] de Lautona quiete clamauit S[ymoni] abbati Cestrie ii dimidias landas in teiritorio de Lautona, iacentes iuxta le Coulone et extensas super marleram prope le Twisse cloch, e. homagium et seruicium vnius denarii annui quod Johannes Haiding sibi facere consueuit pro terra quam de se tenuit in Lautona in campis subscriptis, viz in Quethul, Liueresleghnese, et Parua We[r]sthanl[ey]

792. Quitclaim by William de Lawton to abbot S[imon] of 2 selions in the territory of (Church) Lawton   1265-91

W[illelmus] de Lautona quiete clamauit S[ymoni] abbati Cestrie ii selliones in territorio de Lautona quarum vna iacet in quodam campo qui vocatur Siwardeleg' siue [2] Brodelond et alia iacet in le Ferfeld et abbuttat uersus le Brodeleg'

793. Attornment by William de Lawton to abbot S[imon] of certain rents in (Church) Lawton in return for remission of his rent for a moiety of that vill, saving to the abbot William's homage and suit to his court at Chester, and his licence for alienations   1265-91

Willelmus de Lautona attornauit S[ymoni] abbati Cestrie homagium et seruicium vs et vid quas Willelmus Hard[ing] filius Ricardi Hard[ing] sibi reddere consueuit pro vna bouata terre quam antedictus Willelmus eidem dedit, exceptis mesuagio et gardino cum iiii buttis ex vna parte dicti gardini et aliis quatuor ex altera iacentibus, saluo dicto abbati et domino terre forinseco seruicio   Item dictus Willelmus dedit iid annui redditus quas Adam filius Ade de Lautona sibi solueie tenebatur pro sua parte de Prodeleg' [3] Stanweyerud[ing], et pro vna sellione et dimidia in

---

[1] Willelmus de Lauton, heading

[2] or scilicet   [3] *Sic*   Query for Brodeleg'

le Ferfeld. Pro suprascriptis eciam donacionibus dictus abbas remisit dicto Willelmo imperpetuum vs annui redditus quos pro medietate de Lautona sibi reddere consueuit   Saluis tamen dicto abbati suo homagio, et secta communi ad curiam suam de Cestria, et aliis seruiciis de dicta medietate debitis   De terra eciam quam idem Willelmus tempore confeccionis huius scripti in manu sua tenuit nichil ipse uel heredes sui alienabunt sine dicti abbatis licencia speciali uel impignorabit

793a. Grant by William de Lawton to abbot S[imon] of an oxgang of land in (Church) Lawton, saving the external service, to wit, puture for the abbot and the serjeant of the peace   1265-91

Willelmus de L[autona] dedit S[ymoni] abbati Cestrie vnam bouatam terre in Lauton quam Stephanus Wiger' aliquando tenuit, saluo forinseco seruicio, scilicet pultura eiusdem abbatis et seruient[is] pacis

793b. Grant by William de Lawton to abbot S[imon] of certain lands in (Church) Lawton   1265-91

W[illelmus] de L[autona] quiete clamauit S[ymoni] abbati Cestrie totam terram quam habuit in campo de Barwedes a lacu usque le Chircheruding, excepto assarto quod vxor Thome Lupi de se tenuit, et dimidiam sellionem super le Midilforlong, et duas dimidias selliones subtus ecclesiam, una cum homagio et seruicio quod Willelmus filius Willelmi de Laut' sibi facere consueuit de tota terra quam de se tenuit cum omnibus pertinenciis , ita quod omnimoda seruicia dicto abbati faciet que ante donacionem istam pro tota medietate de Lauton facere consueuit, exceptis vi denariis quod predictus W[illelmus] pro pultura domini abbatis de dicta terra facere consueuit

794. Grant by William de Lawton to abbot S[imon] of his part in the waste below Lawton chapel, in which the abbot had enclosed his houses with a ditch   Also permission to take marl in his demesne land   1265-91

W[illelmus] de L[autona] dedit S[ymoni] abbati Cestrie partem suam quam habuit in vasto subtus capellam de Lautona,[1] in quo dictus abbas domos suas quodam fossato incluserat , concessit eciam marlam capiendam omnibus terris dominicis vbicunque dicto abbati expedient

[1] Carta de medietate situs manerii de Lautona, in heading

795. Grant by William de Lawton to abbot S[imon] of 1¼ acres in Werstonesleg' spone 1265–91

W[illelmus] de Laut[ona] quiete clamauit S[ymoni] abbati Cestrie vnam acram et vnam rodam terre sue iacentes in Werstonesleg' spone, quas Henricus de Bosco de se tenuit

796. Quitclaim by William de Lawton to abbot S[imon] of Everard's Riding and other land in (Church) Lawton 1265–91.

W[illelmus] de L[autona] quiete clamauit S[ymoni] abbati Cestrie totum ius suum et clamium in quadam placea terre que vocatur Euerard' ruding,[1] et in vna sellione que vocatur le Cokshute lond, et in vna placea iacente inter sellionem Roberti filii Ade iuxta Lunthdgate et assartum Symonis filii Alote, saluo tamen seruicio de medietate ville

797. Grant by William de Lawton to abbot S[imon] of a plot and half selion in (Church) Lawton 1265–91

W[illelmus] de Laut[ona] dedit S[ymoni] abbati Cestrie quandam placeam terre in Lauton iacentem inter [2] campum qui vocatur Barwedys et Trhelawenhet, et vnam dimidiam sellionem que vocatur Line Halfland iacentem in campo predicto prope Stappe [f 40 grene

798. Quitclaim by William de Lawton to abbot S[imon] of certain lands in (Church) Lawton 1265–91

W[illelmus] de L[autona] quiete clamauit S[ymoni] abbati Cestrie totam partem suam de terra que vocatur le Barud, et vnam acram terre in Bircheleg', et vnam acram terre et dimidiam in le Lun, quam Symon filius Alote de se tenuit

799. Quitclaim by William de Lawton to abbot S[imon] of 4s. rents in (Church) Lawton. 1265–91

W[illelmus] de L[autona] quiete clamauit S[ymoni] abbati Cestrie tres solidos argenti annuos quos Philippus filius Henrici carpentar[ius] de Lautona et Philippus Harding sibi soluere consueuerunt de ii bouatis terre et pro quodam assarto quod vocatur Salterisbachehurst, et xiid annuos quos iidem homines per manum suam pro pultura domini abbatis soluere tenebantur, vna cum homagio et seruicio eorum.

---

[1] Euerardis, heading   [2] In Barwedys et Trelawenhet, heading

800. Quitclaim by William de Lawton to abbot S[imon] of a moiety of his waste between (Church) Lawton and the Staffordshire boundary.   1265–91.

W[illelmus] de L[autona] quiete clamauit S[ymoni] abbati Cestrie medietatem tocius vasti sui inter villam de Lautona et metas de Staffordschira, cuius vasti aliam medietatem dedit Henrico filio suo, et totam partem suam cuiusdam terre iacentis inter sepem de la Snape et viam altam, sine ullo retenemento. Salua sibi communa fodiendi turbas ad focum suum proprium tantum, sicut vicini fodere solent.

Ormerod (iii. 16) makes Henry de la Snape son of William I., who occurs 1236 (No. 788).

801. Grant by William de Lawton to abbot S[imon] of his part of a certain waste in (Church) Lawton.   1265–91.

W[illelmus] de Lauton[a] dedit S[ymoni] abbati Cestrie totam partem suam cuiusdam uasti in Lautona iacentis infra diuisas subscriptas, scilicet a Salterisbache walle usque ad aqueductum, et sic descendendo per aqueductum usque ad sepem Henrici de Thurlewode, et per eandem ex transuerso usque ad le Merewey, et sic per le Merewey usque ad nouum fossatum, et a dicto fossato usque ad dictum Salterisbachewalle.

802. Grant and quitclaim by William de Lauton to the abbot, etc., of all lands of his assarts and wastes in (Church) Lauton which he had sold or rented to certain men, with their homage, etc.   1265–66 or c. 1275–76.

Willelmus de Lautona concessit et quiete clamauit abbati et conuentui Cestrie imperpetuum omnes terras de assartis et vastis suis in Lautona quas hominibus subscriptis vendidit vel ad firmam tradidit, vna cum homagiis et seruiciis eorundem hominum, ac eciam wardis, releuiis, etc., et approuiamentis omnibus que de dictis terris, hominibus, et heredibus eorum alico modo prouenire poterunt uel accrescere.   Viz., totam terram quam Ricardus Brayn de se tenuit in feodo infra le Sponne et le Ruth pro x*d*. ad festum sancti Martini in hyeme soluendis, et dimidiam acram quam idem Ricardus tenuit ad terminum, et iii acras et dimidiam in Werstanleg' sponne et Sullunhull quas Henricus de Bosco[1] de se tenuit in feodo pro ii*d*. dicto termino soluendis, et dimidiam acram iacentem inter le Longeforde et Liueresleg' euese[2] ad terminum, et totam terram de Litlelond quam Adam filius presbyteri de Lautona

[1] Cf. No. 795.   [2] *Sic*, but cf. No. 791.

de se tenuit in feodo pro ii[d.] ad terminum prescriptum, et terram
quam idem Adam et filii eius, Robertus et Ricardus, de se tenuerunt ad terminum, iacentem in Leysich' hurst ex vtraque parte
ducti usque ad sepem de Werstanl', ac eciam terram quam dicti
Adam et filii eius de se tenuerunt ad terminum inter fossatum propinquiorem ville de Lautona et Stancliffisclouh, vna cum quadam
placea iacente inter Stancliff' et sepem leuatam in le Hurst infra
diuisas suas   Et totam terram quam idem Adam de se tenuit ad
terminum, iacentem in le Halh infra diuisas suas, cum vna placea
inter le Puttes et sepem de Ferfeld   Et quoddam mesuagium
quod Robertus filius Ade de se tenuit in feodo pro vid ad festum
sancti Martini soluendis, idem, scilicet, quod Willelmus de Lund
tenuit, vna cum quadam placea infra sepem, scilicet ad le Lund-
lidgate, et totam terram quam Thomas Lupus tenuit ad terminum,
iacentem infra diuisas a Beterbacheforde sequendo viridem viam
usque fossatum et sic circuieundo usque ad dictum Beterbacheforde   Atque terram del Snape quam Philippus filius Henrici
tenuit in feodo pro vid dicto termino soluendis, iacentem inter
sepem suam et le Brock' cum vna placea ante hostium suum ad
Salterisb[ache]   Et terram de Assenehalh quam dictus Philippus
tenuit ad terminum, iacentem infra diuisas   Ac eciam totam
partem suam de Feyre Pleckes et de Mora quam R filius Ricardi
fabri [1] tenuit ad terminum, iacentem inter magnam viam et Talkhurstesford infra diuisas suas.   Et terram quam Philippus Harding tenuit ad terminum, iacentem inter Assenehalh et le Tvert-
ouercloh infra diuisas   Et terram de Smaleleg' quam Henricus
filius Stephani tenuit ad terminum infra diuisas   Et dimidiam
acram quam Rogerus de Crosseleg' tenuit ad terminum   Unde in
carta dicti W[illelmi] dicitur [2]   Hec omnia predicto abbati et
conuentui ego dictus Willelmus dedi in puram et perpetuam
elemosinam de me et heredibus meis, nichil mihi ex omnibus
reseruans preter oraciones tantum   Preterea obligaui me et
heredes meos hoc scripto praedictis abbati, etc , imperpetuum
quod totum seruicium, consuetudines et sectas curie quas antecessores mei et ego eisdem alico tempore pro medietate ville de
Lautona fecimus imposterum fideliter, sine aliqua diminucione uel
condicione faciemus, nec tamen ipsam terram aut aliquam eius
partem alicui vendemus, inuadiabimus aut vltra terminum xii
annorum ad firmam uel alico modo trademus nisi eisdem abbati,
etc , uel de eorum licencia speciali   Et si ego uel heredes mei
contra formam huius obligacionis aliquid facere presumpserimus,

[1] Cf No 790
[2] Unde   dicitur, in margin , in Harl MS 2062 it is in the text

concedo quod tota terra quam vltra terminum xii annorum alicui quocunque modo tradidero eisdem abbati, etc., imperpetuum permaneat absque reclamacione aliqua. Hiis testibus, Roberto de Hoxl[eg'] tunc vicecomite Cestrisire [et aliis].

Robert de Huxley was sheriff in 1265–66 and again about 1275–76 (Orm. i. 70).

803. Quitclaim by William, son of William de Lawton, to abbot S[imon] of his part of a field called Aschenehalgh with his portion of moor contained within its hedges (cf. No. 817). 1265–91.

(37) *d*.] W[illelmus] filius W[illelmi] de Lauton quiete clamauit S[ymoni] abbati Cestrie totam partem suam cuiusdam campi, scilicet Aschenehalgh, cum tota parte sua more infra sepes dicti campi contente.

804. Grant by William de Lawton to Henry de Walton of all his lands and tenements in (Church) Lawton (heading).

W[illelmus] de Lauton[a] dedit domino Henrico de Waltona omnes terras et tenementa sua cum omnibus pertinenciis, faciendo inde dominis capitalibus seruicia debita.

805. Grant by William de Lawton to abbot S[imon] of land and a house in (Church) Lawton. 1265–91.

W[illelmus] de L[autona] dedit S[ymoni] abbati Cestrie iii acras terre et quartam partem acre terre in assarto quod vocatur le Diches,[1] et dimidiam acram super Trhelowenhet, et dimidiam sellionem cum vna domo in eadem sita iuxta viam ante portam persone de Lautona.

806. Grant by Roger de Crossley (in Buglawton) and his wife Cecilia to abbot S[imon] of all their land in le Diches. 1265–91.

R[ogerus] [2] de Crosseleg' et Cecilia vxor eius dederunt S[ymoni] abbati Cestrie totam porcionem suam cuiusdam placee que vocatur le Diches in territorio de Lautona, cum omnibus pertinenciis.

The grantor's wife was daughter of Ranulf de Lawton (No. 788 *n.*).

807. Quitclaim by Thomas de Rode to abbot S[imon] of his part

---

[1] de ii. acris et de assarto quod dicitur le Diches, heading.
[2] Extended from the heading.

of le Diches in (Church) Lawton in return for confirmation of other lands. 1265–91

Thomas de R[ode] [1] quiete clamauit S[ymoni] abbati Cestrie totam partem suam cuiusdam terre que vocatur le Diches quam habuit ex dono Willelmi filii Willelmi presbyteri, vnde dictus abbas concessit ei licenciam habendi omnes porciones terrarum quas habuit ex dono dicti Willelmi Videlicet infra le Ruth et le Sponne et Sulynhull', Werstanley Sponne, et Werstanleg' Buthinleg', et vna acra super le Barud et in vno crofto apud le Longeforde in forera qua dictas terras tenuit ante presentis carte confeccionem.

For William, son of William the priest, see No 788 n

808. Quitclaim by Ranulf de Lawton (cf 806 n) to abbot S[imon] of all his right in le Diches   1265–91

Ran[ulphus] de Lautona quiete clamauit S[ymoni] abbati Cestrie totum ius et clamium suum in terra que vocatur le Diches

809. Grant by W[illiam] de Lawton to abbot S[imon] of all his demesne rights in the watercourse of (Church) Lawton for fishing and making millpools and mills   1265–91

W[illelmus] de Lautona dedit S[ymoni] abbati Cestrie totum dominium quod habuit in aqueductu de Lautona tam ad piscandum quam ad stagna leuanda, et ad terram suam vbique attachianda[m] et molendina et alia approuiamenta ad libitum dicti abbatis facienda, et ad terram capiendam de solo suo quantumcunque et vbicunque ad dicta stagna facienda et reparanda, cum omnibus pertinenciis et eysiamentis, salua sibi et heredibus suis libertate piscandi per totum predictum aqueductum extra stagna manufacta et quod per nullum opus manufactum refluxus aque cooperiat uel deterioret capitale mesuagium suum in Lauton.

810. Quitclaim by W[illiam], son of W[illiam] the chaplain of (Church) Lawton, to William, son of Adam, of Bik and pannage in Lawton Wood.

W[illelmus] filius Willelmi capellani de Lautona dedit Willelmo filio Ade totum ius suum et clamium in Bik et pannagio [2] et agistiamento in bosco de Lautona et in omnibus approuiamentis de dicto bosco prouenientibus, reddendo sibi ii denarios annuos

See No 807 n   The grantee is said to have been a cousin of William (II), lord of a moiety of Lawton (Orm iii ii, 16)

[1] Extended from the heading   [2] paunagio, MS

811. Grant by Roger and Cecilia de Crossley (cf. No. 806) to abbot S[imon] of their moiety of the watercourse of (Church) Lawton and attachment of a millpool to their land, etc. 1265–72.

Rogerus de Crosseleg' et Cecilia vxor eius dederunt S[ymoni] abbati Cestrie totam medietatem suam aqueductus de Lautona et attachiamentum stagni ad terram suam, cuiuscunque voluerint altitudinis et latitudinis, et agistiamentum aque cum situ molendini super dictum aqueductum vbicunque voluerint a diuisis inter terram domini Jacobi de Audithel[ega] et terram suam de Lautona vsque ad Badilford, vna cum aque refluxu, chimino competenti ad dictum molendinum, et terra de suo solo sufficiente capienda ad dictum stagnum faciendum et quociens necesse fuerit ad eius reparacionem capienda, cum omnibus pertinenciis et aysiamentis et mutacione situs eius infra dictas diuisas, cum necesse fuerit.

James de Audley died in 1272.

812. Quitclaim by Ranulf, son of William de Lawton, to abbot S[imon] of all his right, etc., in the watercourse and land between Brereleyeford and Radilegford for the construction of a mill, etc. 1265–91.

Ran[ulphus] filius Willelmi de Lautona quiete clamauit S[ymoni] abbati Cestrie totum ius suum et clamium in aqueductu et terra iacente inter le Brereleg'forde et Radilegforde ad molendina et stagnum, vbicunque melius viderit expedire, construenda, reparanda et situanda et situm mutanda, cum omnibus pertinenciis et aysiamentis, cum terra et turba in solo suo capiendis ad dicti stagni construccionem et reparacionem, et cum libero introitu et exitu in terris suis dicta molendina adire volencium.

813. Grant by Ranulf de Lawton to abbot S[imon] of a butt and two " eyes " in (Church) Lawton. 1265–91.

Ranulphus de L[autona] dedit S[ymoni] abbati Cestrie quandam buttam terre iacentem in campo qui vocatur Barwedis propinquiorem ecclesie, et ii insulas iuxta aqueductum ad inferiorem extremitatem campi de Barwedis.

814. Grant by Richard, son of Adam de Lawton, to abbot S[imon] of his portion of the watercourse of (Church) Lawton to make a millpool and mill. 1265–72.

Ricardus filius Ade de Lautona dedit S[ymoni] abbati Cestrie totam porcionem suam aqueductus de Lauton a diuisis inter terram Jacobi de Audel[egh] et terram de Lauton descendendo usque ad Radilforde, ad stagnum leuandum cuiuscunque uoluerit altitudinis et latitudinis et aquam super terram suam agistiandum quantum uoluerit, et molendinum ubicunque uoluerit infra dictas diuisas faciendum et ad capiendum terram de solo suo in campo qui vocatur le Lym puttes ad dicti stagni faccionem, emendacionem quociens uoluerit, vna cum chimino competenti et omnibus aysiamentis dictis stagno et molendino necessariis. Vnde dictus abbas dedit dicto Ricardo v partes in acrarum et dimidie in assarto quod vocatur le Heye iuxta Stanchues cloht, faciendo inde dicto abbati homagium et seruicium vi denariorum annuorum

815. Grant by Ranulf de Lawton to abbot S[imon] of the heads of 5 butts   1265–91.

R[anulphus] de La[u]tona [1] quiete clamauit S[ymoni] abbati [f 41 Cestrie capita v buttarum extendencium se versus domos dicti abbatis ad fossandum et includendum et [2] nouum fossatum ab aquilone uersus austrum se extendit, cum toto iure et clamio in tota terra infra dictum fossatum inclusa.

816. Ranulf de Grevelands, having received a toft and land from Roger de Crossley and his wife Cecilia (No 806), proffers to his chief lord abbot S[imon] homage, money, service, and right of pre-emption for licence to enter   1265–91.

Quia R[ogerus] de C[rosseleg'] et Cecilia vxor sua dederunt Ranulpho de Greuelondes vnum toftum in villa de Lautona super le Greuelond', et ii acras et dimidiam in campo qui vocatur le Suthleg', dictus Ranulphus concessit sponte domino suo capitali S[ymoni] abbati Cestrie, pro licencia sua dictam terram ingrediendi, homagium et seruicium xii*d* annuorum de dicta terra soluendorum ad festum sancti Johannis Baptiste et ad festum sancti Martini per equales porciones   Et si dicta terra debeat vendi, abbas Cestrie pre aliis habebit eam precio racionabili

817. Grant by Roger de Crossley (cf. No. 822) to abbot Thomas (I) of all the land in Aschinehalch (Halchinhalgh in heading) field in (Church) Lawton which he bought of William, son of William de Lawton (cf No 803)   1249–65.

Rogerus de Crosseleg' dedit T[home] abbati Cestrie totam partem terre sue in campo qui vocatur Aschinehalgh in villa de Lautona quam emit a Willelmo filio W[illelmi] de Lautona

---

[1] Extended from heading   [2] *Sic*   ? ut

818. Grant by Roger de Crossley and his wife Cecilia to abbot S[imon] of an acre in exchange   1265–91

Rogerus de Crosseleg' et C[ecilia] vxor eius dederunt S[ymoni] abbati Cestrie vnam acram terre in quodam campo qui vocatur le Stanclif in escambium vnius acre iacentis in le Snape inter viam et aliam dimidiam acram terre eorum quam dictus abbas eis dedit.

819. Quitclaim by Roger and Cecilia de Crossley to abbot S[imon] of money services of Richard, son of Ranulf de Greuelands, and of (their son?) Robert de Crossley, clerk (No 820)   1265–91

Rogerus de Crossel' et C[ecilia] vxor eius quiete clamauerunt S. abbati Cestrie seruicium viii denariorum quod Ricardus filius Ranulphi de Greuclond' sibi facere tenebatui de medietate de Buthineleg' et seruicium vnius denarii quod Robertus de Crosseleg' clericus sibi facere tenebatur de medietate de Lautonroue, vna cum iure et clamio quod habuerunt in dictis tenementis

820. Quitclaim by Robert de Crossley, clerk (No 819), to abbot S[imon] of a 1d service   1265–91

Robertus de Crossel' clericus quiete clamauit S[ymoni] abbati Cestrie totum ius et clamium suum in seruicio vnius denarii annui quem percipere consueuit de Ricardo Lupo pro quadam placea terre in territorio de Lauton que vocatur Le Roye, cum omnibus pertinenciis

821. Bond by Ranulf, son of William (No 812), and William (Adam, heading), son of Adam, to abbot Roger for 8s yearly in lieu of lodging in Lawton due to him from them   1240–49.

Ranulphus filius Willelmi et Willelmus filius Ade de Lauton obligauerunt se et heredes suos Rogero abbati Cestrie ad soluendum eidem annuatim in festo sancti Andree viii sol pro hostilagiis ab illis sibi in Lauton quondam debitis

822. Quitclaim by Cecilia, widow of Roger de Crossley, to abbot S[imon] of all right, etc, in the lands, etc, given by her husband and herself to him   1265–91.

Cecilia, filia Ranulphi de Lauton, vxor quondam Rogeri de Crosseleg', in pura viduitate quiete clamauit S[ymoni] abbati Cestrie totum ius et clamium suum in omnibus terris et tenementis cum pertinenciis que dictus abbas habuit ex dono predicti quondam viii sui et eiusdem

823. Grant by Roger and Cecilia de Crossley, and Philip, son of Henry (No 802), with the consent of Adam de Lawton, his sons, and other leaseholders, to abbot S[imon] of a certain portion of moor in (Church) Lawton. 1265–91

R[ogerus] de Crossel[eg'] et C[ecilia] vxor eius, et Philippus filius Henrici, cum consensu Ade de Lauton filiorumque eius et aliorum terminariorum dederunt S[ymoni] abbati Cestrie quandam porcionem more iacentem prope ecclesiam de Lauton, continentem in circuitu xlv perticas, ad includendum et fossandum

824. Grant by Philip, son of Henry de Lawton, to abbot S[imon] of land in le Halgh' of (Church) Lawton 1265–91

Philippus filius Henrici de Lauton dedit S[ymoni] abbati Cestrie totam porcionem suam, scilicet sextam-decimam partem cuiusdam campi qui vocatur le Halg' in territorio de Lauton, cum omnibus pertinenciis

825. Grant by Thomas, son of Roger de Crossley, to Adam, son of Adam de Lawton, of his part of Le Brodeleg', paying 1d to the abbot of Chester yearly.[1]

Thomas filius Rogeri de Crossel' dedit Ade filio Ade de Lauton totam partem suam cuiusdam placee terre que vocatur le Brodeleg', scilicet medietatem illius placee que extendit se in longitudine a le Ferfeld usque ad brueram vocatam Threlowenhet, et in latitudine inter altam viam ex vna parte et le Lunteruding ex altera, sicut diuise demonstrant, cum quodam assarto iacente inter venellam ex vna parte et le Stanweyruding ex altera, et in longitudine a le Lunteruding usque ad domos dicti Ade, cum omnibus pertinenciis, reddendo abbati Cestrie annuatim i denarium in festo sancti Martini

826. Grant by Thomas, son of Roger de Crossley, to (his aunt) Matilda, daughter of Ranulf de Lawton (No 806 *n*), of an oxgang in Lawton.

Thomas filius Rogeri de Crossel' dedit Matilde filie Ranulphi de Lauton vnam bouatam terre cum pertinenciis quam Rogerus le Palmer tenuit, cum curtilagio et edificio, exceptis duobus assartis que vocantur Euerardisrudyng et Hawardisruding, et excepta Morwaldis Medue, reddendo abbati Cestrie iid ad festum sancti Martini

[1] The heading is . Carta Ade de Lautona de terra in eadem.

O

827. Grant by Malka (Matilda) de Lawton to W. de Bruera and Henry de Walton of the tenement conveyed in No. 826, and quitclaim thereof to the abbey by Walton.

Malka filia Ranulphi de Lauton dedit magistro W. de Bruera et Henrico de Walton vnum mesuagium cum edificiis superpositis et vnam bouatam terre cum pertinenciis quam Rogerus le Palmer quondam tenuit, faciendo inde capitalibus dominis debita seruicia. Hanc terram Willelmus filius dicte Malke dictis W. et H. quiete clamauit, vt patet in sua carta.   Item hanc terram dictus Henricus de Walton abbati Cestrie, domino capitali, quiete clamauit, vt patet, etc.

828. Grant by Richard de Hancheriche and his wife Matilda to the abbey of 2 selions in the territory of (Church) Lawton.

(38) *d.*]   Ricardus de Hancheriche et Matilda vxor eius dederunt abbati Cestrie ii selliones in territorio de Lauton extensas ab alta via usque ad fossatum dicti abbatis iacentes inter sellionem Thome filii Rogeri de Crosseleg' et domum Henrici de Westona famuli dicti abbatis.

829. Grant by William, son of William the chaplain of Lawton (No. 810), to abbot S[imon] of his share of a heath in (Church) Lawton.   1265–91.

Willelmus filius Willelmi capellani [de Lauton, heading] dedit S[ymoni] abbati Cestrie totam partem suam cuiusdam bruere in Lauton iacentem inter le Merewey et Rodebache in latitudine et inter Salteresbachewalle et fossatum Henrici de le Snape in longitudine, cum omnibus pertinenciis.

For Henry del Snape see No. 800.

830. Grant by W[illiam], son of W[illiam] the chaplain of Lawton, to abbot S[imon] of the lordship of 1½ acres, etc. 1265–91.

W[illelmus] filius Willelmi de Lauton [capellani, heading] dedit S[ymoni] abbati Cestrie dominium vnius acre et dimidie quas Thomas Lupus de se tenuit, et vnum obolum de eadem terra in festo Anunciationis Dominice annuatim percipiendum, et dominium cuiusdam placee iacentis inter domum Philippi filii Henrici et inter Salteresbachewalle, vna cum tribus obolis annui redditus quos predictus Philippus sibi inde reddere consueuit in festo predicto.

831. Quitclaim by W[illiam], son of W[illiam] the chaplain of
Lawton, to abbot S[imon] of all his lands, etc , in (Church)
Lawton for land in Hulse and 5 marks.   1269–91

W[illelmus] filius W[illelmi] [capellani, heading] quiete clamauit
S[ymoni] abbati Cestrie omnes terras suas et tenementa cum
omnibus pertinenciis in villa de Lauton, sine ullo retenemento
Pro hac eciam quieta clamancia, et pro homagio suo et seruicio
vi*d* , dictus abbas dedit eidem Willelmo totam terram quam
Willelmus de Pulford quondam tenuit in villa de Holys cum iii
sellionibus in campis dicte ville iacentibus, et eciam v marcas
premanibus pacatas

The date is shown to be not earlier than 1269 by Pulford's grant
of the land in Hulse to the abbey (No 728)   William de Lawton made
three grants to it in Hulse (Nos 724, 733–4)

832. Agreement between the abbot of Chester and the rector
of Lawton touching the tithes of 7 acres and the mill,
the abbot consenting to pay a ½ mark yearly, despite
his privileges, but reserving them and tithe of all his
approvements

Rector ecclesie de Lauton a peticione decimarum prouenien-
cium de quibusdam vii acris terre et de molendino de Lauton,
quamdiu rector ecclesie predicte fuerit, desistet, et dimidiam
marcam argenti apud Lauton in festo sancti Martini ab abbate
Cestrie annuatim percipiet, priuilegiis dicti abbatis a summis
pontificibus eidem concessis nonobstante (*sic*)   Hanc composicionem in suo robore permanente (*sic*) hoc adiecto quod, si contingat dictum abbatem aliquid approuiatur de vasto in territorio
de Lauton, de hoc dictus abbas plenarie decimabit, ita quod per
istam composicionem nichil iuris ecclesie de Lauton seu futuris
ipsius rectoribus accrescat, uel dicti abbatis priuilegiis (*sic*)
decrescat

833. Grant by Richard, son of Hugh de Spedur', to abbot
Thomas I. of the messuage and land in Saighton which he
had from Orm the chamberlain in free marriage with his
wife Eleanor, niece of Orm   1249–65.

Ormus camerarius de Saligton dedit Ricardo filio Hugonis de
Spedur' in liberum maritagium cum Alienora nepte sua quoddam
mesuagium in Salighton quod Willelmus filius Prime quondam
tenuit, cum le Holeweylond et vi sellionibus in campo de Salighton,
scilicet iii buttas iuxta le Wodewey et iuxta Lonkediche, vnam

sellionem super Caldewelle forlong, duas dimidias selliones iuxta
Caldewelle Diche, vnam sellionem iuxta viam extensam de villa de
Bruera uersus Cestriam, vnam heuedlond cum dimidia sellione
et cum vna parua butta extensa super dictam heue[d] buttam et
duas dimidias selliones extensas de Merich' usque ad . . . nam
viam que ducit uersus Cestriam, reddendo sibi annuatim i*d*. ad
Natiuitatem sancti Johannis Baptiste. Hanc eciam terram dictus
Ricardus dedit Thome primo, abbati Cestrie, cum consensu dicte
Elianore. Hanc eciam Ricardus filius Thome filii dicti Ricardi
quiete clamauit Thome secundo, abbati Cestrie,[1] vt patet in sua
carta.

An Orm the chamberlain is mentioned in a charter of abbot Hugh
as a former holder of land in Moston (*Journ. Chester Arch. Soc.* x. 17);
but as Eleanor's uncle was living after 1249 (No. 834), he was perhaps a
different person.

834. Quitclaim by Orm de Saighton the chamberlain to abbot
T[homas (I.)] of all the land he held of him in Saighton.
1249–65.

Ormus de Salightona camerarius quiete clamauit T[home]
abbati Cestrie totam terram suam cum pertinenciis quam de dicto
abbate tenuit in Salightona.

835. Grant by Richard, son of Ralph de Dunvile, to the abbot
of the land which he held of him in Cheveley in exchange
for half the land of Meyler, son of Osbert de Broughton,
which abbot Roger bought from Meyler in Broughton
(No. 537), and for 5 lands bought of Maurice Little there.

Ricardus filius Radulphi de Dunvile dedit abbati Cestrie totam
terram suam quam de eo tenuit in Cheueleye, cum pertinenciis,
in escambium pro medietate tocius terre Meyleri filii Osberti de
Brocton quam Rogerus abbas Cestrie emit de dicto Meylero in
eadem villa, et pro v landis emptis de Meuric[io] Paruo ibidem,
saluis domui sancte Werburge xii*d*. annuis in festo sancti Martini
de dicta terra in Brocton percipiendis.

For a similar exchange of land in Broughton for land in Cheveley
in abbot Walter's time see No. 538.

836. Bond by Robert de Pulford, kt., and his son Robert to the
abbot not to raise again their claim (No. 501) to land near

[1] 1291–1323.

the garden of Bruera church, between the road to Steward's
Lee (Lea cum Newbold) and the garden

Robertus de Pulford, miles, et Robertus filius eius obligauerunt se fide media et heredes suos sub pena xx marcarum abbati
Cestrie quod nunquam mouebunt nec moueri permittent per se
uel aliquos de suis questionem uel contencionem contra dictum
abbatem de quadam terra que iacet iuxta gardinum ecclesie de
Bruera, inter viam que tendit ad Lee Senescalli et dictum gardinum, vnde contencio prius fuit inter eos, vnde renunciauerunt
omni iuri et clamio suo in dicta terra, subicientes se archidiacono
Cestrie vt per censuram ecclesiasticam ad penam soluendam eos
compellat, si ista conue[ncio] non, etc

837. Settlement of a suit brought by abbot Simon against Hugh
de Hatton touching rights in the heath near Hatton and
Saighton 1281

Shakerley (Vernon) MSS No 4, f 93e, Somerford Park, Congleton,
collated with the shorter copy in the Chartulary

Anno nono Edwardi I. coram Goncelino de Ballesmere iusti-
ciario Cestrie, Willelmo de Venables, Hamone de Mascy, Petro de
Arderne, Radulpho de Vernon, Uriano de Sancto Petro, Willelmo
Lancelin, Philippo de Benuill, Ricardo de Mascy, Hugone de
Pulford, Rogero de Dumvyle, militibus, Johanne de Wettenhall,
Willelmo de Spurstow tunc vicecomite Cestriscire, Willelmo de
Bonebure, Willelmo de Haworthyn, Johanne de Mersynton,
Ricardo de Wybenbure, etc., inter Symonem abbatem et con-
ventum sancte Werburge per brevia nove disseisine tam de libero
tenemento quam de communa pasture super brueram iacentem
iuxta Hatton et Salhton petentes et purparte dicte (*sic*) usque ad
altam viam que ducit de Christleton versus Golburneford,[1] et
insuper communa[m] pasture averiis suis et hominum suorum de
Salhton in tota dicta bruera ex utraque parte ire usque ad fossata
camporum de Hatton vendicantes ex una parte, et Hugonem de
Hatton def[endentem] ex altera, cessavit contencio in hunc modum
quod bruera inter fossata de Salhton et divisas tempore huius
contencionis factas inculta et extra clausuram remaneat imper- [f 42
petuum, ita tamen quod [tam] dicti abbas et conventus [et]
homines sui de Salhton quam dictus Hugo et homines sui de Hatton
habeant et capiant iampnum et brueram in quadam porcione
iacente [2] inter fossata de Salhton et quandam viam sicut mete et

---

¹ -feld, MS   ² iacentem, MS

divise ibidem posite demonstrant, scilicet a divisis inter Waverton et Hatton descendendo usque ad quandam vallem que vocatur Hessedale,[1] insuper etiam habeant communam pasture omnimodis[2] animalibus suis et hominum suorum de Salhton[3] in tota dicta bruera, scilicet inter fossata de Salhton et de Hatton secundum divisas tempore huius contencionis factas, et etiam habeant dicti abbas et conventus et homines sui de Salhton communa[m] pasture animalibus suis in bruera dicti Hugonis ultra Hessedale[4] infra divisas bruere dicti Hugonis et divisas de Golburne versus Golburneford, salvis tamen dicto Hugoni et heredibus suis iampnum et turbariam[5] [sic in MS.] in bruera sua in porcione bruere predicte. In cuius rei etc. irrotulari in Domesday.

838. Quitclaim by Hugh the priest (No. 847), son of Robert de Christleton, to abbot S[imon] of all the land he held of him in Cotton Abbots; further quitclaim by his brother Robert. 1265–91.

Hugo sacerdos, filius Roberti de Cristilton, quiete clamauit S[ymoni] abbati Cestrie totam terram cum omnibus pertinenciis quam de dicto abbate tenuit in villa de Cotes sine ullo retenemento. Hanc terram Robertus filius Roberti de Cristilton, frater dicti Hugonis, quiete clamauit, vt patet in sua carta.

For Cotes see pp. 33 and 231. It is called Great Cotes in No. 839 to distinguish it from Cotton Edmunds.

839. Grant by Adam de Barrow and his wife Alice to abbot Thomas of 3 oxgangs in Cotton Abbots in exchange for the land of Achston which Thomas the brewer formerly held. 1249–65 or 1291–1323.

Adam de Barwe et Alicia vxor eius dederunt Thome abbati Cestrie iii bouatas terre, cum omnibus pertinenciis, in Magna Cotes, in escambio pro tota terra de Achston quam Thomas braciator aliquando tenuit, tenendas de abbate Cestre per homagium et annuum seruicium iiii den. in festo sancti Martini eidem abbati soluendorum. Hoc escambium irrotulatur in Domesday.

840. Agreement between the abbot and Robert de Pulford and others that a waste plot between Cotton Abbots and

---

[1] Heyedale, Ch.   [2] omnimoda, MS.   [3] Salighton, Ch.
[4] Merexedale, Ch.   [5] iampno et turbis, Ch.

Waverton shall remain as before and a dyke raised on it shall be demolished ? 1273–74

Conuenit inter abbatem Cestrie ex vna parte et Robertum de Pulford, R le Chamberleyn, et Robertum de Huntindon, et Robertum de Heminton ex altera, quod quedam placea vasti iacens inter Cotes et Wauerton eodem modo inter dictas partes iaceat quo prius iacuit, et quod fossatum in ea leuatum prosternatur, saluo iure vtriusque partis cum alias inde loqui voluerint. Datum anno regni regis Edwardi ¹ 2°

Ormerod (ii 787) identifies Robert de Pulford with the rector of Coddington of that name who occurs c 1274–88 and perhaps as late as 1315 (ib 855, 857), whom he takes to be a younger son of Robert (II.) de Pulford

From this and the next deed he infers that he was acting as trustee of the Pulfords of Pulford, to whom the Wavertons alienated (part of ?) their holding in the vill which gave them their name

841. Letter ² from William, son of Robert Pigot, to Hugh de Waverton, instructing him to render to abbot T[homas I.] the homage, etc , which he owed him (William) for a tenement in Waverton   Endorsement that Robert de Pulford, clerk, did homage to abbot S[imon] for that tenement. 1249–65

Willelmus filius Roberti Pigot mandauit Hugoni de Wauerton quatinus homagium et seruicium quod sibi et heredibus suis facere debuit de tenemento in Wauerton T[home] abbati Cestrie de cetero faciat   Scribitur in dorso huius litere quod Robertus de Pulford clericus fecit S[ymoni] abbati Cestrie homagium suum de tenemento de Wauerton coram multis ibi nominatis

William, son of Robert Pigot (of Butley), paramount lord of Waverton, d 1287–88 (No 564)   His grant of Hugh's homage, etc , is in No 568

842. Grant by Robert, son of Hugh de Cholmondeley, to the abbey, with his body to be buried there, of 2 oxgangs in Christleton, which he received from his uncle Simon de Christleton, to whom they had been given by the said Hugh, his brother.   Gift confirmed by Robert's brother Richard This land was granted by abbot S[imon] in fee farm to

---

¹ Holes in the MS here
² Litera attornacionis seruicii Hugonis de W , in heading

Robert, son of Hugh the reeve, of Ham Christleton.
? Before 1250.

Symon de Cristilton quiete clamauit Roberto de Chelmundel',
nepoti suo, totam terram quam habuit in Christ', sc. ii bouatas,
cum pertinenciis, quas dominus Hugo de Chelmund', frater dicti
Symonis, sibi dedit.   Hanc terram dictus Robertus dedit abbati
Cestrie cum corpore suo in cimiterio sancti Werburge sepeliendo,
vt patet in sua carta.   Item, hanc terram Ricardus de Chelmundel',
frater dicti Roberti eidem abbati quiete clamauit, vt patet, etc.
Hanc terram S[ymon] abbas Cestrie ad perpetuam firmam tradidit
Roberto filio Ade prepositi de Hamcristilton cum mesuagio et
pertinenciis, reddendo inde annuatim dicto abbati xxs. ad Anun-
ciaciomen beate Marie et ad festum sancti Michaelis per equales
porciones, vt patet, etc.

See Ormerod, ii. 630, 778.

843. Quitclaim by Simon de Cholmondeley (No. 842) to Robert
de Cholmondeley of his right, etc., in 4 oxgangs in Little
Christleton which his brother John had of the gift of Hugh
de Cholmondeley, brother of Simon and John.   ? Before
1250.

Symon de Chelmundel' quiete clamauit Roberto de Chelmundel' totum ius suum et clamium in iiii bouatis terre in Parua
Christleton, quas Johannes de Chelmundel', frater eius habuit ex
dono Hugonis de Chelmund' [fratris] sui et dicti Johannis.

844. Licence by Hugh de Hoole to abbot T[homas I.] to assart
and cultivate all the land between Boughton Field and the
dyke which abbot Roger began to make, and to finish the
dyke.   1249-65.

Hugo de Hole dedit T[home] abbati Cestrie potestatem as-
sartandi et colendi totam terram iacentem inter campum de
Bochton (Bouhton, heading) et fossatum quod abbas Rogerus
incepit facere, et idem fossatum perficiendi, prout melius viderit
expedire, et omne comodum suum ibidem faciendi ; unde dictus
Hugo et heredes sui in dicta terra nichil vendicare poterunt.

The grantor is not mentioned by Ormerod (ii. 812).

845. Acknowledgement and final concord by which Hugh de
Hoole admitted the equal rights of the abbey in the heath
between Newton Field and Hoole within certain bounds,

and granted to it the right of taking 2 cartloads of furze
in the rest of his heath of Hoole   1267–68

Hugo de Hole recognouit et concessit quod totum illud
bruerium iacens inter campum de Neuton et Hole, a quodam
duplici fossato iuxta viam que ducit a Cestria usque ad pontem de
Trofford ex vno latere, et viam que ducit a uilla de Neuton usque
ad eundem pontem ex alio, est et esse debet imperpetuum commune tam abbati Cestrie et hominibus eius de Neuton quam sibi
et hominibus suis de Hole ad capiendum iampnum, et turbas, et
omnia alia aesiamenta habenda, ita tamen quod neutra pars possit
aliquid de dicto bruerio frussare nec turbam vel iampnum vendere
vel dare sine alterius consensu   Dedit insuper dictus Hugo abbati
Cestrie imperpetuum in reliquo bruerio toto suo de Hole libertatem capiendi iampnum ad abbaciam Cestrie quantum ii carecte
cariare poterunt vbicunque dicto abbati placuerit   Saluis dicto
Hugoni et heredibus suis dominio suo [et] racionabilibus approuiamentis que prius habuit et habere potuit, ita tamen quod dictus
abbas dictam libertatem suam non amittat quam ei dictus Hugo
warentizauit. Super hanc autem recognicionem et concessionem
fuit facta finalis concordia in comitatu Cestrie et in Domesday
irrotulata anno regni regis Henrici patris Edwardi lii

846. Agreement between Master Richard Bernard, rector of
Plemstall, and the abbot (Thomas II) by which the demesne
tithes of Hoole, with certain exceptions, were divided
between them in the proportion of 1 2   1297

Anno Domini m°cc° Non' vii°, archidiacono Cestrie presente
et hanc composicionem approbante et confirmante, conuenit inter
abbatem Cestrie et Magistrum Ricardum Bernard, rectorem ecclesie
de Pleymundestowe, videlicet quod dictus abbas de ii bouatis
terre quas Hugo de Hole ad culturam olim redegit in suo dominico,
siue ab eodem Hugone colantur, siue ab aliis, decimas integraliter
percipiet, de tercia bouata ab eodem Hugone ad culturam redacta
dictus Ricardus integraliter percipiet

Item, dictus abbas ii garbas de aliis dominicis dicti Hugonis
percipiet, et eciam de noualibus dominicarum terrarum ipsius
Hugonis quas ipse propriis sumptibus uel laboribus coluerunt (sic),
set si aliqua eius noualia, priusquam ad culturam redigantur,
alicui dimittantur vel ad terminum vel sine temporis prefinicione,
predictus Ricardus inde decimas integraliter percipiet, quamuis ea [f 42
ad dictum Hugonem reuertantur   Et si noualia dicti Hugonis,
postquam per ipsum ad culturam redacta fuerint, aliis dimittantur,
dictus abbas inde ii garbas decimarum percipiet

It would appear that there had been an unrecorded division of the demesne tithes of Hoole between the abbey and the rector of Plemstall, and that later disputes had arisen as to the application of the arrangement to intakes (*noualia*). The present agreement enforced the abbot's claim except where the intakes had not been made by the lord of the manor himself, but by lease-holders.

847. Quitclaim by Hugh the priest (No. 838), son of Robert de Christleton, of 2 oxgangs in Aldford. ? 1265–91.

Hugo sacerdos, filius Roberti de Cristilton, quiete clamauit abbati Cestrie totum ius suum et clamium in ii bouatis terre cum pertinenciis quas de eodem abbate tenuit in Aldeford.

848. Agreement between abbot S[imon] and Robert de Hockenhull and others by which the abbot quitclaimed his right of taking estovers (timber, etc.) in the woods of Huxley for the abbey, his manors of Boughton and Saighton, his tenants, and his fair at Chester, saving his whole lordship of Huxley and of Shotwick, in return for an annual payment of 40s. in addition to 4s. already due for waste in these woods. 1279.

Conuenit inter S[ymonem] abbatem Cestrie ex vna parte et Robertum de Hokenul, et Willelmum filium Hugonis, et Adam filium Ricardi de Hoxeleg' ex altera, videlicet quod dictus abbas quiete clamauit dictis viris totum ius et clamium suum capiendi estoueria sua in boscis de Hoxel' ad abbaciam Cestrie, et ad maneria sua de Bouhton et Sa[light]ona, scilicet et tenentibus suis, et ad nundinas suas Cestrie, tam ad meremium et clausuram ad housbote et haybote, quam ad focalia, saluo dicto abbati dominio suo integro de Hoxel' et de Schotewic cum omnibus pertinenciis. Pro hac quieta clamancia dicti viri obligauerunt se et heredes suos et omnia sua ad soluendum dicto abbati xl.s. annuos, vna cum 4 solidis quos pro vastis in dictis boscis quondam factis prius soluere tenebantur, videlicet ad festum sancti Johannis Baptiste xxs. et ad festum sancti Martini xxiiii sol., pro quibus non dum solutis liceat dicto abbati tam feodum suum de Hoxel' quam de Schotewic vbicunque et modis omnibus quibus uoluerit distringere. Hec conuencio irrotulatur in Domesday. Data anno domini M°CC°LXXIX°.

For the descent of the Huxleys of Huxley from the Hockenhulls of Hockenhull (near Tarvin) see Orm. ii. 314, 797. William de Hockenhull, father of the Robert of this agreement, had a grant of Huxley (not Hockenhull as *ib.* 797) from the abbey by a deed, for which Ormerod

unfortunately gives no reference, in which the rent of 4s mentioned
above was reserved   It is curious that there seems to be no record of
the acquisition of Huxley by the abbey, for Ormerod's identification
with the Hodislcia of the founder's charter (p 16) is, of course, untenable
That was Hoseley, now in Wales (p. 8)   The association of Huxley
with Shotwick in the abbey fee whose court was at Saughall (Orm. i.
286) was due, doubtless, to the fact that the Hockenhulls were their
tenants in both

849. Grant by Sewall de Titherington to William Sampson of
the lordship of 4 oxgangs in Wervin which the ancestors
of William held of Sewall's ancestors in free marriage
c 1246–58

Sewaldus [1] de Tederinton quiete clamauit Willelmo Sampson
dominium iiii bouatarum, cum pertinenciis et wardis et releuiis,
in villa de Wiruin quas antecessores dicti Willelmi de antecess-
soribus dicti Sewaldi in liberum maritagium tenuerunt

Wervin passed to the abbey from old St Werburgh's (p. xx)   The
Titheringtons of Titherington (near Macclesfield) were its tenants here
and chief lords of Netherpool also, in Wirral (Orm iii 698)   Sewall
transferred Titherington to his son Jordan (Nos 852–3) in 1257–58

850. Quitclaim by William Sampson to abbot S[imon] of the
lordship of 2 oxgangs in Wervin which Anable, daughter
of Richard Sampson, held of him   1265–91.

Willelmus Sampson quiete clamauit S[ymoni] abbati Cestrie
dominium ii bouatarum terre in Wyiuin quas Anable filia Ricardi
Sampson de se tenuit, vna cum seiuicio et homagio et aliis pertinenciis inde sibi debitis, et dicte Anable de dictis seruiciis dicto
abbati faciendis literas attornacionis mandauit.

Ormerod (iii 698 n.) carelessly makes Anabel daughter of Richard
de *Titherington*   She was doubtless the wife of Richard Bradwa of
No 853

851. Quitclaim by William de Glest and Marg[aret] his wife to
Jordan de Titherington of their land in Wervin for 20
marks   c 1258–91.

Willelmus de Glest et Marg[areta] vxor eius quiete clamauit
Joidano de Tederinton totam terram suam quam habuerunt in
Wyruin, cum omnibus pertinenciis, pro xx marcis.   Memorandum

---

[1] Sewardus, heading, in error

quod dictus Jordanus habet aliam cartam huius tenoris ad warantum faciendum et quod Marg[areta] personaliter infra bancum vocata coram iusticiario Cestrie concessit hanc donacionem.

852. Grant by Jordan de Titherington to abbot S[imon] of 2 oxgangs in Wervin bought from William and Marg[aret] Glest (No. 851). 1265–91.

Jordanus de Tederinton dedit S[ymoni] abbati Cestrie ii bouatas terre, cum pertinenciis, in Wyrvin, cum mesuag[io], tofto et crofto, quas emit de Willelmo de Glest et Marg[areta] vxore eius, saluo forinseco seruicio.

853. Grant by Jordan de Titherington to abbot S[imon] of the lordship, etc., of 6 oxgangs in Wervin, and order to Walter, son of William, son of Colbert (No. 355), to do the services to the abbot. 1265–91.

Jordanus filius Sewale de Tiderinton dedit S[ymoni] abbati Cestrie dominium, homagium, et omnimoda seruicia sibi debita de ii bouatis terre, cum pertinenciis, quas Ricardus Bradwa et Anable vxor eius tenuerunt in Wyruin, et de iiii bouatis, cum pertinenciis, quas Matilda filia Reginaldi de Pulle tenuit in eadem villa, vnde dictus Jordanus Waltero filio Willelmi filii Colberti de dictis seruiciis dicto abbati faciendis literas attornacionis mandauit.

854. Quitclaim by William, son of Colbert (Nos. 359, 660), to abbot S[imon] of all his right in 4 oxgangs in Wervin which his father once held, and bond to secure the rights transferred from those detaining them. 1265–91.

Willelmus filius Colberti de Vpton quiete clamauit S[ymoni] abbati Cestrie totum ius suum et clamium in iiii bouatis in Wyruin, quas Colbertus, pater suus quondam tenuit, cum omnibus pertinenciis, sine ullo retenemento. Item dictus Willelmus obligauit se et heredes suos, sub pena xx li. fabrice ecclesie sancti Johannis et sancte Werburge soluendarum, ad persequendum et impetrandum dictum ius et clamium a detentoribus eius, vt in sua obligacione patet.

855. Quitclaim by Robert, son of Hugh de Ince (No. 322), to abbot T[homas] of his share in Ince Marsh. 1249–65 or 1292–1323.

Robertus filius Hugonis de Ynes quiete clamauit T[home]

abbati Cestrie quicquid habuit uel habere potuit in marisco de Ynes iacente vltra Smalreod uersus Frodisham et Hellisby, et in terra que est ultra nouum fossatum dicti abbatis subtus Mucle Dich'

856. Grant by Warin de Vernon to the abbey of 4 marks a year from Picton Mill

Warinus de Vernoun dedit abbati Cestrie iiii marcas argenti annuas de molendino de Picton, percipiendas in festo Purificationis sancte Marie, et in festo sancti Petri ad Vincula per equales porciones

The grantor was probably one of the two successive barons of Shipbrook (and lords of Picton) of that name who lived in the first half of the 13th century (Orm iii 252)

857. Grant by Roger Mainwaring to Robert, son of Ernewey, of 2 oxgangs in Crabwall Field (in Blacon) *c* 1200–50

Rogerus Maynwaring dedit Roberto filio Ernewey ii bouatas terre in campo de Crabbewalle iacentes inter viam et dictam villam, cum omnibus pertinenciis, reddendo annuatim sibi et heredibus suis xii den ad festum sancti Johannis Baptiste et ad festum sancti Martini equaliter

Roger de Mainwaring of Warmingham, chief lord of Blacon, was dead before 1252–53 (*Red Bk of Excheq.* (R.S), 1. 184)   Robert, son of Ernewey or Arnewey, occurs in two of the Aston charters, the first of which may be a little earlier than the editor's date (*c* 1200) and the latter is certainly earlier—? *c* 1244 (*Journ Chester Arch Soc* N S x pp 16, 26)

858. Grant by Roger de Mainwaring to Robert, son of Robert Ernewey, of 1 oxgang in Crabwall (in Blacon)   *c* 1200–50.

Rogerus de Maynwaring dedit Roberto filio Roberti filii Ernewey vnam bouatam terre in Crabbewalle, iacentem inter terram quam prius dedit Roberto filio Ernewey patri suo et croftum quod domus hospitalis sancti Johannis Baptiste de se tenuit, reddendo sibi annuatim vnam libram cimini uel iid ad festum sancti Johannis Baptiste

The grantee occurs before 1228 (*Journ. Chester Arch Soc* N S x p 20 , cf. No 390)

859. Grant by Roger de Maynwaring to Robert, son of Robert, son of Ernewey, of a messuage and croft, etc., in Crabwall in exchange for other land. *c.* 1200–50.

Rogerus de Maynwaring dedit Roberto filio Roberti filii Ernewey vnum mesuagium, cum quodam crofto, que iacent iuxta viam tendentem versus Molinton, et vnam sellionem in campo de Crabbewalle, iacentem iuxta mesuagium quod fuit Cordiani, in escambium pro ii buttis in frussuris de Crabbewalle, reddendo sibi annuatim [1] . . . vel vnum denarium in Natiuitate sancti [f. 43 (40).] Johannis Baptiste.

860. Grant by Thomas de Mainwaring to John, son of Robert Ernewey, of 3 oxgangs in Crabwall (in Blacon). 1250–78.

Thomas de Maynwaring dedit Johanni filio Roberti Ernewey iii bouatas terre, cum pertinenciis, in Crabbewalle, quas Robertus filius Ricardi Brun et Philippus filius Suani et Yarridus de se tenuerunt, cum toftis et croftis et mesuagiis, reddendo inde annuatim sibi vnam libram cimini ad Natiuitatem sancti Johannis Baptiste pro omnibus secularibus seruiciis, wardis, releuiis, et sectis curie, et omnibus demandis.

Thomas de Mainwaring, son of the Roger of the last three deeds, and brother of the progenitor of the Mainwarings of Over Peover, occurs in 1252–53 (*Red Bk. of Excheq.* (R.S.), i. 184). The grantee seems to have been the Sir John Arneway, mayor of Chester 1268–76 (Orm. i. 207), in whose mayoralty the Chester plays are said to have been first performed (*ib.* i. 383, 385–6 ; ii. 577). He died in 1278 (*Ann. Cestr.* 106).

861. Grant by Thomas de Mainwaring to John, son of Robert, son of Ernewey, of 3 oxgangs in Crabwall (as in No. 860), etc., saving the service of guarding the ford of the Dee in war time. 1250–78.

Thomas de Maynwaring dedit Johanni filio Roberti filii Ernewey iii bouatas terre in Crabbewalle quas, etc. (as in No. 860 down to mesuagiis), et ii bouatas terre iacentes inter viam et predictam villam, et vnam bouatam iacentem inter terram quam Rogerus pater suus dedit Roberto filio Ernewey et croftum Stephani ; dedit eciam vnum mesuagium, cum quodam crofto, iacens iuxta viam tendentem versus Molinton, et vnam sellionem iacentem iuxta mesuagium quod fuit Cordiani, cum omnibus pertinenciis et libertatibus, et asiamentis, reddendo sibi annuatim vnam libram cimini vel vnum denarium ad Natiuitatem sancti

[1] Corner torn off.

Johannis Baptiste pro omni seculari seruicio, wardis et releuiis, et sectis curie, salua custodia vadi de Dee, prout custodiii consueuit tempore guerre

862. Grant by Roger de Mainwaiing to Robeit, son of Robeit, son of Ernewey, of part of his meadow of Blacon Regrant by Thomas, son of Roger c 1200–50 and 1250–78

Rogerus de Maynwaring dedit Roberto filio Roberti filii Ernewey quandam partem prati sui de Blakene iacentis inter lacum de veteri prato in longitudine et pontem lapideum qui appellatur Wyardesbrugge, et per illas diuisas in latit' a via usque ad pratum domini abbatis sancte Werburge, sicut riuulus diuidit, reddendo sibi annuatim vnam libram piperis vel vid at Natiuitatem sancti Johannis Baptiste pro omni seruicio. Hoc piatum Thomas Maynwaring dedit et confirmauit dicto Johanni (sic), reddendo sibi annuatim xx vnum denarios ad Natiuitatem etc (as above) et ad festum sancti Martini equaliter

863. Grant by John, son of Robert Arnewey, to abbot S[imon], with his body to be buried in the monastery, of the lands in Crabwall and Blacon in which he and his father and grandfather had been enfeoffed by the Mainwarings Confirmation and grant by Thomas Mainwaring 1274–78

Johannes filius Roberti Arnewey dedit sancte Werburge et S[ymoni] abbati Cestrie, cum corpore suo in monasterio dicte virginis sepeliendo, tres bouatas terre in territorio de Crabbewalle, cum toftis et croftis, et mesuagiis, et aliis peitinenciis, quas Robertus filius Ricardi Brun, et Philippus filius Suani, et Yoiuerth quondam tenuerunt, et alias duas bouatas iacentes inter viam et dictam villam, et sextam bouatam iacentem inter terram quam Rogeius de Maynwaiing dedit Roberto Arnewey, patri dicti Johannis et croftum Stephani, cum vno mesuagio et quodam crofto iacentibus inter viam tendentem versus Molinton et terram que fuit Willelmi Beatricis, et vnam sellionem que fuit de bou[ata] Vlfi, iacentem iuxta mesuagium Jordani, et eciam pratum suum in Blakene quod habuit de dono Thome Maynwaiing Hec omnia dedit cum omnibus pertinenciis, sine ullo retenemento, saluis dicto Thome et heiedibus suis xxid annui iedditus de dicto prato, et vna libra cimini annuis de dictis terris in Crabbewalle pro omni seiuicio, excepta custodia vadi de Dee in tempore guerre consueta. Has omnes terras, scilicet medietatem ville de Crabbewalle et dictum pratum de Blakene dictus Thomas Maynwaring Deo et sancte Werburge sine ullo retenemento concessit et confirmauit, et totum dictum redditum imperpetuum quiete clamauit. Salua custodia dicti vadi. Teste G[uncelino] de Badlesmere tunc iusticiario Cestrie.

864. Grant by Robert, son of William Arnewey, to Hamon, son of Guy, of land in Northgate Street.   ? 1208–29.

Robertus filius Willelmi Arnewey dedit Hamoni filio Guydonis, pro homagio et seruicio suo, terram illam que iacet inter terram eiusdem Hamonis et terram Ricardi filii Osgoth' in Norgate strete, reddendo inde annuatim sibi et heredibus suis iis. in Natiuitate sancti Johannis Baptiste et in festo sancti Martini per equales porciones.   Teste Philippo de Orreby.

The father of the grantor was perhaps brother of Robert, son of Arneway (No. 857).   See No. 866.   His own brother Bertram appears in No. 873.   For Hamon, son of Guy, see Nos. 638 and 878.

865. Grant by John, son of Hugh Tardif, to John Arnewey of half his shop in Bridge Street, Chester.   Late 13th century.

Johannes filius Hugonis Tardif dedit Johanni Arnewey totam medietatem suam sue selde in Bruge strete ciuitatis Cestrie que iacet inter seldam lapideam et seldam Roberti le Mercer', que quidem medietas selde iacet propinquior selde lapidee, in longitudine lii pedum et in latitudine x pedum, reddendo annuatim ecclesie sancte Werburge xviii*d.* ad festum sancti Andree Apostoli, et sibi et heredibus suis vnum obolum in Natiuitate sancti Johannis Baptiste.

Hugh Tardif occurs *c.* 1255–69 (*Journ. Chester Arch. Soc.* N.S. x. pp. 25–30) (misspelt Cardi), and his son John, *c.* 1271 (*ib.* 31).

866. Grant by Jordan de Bristol to Robert, son of Robert Arnewey, of land in Crokeslane, Chester.   *c.* 1220–50.

Jordanus de Bristowe dedit Roberto filio Roberti Arnewey quandam partem terre sue in Cestria, habentem in latitudine xiii pedes in fronte uersus vicum de Crokeslone et eadem latitudine, extensam usque ad terram que fuit Ricardi filii Philippi, reddendo sibi annuatim vnum denarium in Nat. sancti Johannis Bapt.

867. Quitclaim by Roger, son of William Hodard, to Robert, son of Robert Ernewey (No. 858), of all the land in Chester which he held of the abbot of Chester.   ? 1213–19.

Rogerus filius Willelmi Hodard quiete clamauit Roberto filio Roberti Ernewey totam terram suam in Cestria quam tenuit de domino abbate Cestrie, iacentem inter terras Petri clerici comitis Cestrie et terras Willelmi filii Ernewey de feodo Thurstani Banastre, reddendo annuatim dicto abbati vi*d.*, et sibi et heredibus suis vnum denarium in festo Apostolorum Petri et Pauli.

The Thurstan Banaster mentioned can hardly be the second of that name in the main line, who died by 1199, and is more probably to be identified with his nephew, baron of Newton (Lancs.) 1213–19, or (less probably) with the second son of this nephew, who received a grant of land in Newton (cum Larton) in Wirral from his elder brother between 1219 and 1241 (Orm. ii. 499, 574, *V.C.H. Lancs.* i. 371).

868. Sale by Ralph, son of Robert Turnebacin, to John Ernewey, of all his land in Northgate Street, Chester. *c.* 1250–78.

Radulphus filius Roberti Turnebacin vendidit Johanni Ernewey totam terram suam in Nortgate strete ciuitatis Cestrie, iacentem inter terram que fuit Willelmi Kenewrec et terram que fuit Roberti de Bristow, reddendo inde annuatim priorisse Monialium Cestrie xvi*d.* ad Natiuitatem sancti Johannis Baptiste et ad Natiuitatem Domini per equales porciones, et sibi et heredibus suis vnum obolum ad festum sancti Johannis Baptiste.

869. Grant by Alice, daughter of Picauoys, and her sister Janne to John Arnewey of land in Northgate Street opposite the abbey. *c.* 1250–78.

Alicia filia Picauoys (filia omitted in heading) et Janne soror [f. 43 sua dederunt Johanni Ernewey quamdam terram suam in Nortgate strete Cestrie ex opposito abbathie, iacentem inter terram que fuit Ricardi Pilate et terram que fuit Johannis de Wigornia, reddendo annuatim heredibus Rogeri le Duc xii*d.* ad festum sancti Johannis Bapt. et ad festum sancti Martini per equales porciones, et sibi et heredibus suis vnum obolum pro omni seruicio, saluo hostilagio dominorum de Thurstanton.

The lodging right of the lords of Thurstaston in the tenement which is reserved here was quitclaimed by the then lord (No. 871).

870. Ratification by Matilda de Coddington, widow, of the sale of land in Northgate Street, Chester, to John Arnewey by her daughters, Cecily and Agnes (No. 871). *c.* 1250–78.

Matilda de Codinton in viduitate sua ratam et gratam habuit donacionem quam Cecilia et Agnes, filie sue et heredes, fecerunt

P

Johanni Ernewey de quadam terra in Norgate strete, iacentem inter terram que fuit Philippi Moule et terram que fuit Roberti Thurstan.

871. Quitclaim by Patrick de Heswall and Agnes (de Thurstaston) his wife to John Arnewey of lodging right and suit of court, etc., from lands bought by Arnewey (Nos. 869–70). *c.* 1250–78.

Patricius de Hasilwelle et Agnes vxor eius quiete clamauerunt Johanni Ernewey hostilagium et sectam curie sue et creanciam xs., et omnia alia que eis competere solebant de terris quas dictus Johannes emit de Alicia filia Picauoys et Johanna sorore sua, et Cecilia filia Roberti de Codinton, et de Agnete sorore sua, in Cestria, reddendo sibi annuatim xviii*d.* ad festum sancti Johannis Bapt. et ad festum sancti Martini per equales porciones.

872. Quitclaim by Hugh de Brickhill and his wife to abbot Thomas (II.) of fishing rights in the Dee at Chester. 1291–1323.

Hugo de Brichulle et Marg[areta] vxor eius quiete clamauerunt Thome abbati Cestrie imperpetuum totum ius et clamium suum quod habuerunt in quadam libertate habendi vnum batellum ad piscandum in aqua de Dee, cum pertinenciis in ciuitate Cestrie, quam asseruerunt aliquando pertinere tenementis que Johannes Arnewey habuit ex dono Ricardi filii Reginaldi Arneys et Willelmi de Winchecumbe in Bruggestrete.

873. Title of a tenement in Bridge Street acquired by John Arnewey from Geoffrey de Tarvin. 1250–78.

Bertramus filius Willelmi Ernewey dedit Magistro Andree de Tawelle totam terram suam iacentem in Brugge strete inter terram que fuit Germani Dubbilday super capud cuiusdam viculi tendentis uersus terram que fuit Ricardi de Pereponte. Reddendo inde annuatim domino Cestrie vii*d.* et obolum ad Longable, et ei et heredibus suis vnum obolum ad Natiuitatem sancti Johannis Bapt. pro omni seruicio. Hanc terram dictus magister Andreas dedit Marg[arete] de Tawelle et heredibus suis de corpore suo matrimonialiter procreatis. Reddendo sibi iii obolos annuos in Nat. S. Joh. Bapt. et vii*d.* ob. ad Longable, vt patet in sua carta. Item, hanc terram Johannes Austyn maritus dicte Marg[arete] cum eius assensu in comitatu Cestrie dedit Galfrido de Taruin, vt patet in sua carta, que irrotulatur in Domesday. Hanc eciam terram dictus Galfridus dedit Johanni Ernewey cum quodam annuo redditu vnius oboli de terra Ranulphi Dubbilday percipiendo, quam de Johanne Austyn et Marg[areta] vxore sua emit, vt patet, etc.

See No. 864 *n*.

874. Grant by Alexander le Beel and Agnes Arnewey, his mother, to Margaret de Stanlow, widow of John Arnewey, of their land longways between a common land-plot of the city of Chester and the rear of the chapel in the lane of Richard Little (?), formerly sheriff. 1278– [See Addenda.]

Alexander le Beel et Agnes Arnewey, mater eius, dederunt Marg[arete] de Stanlowe, quondam vxori Johannis Arnewey, totam terram suam iacentem inter terram que fuit Willelmi Gisehors et terram dicte Marg[arete] in latitudine et longitudine, inter communem placeam terre ciuitatis Cestrie et posteriorem partem capelle in venella Ricardi quondam parui (*sic*) vicecomitis Cestrie, que quidem terra [1] continet in latitudine usque ad predictam capellam xxxviii pedes, et inter ipsam capellam et terram predicti W. Gisehors xxx pedes, cum omnibus pertinenciis, et cum tanta largitate ad portam predicte terre per quam vna carecta possit intrare. Reddendo inde annuatim eis vnum par albarum cirotecarum vel vnum obolum ad Nat. S. Johannis Bapt.

875. Grant by Agnes Arnewey, widow of William le Beel, to Margaret, widow of John Arnewey, of her land on which a chapel was built, with houses and herb-garden (?) etc. 1278–

Agnes Arnewey, quondam vxor Willelmi le Beel, in viduitate sua dedit Marg[arete] de Stanlowe, quondam vxor Johannis Arnewey, totam terram suam super quam capella constructa fuit cum domibus et herbario adiunctis, que quondam fuerunt Alexandri Harre, et cum quodam gardino retro predictam capellam iacente in longitudine inter gardinum quod fuit Willelmi Gisehors et quandam terram dicte Agnetis, et in latitudine inter gardinum quod fuit Ade Godeweyt et capellam dictam, quod quidem gardinum continet in latitudine xl pedes et in longitudine c et xv pedes. Reddendo sibi annuatim vnum par albarum cirotecarum vel vnum obolum ad Nat. S. Johannis Bapt.

876. Grant by Marg[aret], widow of John Arnewey, to S. Werburgh's of the land which she bought from Alexander le Beel and Agnes his mother (Nos. 874–5). 1278–

---

[1] terram, MS.

Marg[areta] quondam vxor Johannis Arnewey in viduitate sua dedit ecclesie sancte Werburge totam illam placeam terre quam emit de Alexandro le Beel et Agnete matre eius, et eciam capellam cum herbario et toto gardino quam emit de dicta Agnete post mortem viri sui. Reddendo inde annuatim duo paria albarum cirotecarum heredibus dictorum Alexandri et Agnetis.

877. Quitclaim by Richard Fitton to abbot Thomas (II.) of all right, etc., in the burgage, with chapel and well, which John Arnewey formerly held in Little Parsons Lane. 1291–1323.

Ricardus Fiton quiete clamauit imperpetuum Thome abbati Cestrie totum ius suum et clamium quod habuit in burgagio illo, cum capella et fonte et ceteris pertinenciis, quod Johannes Arnewey quondam tenuit in vico qui vocatur Petit Personeslone.

878. Grant by John Arnewey to the abbey, with his body to be buried there, of lands and rents in Chester bought from Geoffrey de Tarvin (No. 873), John Tardi[f] (No. 865), Ralph Turnebacyn (No. 868), the daughters of Picavoys (No. 869), etc., rendering the services due to the chief lords. Before 1278.

Johannes filius Roberti Arnewey, ciuis Cestrensis, dedit monachis Cestrie, cum corpore suo in monasterio eorum sepeliendo totam terram suam quam emit de Galfrido de Teruin, et redditum vnius oboli de terra Ranulphi Dubbilday percipiendum, et medietatem suam cuiusdam selde in Brugge strete quam emit de Johanne Tardi, et totam terram in Nortgate strete quam emit de Radulpho filio Roberti Turnebacyn, et quamdam terram suam (41).] quam emit de filiabus Picauoys in Nortgate strete, et quamdam terram suam in Bruggestrete quam emit de abbate Cestrie, iacentem inter terram que fuit Hugonis Cissoris et terram que fuit Thome de Bocthon pelliparii, et duos solidos annuos percipiendos de quadam terra iacente inter terram que fuit Hamonis filii Guydonis de Neuton et terram Ricardi filii Osgot. Omnia hec tenementa, cum omnibus pertinenciis, dedit dictus Johannes monachis Cestrie faciendo dominis capitalibus debita inde seruicia que in cartis superioribus continentur.

879. Delivery by abbot T[homas] (II.) at a perpetual rent to Robert the chamberlain, senior, of land in Bridge Street, Chester, given by John Arnewey. 1291–1323.

T[homas] abbas Cestrie tradidit [1] ad perpetuam firmam
Roberto Camerario, seniori, totam terram in Bruggestrete ciuitatis
Cestrie quam habuit de dono Johannis Arnewey iacentem inter
terram que fuit Ranulphi Dubbilday et venellam que tendit ad
terram que fuit Roberti [2] de Perponte, cum omnibus pertinenciis,
et totam terram suam in fine dicte venelle versus Fratres Car-
melinos, cum omnibus pertinenciis   Reddendo inde annuatim
dicto abbati xxx[ta] solidos ad Nat. sancti Johannis Bapt et ad
Natale Domini per equales porciones, ad quam solucionem integraliter et fi[deli]ter faciendam dictus R obligauit pro se et
heredibus suis tam terras suas quas tenuit in Cristilton quam
terras prenominatas per ministros abbatis Cestrie distringendas

Robert le Chamberleyn attests Chester charters in 1292–93 (*Journ
Chester Arch Soc.* N.S x. pp 48–9).   For the position of the Carmelite
Friary see Morris, *Chester,* p 146

880. Bond by abbot S[imon] and the convent to maintain two
secular chaplains celebrating for ever for the souls of John
Arnewey and his wife, etc , one at the altar of St Leonard
in the abbey church, and the other in the church of
St. Bridget, with music on Mondays, Wednesdays, and
Saturdays, and without music on the other days of the
week   1265–78.

S[ymon] abbas Cestrie et conuentus eiusdem obligauerunt se
et successores suos ad sustentandum sumptibus suis ii capellanos
seculares imperpetuum celebrantes, scilicet vnum in ecclesia sua
conuentuali ad altare sancti Leonardi pro animabus Johannis
Arnewey et Marg[areta] vxoris sue et antecessorum et successorum
suorum et omnium defunctorum, et alium capellanum in ecclesia
sancte Brigide Cestrie de beata Maria, scilicet singulis septimanis
feria secunda, quarta et sabbato cum nota, reliquiis autem diebus
sine nota continue quantum humana fragilitas permittit celebrantes, et vnam lampadem coram predicto altari sancti Leonardi
sicut idem Johannes eam sustentare solebat   Et ad hanc obliga-
cionem conseruandam dicti abbas et conuentus subdiderunt se et
successores suos cohercioni Couentrensis et Lichefeldensis episcopi
et archidiaconi Cestrie vel eorum vices gerentibus [vt per sim-
plicem que]rela[m] [3] maior[i] Cestrie qui pro tempore fuerit
possint eos ad pred[i]c[ta] [obseruanda] [3] compellere   Pro hiis

---

[1] Convencio inter abbatem et Robertum, etc , heading
[2] Ricardi in No 873
[3] Fold in text   Portions in brackets supplied from Harl 2062

imperpetuum sustentandis dictus Johannes dedit dictis abbati, etc., imperpetuum terras suas de Crabbewalle et pratum suum de Blakene, et tenementa sua in Cestria, prout superius in aliis cartis suis continetur (Nos. 863, 878).

881. Grant by Richard Bussel of Penwortham to the abbey of 3 oxgangs in (North) Meols (Lancs., now partly in Southport). *c.* 1150–64.

Ricardus Bussel dedit Deo et sancte Werburge Cestrie iii bouatas terre in Moelis cum hominibus eas tenentibus, solutas ab omni accione.

The editors of the *V.C.H. Lancs.* (iii. 230, cf. i. 335) remark that this gift seems to have been surrendered or repurchased, for in 1311 Thomas de Sutton held the three oxgangs. It is not recorded in the Inquest of Service of 1212 as given in the Testa de Neville.

882. Confirmation by Albert Bussel of Penwortham to the abbey of his father Warin's gift of Rufford (Lancs.) and his brother Richard's of 3 oxgangs in (North) Meols (No. 881). 1164–1193.

Albertus Bussel concessit et confirmauit donacionem antecessorum suorum, scilicet Ruthford de donacione patris sui Warini Bussel, et iii bouatas terre in Moelis, cum hominibus eas tenentibus de dono fratris sui Ricardi Bussel, Deo et sancte Werburge Cestrie, in puram et perpetuam elemosinam.

In the Inquest of Service of 1212 the grant of Rufford is ascribed to *Richard* Bussel (*Lancs. Inqs. and Extents* (Rec. Soc.), i. 32). But the scribe of the chartulary doubtless had the original charter before him.

883. Final concord between abbot [Thomas II.] and William Hesketh by which the former recognised the manor of Rufford to be the inheritance of Matilda, wife of William Hesketh, and Anabil, wife of Edmund de Lea, in return for an increased rent of 40s. yearly (instead of 5s.) and a payment (orig. fine) of £10. No other service (except forinsec). July 1, 1293.

Abbas Cestrie et conuentus recognouerunt et concesserunt manerium de Ruthford', cum pertinenciis, esse ius et hereditatem Matilde vxoris Willelmi de Hesket et Anabilie vxoris Eadmundi de Lega, tenendum sibi et heredibus suis de dictis abbate et conuentu imperpetuum pro seruicio xl solidorum annuatim reddendorum in abbathiam sancte Werburge Cestrie per manus ipsarum Matilde et Anabilie et heredum suorum uel certorum attornatorum suorum sumptibus piopriis et propria missione, ad Nat sancti Johannis Bapt et ad festum sancti Martini per equales porciones, faciendo inde dominis capitalibus debita seruicia ; et ad hec omnia obseruanda subdiderunt dictum manerium districcioni dictorum abbatis et conuentus tam pro dampnis et expensis ibidem leuandis que sustinuerunt occasione arreragii dicti redditus non soluti quam pro ipso redditu   Nec dicti abbas, etc , possint in dicto manerio aliquid clamare nisi seruicium dicti redditus cum pertinenciis.   Hec concordia fuit facta in Curia Regis vbi irrotulatur.

The wives of Hesketh and Lea were daughters of Richard Fitton of Great Harwood, who was enfeoffed in Rufford by the abbey before 1260 (*V C H Lancs* vi 120 , *Lancs Fines* (Rec Soc), i 177)   The rent of 40s was transferred at the Dissolution to the dean and chapter of Chester, to whom it is still paid by the lord of Rufford

In Harl MS. 2062, f. 28, this entry is put into brackets, because a fuller copy of the fine has been entered in a later hand on f 29   The latter is now much rubbed and partly illegible

884. Grant by William de Mesech' to the abbey of a tenement in Dublin, outside the walls of the city near the bridge opposite the church of St Andrew, which Silvester de St. Patrick held

Willelmus de Mesech' dedit ecclesie sancte Werburge Cestrie vnam mansuram integre cum omnibus pertinenciis in Dublinia, extra muros ciuitatis iuxta pontem contra ecclesiam sancti Andree, quam Siluester de sancto Patricio tenuit

885. Licence by Roger, bishop of Coventry and Lichfield, to the abbot of Chester, to construct oratories in his manors in Cheshire in which he may celebrate seivice for himself, his fiee household, without prejudice to the rights of others. 1130–48 or 1245–95

Rogerus Couentrensis et Lichfeldensis episcopus concessit abbati Cestrie vt in maneriis suis in Cestresir' oratoria construere valeat in quibus sibi sueque libere familie sine iuris alieni preiudicio diuina possit celebraii

886. Grant by John de Courci to the abbey, of " Hurmach," with 10 carucates of land within the "thewet" of "Cheuel-

ferna," in order that they may find him from their house
a prior and monks for the construction of an abbey of their
order in the church of St. Patrick at Down[patrick], to be
free of all subjection to their church.   ? 1183.

Johannes de Curci dedit ecclesie sancte Werburge Cestrie
Hurmach, vna cum x carucatis terre infra thewet de Cheuel-
fernam [1] in perpetuam elemosinam, cum omnibus pertinenciis, ea,
scilicet, de causa quod conuentus Cestrie inueniet sibi de domo sua
priorem et ord[inem suum], ad construendam abbaciam sui ordinis
in ecclesia sancti Patricii apud Dun [2] ; [ita quod prefata ecclesia
Dunensis] libera permaneat ab omni subieccione Cestresir' [3]
ecclesie [per decem carucatas] predictas.   Teste Malachia Dunensi
episcopo, etc.

Some illegible words in this entry are restored from Dugdale's copy
made from a Register of St. Werburgh's penes Dec. et Capit. eccl. Cath.
Cestriae, anno 1640 fol. 28a (*Mon.* vi. 1124), *i.e.* Harl. MS. 2062, which
has also been collated.

Dugdale's copy is headed "anno domini MCLXXXIII," but his
account of the foundation ascribes it to 1185.   The former is the date
given by the Irish authorities (Archdall, *Mon. Hib.* 114).   The first
prior was Henry of Hassall (Etleshall), near Sandbach.

887. [4] Grant by William, son of William Lancelyn, to abbot
T[homas] (II.) of homage, etc., from Hatherton (Nantwich
hundred), which Sir John de Orreby formerly held from
him.   1291–1323.

[f. 44 (41) d.]   Willelmus filius Willelmi Lancelyn dedit T[home] abbati
Cestrie homagium et omnimoda seruicia pertinencia de villa de
Hatherton' quam quidem villam dominus Johannes de Orreby
quondam de se tenuit pro seruicio vnius denarii, vt dictus abbas et
successores sui dicta homagium et seruicium et redditum habeant
imperpetuum, cum omnibus pertinenciis, vnde dictus Willelmus
dicto S'. (*sic*) de Orreby,[5] ad dicta seruicia et homagia facienda
literas attornacionis mandauit.

See Orm. iii. 504, 548.

888. Agreement arranged by the priors of Clavercote (? Clattercote, Oxon.) and Winchcombe between the abbot and
convent of Chester and the rector of Stoke, the former to

---

[1] Chenelfernam, MS.   [2] Or Duni.   [3] Cestrensis, Harl. 2062.
[4] No Latin headings rubricated in the text in red after this.   They are
supplied in the margin in black ink.
[5] He is perhaps mentioned in the marginal note, most of which is torn off.

retain all the tithes and ecclesiastical profits of Croughton in the name of their parish church of St Werburgh, Chester, and their chapel of Wervin, and to have the right of admitting to burial in the cemetery of St Werburgh's any dying in Stoke and (Little) Stanney with the Holm, a moiety of Whitby and Croughton, and of taking their mortuaries, etc , the rector to receive, as before, from the abbey 2 marks yearly   Also another similar agreement with regard to the tithes, etc , of Croughton   Pd (incorrectly) in Orm ii 389   ? c 1270–1316

Abbas et conuentus sancte Werburge Cestrie omnes decimas et prouentus ecclesiasticas prouenientes de villa de Crochtona capi * ipsius nomine ecclesie sue sancte Werburge parochialis et capelle sue de Wyrvin [1] imperpetuum retinebunt necnon corpora defunctorum in villis de Stoke et Staney cum le Holm, medietate de Wytebi et villa de Crochton in cimiterio ecclesie sue sancte Werburge Cestrie libere ad sepulturam admittent et mortuaria et oblaciones que offerrentur pro dictis defunctis, sine reclamacione rectoris ecclesie de Stoke et successorum suorum libere percipient imperpetuum.   Dictus uero abbas et successores sui dicto rectori ii marcas argenti imperpetuum annuatim in Nat. S Johannis Bapt. in abbacia Cestrie soluent secundum ante litem motam soluere consueuerunt sub pena xx solidorum dicto rectori soluendorum infra viii dies a termino solucionis predicte simul cum debito principali, dummodo a dicto rectore vel procuratoribus suis dictus abbas super dicta solucione fuerit requisitus   Hec uero composicio iudicialiter fuit declarata et cum sigillis iudicum, videlicet virorum religiosorum prioris de Clauercote et prioris Winchecumbie, necnon domini Rogeri de Schoterleg' patroni ecclesie de Stoke, et eciam dicti rectoris consignata   Item alia composicio inter abbatem Cestrie et quendam rectorem ecclesie de Stoke super percepcione decimarum et prouentuum ecclesiasticarum ville de Crouhton a dicto abbate imperpetuum percipiendorum fuit facta et iudicialiter declarata, vnde rector de Stoke imperpetuum percipiet ii marcas argenti annuas, vt superius dictum est   Priore sancte Fredeswide et cancellario Oxonie, iudicibus domini pape delegatis super hiis ex[eque]ntibus et dictam composicionem suis sigillis vna cum sigillo dicti rectoris roborantibus

* This proves to be a misreading of " et campo "
[1] Partly illegible, and an attempt seems to have been made to correct to Wytebi, but it was clearly Wyrvin in Ormerod's time, and Harl MS 2062 has Wirvin

Little is known of the Soterley family (no doubt from Sotterley, co. Suffolk, a manor of the earls of Chester, the demesne tithes of which were given to the abbey (No. 487)), who were patrons of Stoke church. Edmund de Soterleghe held a knight's fee in Cheshire in 1252–53 (*Red Book of the Exchequer* (R.S.), i. 184). Roger de Soterley, probably the signatory of the above document, was lord of Arrow in Wirral under the barons of Mold in 1277–78 (Orm. ii. 526), and had been succeeded by an Edmund de Soterley before October 1316 (*ib.* ii. 388).

889. Decision of Master S[imon de Baliden (No. 78)], official of the bishop of Coventry, that all the tithes of assarts, etc., in the demesne of Poynton, except from one assart, belonged to the parish church of Prestbury, and imposing silence thereon upon Alan, the chaplain ministering in Poynton Chapel. (Similar judgement by the official of the archdeacon against John Malyns, another chaplain of Poynton.) 1276.

Anno Domini M°CC°LXX°VI° Magister S[ymon] Couentrensis et Lychfeldensis episcopi officialis sentencialiter adiudicauit quod omnes decime, tam maiores quam minores tam personales quam prediales, de omnibus assartis et frussuris in terris dominicis ville de Poninton' factis, habitatoribusque in eisdem, prouenientibus, preterquam de vno assarto quod [Henricus] [1] de Worth [quondam excoli fecit in] [1] le Hope, ecclesie parochiali de Prestebur' pertineant imperpetuum, Alano capellano in capella de [Pon]inton' ministranti super percepcione earum imperpetuum imponens silencium.

Sciendum est quod idem capellanus in dicta capella ministrans qui vocabatur Johannes Malyn quasdam decimas de noualibus et assartis de nouo ad culturam redactis in territorio manerii de Poninton prouenientibus asportauit qui eas ecclesie de Prestebur' per iudicium magistri Roberti de Frodesham officialis domini Archidiaconi Cestrie restituere compellebatur, et ne de cetero aliquas decimas in noualibus dicti manerii uel eorum habitatoribus vendicaret uel aliquis ipsius successor exigeret, predictus officialis eis silencium perpetuum imposuit.[1]

This document refutes Ormerod's suggestion (iii. 684 *n.*) that Poynton Chapel was founded in 1312, soon after abbot Thomas had established his right to its advowson before Robert de Holland, justice of Chester. It was unknown also to Earwaker (*East Cheshire*, ii. 282). Robert de Frodsham was probably the vicar of Frodsham who occurs 1276–1301 (Orm. ii. 48).

[1] Illegible. Supplied from Harl. MS. 2062.
[2] The hand which begins with No. 3 (p. 15) ends here.

890. Settlement of disputes between Henry de Lacy, earl of
Lincoln, and the abbot and convent of Chester, arising in
their respective manors of Castle Donington and Weston
(with Shardlow and Wilne), separated by the river Trent,
the earl conceding to the abbot, etc , one-third of the profits
of his ferry at the Bargeford between Derbyshire and
Leicestershire, with access for their men, etc , from the ford
and Castle Donington to the Leicester high road, and free
passage for their grass and hay to and over Langholm ford
(or the nearest possible, if that becomes too deep), rendering
for such passage 12*d* yearly , also the right to save their
meadows and pastures in Weston, etc , not yet penetrated
by the flow of the river, saving to the earl his demesne
rights and fisheries in the waters of the Trent , the abbot,
etc , conceding to the earl a contribution of one-third of the
cost of repairing and rebuilding the boat and barge at the
Bargeford, free landing there for his men, etc , and free
access for them through their land in Wilne to the high road
to Derby   February 17, 1309

Cum mote essent contenciones inter dominum Henricum de
Lacy comitem Lincolnie in quibusdam locis et placeis terre, prati
et vasti ipsius comitis in Casteldonigton' ex vna parte aque de
Trente infra comitatum Leycestrie et dominum Thomam abbatem
[et] conuentum abbatie sancte Werburge Cestrie de quibusdam
aliis locis et placeis terre et vasti ipsorum abbatis, etc , in manerio
de Weston' et hamelettis de Schardelowe et de Wilne, ex altera
parte aque de Trente in comitatu Derbeie, Tandem decimo vii die
Februarii anno gracie Domini M°CCC°IX° contenciones predicte
vtrique conquieuerunt in forma subscripta, videlicet quod predictus comes concessit pro se et heredibus suis quod predicti
abbas et conuentus et eorum successores de cetero percipiant et
habeant terciam partem proficui prouenientis de baigea et batello
ipsorum comitis et heredum suorum facientibus passagium vltra
aquam de Trente vsque ad comitatum Derbeie, et similiter facientibus passagium de comitatu Derbeie vsque ad comitatum Leycestrie iuxta vadum quod vocatur le Bargeford', et similiter predictus comes concessit pro se, etc , quod predicti abbas, etc , de
cetero habeant viam competentem cariandi herbam et fenum
suum de quadam placea prati ipsorum abbatis, etc , que vocatur
le Steure per pratum et pasturam ipsius comitis quod vocatur
Langholm cum equis et carectis et plaustris vsque ad quoddam
vadum quod vocatur Langholm Ford' vltra aquam de Trente
vsque ad maneria et hameletta ipsorum abbatis, etc . in com

Derbeie, et si vadum illud temporibus futuris tam profundum deuenerit quod herbam et fena sua de predicta placea prati per vadum illud cariare non poterunt, predictus comes pro se, etc., concessit quod predicti abbas, etc., habeant· viam competentem cariandi herbam et fena sua de predicta placea prati que vocatur le Steure vsque ad aliud vadum propinquum et congruum adiacens prato domini [comitis], etc., vltra aquam de Trente predictam, si tale vadum inueniatur ; pro qua via habenda dicti abbas, etc., reddent dicto comiti, etc., xii*d*. annuatim apud Casteldonyngton ad festum Natiuitatis beati Johannis Bapt. inperpetuum.   Con-

[f. 45 (42).] cessit eciam predictus comes pro se, etc., quod predicti abbas, etc. de cetero pacifice et sine impedimento aliquo possint saluare et defendere terras, prata, et pasturas suas de manerio suo de Weston' et hamelettis de Schardelowe, Wylne et Aston' per cursus aque de Trente non penetrata die confeccionis huius scripti in predictis manerio, etc., saluis tamen dictis comiti, etc., dominiis suis in aquis de Trente et in piscariis suis vbique in predictis aquis, sicut ipse et antecessores sui habere consueuerunt ante confeccionem huius scripti.   Et similiter concessit dictus comes pro se, etc., quod homines, animalia et alia bona per batellos et bargeas predictos transeuncia aquam de Trente predictam apud le Bargeford et infra terram et feodum ipsorum comitis, etc., apud le Bargeford et subtus le Bargeford in Casteldonigton' applicancia habebunt viam sufficientem vsque ad altam viam que ducit apud Leycestriam et homines, animalia et alia bona predictam aquam de Trente per batellos et bargeas predictos transeuncia et in Casteldonigton' applicancia sine dampno quantum in ipsis est conseruabuntur.   Et pro suprascriptis concessionibus concesserunt prefati abbas et conuentus pro se et successoribus suis quod ipsi inperpetuum inuenient terciam partem sumptuum omnium et misarum ad predictos batellum et bargeam de nouo construendos et reparandos quocienscunque necesse fuerit, et quod batelli et bargee illi possint applicare super terram et feodum ipsorum abbatis, etc., et tenencium suorum in Wilne vltra aquam de Trente apud le Bargeford' et subtus le Bargeford' sine contradiccione vel impedimento aliquo, . et similiter inuenient viam competentem omnibus transeuntibus cum animalibus et aliis bonis vltra predictam aquam de Trente et infra terram et feodum ipsorum abbatis, etc., in Wilne subtus le Bargeford' applicantibus vsque ad altam viam que ducit del Bargeford' vsque Derbeiam vbique infra terras et feodum ipsorum abbatis, etc., et tenencium suorum in Wilne, et homines, animalia et alia bona predictam aquam de Trente per batellum et bargeam predictos transeuncia et in Wilne applicancia indempnes conseruabunt, quantum in ipsis est   Et in omnium suprascriptorum testimonium parti huius scripti cirographati penes predictum comitem remanenti sigillum capituli sancte Werburge Cestrie, et similiter sigillum predicti abbatis sunt apposita, et alteri parti penes predictos abbatem et conuentum sancte Werburge Cestrie remanenti sigillum dicti comitis est appositum [1]

For the lands of the abbey in Weston-upon-Trent, etc , see No 128 ff.

891. Recovery by abbot Simon in the county court of Chester of the homage, wards, reliefs, etc , of Hugh de Raby, lord of Raby   November 20, 1268

Comita[t]u Cestrie tento die sancti Edmundi regis anno regni regis Henrici patris domini Edwardi [quinquagesimo] tercio per iudicium Curie abbas Symon et conuentus Cestrie recuperauerunt homagium, wardas, releuia, et aliquem [2] redditum xiii , cum aliis consuetudinibus, etc , de Hugone de Raby, domino de Raby, vnde placitum erat inter eos ibidem ad tunc motam [3]

The abbey originally held Raby in demesne (No 351), but at some unrecorded date enfeoffed a family which took the local name   Ormerod does not mention the Hugh of the present entry, who may perhaps have been father of the Robert de Raby who occurs c 1302–1349 and held the office of gardener of Chester Castle in fee and the serjeanty of the Bridge Gate (Orm 1 356, ii 547–8, Stewart-Brown, *Chesh Chamberlains' Accounts* (Rec Soc), 59, pp 6, etc)

892. Incomplete copy of the same *inspeximus* as that (also imperfect) in No 2 *supra,* giving the salutation clause in full, inserting "Dei gracia" after "Henricus" and "et Aquitanie" after "Normannie," and ending with "Ranulphus comes"

893. Final concord in the county court of Chester between abbot Simon and Ranulf, son and heir of Peter de Thornton, by which Peter, in consideration of a payment of 5 marks, agreed for himself and his heirs to make, repair, and maintain the bridge and causeway at Fulford on the high road from Chester to Ince   August 29, 1284

From the Chartulary, collated with the copy in the Shakerley (Vernon) MSS. No 4, f 94a (V) at Somerford Park, Congleton.

---

[1] This document is in a different hand from what precedes, and in darker ink In Harl MS 2062 it is in the same hand as the latter half of the MS.
[2] Rubbed and doubtful   Only a word or two are legible in Harl MS 2062, f 29
[3] In a different hand from that of No 890

Hec est finalis concordia facta in pleno comitatu Cestrie die Decollationis sancti Johannis Baptiste anno regni regis Edwardi filii regis Henrici duodecimo, coram domino Reginaldo de Grey tunc iusticiario Cestrie, dominis Johanne de Grey, Petro de Ardena, Warino de Maingarin, Johanne Boydell', Ricardo de Stokport, [Ricardo] [1] de Mascy, Hugone de Pulford, Rogero de Domvill', militibus, Roberto Grosso venatore tunc vicecomite Cestrie et aliis fidelibus domini regis tunc ibidem presentibus.   Inter Simonem abbatem sancte Werburge Cestrie petentem et Ranulphum filium et heredem Petri de Thornton defendentem faccionem refaccionem et sustentacionem pontis et calcete [2] in alta via que ducit de Cestria usque Ines,[3] in loco qui vocatur Fulford', unde placitum fuit inter eos in eodem comitatu, scilicet quod predictus Ranulphus pro se et heredibus suis recognouit se et heredes suos ad faccionem, refaccionem et sustentacionem dictorum pontis et calcete [2] imperpetuum teneri.   Ita quod homines pedites et equites, plaustra, bige, et omnia que transitu ibidem indigent libere et sine impedimento transire valeant, et ipsum abbatem et successores suos pro faccione, reparacione, et sustentacione dictorum pontis et calcete quietos clamauit imperpetuum.   Pro hac autem recognicione idem abbas dedit predicto Ranulpho quinque marcas.   Et irrotulata est hec finalis concordia de consensu parcium in rotulo qui vocatur Domesday.[4]

A copy of this document has been entered in a 16th-century hand, perhaps that of Henry Birkenhead (above, pp. xxix, xxxi), on the *verso* of the same folio (*i.e.* 45 (42) *d*).   Below it in the same hand is the sentence : "All that is in this bok of the pope of Rome is clerely abjegate and extincte."

Mr. Fergusson Irvine informs me that Mr. Slater of Ince thinks that Fulford (*i.e.* foul ford) Bridge was what is now called Cryers Bridge, over the Thornton Brook on the boundary of Elton and Thornton.   In some maps it is called Thornton Bridge.   Mr. Slater also states that two fields in Ince on either side of the main road to Chester are still called Portway Heys (cf. p. 205 above).

[1] Supplied from V.   [2] calcee, V.
[3] Yns, V.   [4] 892–3 in another hand.

APPENDIX

894. Verdict of a jury in the county court of Chester that the
abbots of Chester were bound by ancient usage to find a
clerk in the exchequer of Chester at their own expense
November 13, 1257

Harl MS 2071, f 46 (old 32) *d*

Placita comitatus Cestrie die Martis proximo post festum
sancti Martini anno xlij° Henrici tertii. De tempore Rogeii de
Montealto iusticiario.

M^d quod die Martis proximo post festum sancti Martini anno
regni regis Henrici xlij° facta fuit inquisicio per subscriptos utrum
abbas Cestrie et antecessores sui consueuerunt et debent inuenire
quendam clericum idoneum super custum suum proprium ad
scaccarium Cestrie · scilicet per dominos Thomam de Crue et
Willelmum de Mascy, Radulfum de Wetenhale, Ranulfum de
Ruston, Robertum de Pulle, Robertum de Moldesworth, Robertum
de Bulkelegh, Willelmum de Brey, Adam de Kelsale, Mattheum
de Holegraue, Willelmum de Lostock, Willelmum de Bonebury et
Hamonem de Brett, qui dicunt super sacramentum suum quod
sciunt et uiderunt quendam clericum, Adam de Christleton
nomine, Robertum de Thurstaneston, Galfridum clericum et
Johannem de Willelegh, clericos abbatum Cestrie, exstantes [1]
ad scaccarium Cestrie ad iirotulandum et certificandum factum
camerarii Cestrie et hoc super custum dictorum abbatum. Dicunt
etiam quod dicti abbates [2] talem clericum de iure tenentur
inuenire.

[1] exantes, MS   [2] dictum abbatem, MS

INDEX I · PERSONS AND PLACES

The names of towns and townships are given in their modern forms As the value of the older forms in the text for their interpretation varies according as they occur in original charters, in the chartulary (c 1310) or in 17th century transcripts, direct reference to the printed document is in such cases necessary The same caution applies to field names, which, however, are here given in the forms of the text, their modern forms being often unknown

Abbey, Anketill of the, 210 , Guy of the, 336 , Hugh his br , 336
Abbots *See* Chester, Combermere, Dieulacres, Haughmond, Pulton, Radmore, St Evroult, Stanlaw
Acard, 19
Achston, 454
Acke, Geoff s of, 96
Acton, 137, 285-6
Adam, justice of Chester, iv, 234
——, Rob s of, 441
Adderley, Amicia de, 179 , Wm , 179
Aete, Wm de, 144
Agnes, Wm s of, 371
Aguillen, Rob , 144
Aigle (Aquila), Rich de l', 71, 235 , Rog s of Rich , 71
Aistun, Ad de, 315 , Hen , 315
Alan, Master, 338 *See* Tawell
——, Ralph s of, 158 , Wm s of, 245
Albini, Hugh de *See* Arundel
Albo Monasterio (Oswestry ?), Rog de, 373 , Sim , 373, and *see* Chester, abbots of , Wm , 373
Aldford, 3, 394, 458
——, Ad de, 319 , Rog , 319
——, Gilb de Ardeine, rector of, 369, 371 (?)
Aldhelm, 11
Alexander, tutor of earl Ranulf III *See* Ralph, Alex s of
——, Thos s of, 265
Alota, Sim s of, 441
Alpraham, 227-8
——, Matt de, 227-8, 230
Alrichesholm *See* Holm House

Alvanley, 267, 394 , Ichincote, Huchenescote, in, 4, 391, 394
Amundeville, Wm de, 235
Andesacre, W de, 131
Andrew, canon, 94, 336
——, chaplain, 79
——, Wm s of, 49 , Wilym s of, 372
Anglesey, 17, 21, 30, 55, 57
Anglicus *See* English
Anketil, Geva d of, 275 , Leuka d of, 274
Anschetill, Ivo s of, 235
Anselm *See* Canterbury
Aichei, Agnes d of Rob le, 184 , Rob le, 186
Arderne (Arden), Agn de, 97 , Gilb , 369 , Sir John, 229, 264, 394 , Sir Pet , (xxx), 205, 264, 296, 324-5, 329, 394, 423, 425, 431, 433, 453, 478 , Thos , 369-70 , Thos (of Ratley), 369 , Sir Walkelin, (xxix), 82, 369, 400, 409, 412
Ardreshill, Rob de, 338
Ardulph, Sim s of, 167
Arneway, Agn , (xxxvi), 347, 467-8 , Bertram s of Wm , 466 , Sir John, 7, 340, 462-70, Marg , 467-468 , Rob , 461, 463 , Rob s of Rob , 461-5 , Rob s of Wm , 464 , Wm , 465
Arneys, Rich s of Reg , 466
Arrecio, Norman de, 19, 56
Arrow (Wirral), 283, 474
Arundel, Hugh, earl of, 138 , Wm. earl of, 143

Ascchetil, 336

Ashton (by Tarvin), 19, 33, 56

Astbury, 6, 7, 20, 36, 61, 127, 217-22, 252-3, 271, 309
——, Alex., rector of, 419 ; Ran. his br., 419 ; Master John de Stanlegh, rector of, 427 ; Rich., clerk of, 419

Astle (in Chelford), 5, 319-24
——, John de, 323, 328, 428

Aston (by Sutton), 163. See Middleton Grange

Aston upon Trent, 6, 17, 30, 55, 87, 110, 116, 136-7, 142 ff., 145-70, 174, 181, 194, 231, 252, 476
—— Field names, etc. : Blodi londes, 158 ; Bortefoxoles, 158 ; Cokeswell, 151 ; Crombehalfacres, 157 ; Dunclavestr', 152 ; Flinticlif, 157 ; Forkedemere, 151 ; Foxoles, 155 ; Galowoe, Altam, 151, Litel, 151, Long, 163 ; Gillemedewe, 152 ; Gostineslondes, 157 ; le Grene, 158 ; Harneford, 153 ; le Heed, 162 ; Heyethurne, 151 ; Hipelmereholm, Ylemereholm, 151, 158 ; Horsfeld, 157 ; Hundeland, 155 ; Lonedui, 157 ; Longerudinck, 162, 168 ; Mewinesflatt, 152 ; Middesforlong, 151 ; Middilfeld, 163 ; Mordicheforlong, 153 ; Mordichesende, 162, 168 ; Mordicheswall, 151 ; Pastineslondes, Curtes, 153, Long, 153 ; Redeput, 157, 188-9 ; Snechedoles, 157 ; Teterside, 153 ; Thornberlin, 157 ; Thornleiesiche, 151 ; Wadesute Thorn, 157 ; Waringores, 160, 162 ; Wittinmere, 158
——, Roger the cementer of, 194
——, Roger the chaplain of, 157 (?), 158-9, 165
——, Alan s. of Alan de, 155 ; Arnold, 147, 152-4, 158-9 ; Emma his wid., 154, 159 ; Gilb., 175 ; Hugh s. of Rich., clk., 159 ; John, clk., s. of Rog., 162, 168 ; Ralph s. of Hen., 170 ; Rich., 159, 175 ; Rich. s. of Gilb., 186 ; Rose wid. of Thos., 430 ; Sara wife of Rich., 159 ; Thos. s. of Arnold, 159, 165 ; Wm. s. of Ralph, 171

Aubrey, Rob. s. of Rob., 244

Audlem, Thos. de, (xxxi)

Audley (Aldithelega, Aldidele), Clemence de, 184 ; Hen., 80, 106, 338 ;

Hen. (II.), 431 ; Hugh. just. of Chester, 379 ; Jas., just. of Chester, 322, 413, 446-7 ; Wm., 184, 187

Aula, Wm. de, 314

Austerson, 285

Austyn, John, 466-7 ; Marg., 466-7

Aylward, Alan s. of, 350

Azo, 280

Bache, la, 40, 43, 51, 58, 274-5, 352, 357
—— pool, (xxxiv)
——, John de, 268

Backford, 3, 8, 59, 67, 118, 368-71
—— Cross, (xxxiv), 285
——, Ad. s. of Agn. de, 355

Badington, 285

Badlesmere, Sir Guncelin de, just. of Chester, xxxi, 25, 85, 89, 196, 205-8, 375-7, 403, 428, 453, 464

Baguley, Sir Wm. de, 90, 324, 329

Baiunville, Fulk de, 19, 56

Bakepuz, Ralph de, 144

Baldric, Billeheld wife of, 19, 34, 56

Baldwin, monk, 17, 55

Baliden, Sim. de, 119, 128, 130, 474

Balliol, Jocelin de, 83

Bamville, Agn. de, 387 ; Alex., 90, 207, 296, 425, 427 ; Sir Phil., (xxxii), 205, 207, 387, 453 ; Thos., 387

Banastre (Banaste), Rich., 18, 50, 55, 57-8 ; Rob., 58-9, 217 ; Thurstan, 70, 73 ; Thurstan, 465 ; Warin, 58

Bangor, bps. of : Guy, 278 ; Hervey, 17, 22, 55
——, debts, etc. of the abbey in dioc. of, 7

Barbe d'Avril, Ralph, 80 ; Wm., xlviii

Bardulf, Hamelin de, (xxx), 95 ; Kath., 95 ; Rob., 95 ; Wm., 187

Barnshaw (in Goostrey), 4, 7, 231, 417 (chap.), 418-22, 428-30
——, Rog. de, 322, 324, 401, 403, 411, 413-15, 417, 423-5, 428-31 ; Rob. 401 ; Rob. s. of Rog., 430
—— Field names, etc.: Sercroft, 419 ; Syddenale, 419

Barnston, 19, 34, 56, 275-6, 282-3
——, Gilb. de, (xxxii), 275 ; Hugh, 296, 368 ; Ralph, 361-3

Baro, Waleran de, 21, 57

Barre, Alice, 350

Barrow, xviii, 4, 9, 12, 313
——, Ad. de, 454 ; Alice, 454

Barthomley, 44
——, Thos (de Praers) de, 91, 365, 376
Barton, Patr de, 296, 314
Basingwerk abbey, (xxxiii), xxvii, 30, 44, 232 n, 292, 294-6
—— ——, Hugh, abbot of, 294-6
Basset, Phil, 144, Rob, 78
Batail, Andr, 313
Batecok (Badok, Badek), Sim s of, 425-6
Bath and Wells, Rob Burnell, bp of, 89, 90, 99, 100, 213, 222-3
Beatricis, Willelmus, 463
Bebington, 4, 8, 20, 35, 41, 56, 58, 127-128, 137, 282, 337, 376-82
——, Nether, 4, 35, 214, 388
——, Rob de, 379
—— Field names, etc le Bruche, (xxxv), 381, domus Leprosorum, (xxxv), 126, 381, le Lym Put, 381, Pulton Mulnewey, (xxxv), 381
Bech' (Beth'), despenser, 75
Bechene (co Flint), 305
Beck, lady Mabel de, 280
Beel, Agn le, 467-8, Alex, (xxxvi), 467-8, Wm, 467
Beleton, Hawise de, 175, Rich, 175
Benedict, Nich s of, 237
Benfre (?), Rich, 401
Benton, Rob de, 125
Berlei, Rich s of, 58 (bis)
Bernard, J, 314, Rich, 304, 408, 412, 420, Mast Rich, 457, Wm, 90, 205, 208, 318, Agnes w of, 248
Berneres, Wm de, 19
Bertram the chamberlain, xlv, 74, 80
Beton, Rich s of, 188-9
Beurell See Burel
Bidston, (xxxiv), 4, 8, 375
Bigod, Barthw le, 144, Rog, 22, 24
Birches (nr Lostock Gralam), 398
——, Wm de, 398
Birkenhead priory, 336
——, Hen, xxix, xxxi, 139, 478, Rich, xxix
Birtles (Birchel, Burchells), 330
——, Hen de, 322, 324-5, 421, 428, John, 322, 421, 437 (?), Thos See Chester, abbots of (Thomas II)
Bistre (co Flint), Bissopestred, 17, 31, 55
Blacon, 3, 20, 36, 57, 461-3, 470, —— ford, 463, Wyardsbrugge in, 463

Blay (Bloy), Alice, 258, 349, 372-5, Alina, 344, 348, 372, Amaria, 344, 348, Gilb, 258, 344-5, 372
Blayne, Gilb de, 19, 56
Blobbe, Wm, 405
Bloy See Blay
Blund, Alice, 277, Master John, 121, John, 277, Walt, 189
Blundel, Rob, 193-4, Rob s of Rob, 194
Bochard, Walter, 244, Hugh s of Walt, 244
" Bochtunestan," 18, 33, 55
Bodfari (Butavari), 41, 45, 58, Alfred, chief lord of, 41, 45
Bolingbroke (Lincs), court of, 177
Bollin, riv, 330, 333
Bolour, Wm le, 239
Bolton, Thos de, just of Chester, (xxx), v, 84, 219, 396-7
Bonetable, Felicia, 425-7, Hen, 425-7, Rich, (xxxvi), 322, 324, 397, 403-4, 411, 413-14, 420, 423, 425-8, Wm, 420
Booths, 5
——, Ad de, 322, Thos, 322
Bor, Rich s of Rob le, 434
Bordesley, abbey of, 139
Bordland See West Kirby
Bordon See Burdon
Boscherville (Buschervile), Rob de, 232
Bosco, de See Wood
Bostock, Hugh de, 404, Wm, 404
Boston, John de, 121
Boughton, xix, 2, 16, 54, 110, 119, 223-4, 231, 456, 458
——, lepers of, 96, 211
——, Hugh de, 341, Thos, 468
Boydell (de Bosco Ale (Bois d'Elle)), Alan de, 74, 92-3, 122, Heute, 91-2, 128, 335, 337, Hugh, 74-5, 92, Idonea, 91-2, Sir John, 93, 220, 222, 279, 316, 478, Wm, 82, 92-3, 122, 315, Sir Wm, (xxxi), 279, 307, 412
Boydin, Agn, 163, 166, 168
Bradford (in Shurlach), 41, 45, 57
Bradley (in Frodsham), 370
Bradshaw, Henry, author of Lyfe of St Werburgh, x, xv, xxii f
Bradwa, Anable, 460, Rich, 460
Brai, W de, 131
Braose, Wm de, 362
Bras, Rob, 249, 273
Brayn, Rich, 442
Breaston (co Derby), 190-94
——, Ismay d of Beatrice de, 191
Bredon, Wm s of Ralph de, 193

Brereton, 219 *n.*
——, Ralph de, 311 ; Sir Wm., 219, 221-2, 426
Brescy, Rich. de, 107 ; Rob., (xxxi), 207, 427
Bretby (co. Derby), 59, 67
Brett, Hamon de (? le), 479
Brewer (Bruer), Rich., 435 ; Wm., 143
Brexen. *See* Broxton
Brey, Wm. de, 479
Briceio, Rich. de, 20
Brickhill, Hugh de, 276, 466 ; Marg., 466
Brid, Hugh, 241
Bristol (Bristowe), Jord. de, 464 ; Rob., 465
Bromborough, xxvii, 4, 8, 113-15, 129-131, 133-5, 212, 214-15, 232-3, 236, 259, 344, 376, 378, 381, 388-390
—— Field names, etc. : le Chirche-croft, 389 ; Manislawe feld, 389 ; Ranesfeld, (xxxv), 388 ; the Seeches, (xxxv); Suchacresendes, 389
——, John, clerk of, 388
——, Agn. d. of Reginald de, 389 ; Alan (Alcok) s. of Reginald, 389-90 ; Andr. s. of Dandi, 389 ; Hen., 371 ; Hen. s. of Raven, 389 ; John, 389; Raven (Raban) s. of Raven, 389 ; Rob. s. of John, 388 ; Wm., 340 ; Wm. s. of Reginald, 389
Bromhall (in Wrenbury par.), 20, 35, 56, 282, 285
Broughton (co. Flint), 3, 6, 19, 34, 56, 110, 305, 308, 452
Broun, Brown. *See* Brun
Broxton (Brexen), Wm. de, 207, 296
Bruera, (xviii), (xxxii), 3, 110, 112, 115, 118-19, 131, 133, 252, 287-8, 307, 453
——, Wm. de, 314 ; Master Wm., 345, 450
Brun, Arnewey le, 330 ; Cecilia, 311, 431 ; Pet. s. of, 184 ; Reg., (xxxiv), 311, 413, 431 ; Rich., 350 ; Rob. s. of, 184 ; Rob., 310, 314, 455 ; Rob. (Barnshaw), 420-21, 431 ; Rob. s. of Rich. (Crabwall), 462-3 ; R. (Bruen Stapleford), (xxxiv); Serlo, 330 ; Thos. s. of Reg., 311, 413, 431
Brunston, Rich. de, 351
Buchard, Ralph s. of, 336
Buglawton, 122-3, 444
Buildwas, Ralph, abbot of, 196

Bulkeley, Rob. de, 304, 479 ; Wm., 207, 229
Bullock, Wm., 373
Bunbury, Humphr. (I.), 269 ; Humphr. (II.), (xxxi), 269 *n.* ; Wm., (xxx), 205, 208, 296, 314, 318, 423, 425, 453, 479
Burcy, Nigel de, 19, 33, 56 ; Garacin, 19, 56 ; Ranulf, 19
Burdon, Wm., 190-91, 193
Burel, Ranulf (de), 20, 41, 45, 57-8, 236
Burgh, Marg., d. of Thos., 347 ; Sara, 347
Burmingham, Marg., 314 ; Wm., 314
Burnell, Isabel de, 222-5 ; Sir Phil., 222-5 ; Phil., 223 ; Rob. *See* Bath and Wells ; Wm., 223
Burwardsley, xix, 16, 28, 54, 246, 251
Bussel, Albert, 470 ; Rich., 470 ; Warin, 470
Butler. *See* Richard, Thomas, William
Butley, 319, 330
—— Field names, etc. : Heyebirches, 332-3 ; Nouthercuese, 333
——, Wm. de, 330
Buxeria, Geoff. de, 74
Byley, 406

Cademon, Matilda d. of Rich. s. of Hugh, 346 ; Reg., 159
Cadwalader, rex Nortwaliarum, 59, 65
Caldecote, Sim. de, 394
Caldy, Great, 19, 34, 61, 283, 294-5
——, Little, 283
——, Hundred of, 297-8
Caletot (Kaletoft), Ivo de, 106
Calke, Rob., prior of, 232
Calveley, Rich. de, 420
Camera, Osbert de, 120
Campden, Chipping, 5, 17, 31, 55, 110, 138-9, 140, 237, 282 ; Combe in, 139
——, Peter, rector of, 140 ; R. de Stainsby, rector of, 139 ; Stephen, rector of, 138
——, Patrick de, 166-7
Candelan, Thos., 255
Canterbury, archbishops of : Anselm, xxiii-v, 15, 17, 22-4, 31, 38, 54-5, 57 ; Baldwin, 335 ; Hubert, 237 ; John, 133 ; Lanfranc, 64 ; Theobald, 39, 61, 65-6, 75, 129 ; Richard, 121, 126-7 ; Stephen, 118
Cantilupe, Wm. de, 143
Capenhurst, 3, 208, 368
——, Amauria de, 368 ; Thos., 368 ; Wm. s. of Rich., 368

Carlisle, Alice de, 241 , John, 241
Case, Thos , 62 n
Castle, Hugh s of Rob de, 313 ,
Rob , 313
Castle Donington See Donington
Catchpoll, Andr , 282
Catel, John, 373
Cattenhall (in Kingsley), 4 , chapel of,
94, 337-8
Caughall, 207
Cepmondswich (in Over Peover), 312
Chaldel (Chaundell), Nigel, 49, 59
Chamber See Camera
Chamberlain, Alice wid of John le,
351 , John s of Rob , 348 ,
R , 455 , Rob , 469 , Thos
s of Rob , 274, 344, 346-8 ,
Thos s of Thos , 347
Chancellor, Pet , 147 , Rog , 146-8,
153, 184 See Chester
Chaumpvent, Pet de, 89
Cheadle, Sir Geoff de, 84, 90, 329
Chel, Haagne (Hagene) de, 59, 95
Chelford, 5, 87, 319-28 , chapel of,
321
—— Field names, etc Crakemers,
326 , Leylache, 327 , Longe-
fordecroft, 321 , Merecloh, 327 ,
Puttes, 326
Chellaston (co Derby), 157
——, Hugh s of Rob de, 165
Chelleia, Thos de, 367
Cheshire, avownies of, 103, 108
——, barons of, 18, 31-2, 42, 55, 67,
69 ff , 101 ff , courts of, 102-3 ,
privileges in earl's court, 103-4 ,
forest rights, 104, 106 , judicial
duties of their men, 104 , military service of, 103-5 , natives
of, 103, 105 , retainers of, 103 ,
limitation of numbers and entertainment of earl's serjeants at
their request, 104-5 , stewards
of, 104, 108 ; wills of, to be
executed, 105 , widows and
heirs of, 105 , petitions of,
refused, 106 , undertenants of,
protected, 106
——, Domesday Book of See Index
II
—— Field system See Index II
——, the lord of, 91, 324, 341, 347, 383,
393
——, " Magna Carta " of, 6, 101-9
——, sheriffs of
Richard (Rich de Pierrepont or
Rich son of Liulf), 338 (?),
367, 409 (?)

Cheshire, sheriffs of—contd
Wybunbury, Rich (I) de, (xxxiv),
82 (1233), 401, 408-9 (1244),
420
Bernard, Rich (c 1247-8), 412
Clerk, Steph (1263), (xxxii)
Huxley, Rob de, 444 (1265-6 or
1275-6)
Puleston (Peulesdon), Jordan de,
322 (1267), 413
Wilbraham, Rich de, 318 (1270-
1271), 349, 397 (1269-70), 402-3
(1270-71)
Hatton, Hugh de (c 1271-74), 328,
404, 411, 414, 432-3 (1274)
Massey, Sir Rich de, 207 (1278)
Hawarden, Wm de, 205 (1279)
Spurstow, Wm de, 329, 415, 453
(1281)
Grosvenor, Rob le, 296 (1286-7),
311, 325, 394, 425 (1287), 431,
478 (1284)
Praers, Wm de, 316, 415 (1287-91)
Egerton, John (? Philip) de, 430
(? 1294-6)
Brescy, Rob de, 427 (1305)
Fouleshurst, Rich de, 229 (1310-
1311), 379 (1313)
Chester, archdeacons of Rob , 336 ,
Ad de Staunford, 433 , Wulmar (?), 56 , official of See
Tawell
bishops of, 70 See Coventry
official of See Baliden
S " Wilfricus," bp, of, xv
burgesses of, 17
castle, 81 , constables of Nich de
Willilegh, 408-9 (1244) , Hen
de Torbock (1245-9), 400, 412 ,
R de Pulford, (xxxii), Rob de
Stockport, 413 (1266-7) , Rob
de Huxley, 324, 328, 397 (1269-
1270), 404 (1271-5), 432-3
(1274), 435 (1270-71)
chamberlains of, xlv-vi, 48, 299, 479
Orreby, Rich de (1263), (xxxii) ,
Brickhill, Wm de, 435 (1270-71)
chancellor of Geoffrey, xlvii n ,
Simon Diggons, (xxix) See
Peter the Earl's Clerk
" chancery " of, xlvii-ix
charters to city of, 13, 477-9
constables of William I (fitz
Nigel), (xvii), xx, xxv, xlvi,
18-19, 20, 22, 28, 34, 40, 42-4,
50, 55-8, 233-4 , William II ,
233-5 , Eustace fitz John,
232 , John (de Lacy), 214 ,

Chester, constables of—*contd.*
 Roger (de Lacy), 74, 201-2, 216,
  338. *See* Lacy
 baronial claim of, 102-3
 countesses of : Bertrade (Bertrude),
  74, 80, 332 (?) ; Clemence,
  332 (?) ; Ermentrude, xxiv,
  16-19, 21, 54-7, 75, 140 ; Lucy,
  58, Matilda, 78, 80-81
 dispensarii, (xvii). *See* Bech', Geoffrey, Henry, Hugh, Robert, and
  Thomas
 earls of, iii-iv :
  Hugh I., xxiii-v, 15 ff., 38, 47,
   54-8, 60, 75, 83, 110, 141-2, 217,
   224, 367, 380
  Hugh II., xlviii, 73-4, 77-9, 82,
   95, 231, 236, 279-80, 291, 313,
   328
  John, 81, 96, 299
  Ranulf I., (xvii), xxvi, 46ff., 58-60,
   83
  Ranulf II., (xvii), (xxix-xxx), xi,
   xxvi-viii, xlv, xlvii, xlix, 30,
   36 *n.*, 52-73, 76, 95, 122-3,
   139-40 *n.*, 215, 232-3, 235, 247,
   280-81, 286, 295
  Ranulf III., xlvi-viii, 30, 72, 74,
   80, 83, 96, 102 ff., 138, 149, 201,
   211, 216, 236, 247, 251, 267,
   281, 295, 338, 477
  Roger brother of, 74
  Ranulf (doubtful), 149
  Richard, xxv-vi, 21, 23, 39 ff.,
   57-8, 60-61, 83

         2nd Line
  Edward, 82, 90, 230, 375
 early history of, xiv-xvii
 exchequer of, 479
 honour of, xliv
 illuminator of, Master Augustus,
  210
 justices of (xxxii), xliv, 52, 70, 81, 84-
  85, 90, 97, 196, 200, 202, 205, 208,
  212, 219, 229, 234, 294, 303.
  See pp. iv-vi and the names of
  individual justices in the Index
 mayors of, 273, 469
 official of, Master Alan de Tawell,
  200, 202, 367
 palatinate of, xliv ff. ; law of the,
  32 *n.*
 parishes of, 300
 portmoot of, 239, 341, 353
 sheriffs of (city), xlix, 48, 53, 59 (?),
  70, 211, 467 (Rich. Little)
  Rich., 338, 409 (? error for Cheshire)

Chester—*contd.*
 tithes of, 137
 topography : churches :
  St. Bridget, 469
  St. John, xvi-xvii, 7, 300-301, 460
   Andrew and Philip, canons of,
    94, 336
  St. Martin Ash, 210
  St. Mary of the Castle, xxvii, 1,
   6, 59, 252-3, 286
  St. Nicholas, (xix)
  St. Nicholas (chap.), 210
  St. Olave, 41, 45, 57
  St. Oswald, (xviii), 114, 117-19,
   131, 133-5
  St. Peter, xv, 6, 252-3, 288-90
   rectors : Alex., 289 ; Walter, 345
  " St. Peter and Paul," xv-xviii
  St. Thomas the Martyr (chap.),
   132, 274
  Holy Trinity, (xxxvi), 342
  St. Werburgh, xv-xxii, 113-14,
   118, 299-301, 352, 460 ; canons
   of, xv-xxii ; gifts of earl Leofric
   to, xix ; Ulminus, canon of,
   xxii. *See* Abbey of St. Wer-
   burgh below
  Chapel in Venel of Richard Little,
   467-8
 topography : gates, streets, religious
  houses, etc. :
  Bagge Lane, 213, 348-50
  Battlecroft, 374
  Bernelone, 347
  Blackfriars, (xix), (xxxii), 7, 210,
   301
   Hen., prior of, 199
  Bridge, 41, 70, 91 ; — gate, 477 *n.* ;
   — street, 276-7, 341, 464, 466,
   468
  A burgage with chapel, well, etc.,
   468
  Carmelite Friary, 469
  Castle Lane, 166, 256
  Piece of City land, 467
  Clippe Gate, 49
  Crofts, The, 346-8
  Crokeslone, 464
  Cuppings (Copines) Lane, 210
  Ditch, The, 213
  Eastgate, 277 ; —— street, 340
  Fles(h)monger Lane, 243-4, 276,
   279, 342
  Flookersbrook (Flokersbroc), 253-
   254, 357
  Fulchard's Lane, 277-8
  Hospital of St. John, 7, 273, 299-
   300, 346, 348, 350, 461

Chester, topography · gates, etc —
  contd
  Ir[o]nmonger Street, 273
  Kingseye meadow, 48, 61
  (Dee) Mills, 41, 55
  Le Leure (? L'Oeuvre), 59
  Leper Hospital (Boughton), 96,
    211
  Lonewalthon, 346
  Market-place, 41, 49, 251
  Nicholas Street, 302 *n*
  Northgate Street, 16, 55, 213,
    237 ff , 267-9, 344, 357, 464-6
  Parson's Lane, 119, 242, 255, 344-5
  Petit, 468
  Pepper Street, 339
  Portpool (?), 352
  " Redcliff," 19, 34
  Roodeye (?), 369
  St Mary's Nunnery, 7, 301,
    465
  Stone Bridge (?), 352
  St Werburgh Street, 343
  Trinity Street, 342
  Venella Ricardi Parvi, 467
  Wall, The, 226, 344-6
  Walleforlong, 350 , Welle —, 357
  Wulfad's Gate, 339
Chester, Abbey of St Werburgh —
  abbots of . Geoff , 125, 133, 142,
    163 (?), 167, 177, 209, 210
    (Rich , clerk of), 242, 250 ,
    Hugh, (xviii), 106, 132, 137,
    145-7, 158-9, 164, 169, 174-6,
    185, 201, 203, 243, 249, 251-2,
    309, 346, 367 , Ralph, xvii, 70,
    73, 88, 247 , Rich , xxii, xxiv-v,
    38, 234, 247 *n* , 287 , Rob I or
    II , 74, 114, 120 , Rob II or
    III , 196 , Rob I , II , or III ,
    214, 252, 282, 286 , Rob III ,
    109, 124, 138, 179, 196, 214,
    246, 368 , Rog , 88, 147, 149-
    150, 159, 170, 175, 189, 198,
    245, 259, 276, 279, 283, 286,
    308, 357, 361, 384-5, 400, 409,
    411-12, 448, 452, 456 , Sim ,
    (xxxi), 88, 90, 165-70, 172-3,
    176, 178-83, 190-94, 196, 218,
    222, 241, 257, 270, 311, 314,
    321-5, 327, 329, 339-51, 357-62,
    364-6, 373-6, 385, 387-400, 402-7,
    410, 413-15, 422-3, 426, 428,
    431-7, 439-42, 444-51, 453-6,
    458-60, 463, 469, 477-8 , Thos
    I , (xxxii), 163-4, 172 (?), 175,
    250, 279, 303, 307, 317, 346, 358,
    361-3, 397 , Thos II, 8, 97,

Chester, Abbey of St Werburgh,
  abbots of—*contd*
    180 (?), 183, 185 (?), 219-22, 225,
    227-9, 248, 276, 316, 339 (?),
    341-3, 352, 363, 365, 368, 371-2,
    377-9, 387, 394, 397, 405, 417,
    427, 429-30, 466, 468-9, 470,
    474-7 , Thos I or II , 160, 162,
    172-3, 180, 185, 345, 375, 388,
    454, 460 , Walt , 88, 133, 145,
    150-52, 169, 176, 179-80, 184-5,
    188-90, 219, 259, 308-9, 419,
    437 , Will I , xxvi, 93 , Will
    II , 183, 249, 275, 351, 353-4
  their houses in the earl's manors,
    247
  economy of almonry, 131 f , 260-
    271 , altar of St Leonard, 469 ,
    altar of St Mary, 251, 259, 278-
    279 , ancient alms, 70-71, 91 , re-
    lations with bishops, 110, 115 ,
    bridge penny, 70, 91 , build-
    ings, (xviii), xxviii, 16, 47, 72,
    260, 274-5, 281-3, 285 *See*
    Fabric , burial in, 47, 92, 111,
    113, 272, 277, 336, 456, 468, 473 ,
    chamber, 249, 259, 339 , chan-
    try, 251-2 , chapel of St
    Nicholas, (xviii), charities, 237-
    250, 259 , charters, (xvii), (xxx),
    xxviii ff , 53-67 , conduit, 225-6 ,
    clerk in exchequer, 479 , master
    cook's fee, 353-6 , court, 21, 23,
    39, 42, 48-9, 53, 67, 74, 246, 357,
    440, 443, 459 , daughter priory
    of Downpatrick, 472 , fabric,
    277, 460 , master of fabric, 277 ,
    fair, 21, 23, 47, 53, 57, 59, 68-9,
    201, 251-2, 458 , ferry rights,
    475-7 , privileges in earl's forests,
    88, 90 , foundation, xxiii-v ,
    garden, 212, 242 , houses in
    earl's manors, 247 , income,
    xxviii , infirmary, 122 , free
    trade with kingdom of Isles, 211 ,
    kitchen, 257-9, 271 , monks,
    names of Andrew s of Wm ,
    59 , Baldwin, 17, 55 , Bernard,
    xxv *n* , Hen Bradshaw, x ,
    Eustace, 18 , Guy de Main-
    waring, 41, 57 , Hugh (sub-
    prior), 367 , Heldebald, 18 ,
    Ran Higden, ix , Leofnoth, 73 ,
    Leofwine, 73 , Rich de Cruce,
    48 , Sim de Rhuddlan, 48 ,
    Sweyn de Wettenhall, 48 ,
    William, xxv *n* , Wm le
    Palmer, 73 , number of monks,

Chester, Abbey of St. Werburgh, economy of—*contd.*
  xxviii, 259 ; Orreby's postern, 338 ; pannage in Cheshire and Englefield, 86, 338 ; prebends of old St. Werburgh's absorbed, xxii, xxiv, 29, 234-5 ; precentor, 250 ; refectory, 254-6 ; registers, xxx-v, 32 ; sacrist, 259 ; tenth salmon, 41, 43, 70, 91 ; salt, 215-16 ; serfs. See *Nativi* in Index II. ; the sprice, 225 *n.* ; demesne tithes, 17, 31, 55, 77, 137, 282-4 ; tithe of mills, 76, 91, 96 ; freedom from toll in Shropshire, 73 ; royal rights on vacancy of the abbacy, 87 ; wardrobe, 252-4 ; losses in Wales, 30, 45, 127, 278 ; in Barons' War, 213
——, Philip de, clerk, 205
——, Rich. de, clerk, 265
——, Master Hugh de, (xix), 125, 202 ? *See* Hugh and Young
——. *See* Leiacestria
Chetwynd, Ad. de, 208
Cheveley, xviii f., 2, 9, 16, 54, 62, 81, 110, 223-4, 230, 309, 452. *See* Edwards
Chevelferna, thewet of, 472
Chew, Agn., 252 ; Wm., 252
Childer Thornton, 97-9
Chipping Campden. *See* Campden
Cholmondeley, Hugh de, 244, 408, 410, 456 ; John, 456 ; Rich., 456 ; Rob., 408, 410, 456 ; Sim., 456 (*see* Christleton)
Chorlton (Cherliston, Churlston), 3, 208-9, 368-71, 381, 393
——, Ellis de (Venator), 257, 353-6 ; John s. of Ellis, 353-4
Christleton, 3, 18, 33, 55, 110, 225-6, 252-3, 271, 348, 453, 456, 469 ; Abbots Well in, 225
——, Ham, 456 ; Rob. s. of Ad., reeve of, 456
——, Ad. de (clk.), 479; Hugh the priest s. of Rob., 454, 458 ; Rob. s. of Ad., 226 ; Rob. s. of Rob., 454 ; Sim., 456 ; Wm. s. of Rob., 226
Churchenheath. *See* Bruera
Clare, Gilb. s. of Rich. de, (xix)
——, Rog., earl of, 140-41, 280
—— ——, Adeliz (of Chester) mother of, 140
—— ——, Adeliz (de Clermont) grandmother of, 140-41

Clattercote (MS. Clavercote), priory of (co. Oxon), 473
Clayton (co Flint), 18, 32, 44, 55
Clech, Godwin, 217
Clerk, Rich., (xxxiv), 340, 358-9, 362, 467 (?) ; Rich. s. of Rich., 359 ; Steph., (xxxii) ; Thos., 225, 329 ; Wm., 358 ; Wm., mayor of Chester, 273
Clifford, Rog. de, 84
Clifton, xx, 5, 16, 54, 214
——, Geoff. de, 412
Clotton, 19, 34, 56, 282
Cnoctirum. *See* Noctorum
Coddington, 3, 19, 56, 110, 252, 307
——, Master Hugh de Chester, rector of, 125
——, Agn. de, 465-6 ; Cecilia, 465-6 ; Matilda, 465 ; Rob., 466
Cokeswall, John de, 148, 150 ; Rog., 148, 150
Col, Wimund de, 20, 56
Colbert. *See* Upton
Coleshill (co. Flint), 17, 31, 55, 110
Collan, Amaria, 344 ; Rob., 344
Columbe, Hugh de, 107
Combe. *See* Campden and Cumbe
Combermere, abbey of, 285
——, John, abbot of, 196
Conan, 291
Cook. *See* Robert, Geoffrey s. of
Copston, Rog. s. of Rog. de, 258
Corbia, Ralph, 303
Corbin, 40, 44
Cordian, 462
Cornwall, Reginald, earl of, 233
Corona, Hugh de, (xxxi)
Cosin, Hamon, 356, 358
Costentin, Humphr. de, 19, 56
Coterel, Brice, 313
Cotes, Hugh (clerk), 413
Cotton Abbots (Ordrichescotes, Cotes), 3, 18, 55, 110, 231, 454-5
——, Hugh de, 396, 404 ; John, 407
Coudray, Benedict de, 319, 322 ; Hen., 322 ; Matilda, 257 ; Matildis, 280 ; Rich. (rector of West Kirby), (xxxiii), 199, 200, 304, 317, 401, 408-10, 431 ; Rich. (son-in-law of Geoff. the Cook), 257, 353-4 ; Rob., 106, 280, 338
Courcy, John de, 472
Coventry (and Lichfield), bishops of : Alex., 119, 136-7 ; Geoff., 122, 136, 300 ; Hugh I., 124-5, 286 ; Hugh II., (xvii), 286 ; Rich., 120, 126, 215, 286, 309, 325, 337 ; Rob., 38 ; Rog. I., 94 ; Rog. II.,

(xvii) , Rog III , 119, 130, 135,
332 , Rog (doubtful), 117, 127,
131, 253, 286, 471 , Walt , 129,
232-3 , Wm , 118, 129, 131-4,
309, 332
Coventry, priors of Geoff , 132-3, 135 ,
Thos , 134 , Wm , 134, 136
——, Rich de, 178 , Walt , 106, 178
Crabwall (in Blacon), 3, 374, 461-3, 470
Craket, Alex , 404
Cranage (Craunache, Craulache), (xxxv-
xxxvi), 4-5, 400, 402-7, 418, 429
—— Field names, etc Bradeclif,
407 , Crewe Wood, 416 , Elif,
416 , Ermitage, 400, 405 , le
Leyes, 405 , Netherwode, 405 ,
Overwode, 405 , Rudheath mine,
401-3, 407 , Saxeruding, 416 ,
Saxirudingsclow, 416 , Serle-
croft, 402 , Stanilands, 402-3 ,
Witesiche, 406 See Hermitage
——, Ad , clerk of, 405, 423 , Brun de,
409 , Felice, 405-6 , Hen (c
1210), 416 , Hen , 311, 315, 327,
401, 403, 405-6, 411, 414, 425-8,
431 , Randle, 327 , Reg (le
Brun), 311, 413 , Rich , 311,
315, 324, 403-6, 411, 414, 425-8,
430-31 , Thos , 401, 405, 430 ,
Wm , 400, 412
Crew (in Farndon), 3, 18, 33, 56, 110
——, Thos de, 479
Crist', Wm , 79
Cromwell, Ralph de, 179
Crossley, Cecilia, 444-9 , Rob , 448 ,
Rog , 443-9 , Thos , 449-50
Croughton, xx, 16, 54, 110, 473
Crowther, Alice d of Alan le, 187
Croxton, Liulf de, 327 See Twemlow ,
Rich , 403, 407, 416, 419 , Rich
(1271), 423 , Rob , 322, 401-4 ,
Wann, 322, 327, 401-2, 405,
410 11, 414, 415 (?), 419, Wann
br of Rich , 415 (?), 423 , Wm ,
200
—— family, 311
Cruce, Norman de, 48 , Rich , 48, 58
Cumbe See Campden
——, Amicia de, 169 , Thos , 169
Cumbray, Albric (?) de, 94 , Alfred, 20,
69, 94 (?), 122-4, 246, 291 ,
Basilea, 122-3 , John, 124 ,
Rich , 291 , Rog , 123, 246
Curtis, Rich , 146, 157
Cutler See William

Darvil, Rob de, 80, 107 , Walt , 80,
106, 338

Dalam, Rich de, 130
Dane, riv , 332, 415-16
Daniell, Pet , 223
Danne, Hen de, 437
Daresbury, 137
——, Marg de, 339 , Ran , 339
Davenham, Ran de, 103
Davenport, Rog de, 324, 328, 401,
403, 418, 420, 426, 428 , Vivian,
319
David, Pain s of, 210
—— the miller, 341
Dedishay, John, 417
Dee, riv , 17, 110, 463, 466
——, service of guarding Blacon ford
on, 463
Delamere, forest of, 89, 91, 94
Denford (Northants), (xix), 5, 17, 31,
55, 110, 116, 140-42, 252, 373,
425
——, Rog de Albo Monasterio, rector
of, 373
——, Thos , rector of, 142
Derby, 6, 142, 147, 149, 165-6, 476
—— (Froger), archdeacon of, 233
——, Hugh s of Phil de (? Philip
s of Hugh See Abbreviatio
Placitorum, 95 b), 175 n ,
Rugeram (rect Ingeram) le
Dubler, 165 , Steph , 427 , Wm ,
174
Derwent, riv , 189
Despenser See Bech', Geoffrey, Henry,
Hugh, Robert, Thomas
Dieulacres, abbey of, 284, 332
——, W[illiam], abbot of, 416
Dodleston, 122, 243 n
Dom, Thos , 182
Domvile (Dounevill, Dumvile), Ad de,
302 , H de, 265 , Sir Rog de,
(xxxii), 196, 205, 207, 296, 329,
361, 379 (1313), 415, 453, 478.
See Dunvile
Done, 394
——, Rich de, 246, 435
—— fam , 393
Donington, Castle (co Leic), 8, 214,
475-6
—— Field names, etc le Bargeford,
475 , Langholm, 475 , Lang-
holmford, 475 , le Steure, 475-
476
——, Master John de, 199, 200
Doubleday (Dubbilday), German, 466 ,
Ran , 467-8
Downes, Rob de, 322
Downpatrick (Dun), priory of, 472
—— Hassall, Hen de, prior of, 472

Draycote, Rich. de, just. of Chester, (xxix), v, 190
Dublin, 471 ; church of St. Andrew in, 471
Duc, Thurstan le, 356-7. *See* Leduc and Thurstan
Duck, John le, 343 ; Rog., 343
Dugdale, Sir Wm., 15, 25
Duncan, Wm. s. of, 59, 70-71
Dune, Rob. de, 169
Duning, Wm. s. of, 59
——— ———, 210 (*c.* 1200)
Dunvile, Ralph de, 452 ; Rich., 452. *See* Domville
Durham, Antony Bek, bp. of, 89, 213
———, Hugh de, 208
Dutton, 282, 284
———, Ad. de, 315, 408 ; Geoff., 199, 200 ; Hugh (t. Hen. II.), 77, 94 ; Hugh (*c.* 1200), 315, 408 ; Sir Hugh (*c.* 1230), 257 ; Sir Hugh (1272, 1287-8), (xviii), (xxxi), 90-91, 296
——— fam., 43, 282, 337
Dyserth (co. Flint), 6, 48, 51, 58, 93

Eastham, xxvii, 3, 8, 17, 55, 97-9, 110, 114-15, 129-30, 133-5, 196, 232-3, 236, 253, 259, 282, 383
——— Border names : le Blakestret, 97-8 ; Bradesiche, 97 ; Estham-dale, 97 ; Mukeldale, 97 ; Stok-welsiche, 98 ; Street Heys, 99
Eaton, 17, 31, 55, 110, 282
——— Hall, charter of Ranulf II. at. *See* " Manuscript " in Index II.
Eccleston, 137
———, Wm. s. of Reg. de, 436
Eddisbury hundred, 270
Edgar, king, charter of, to St. Wer-burgh's, 8
Edusa widow (Manley), 391
Edward I., king, 83, 86-9, 212-13, 215, 226, 231, 283, 331. *See* Chester, earls of
Edwards, John, xxix, 62
Egerton, John (?) de, 430 ; Phil., 222, 430
Eilevin, Alan s. of, 273
Eleanor, queen of Edward I., 331-2
Ellis (Elias), Gilb. s. of, 80 ; Hen. s. of, 155, 166
——— the hunter. *See* Chorlton
Elton, 252, 260-67, 394
——— Field names, etc. : Assefeld, Aysefeld, 263-4 ; Bothumfeld, 261-3 ; Brodelond, 263 ; Brom-feld, 261-3 ; Crabbelond, 264 ;

Crabbelondfurlong, 264; Crougre-flont, 261 ; the Cross, 266 ; Crowegravefeld, 262-3 ; Drite-gravelond, 264; Egmundesheved, 266 ; Eltonmos, 264 ; Flahe-lond, Flaylond, 261-3 ; Fulford Bridge, 478 ; Hoklone, 265 ; Longethornfeld, 261, 265 ; Mor-feld, 261, 263 ; Muche Hadlond, 262 ; the Rock, (xxxi), 262 ; Roggedelond, 262 ; Sevene-londes, 265 ; Spertes Deynes, 263 ; Stanewaye, 262-3 ; Walle-waye, 264 ; Wille, 264 ; Wit-feld, 263
Elton, H. de, 262 ; John, 263-4 ; Juliana, 265; Ralph, 265; Sim., 260-64 ; Thos., (xxxi), 265-6 ; Wm., 260-64
Elvaston, Rob. de, 186 ; Wm., 185
Ely, abbey of, vii-ix, xi-xii
England, knights of, 105
Englefield (co. Flint), 86, 338
English, Rob., 20
Ermewine, Ralph s. of, 19, 34 ; Claricia his w., 19, 56
Erneis the hunter, 18, 163 (?)
Esseburn, Rog. de, 245
Essex, Hen. de, 233
Eston. *See* Middleton Grange
———, Suan s. of Alan de, 237, 239
Eustace the monk, 18
Eversley, Walt. de, 89
Evesham, Walt. de, 91
Eynon the Hooper, John s. of, 342

Fallybroom, Rich. de, 334
Fancham, Wm. de, 144
Fauld. *See* Hanbury
Fawdon (in Over Peover), 327-8
Fitton, Anabil de, 470-71 ; Hugh, 82, 97 ; Sir Edm., (xxxi), 430 ; Matilda, 470-71 ; Rich., 59, 97, 106 ; Rich., just. of Chester, 81 ; Rich., 468
Fitzalan, John s. of Wm., 210, 267
Fleming, Wm., 48, 58
Flint, 215
Foden. *See* Fawdon
Fouleshurst, Rich. de, 229, 379, 427
Franceys, Eve, 240-41 ; Nich., 239-241 ; Rob. s. of Sim., 158, 169 ; Wm., 240-41
Freeman, Walt., 145, 148, 154
Freg', Hugh, 79
Frend, Rog., 367. *See* Chester, St. Werburgh's, abbots of
———, Wm., 250

Frodsham, 17, 55, 110, 137, 162, 237 n , 283, 370
——, Rob (de Frodsham), vicar of, 474
——, Walter, rector of, 371
——, John de, 368 , Nich s of John, 352 , Pet , 237-40 , Ran (or Rad), 277-8 , Thos s of John, 352
Froger   See Derby
Frombald   See Ridefort
Fulbert, 20
Fulford Bridge, 478
Fulk, Rob s of Adam s of, 242
Fullwich, 18, 33, 55

Gamel, John, 350
Gast, Geva, 352 , Gilb , 274 n , 275 , Gunwara, 275, 352
Gawsworth, 7, 437
——, John de Birtles, rector of, 437
Gemme, Rich , 264
Geoffrey the chaplain, (xvii), 50
—— the clerk, 121
—— ——, 408, 410, 479 (?)
—— the cook (of the abbey), 257-8, 343-4, 346, 354-5
—— ——, Agn d of, 257, 355 , Gunwara m of, 355 , Matilda d of, 353-6
—— the despenser, xlvii, 75
——, Gilb s of, 367
——, John s of, 144
——, Rob s of, 381
Gernun, Wm , 144
Gerold the usher, 80
Gerrard, Wm , 222, 337, 427 (same ?)
Giffard, Andr , 120
Gilbert, 20, 56
—— the chaplain, 234
——, Rich s of, 175
Giliend, Wm s of, 336
Ginges (Giuges, Ginoes), John de, (xxx), 121, 131
Girard, Master, 121
Girgkin, Gamel s of, 243-4
—— ——, Cecilia, 342
Gisehors, Wm , 467
Glest, Marg , 459-60 , Wm , 459-60
Gloucester, Wm , archdeacon of, 121
Gobaud, John, just of Chester, (xxix)
Gocehn, Ranulf s of, 36, 57
Godeweyt, Ad , 467
Godfrey the merchant, 20, 56
Godusa, Hugh s of, 391
Golborne, 454 , Assedale in (?), 225 , Golborneford, 453-4
——, John de, 225 , Wm , 225 n

Goostrey, 4, 40, 44, 57, 231, 307, 310-12, 413, 417-30
—— Field names, etc   Blakedene-broc, 424 , Brerehey, 424, 429 , Bromicroft, 424 , Bystowes-nabbe, 418, 429, 430 , Ewode, 418 , Gostreschawe, 418 , Longe-sthayecloch, 424 , Rogensweye, 418, 420, 424, 429-30 , Saltens-wey, 424
——, Mich de, 322, 401, 413 (1266-7), 420-21, 425, 430 , Thos , 311, 324, 403-4, 414-15, 418, 422-5, 427, 429-31
——, Rob , chaplain of, 419
Gowy, riv   See Tarvin Water
Grandison, Otto de, 89
Grant, Hen le, 189-90
Grave, Nich de la, 151
Greasby (Gravesberi), 4, 19, 34, 56, 78-9, 110, 231, 375
Greetham (Graham), co Lincs, 42
Grefesac, Rob , 59
Grendun, Rich de, 242, 367
Gresley, Wm de, 68, 232
Grevelands, Ran de, 447-8 , Rich , 448
Grey, John de, just of Chester, v, 144, 200, 219, 222, 319, 383, 400, 412 , John s of Reg , 329 , Reginald, just of Chester, v, 89, 90-91, 219, 296, 311, 318, 324-5, 328-9, 349, 402, 411, 414-15, 423, 425, 432-3, 435, 478 , Will , 144, 200
Griffin, Rich s of, 308
Grosvenor, Marg le, 298 , Rich , 395, 397 , Rob , 296, 298, 311, 325, 394, 415, 425, 431, 478 , Wann, 404
——, Rob , clerk of Rich le, 395-7, 435
Gud, Wm s of, 20
Guy the carpenter, 244-5
——, Hamon s of   See Newton
——, Ralph s of, 342 , Christiana his w , 342
Guilden Sutton, 118
Gurney, Hugh de, 184, 186 , Rich le, 187
Gutha, 57

H the baker, Sim s of, 249
Halmar   See Wulmar
Halton, Rich de, 394
——shire, 5, 102-3
Hamon, 49
—— the clerk, 315
——, Guy s of, Wm s of   See Newton

Hanbury (Staffs), nunnery of, ix-xiv, xix

Hancheriche, Matilda, 450 ; Rich., 450 ; Wm., 450

Handforth (Haneford), Wm. de, 77

Handley, 3, 7, 92-3, 122, 128, 253, 271, 335, 337

Hapsford, Ad. de, 265

Harding, John, 439 ; Phil., 441, 443 ; Rich., 439 ; Wm., 439

Hardmer, 79

Hardredeshill (Hartshill). See Ardreshill

Harold, king of Danes, xxii

Harre, Alex., 467

Hassall, Hen. de, 472

Hatfield, Wm. de, 121, 131, 134

Hatherton, 5, 472

Hatton, 3, 19, 34, 56, 326, 453-4 ; Hesse (Heye) dale in, 454

——, Hugh de, 314, 328, 404, 411, 414, 432-3, 453

Haughmond (Salop), Rich., abbot of, 302

Haunville, Ellis de, 213

Hauterive, Wm. de, 193

Hawarden, 17, 31, 55, 110, 282, 305-6, 309

——, Wm. de, 205, 453

Hawise, Hen. s. of, 179

Haylward. See Aylward

Heldebald, monk of Chester, 18

Helsby, 4, 265, 393 ; Ernutisfeld (? Ermitisfeld) in, 393

——, Ad. de, 199, 408, 420 ; Ad., 371 ; Hugh, 276 ; Joceraline, 107, 370 ; Ralph, 265 ; Wm., 370, 393

Hemington, Rob. de, 455

Hengham, Ralph de, 222

Henry II., 82, 142, 233 ; Henry III., 143, 230

Henry the chaplain, 120

—— the despenser, 202, 338

——, Alan s. of, 153 ; Phil. s. of (carpenter), 441

Herbert the carter, 351

—— the jerkinmaker (Weambasarius), 41, 45, 58

——, John s. of Nich. s. of, 273 ; Rich. s. of, 297

Hermitage (in Cranage), Marg. del, 405 ; Rich., 400 ; Wm. s. of Rog., 416 ; Wm., 405

Herwart, Hereward, Rob., 346 ; Thos., 237-41, 346 ; Eve aunt of Thos., 240-41

Hesketh, Matilda de, 470-71 ; Wm., 470-71

Heswall (Heselwall), 8

——, Agn. de, 466 ; Sir Patrick de, (xxxii), 90, 196, 205, 207, 220-21, 296, 303, 425, 432-3, 466 ; Wm., 338, 387, 403

Heyham, John de, 328

Hilbre Island, chapel and cell of, 4, 118, 289, 296-9

——, Heypol in, 298

Hildebrand, monk of Chester. See Heldebald

Hiraddug (Yraduc), co. Denbigh, 18, 32, 55

Hockenhull, Rob. de, 349, 458 ; Wm., 458

Hodard, Rog. s. of Wm., 465

Hodresham, Hub. de, 347

Hoke, Rich. del, 401

Holbeach, Sim. s. of Martin de, 170 ; Wm. s. of Sim., 170

Holgrave, Matth. de, 479

Holland, Alan s. of John de, 245

Holm, le (in Ince), 215

Holm House (Alrichesholm), 4, 201-4, 269-70, 473

Holme, Randle, (xxix), xxix ff., 61 ff., 85, 100, 125, 223, 270, 408 ; Wm. de, 270

Holt, John de, 418 ; Sir Rich. de, 90

Holywell (co. Flint), 6-7, 41, 45, 58, 232 n., 236-7, 295

Hoole, 3, 7, 41, 45, 58 ; tithes of, 457

——, Hawise de, 278 ; Hugh, 456-7 ; Rob., 342-3, 347 ; Rog., 349, 427, 434

Hooper. See Eynon

Hooton, 383-4

——, Alice de, 387 ; Nich., 387 ; Secherith, 387 ; Wm., 90, 303-4. See Walsh

Hope (? in Bradwall), 335

Horseley, John de, 191

Hoseley (co. Denbigh and Flint), xviii, 9, 11-12, 16, 54, 459 n.

Hotot, Hen. de, 168 ; Wm., 168

Hough (in Mere), 5, 209

Hubert, Wm. s. of, 19, 56

Huchenescote. See Hychenescote

Hudard, 94

Hugh the chamberlain, xlv, 21, 57

—— the clerk, 97

—— the despenser, 106, 323

—— the hawker, 67, 75, 232

—— the priest, 59

—— the smith, 273

—— the waterman, 277

——, Master, (xx), 210. See Chester

Hugh, Ad s of, 362-4, Dear s of, 419,
 Hamon s of, 361, 363, Hay-
 trop s of, 302, John s of, 419,
 Osbern s of, 42, 50, 58, Rob
 s of, 18, 22, 28, 32-3, 55,
 Rob s of, 232, Wm s of, 341
—— See St Angelo
Hulle, Agn de, 163, 166, 168, Edm,
 162, Ellis, 171, Emmeline,
 162, Hugh, 162, Rob, 162
Hulm, Hen de, 401
Hulse, 394-9, 451
—— Field names, etc Bacforlong,
 395, Hewesfeld, 399, le
 Leveth, 395, highway to Mac-
 clesfield, 398, Pilotescroft, 395,
 Porteford, (xxxv), 398, Su-
 line(s)feld, 395, 398, le Wyte-
 weye, 398-9
——, Ad s of Hawise de, 399, Herb,
 394, Jonas, 395, Ralph s of
 Herb, 399, Rob s of Herb,
 394-5, 398-9, Wm s of Eva,
 395-7 See Turnevileyn
Hulton, Rob de, 200
Humez, Rich de, 233
Huntington, xvi, xviii, 2, 9, 10, 54, 81,
 110, 223-4, 230, 355
——, Rob de, 455
Hurdsfield, 334
Hurel, Alex, 350
Hurmach (Ireland), 472
Hurne, Isabel, 226, Rog, 226
Hutred, Wm, 182
Huxley, 3, 458-9
——, Ad s of Rich de, 458, Rob,
 314, 318, 322, 324, 328, 396-7,
 403-4, 411, 413-4, 423, 432-3,
 435, 444
—— family, 458
Hychenescote, 4 See Alvanley and
 Manley

Ichincote See Alvanley
Iddinshall (Edinchale), xx, 4, 16, 29,
 54, 116, 118, 231, 434-6
—— Field names, etc Blakesiche,
 436, Boteokweye, 436, Bradesunderlond, 434, Colemon leye,
 434, Cokschutehavedlond, 434,
 Derneforde, 436, Fildingeshurst, 436, Flaxyord, 436,
 Gatebrugg, 434, Geylmaresiche, 436, Holefeld, 434, Morichbuttes, 434, Netstallis, 436,
 Peverlishurst, 436, Saweheved,
 434, Tounstede, 434, Witeo-
 kestonel, 436

Iddinshall, Helemunt de, 234, John,
 434-5, Rich, 434-5, Rob, 434-5
Ince, xx, 4, 16, 54, 110, 113, 132, 203-6,
 211, 261-2, 264, 270-71, 461
—— Field names, etc le Holm, 215,
 Marsh, 461, Muchele Medewe,
 215, Mucle dich, 461, le Port-
 wey, 205, Portway Heys, 478 n,
 Smalreod, 461
——, Rob, 314, 349, 434, 460, Rob
 s of Hugh, 215, Walt, 266
Infirmary, John of the, 345, Lucia,
 345, Master Rich, 345
Ingeram le Dubler, (xxx), 165
Irby (Erbeia), 4, 17, 55, 110, 236, 375,
 387
—— Field names, etc Knukyn, 387,
 Londymere, 387
——, John s of German de, 387
Ireland See Downpatrick
——, Wm de, 374
Isles, the king of the, 211

Jevenat, John s of, 161
Jocelin See Gocelin
John, king, 142
——, 234
—— the chamberlain, 348, 351 See
 Chamberlain
——, chaplain of Ranulf II, 68-9, 232
——, clerk of Ranulf III, 75
—— the clerk, 162
—— the smith, 268
——, Eustace s of, 232
——, Rob s of, 89
——, Thos s of, 244
Jordan, 463
——, Alan s of, 186
Juhel the priest, 94
Jukel (Jokel), Wm, 312, 421, 431
Julian, Ad s of, 427
Juliana, lady (of Elton), 265

Kachepol See Catchpoll
Kaletoft See Caletot
Kegworth, Rich de, xlvi, 317, 409
Kelsal, Ad de, 90, 479
Kenewrec, Wm, 465
Kenil, Hugh, 271
Kent, Walt de, 329, Wm, 94
Kermincham See Mainwaring
Ketin, Hen de, 401
Kidsley (co Derby), 30, 175, 177, 231
King, Marg le, 273, Rob, 273
Kingsley, 282, 337
——, Rand de, 279, Rich, 94, 107, 199,
 276-7, 310 (c 1200), 337-8, 393,
 408, 420, Rich (c 1300), 264

Kinnerton family, 357
Kirkby. *See* West Kirby
——, Rich. de, (xxxii), 293-4
Kyme (Lincs), Phil. de, 287 ; Sim. s. of Wm., 232, 287

Lache, Crooked, 5, 400, 406-7 ; Ammerlache in, 406 ; Chippebroc in, 406
——, Dennis (formerly Malbank), 5, 406-7
—— ——, Matilda de, 407
—— (in Marlston), Leche, xx, 16, 30, 54
——, Wulfric de, (xxxv), 418-9
Lacy (Lasci), Edm. de, 198-9 ; Hen., 8, 207, 213, 475-7 ; Hugh I., 40, 57 ; Hugh II., 77, 217 ; John I., 114 ; John II., 198-9 ; Roger, 338 ; Wm., 97
Lambert, 57
—— (native), 148, 152
——, Wm. s. of. *See* Weston-upon-Trent
Lancelyn, Anable, 248 ; Ran., 248, 382 *n.*; Rich., 35, 79, 380 ; Rob. I.,92, 127, 243(?), 337, 380 ; Rob. II., 297, 377 *n.*, 380, 382, 400, 412, 453 ; Thos., 248 ; Sir Wm. I., (xxx-i), (xxxv), 205, 207, 214, 248, 298, 376, 380-82, 388 (?), 393 (?), wrongly called Wm. II. in some notes ; Wm. II., 377 *n.*; Wm. III., 297-8, 377-9, 381, 388 (?), 393 (?), 472
Landican, 283, 363, 365
Lasselys, Wm. de, 379
Latthon (? Leighton), Hen. s. of Ad. de, 364
Lawton, Church, Lawton under Lyme, 4, 7, 40, 44, 57, 231, 307, 309, 437-51
——, chapel of, 440 ; tithes of, 451
—— Field names, etc. : Aschenehalgh, Assenehalh, 443-4, 447 ; Badilford, 446 ; Barud, 445 ; Barwehedys, 439-41, 446 ; Beterbacheforde, 443 ; Bik, 445 ; Bircheleg', 441 ; Brereleyeforde, 446 ; Brock, 443, 449 ; Brodeleg', 439, 449 ; Brodelond, 442 ; Buthinleg', 448 ; Chircheruding, 440 ; Cokshutelond, 441 ; Coulone, 439 ; le Diches, 444, 445 ; Everardisruding, 441, 449 ; Ferfeld, 439, 443, 449 ; Feyre Pleckes, 443 ; Grevelond, 447 ; le Halg', Halh, 443, 449 ; Hawardisruding, 449 ; le Heye

juxta Stanclives, 447 ; Hurst, 447 ; Lautonroue, 448 ; Leysichehurst, 443 ; Line Halfland, 441 ; Litlelond, 442 ; Liveresleghnese (-evese), 439, 442 ; Longeforde, 442, 445 ; Lun, 441 ; Lund(Lunt-)lidgate, 441, 443 ; Lunteruding, 449 ; le Lym Puttes, 447 ; Merewey, 442, 450 ; Midilforlong, 440 ; Mora, 443 ; Morwaldis Medue, 449 ; Puttes, 443 ; Quethul, 439 ; Radilforde, 447 ; Radilegford, 446 ; Rodebache, 450 ; le Roye, 448 ; le Ruth, 442, 445 ; Salterisbachehurst (-walle), 441-442, 450 ; Siwardeleg', 439, 442 ; Smaleleg', 443 ; la Snape, 442-3, 448 ; le Sponne, 442, 445 ; Stanclif, 443, 448 ; —— isclouh, Stanclives cloht, 443, 447 ; Stanweyruding, 439, 449 ; Stappe grene, 441 ; Sullunhull, 442, 445 ; Suthleg', 447 ; Talkhurstesford, 447 ; Threl(Trel-)owenhet, 441, 444, 449 ; Tvertoverclouh, 443 ; Twisse cloch, 439 ; Werstanley, 443 ; Werstanley Buthinleg', 445 ; Little Werstanley, 439 ; Werstonesleg' spone, 442, 445
——, rectors of : Edward, 309 ; William (de Massey), clerk of Rostherne, 309
——, Ad. de, 309, 437 ; Ad., 427 ; Cecilia, 444-9 ; Ad. s. of Ad., 439, 449 ; Ad. s. of the priest of, 442, 449 ; Hen., 442, 450 (?) ; Matilda, 449-50 ; Phil. s. of Hen., 443, 449-50 ; Ran. s. of Wm., 309, 438, 444-8 ; Rich. s. of Ad., 446 ; Rich. s. of Ad. s. of the priest of, 443, 449 ; Rob. s. of Ad. s. of the priest of, 443, 449 ; Wm. s. of Ad., 309, 437, 439-48 ; Wm. s. of Ad., 445 ; Wm. s. of Wm., 438-9, 440, 444, 447 ; Wm. s. of Wm. of, the priest, 309, 395, 397-9, 438, 445, 447
Lea (by Backford), Wisdeleth (*D.B.* Wisdelea), xx, 3, 16, 54, 354-5, 368 ; Lensethorn in, 368
—— (cum Newbold), Steward's, Le Lay, 19, 33, 51, 56, 58, 118, 287-8, 302, 453
——, Anabil de, 470-1 ; Edm., 470-71
Lectone, wood of (co. Flint), 41, 45, 58 (Lestone)

Ledesbera, Agn de, 366 , Rich s of Leuca, 366
Ledsham, 20, 35
Leduc, 245 *See* Duc
Leek (Staffs), 7, 17, 55, 76-7, 110, 137, 282, 284, 332
Lees, 5, 231, 400, 405-6, 407-15
—— Field names, etc la Bruch, 409 , Claycroft, 413 , Dernelehegreue, 408-9, 411 , Hethfeld, 414-15 , Littlecroft, 414 , Perde juxta Ruhelawe, 409
——, Agn de, 410 , Marg , 411 , Rich s of Hen , 409 , Rob , 317-18, 400, 409-10
Legbourne (Lincs), 178
Legh, H[enry ?] de, 200 , John, 229 , Ran , 80
Leiacestria (=Chester), 9
Leicester, 476
——, Rich of, abbot of St Evroult, 292-3
Leighton *See* Latthon
Lene, Len (? Lleyn), (xxxiv) , Hugh de, 350 , John s of Mayler, 350 , Rob , 350
Lenton, Master Geoff de, 120
Leoff', the sheriff *See* Liulf
Leofnoth (Leoventh), the priest, 73
Leofric, earl, xix
Leofwine (Leovinus), the priest, 73
Leuca d of Rich , 313
Lexington, John de, just of Chester, (xxix), v
Leycester, Sir Pet , 15, 25
Lichfield, bishops of *See* Coventry , deans of Rich de Dalam, 130 , Ralph de Neville, 130
Lime *See* Lyme
Lincoln, earls of *See* Chester, Ranulf III , earl of, and Lacy
Lindsey, (xxix), 5, 17, 30, 55, 282
Little, Rich , 467
Liulf, the sheriff *See* Twemlow
Liverpool, 245
Livet, Rich de, 291 , Rog , 291 , Walt , (xxxiv), 339
Lleyn *See* Lene
Loges, Bigod de(s), 18, 22, 44, 55-6
—— ——, Rob s of (?), 50 , Rose w of (?), 40, 44-5
Lombe, Matilda, 279, 342 , Wm , 279
London, Rich de, 121
Long, Rob , 351 , Thos , 244
Longchamp, Hen de, 338
Lostock, 19, 33, 56, 398 *n.*
—— (Gralam), Geoff de, 427 , Gralam *See* Rundchamp , Matilda d

of Gralam, 409 , Rich s of Gralam, 394, 396-7, 400, 411-12, 414, 418, 425 , Rich s of Rich , 397, 399 , Thos , 434 , Wm , 479
—— fam , 398, 401
Lovecock, Hen , 414
Lucy, Rich de, 338
Lund, Wm de, 443
Lupus, Thos , 440, 443, 450
Luvetot, Rich de, 217
Lydiate (Halsall par , Lancs), 59, 67
Lyme, the, 105
——, Lawton under, 307 *See* Lawton
—— Wood (co Derby), 169, 179
Lymm, Alan de, 90 , Alex , 349 , Gilb , 388 , Hugh, 400, 412 , Mabel, 388 , Rog , 361

Macclesfield, 5, 21, 36, 57, 282, 335, 398
——, bailiffs of Benedict de Coudray (c 1250), 319 , John de Heyham (c 1272), 328 , Thomas Clerk (c 1285), 325, (1289), 329
——, chapel of, 331-2
Madiou, Rich s of, 94
Maidstone, Master Ralph de, 134
Maillard, Rich , 49, 59
Maine, Friar (Dorset), 20, 35, 56
——, Little (Dorset), 20, 35, 56
Mainwaring (Mesnilwarin), Geoff neph. of Rog de, 94 , Guy, 41, 57 , Hen , 233, 350-51 , John, 343 , Mabel, (xxxvi) , Matilda, 97 , Ralph I , 235 , Ralph II , 74, 80, 94, 216, 291, 310 (just of Chester) , Rich , 20, 57 , Rob , 310, 408 , Rog , 20, 41, 57 , Rog , 94 , Rog , (xxix), 310, 338, 409, 461-3 , Sir Thos , (xxx), 84, 307, 318, 324, 328, 401, 404, 411, 413, 428, 431, 433, 435, 462-3 , Sir Warin, 97, 99, 318, 425, 428 , Wm , 41, 57, 59 , Wm , 94 , Wm (1267), 322, 328 , Wm , 418, 421, 425, 428, 430, 478
—— of Kermincham, (xxv), 432
Malbank (Maubanc), Adaliza, 57 , Annora, 95 , Hugh I , (xvii), 32, 42, 50, 57-8, 60-61 , Phil , 94 , Wm I , 18-19, 20, 22, 28-9, 32, 34-6, 42, 55-7, 60-61, 215 , Wm II , 59, 94, 215 (?), 215-7
Malehunte, Rob , 191, 194
Malgar, Hen , 413
Mallanel, Steph , 302
Malmac', Wm , 217

Malpas, David de, 338 ; Gilb., 302 ; Hen. s. of Gilb., (xxx), 269 ; Leticia, 49, 51, 58, 60 ; Wm., 82, 97, 420 ; Wm. s. of David, 338
——, Rich., lord of, 49, 59. *See* Patrick
Maltby (Lincs), 5, 30, 110, 177-8, 282
Malvodan, Edusa, 268
Malyns, John, 474
Mancetter (Manecestria), Master William de, 121
Manley, (xxxv), 4, 390-93
—— Field names, etc. : Aleynes Hadde (Heved)lond, 391-3 ; Aspone(s)-forlong, 391-3 ; Blake Lake, 390 ; Bernullisleg', 391 ; Cakebroc, 390-91 ; Chircheweye, 391 ; Fouleslecheved, 392 ; Gerardesweye, 392 ; Gosebuttes, 391 ; Grenewalle, 391 ; Hullesholm, 392 ; Huchenescotc, 391 (*see* Alvanley) ; le Hullond, 391 ; Lamblachelond, 391 ; la Lee, 390 ; le Leylond, 392 ; Leysigesmulnebroc, 391 ; Mosewalle, 390 ; Salterestrete, 392 ; Schadlond, 391 ; Siridac, 390 ; Stokenewalle, 390 ; Teytesfeld, 392 ; Ynumhoc, 392
Manners, Oliver de, 235
Manualätt, Ad., 426
Mara. *See* Delamere and Mere
——, Hugh de, 19, 34, 56
Marisco, Hen. de, 390 ; Ralph, 391-2 ; Rich., 143 ; Rob., 134 ; Rob., 391 ; Rob. s. of Rog., 392-3 ; Rog., 390-91
Martin, Rich. s. of, 274-5
Massey (Masci, etc.), Gilb. de, 175 ; Hamon (I.), 18, 22, 40, 44, 55-57, 281 ; Hamon (II. or III.), 94, 217 ; Hamon (III.), 310-11, 409 ; Hamon (IV.), 81, 97, 199, 307 (?) ; Sir Hamon (V.), 205, 296, 425, 453 ; Hamon (V. or VI.), 222 ; Sir Hamon (VI.), 329, 418, 429 ; Hamon (uncertain), 247, 375 ; Sir Rich. (of Tatton), 205, 207, 220-22, 296, 316, 329, 370, 415, 418, 425, 429-31, 453, 478 ; Rich. (of Moreton), 207 ; Rob. (*c*. 1125), 50 ; Rob. (*c*. 1150), 59, 67, 369 ; Rob. (*c*. 1215), 107 ; Rob (*c*. 1250), 319 ; Rob. br. of Sir Rich., (xxxi ?), 370-71 ; Rob. (of Sale), 370-71 ; Wm. (clerk of Rostherne), 309 ; Wm. (1257), 479

Massey, baronial claim of, 102 *n.*
Master, Hen., 183
Matilda, Rob. s. of, 274-5
Matthew the goldsmith, 343
——, Rob. s. of, 255
Mayler. *See* Lene
Maynes. *See* Maine
Mazelyn, Geoff., 347
Meols, North (Lancs), 5, 470
Meolse, Gt. and Lit., 283, 297-8, 382
——, Bertram de, (xxxii-iii), 90, 207, 304, 388 (?) ; Bertram s. of Hen., (xxxiii), 297 ; Bertram s. of Rich., 297 ; Fulk, (xxxiii), 297, 379 ; Marg., 272 ; Rich. s. of Herb., (xxxiii) ; Rob., jun., 272 ; Rob. s. of Geoff., 388
Mercer, Rob. le, 213 *n.*, 272, 340, 464 ; Wm. s. of Hugh, 347-8
Mere (in Rostherne par.), 209 ; priests' cartway in, 209 ; Roger's Crosses in, 209 ; Hough in, 209 ; Strettle in, 209
——, Rob. del, 209
Mersey riv., 269
Mersynton, John de, 453
Merton, Ran., 298
Meschin, Osbern, 42 ; Ranulf, 42. *See* Chester, earls of ; Ranulf (de Rhuddlan s. of William), 48, 58, 93 ; William, 42, 48, 50, 58, 93
Mesech', Wm. de, 471
Middleton Grange (Midestune, Estune), (xxix), xviii, xx, 9, 11, 16, 54
Middlewich, fair of, 405 ; saltworks at, (xxxv)
Midgebrook (Mugebroc), Rob. de, 324-326 ; Wm., 325-6
—— fam., (xxxiv)
Miller. *See* David, Richard
Millington, Avdrop de, 207
Minshull, Rich. de, 90
Mobberley, Pat. de, 310 ; Ralph, 327 ; Wm., 229
Mold (*Monte Alto*), John de, 329 ; Leuca w. of Rob. I., 302 ; Ralph I., (xvii), xlvi, 18-19, 40, 50, 55, 57, 287 ; Ralph II., 51, 120, 134, 287, 302 ; Ralph III., 216 ; Ralph, 205 ; Ralph, rector of West Kirby, (xxxiii), 304-6 ; Ran., 303 ; Rob. I., 50, 58-9, 67, 70, 73, 234, 287-8, 302, 307 ; Rob. II., (xxxiii), 302, 310, 311 (?) ; Sir Rob., (xxxi ?), 431 ; Rog. I. (xxxiii), 248, 311 (?), 338, 409 ; Rog. II.,

144, 200, 288, 304-7, 309 (?), 400, 412, 479, Wm, 51, 58, 60, 287-8, Wm, rector of Neston, 120, 287-8, 302
Mollington, 208, 462
Mooresbarrow, Gilb de, 420-21, Rose, 420-21
Moreton (Morton), Geoff de, 90, 433, Ralph, 426-7
Morice, 79
Morley (co Derby), o, 30, 165, 169, 174-7, 179, 185-6, 231
—— Field names Saxesichis, 177, Smalleysty, 185
——, Gilb de Masci de, 175, Hugh s of Hugh, lord of, 169, 175, 185, 188, Hugh, 176, 189, Hugh, jun, 179, Milisande, 175, Nich le Lou, 175, Rich, 174-7, Rob s of Nigel, 175, Rog s. of Ralph, 175
Moston (Morseton), 3, 48, 58, 242, 366-7
——, Agn de, 366, Marg, 366, Ralph, 366, Rich, 366, Swein, 367
Mottram St Andrew, 5, 333-4, Haukeshert in, 333
——, John de, 329, 333-4, 431, Rich, 319, 325, 329, 333-4, Rich his s, 325
Mouldsworth, Rob de, 479, Rog, 391
Moule, Phil, 465, Rob, 343
Mudle, Wm de, 345
Mug', Reg de, 388, Seyerith, 388
Mundrei, Gilb de, 234

Nantwich (Wich (Malbank)), 4, 18, 32, 60-61, 106, 110, 215, 217 See Wich
——, Rob, clerk of, 80
——, Ralph de, 322
Ness, (xxxi), 20, 35, 56, 257, le Houtrake in, 257
——, Wm s of Rich de, 355, Agnes his w, 355
Neston, xx, xxii, 3, 8, 29, 54, 110, 113, 120-21, 130-31, 133-5, 234, 249-250, 259-60, 287, 302-7
——, Pat de, 303-4, Rich, 303-4, Wm s of Hen, 306-7
Netherpool See Poole
Nevell, Sim de, 134
Neville, Rob de, 349 See Lichfield
Newball (Lincs), Idonea de See Boydell
Newcastle, 259

Newton (by Chester), 3, 40, 43, 57, 226, 231, 244, 254, 354-5, 357-8, 457
——, Agn de, 356, Guy s of Hamon, 271-2, 356, 358, Hamon s of Guy, 350, 356, 464, 468, Phil, (xxxiv), 356-8, 409, Rob, 357, Sim, 420, Wm (chaplain), (xxxiv), 357-9, Wm s of Hamon, 233
Nigel, 56
——, Rich s of, (xvii), 18 (bis), 42, 50, 56, Wm s of See Chester, Constables of
Noctorum (Wirral), (xxxiv), 40, 44, 57, 110, 283
Norfolk, Rog le Bigod, earl of, 144
Norman the clerk, (xvii), 234 (?)
——, Bertram s of John, 344, Hugh s of, 18-19, 22, 33, 40, 44, 56-7, 287, 307, John, 344, Ralph s of, 19, 33, 40, 56, Ralph s of John, 268, 271, Rog s of, 40, 57, Wm s of Hugh, 50
Northenden, 5, 40, 44, 57, 124-5
——, Rob de Benton, rector of, 125
——, Rob de, 124
Northwich, 4, 216
Norton priory, 284
Norwich, Sim de, just of Chester, (xxix)

Occleston (Aculveston), John de, 315, 401, 409
Odard See Udard
——, Roald s of, 277-8, Alan s of Roald s of, 278
Odo, Rob s of, 159
Oliver, Hugh s of, 71, 79
Olres, 335
Ordric, 18, 55
Ordrichescotes See Cotton Abbots
Oreng (?), Auvered de, (xx)
Orm the chamberlain, 367
—— the harper (sithareda), 234
——, Wm s of, 330-31
Orreby, Agn de, 99, Fulk, just of Chester, 277, 307, 400, 412, Sir John, 339-40, 472, Phil, just of Chester, (xxix), v, 80, 106, 167, 202, 267, 303, 310-11, 338, 367, 408, 464, Rich, (xxxii), 90, 304, 318, 322, 324, 328, 349, 396, 403, 411, 413-14, 433, Thos (c 1210), 303, Thos, just of Chester, 319, 360, Sir Thos, (xxxi), 307, 318

R

Osbern (Osbert), Hugh s. of, 18, 20, 42, 50, 52, 55-6, 58-9, 60, 243, 279; Juliana d. of, 253; Meyler s. of, 308, 452; Sim. s. of, 232, 288-9; Rob. s. of, 253, 358; Wm. s. of, 42, 243

Osgot, Rich. s. of, 253, 464, 468

Osmund, Hen. s. of, 188

Other, Leticia (Leca) d. of Wm., 359-61; Madock s. of Leticia, 359; Matilda (de Pensby) d. of Wm., 360; Wm., 360; Wm. s. of Wm., 361

Otto, Hugh s. of, 213, 222

Outred, Edwin s. of, 282

Over, 31, 55, 137, 282

Overpool. See Poole

Oxford, Rob. earl of, 144

——, chancellor of, 473

Pacy (Pascy), Hugh de, 80, 107, 338

Pain (Paganus), Rich., 58, 68

——, 94

——, the sheriff, 79

Paker, Rob. s. of Wm. le, 331

Palmas, Rob. de, 50

Palmer, Cecilia le, 311, 431; John, 244; Rob. s. of Rog., 417; Rog. s. of Ralph, 417-18; Rog., 449-50; Thos., 311, 431; Wm., 73; Wm., 181, 183; Wm., 185

Panton (Paunton, Pantulf), Brice, 303, 310; Brice s. of John, 313; John, 313; John, 313; Leuca, 313; Norman, 107, 202, 338

Paris, Ad. de, 273; Felicia, 274

Patemon, 312

Patrick (Patric), Beatrice, 225; Isabel, 222-5; Rob., (xviii), 202, 338; Wm. (d. 1184), (xviii), 73, 217, 269; Wm. (1184-), (xxxi-ii); Wm. (c. 1268), (xxx-i), 225; Wm., 312

Peatling Magna (co. Leic.), 290-1, 293

Pecch', Geoff., 120

Pecke, Wm. de, 342

Peckforton, 19, 34, 56, 269

Pelter, Hugh, 245

Penchester, Steph. de, 213

Penkridge (Staffs), 9

Pensby, Madock de, 360; Matilda, 360

Percy, Alan de, 22, 24; Wm., 24

Peter, clerk (chancellor) of the earl of Chester, xlviii, 75, 107, 147 (?), 166-7, 202, 210, 216, 252, 267, 310, 338, 367, 408-9, 465

Peter, clerk (chancellor) of the earl of Chester, Mathania, d. of, 166; Patrick s. of, 166-7

——, Gilb. s. of, 276

Peulesdon. See Puleston

Philip the chamberlain, xlv, 68-9

—— the clerk, 349

—— the serjeant, 344

——, Rich. s. of, 464

Pica, Gilb., (xxix)

Picavoys, Alice d. of, 465-6, 468; Jannie d. of, 465-6, 468

Picton, 3, 19, 56, 461

Pierrepont, Pereponte, Perpunt (Petraponte), Hugh de, 59; Rich., 107, 338, 367, 409 (?), 466, 469

Pigot (Picot), Gilb. (1267), 323; Gilb. s. of Rob. s. of, 59; Isabel, 326; Rob. s. of (c. 1200), (xxxiv ?), 210, 216, 310; Rob. (c. 1250), 319, 326; Rose w. of(?), 40; Wm. s. of, 80; Wm. s. of Rob. (c. 1270), 323, 325-6, 330, 332, 401 (?), 455; Wm., 329

Pilate, Rich., 465

Pimmere, Rich. s. of, 374

Pinchbeck, Rich. de, 358; Rob., 367; Suet, 161, 193

Plemstall, 7, 118, 457-8

——, Master Rich. Bernard, rector of, 457

Plesel, Thos. de, 80

Plumley, 5, 41, 45, 57, 431-4

——, Agn. de, 432, 434; Hen., 432; Leticia, 434; Rich., 434; Walthew, 432, 434. See Sladehurst and Smith

Pohenhale, Wm. de, 280

Poimton. See Poynton

Poole, Nether, 352 (?), 356, 384-6. See Chester, s. Portpool

——, Over, 3, 95, 282

——, Jas. de, (xxxi), 222, 296, 356, 368; Marg., 387; Matilda, 460; Reg., 354, 356, 384; Rob., 90, 205, 207, 356, 384-6, 479; Rob. (Storeton), 387; Walt., 387

Poor, Sim., 166

Popes: Alexander III., 112 (?), 114, 116 (?); Alexander IV., 112 (?), 116 (?); Clement III., 109, 113 (?), 115; Clement IV., 113 (?); Gregory IX., 115, 117 (?); Gregory X., 117 (?); Honorius II., 112; Honorius III., 112-14; Martin IV., 117; Nicholas III. or IV., 116

Porter, Rich., 367

Poulton (Lancelyn), 4, 35, 126, 214, 248, 376-82
—— Leper hospital   See Bebington and Spital
—— Field names, etc   Crosdale, (xxxv), 379, le Pul, 376-9, Pulton Bridge, 376, 378, Pultundale, 376-8, Pulton Mulnewey, (xxxv), 381
——, Avicia de, 376
——   See Lancelyn and Pulton
Poun, Gilb, chamberlain, 120
Poynton, 5, 7, 329, 334, 474 (tithes), le Hope in, 474
——, chapel of, 474
——, chaplains of   Alan, 474, John Malyn, 474
——, Gilb de (?), 349
Praers, Ad de, 40, 44, 50, 57, 68, Ad (Baddiley), 240-41, Ran, 310, Ran, s of Thos, 365, Rich, 40, 44, Thos, 365   See Barthomley, Wm, 40, 57, Wm, 316, 415, 427
Préaux (Pratellis), John de, 80, 202
Prenton (Preston), 20, 35, 56
Prestbury, 5, 6, 79, 80, 113, 115, 128, 131, 133-5, 231, 283, 328-36, 437, 474
——, chapel of St Nicholas in church of, 321
—— Field names, etc   Booths, 437, Cokemonscloht, 437, Freistelache, 437, Frewineslache, 331, Harebarwe, 437, Presteslache, 437, Spelenford, 437
——, Walter de Kent, rector of, 329
——, Ralph Mansel, rector of, 437
——, Master Hugh, vicar of, 421
——, Serlo de, 330
Preston (by Dutton), 282, 284
——, Gilb de, judge, 170-71, Norreys s of Hugh, 259, 278
——   See Prenton
Prime, Wm s of, 452
Priors   See Calke, Lichfield, Trentham
Proud, Wm the, 78-9, 94
Puddington, 247, 281, Flodgeard in, 247
——, Ad de, 208
Puleston (Peulesdon), Jord de, 322, 413
Pulford, xx, 16, 29, 54, 266
——, Hugh, clerk of, (xxxi), 266-7
——, Hen de, 266, Sir Hugh, (xxxi), 91, 453, 478, Ralph, 266, Rich, (xxxii ?), 396, Rob, 107, 200, 288, Sir Rob, 229, 453, Rob, rector of Coddington (?), 455, Rob s of Sir Rob, 453, Wm s of Rich, 396, 399, 451

Pulle, 352, ? Portpool, Chester
Pulton (Poulton), by Pulford, R[ich], abbot of, 408, 411   See Dieulacres
Pultrel (Putrel), Rob de, 21, 36, 57
Punterley (Punterlin), Herb de, 41, 45, 58, Wm, 41, 45, 58
—— family, (xxx), 45-6

Quarndon Park (co Derby), 149
Quarreyer, John le, 268, 274

R the chamberlain, 455
Raby, xx, xxii, 3, 8, 16, 29, 54, 84, 110, 234
——, Hugh de, 8, 477, Matth, 303, Rob, 477 n
Radmore (Staffs), Wm., abbot of, 232
Raithby (Lincs), 178
Ralph the chaplain, 76
—— the clerk, 121, 131
—— the hunter, 19, 34, 56
——, justice of Chester, (xxix)
—— the salter, 244
—— the smith, 355
——, Alex s of, 74, 281
——, Serlo s of, 308
Ranulf the hunter, 18, 41, 55, 57, 94
—— the sheriff, 67
——   See Chester, earls of
Ratcliffe, Emma de, 190, Gilb, 190
" Redcliff " (in Chester), 19, 34, 56, 110
Redemor, John de la, 394
Repton (Rapentune), Nigel de, 21, Wm, 168
Rhos (Ros), co Denbigh, 17, 30, 55
Rhuddlan (Rodelent, Ruelent), co Flint, 17, 55, 86, 338
——, Hen de, 343, Matth, 48, 51, 58, 60, 125, Ran   See Meschin, Rob, 288-90, 292, Sim, 48
——, Wm, clerk of, 48, 58
Richard the butler (pincerna), 18, 45, 55, 57, 59, 68-9, 71, 232
—— the chaplain, 71
—— the marshal, 260
—— the miller, 187, 351
—— the porter, 237, Isoult, wid of, 237
—— the young (iuvenis), 238
——, 76
——, Bertram s of, 297, Gilb s of, 275, Leuca d of, 313, Reg s of, 355, Yon s of, 404
Ridefort, Frombald de, 80
Ridley, Wm de, 304, 314
River', John de, 121
Robert the baker, Sim s of, 273

Robert the chamberlain. *See* Chamberlain
—— the cook, Geoff. s. of, 343-4, 346, 354-5
—— the despenser, 107
—— the hunter, 149, 163
—— the priest, Wenthilian d. of, 309
—— the sheriff, 255
—— the smith, 188
—— the steward (*dapifer*), 20, 56
—— the tailor, John s. of 254
——, Rich. s. of, 177, 313 (?) ; Rich. s. of, 263
Rocester (Staffs), 7, 17, 55, 110, 137, 279, 282
——, John, vicar of, 279
Rode, Thos. de, 445
Roger brother of earl Ranulf III., 74
——, chaplain of earl Hugh II., 78
—— the cementer, 194
—— the dean, 121
—— the despenser, 202 (erroneous extension for R[obert])
——, Ralph s. of, 162, 169, 302 (?)
Rolleston, Master Roger de, 121
Roodeye, 369
Rostherne, priests of, 209
——, Rich. de, clerk, xlix, 210, 249, 315, 409
——, Wm., clerk of, 309
——, Alan s. of Rich. de, 351 ; Wm. s. of Walt., 209
Roter, Pet. le, 166
Rothwell (Northants), 140-41
Rudheath, 5, 397 ; mine on, 401-2, 407
Rufford (Lancs), 5, 470-71
Rugeram. *See* Ingeram
Rullos, Rich. (I.) de, 18-19, 33, 55-6 ; Rich. (II.), 78, 231 ; Rob., 78, 231
Rundchamp, Gralam (Gralan) de, (xxx), 404, 408 ; Mabel, (xxxvi)
——, Rich., (xxxvi), 408. *See* Lostock (Gralam)
Rushal', Rich. de, 120
Ruston, Ran. de, 479

Sage, Ralph, 234
Saighton, (xviii), xix, xxvi, 2, 16, 54, 110, 112, 223-4, 230, 451-3, 458
—— Field names, etc. : Caldewelle, 452 ; Caldewelle diche, 452 ; Caldewelle forlong, 452 ; Holeweylond, 451 ; Lonkediche, 451 ; Merich', 452 ; Wodewey, 451
——, Alienora de, 451 ; Orm (chamberlain), 451-2

St. Angelo, Hugh, card.-deacon of, 328-9
St. Asaph, bps. of : Anian, 331 ; Reiner, 127
St. Evroult (Orne, France), abbey of, (xxxii), 288-93
——, Nich., abbot of, 292-3 ; Rich., abbot of, 291-3 ; Rich., monk of, 290-92
St. Frideswide, Oxford, prior of, 473
St. Lice (Licio), Sim. de, 134
St. Martin, Rog. de, 41, 58
St. Mary, Master Andrew de, 199
——, Master John de, 202, 210, 310
St. Maure, Nich. de, 144
St. Patrick, Silvester de, 471
St. Pierre, Urian de, 205, 431-2, 453
St. Thomas the Martyr, chapels of : in Wirral, 126 ; in Chester, 132, 274
St. Werburgh, vii-xiv, 16 ; 72 (Gwerburge)
——, *Lyfe and Hist. of* (by Hen. Bradshaw), x
——, dedications to, xii
——, feasts of, xiii, 21, 339
——. *See* Chester, abbey of
——, Master Hugh de, 202
St. Wilfric. *See* Chester, bishops of
Salamon, Gilb., 435 ; Thos. s. of Andr. s. of, 244
Sale, Rob. de, 370-71. *See* Massey
Salisbury, Walter Scammell, bp. of, 89
Sallowe, Rob. de, 192
Salter, Ralph lc, 244
Sampson, Anable, 459-60 ; Rich., 459 ; Wm., 459
Sandbach, Thos., rector of, and John his br., 315
——, Rich. de, 82, 315, 401, 409 ; Sir Rich., 219-21, 325
Sandon, Master Rob. de, 121, 134
Saracen, Alex., 346 ; Ralph, (xx), 345 ; Rich., 268-9, 345-6 ; Rob., (xx), 336, 345 ; Wm., 336 ; Wm., xlix
Sartes, Geoff. de, 20, 36
Saughall, xx, 3, 16, 18, 28-9, 32, 54-5, 110, 251, 459 *n.*
——, Little, 258, 372-5
——, ——, Field names, etc. : Longe Acre, 373 ; Renesfeld, 374 ; We forlong, 258 ; Wildemarelode, 373 ; Wodeforlong, 373
—— Massey, 375
Sauncheverel, Oliver, 153
Sauvage, Alan, 78, 280-81 ; Annabella, 281 *n.* ; Rob., 280-81

Say, Rob de, 107
Scales   *See* Tiresford
Schail, Wm , 373
Scirard (Sirard), 18, 20, 32 *n* , 35, 55-7, 380
Scoct', Hugh, 388 , Matilda, 388
Sedulius, " Carmen Paschale " of, 11
Segrave, Steph de, 338
Serlo the hunter, 308
——, Rob s of, 18-19, 33
Seward, Rog s of, 145-6, 152-4
Shardlow (co Derby), 6, 30, 160, 162, 164-6, 168-9, 179-80, 184-7, 193, 231, 475-6 , Longepol in, 186 , Schotsroyndegrene, 184
——, Hen the smith of, 160, 162
——, Rich s of Alwine de, 184, 186
——, Wm de, 187
Sheppey, abbey of, vii
Shirburne, Rich de, 84-5, 90-91
Shotwick, xx, 8, 16, 28-9, 54, 110, 113, 131, 133, 258-9, 458-9
Shrewsbury, abbey of   charters, 27 , freedom from toll in Cheshire, 73
Sibsey (Lincs), 5, 96, 164
——, Martin de   *See* Weston
Silvester   *See* Sauvage
Simon the clerk, 419
—— of the writs or briefs (*Brevitor*), 271   *See* Index II *s* Brevitor
——, Lucas s of, 273 , Ralph s of, 74 , Rob s of, 158   *See* Franceys
Sirard   *See* Scirard
Skinner, Wm s of Rich , 331
Sladehurst, Leticia de, 434 , Rich de, 434
Smalley (co Derby), 6, 30, 175-7, 184-6, 231
Smith, John s of Hugh, 242 , Rich , 439 , Thos , 432-3 , Wm , 242, Wm , 349, Wm (of Plumley), 432-3
Snape, Hen de la, 442, 450
Snelson, 327
——, Wm , lord of, 327
Somerford, Wm , lord of, 419
Sorel, Wm (of Spalding), 242
Sottendon, Wm de, 121
Sotterley (Suffolk), Soterley, 282
——, Edm , 474 , Edm (II), 474 , Rog , 474
Spalding   *See* Sorel
——, Gilb s of Geoff de, 274 , Sim s of Wm de, 367
Spedur', Rich s of Hugh de, 451
Spendlove, Sim , 267
Spileman the chamberlain, xlv, 71

Spital, in Bebington, now in Poulton, (xxxv), 126, 381 , chapel, 126
Spon chapel (in Buckley, co Flint), (xxxiv), 305
Sproston, 415
——, Hugh de, 415 , Ran , 413-14
Spurstow, Wm de, 329, 415, 453
Stamford, Rog the chaplain of, 157-9
—— Mill (on the Gowy), 18, 55, 110, 112
Stanlaw, Stanlow, abbey of , agreements with Chester abbey, 3, 195-209, with Wm de Bunbury, (xxx) , roads, etc , (xix)
—— abbots of   Chas , 198 , Ralph, 201 , Rob , 196, 203
——, John de, 342, 347 , Lucy, 347 , Marg , 417 , Thurstan s of Ivo, 342
Stanley, Master John de, 208, 329, 403, 425, 427-8 , Wm , 296, 379
Stanlow   *See* Stanlaw
Stanney, Great, xix, 7, 16 *n* , 24, 54, 60, 195-6, 206-9, 214
——, ——, Local names   Biflet, 198 , Elpul, 197 , Fliddale, 207 , Holmlache, Holmlake, 201 , Holpol, 201, 263
——, Little, 207-8, 269-70, 473
Stapley, Phil de, 90
Starky, Rich , 90, 433
Staunford, Ad de, 433
Steinolf, Wm the priest, son of, 79
Stephen, 463
——, Hen s of, 443
Stockford (Stockport), Rog de, 431
Stockport, Joan de, 329 , Sir Rich , 329, 334, 478 , Sir Rob , (xvii), (xxxi), 84, 324, 328, 411, 413-14, 432-3 (1274) , Rog, 334, 431 (?)
Stoke (Wirral), rector of, 7, 8, 270, 473-4
——, tithes, etc , of, 473
Storeton, 19, 34, 56, 78, 280-83   *See* Poole
——, Agn de, 387
Strange, Sir Rob le, (xxxi)
Stredeleye, Hugh de, 191
Strettle   *See* Mere
Stretton, Wm de, 322
Struencle, H de, clerk, 82
Stubbs, Agn de, 410 , Hen s of Wm , 415 , Jord , 400 , Wm , 410, 413-15
Stublach, 414
Suan the clerk, 238-41, 251, 273
—— ——, Isoult wife of, 238-41, 251, 273

Suan, Phil. s. of, 462-3 ; Wm. s. of, 167
Suargar the skinner, 59
Suligni, Alfred de, 338
Superbus. *See* Proud
Surrey, John de Warenne, earl of, 89 ;
    Wm., earl of, 143
Sutton (by Macclesfield), Ad. de, 319
——— (in Wirral), xx, 16, 54, 110, 207-8,
    236, 368, 386
———, Maria de, 388
———. *See* Guilden Sutton
Swein the smith, 59
——— (of Moston), 367
Swereford, Alex. de, 134
Swettenham, Pet. de, 310, 315, 419 ;
    Rich., 311, 325, 423

Tabley, Over, 5, 94
———, Hen. de, 388 ; Rob., 408 ; Wm.,
    315
Tama, Manasser de, 120
Tamworth, Wm., dean of, 134
Tardif, John s. of Hugh, 340, 464, 468
Tarporley, the Hermitage in, 436
———, bounds of. *See* Iddinshall
———, Hugh de, 314, 435 ; Matilda,
    405 ; Ralph, 265 ; Rich., 262.
    See Done and Tiresford
Tarvin, Geoff. de, 466, 468 ; Phil.,
    107 ; W., 256
——— Water (Gowy), 198, 201-2, 270
Tathwell (Lincs), 140, 178
Tattenhall, 18, 32, 55, 110, 122, 124,
    252, 346
———, W., clerk of, 124
———, Rob. s. of Matth. de, 255
Tatton, 370-71
Tawell, Master Alan de, 200, 202, 367 ;
    Master Andrew, 466 ; Marg.,
    466
Taylor, Hugh, 468
Teck, John, 408. *See* Thece
Tellesberia, Master Walter de, 120
Tesson, Osbern s. of, 35, 92
Teyt, Punne, 390
Thece, John, 410. *See* Teck
Thicknesse (Thighnes), Hen. de, 427 ;
    Ralph, 427
Thingwall, Gerard de, 362 ; Hawise,
    361 ; Thos., 361-2, 364
Thomas the brewer, 454
——— the butler (*pincerna*), 80
——— the carver (*incisor*), 273
——— the chamberlain. *See* Chamber-
    lain
——— the chancellor of Hen. II., 83, 233
——— the clerk, (xx)
——— the despenser, 106, 202, 310

Thomas the tailor, 253.   *See* Taylor
Thored, Wm., 94
Thornton (le Moors), 260-61, 270 ;
    Fulford Bridge in, 478
———, Sim. de Elton, rector of, 260-64
———, Hawise de, 264 ; Matth., 356 ;
    Pet., 205, 478 ; Ran., 478 ;
    Rich., 90. *See* Peter the clerk
    and Roter
Threckingham (Lincs), nunnery of,
    (xxix), ix-xiii
Thurchever, Wm. de, 169
Thurlewode, Hen. de, 442
Thurlston. *See* Chorlton
Thurstan the priest, 79
———, Rob. s. of, 276, 466 (?)
——— s. of Leca, Rob. s. of, 342-3
Thurstaston, (xix), 8, 48, 58, 125, 387,
    465
———, Knukyn in, 387 ; Londymere in,
    387
———, Ad. de, 380-81 ; Matth., 125 ;
    Rob., 479 ; Wm., 125
Tibotot, Pain, just. of Chester, vi,
    229 ; Rob. de, 213
Tilstone (Fearnall), 4, 20, 34, 56, 110,
    227-30, 313-14
———, le Bruches in, 314 ; Dedelache in,
    227 ; Henneshawe in, 227-8 ;
    Tilstone (Tidulstan) Pol, 227-8
———, Rich. s. of Sim. de, 314
Tiresford (in Tarporley), 246
———, oxgang called Scales in, 246
———, Wm. s. of Hen. de, 246
Titherington, 332-3
———, Jord. de, 322, 459-60 ; Sewall,
    319, 459
Tiverton, 436
Toft, Rich. de, 245, 255 ; Rich., 317,
    372 ; Rich. s. of Rich., 372 ;
    Rog., 200, 322, 400, 412-13 ;
    Wm., 394, 415
Toinehag' (? Tornehag'), 69
Toki, Rob. s. of, 190
Torbock, Sir Hen. de, 200, 307, 400,
    412 ; Sir Rob., (xxx), 124 ;
    Thos., (xxx), 124
Touchet family, 36 *n.*, 122 *n. See*
    Tuschet
Trafford (Bridge), xx, 16, 54, 110, 457
———, Ad. de, 265 ; Alan, 268 ; Rob.,
    349, 433 ; Rog., 263 ; Wm.
    s. of Alan, 269, 271 ; Wm., 427
Trane, Ralph, 268, 271
Tranmere, 248
Tremons, Ran. de, 20, 56 ; Rob., 20,
    34, 56, 228 ; Wm. (?), 35
Trent riv., 214 ; ferry over, 475-7

Trentham, priory of, x, xi, xiii
——, ——, John, prior of, 79, Sampson, canon of, 79
Trickingham *See* Threckingham
Trussell, Sir Wm de, just of Chester, v, 97, 427, Wm his son, 97-9
Tudalee, Thos de, 331
Tuddenham, Thos de, 347
Turgis the doctor, 50
Turnebacin, Ralph s of Rob, 465, 468
Turnevileyn, Ralph, 395-7, 409, 412, 421, 431, Ivo his uncle, 399, Ran his uncle, 396, Wm s of Eva his nephew, 396
Tuschet, Josc, 36, 123, Matth, 123, Sim, 123, 310
Twemlow (Twamlow), 424, 427, 429
—— ——, Gilb de, 417-18, Liulf de, (xxxv), 107, 310-11, 315-16, 408-9, 417-18, 420 (Lidulphus vicecomes), Mabel, 316, 408, 410, Rich, 409, Rob s of Liulf, 315-16, 408-10, Reg (le Brun), 412, Thos, 311, 412-13, Cecilia, d of Thos, 311

Udard, Hugh s of, 43 *See* Hodard
Uerulestane *See* Worleston
Upton (by Chester), xviii-xix, xxvi, 1, 3, 9, 17, 47, 51, 55, 58, 71, 83, 231, 356, 358-9
——, Colbert de, 237, Wm s of Colbert, 237-9, 241, 364, 460, Walt s of Wm, 460

Valence, Wm de, 144
Vale Royal, abbey of, 283-4, 406-7
Venables (of Kinderton), Gilb (I) de, 18-19, 20, 55, 216-19, Gilb, 36, 59 (?), Hamon, 107, Hugh, 82, Hugh, 220, Sir Rog, 218-219, 307, 401, 435, Thos, 426, Wm (I), 28, 128, 216-19, Wm (? II), 81, 202, 219 *n*, 310-11, 338, 408-9, Sir Wm, 205, 218-19, 296, 311, 329, 397, 404, 425 (1287), 431, 453
—— (of Newbold), Rich de, 220-21, Rich, 220-21, Rich, 220-21, Rob, 220-21, Thos, 220-21, Thos, 220-21, Wm, 219-22
Verdon, Arnold de (of Aston upon Trent), 163-5, Bertram, xlvi, 338, John (Aston), 146, 150, 157, Norman, 59, 67-9, 70, 235, Will, 216, Sir Wm sen (Aston), (xix), 144-9, 174, 179, 186-9, Wm jun (Aston), 145-

160, 163-5, 173-5, 179-81, 184, 186-90, Wm s of Arnold, 173-4, Alice mother of Arnold, 165, Alice wife of Sir Wm sen, 186, 144
Vernon (Vernun), Hugh de, 57-8, Felicia, 405-6, Joan, (xxxv), John, 394, Matth, 107, Nich, 405-6, Sir Ralph, (xxxi), (xxxv), 205, 219, 222, 296, 319, 425, 428-9, 453, Rich (I), 18-19, 33, 55-6, Rich (c 1200), 310, 315, Rob, 200, Rog, 324-5, 328, Wacelin (?), 20, 24, 35, 56, Walt, 20-21, 35, 40, 57 (*bis*), Warin, 217, Warin, 81, 97, 202, 310-11, 338, 408-9, 461 (?), Wm, just of Chester, v, 199, 401 (?)
Vescy, John de, 89
Vilers, Alan de, 59, 67

Waland, Hugh s of, 79, 94
Walbrun, Ran de, 20, 57
Walensis *See* Walsh
Waleraund, Rob, 144
Wales, losses of the abbey in, 30, 45, 127, 278, wars with, 105, 108, 212, 215
Waley (Wallasey), Alan de, (xxxii), 107, Rob s of Alan, 275, Rob s of Rob, 387-8, Wm s of Rich, 128, 275 *n*, 336-7, Wm (de Waley), 367
Wallasey (Waley, Kirkby in Waley), 4, 7, 8, 20, 35, 56, 137, 275, 282, 336-7
Walsh, Barnard, 126, Emma, 362, 364, Isoult, 383, Randle, 126, Rich, 383, 387, 420, Utred, 59, Walt, 362, Wm s of Rich, 384, 388
Walter the parmenter, 245
——, John s of, 190, Rob s of, 144, 175, 179
Walton, 80
——, Alice de, 351, Henry, 444, 450, Marg, 411, Wm, 255, 271, 351 (?), 411
Warburton, 52, 59, 60-61, 123
——, Reg de, 245
Ware (Herts), priory of, 250, 290
Warenne, Wm de, 217 *See* Surrey
Warford (Old), 317, 327
—— family, 317
Warin, Geva sist of Ralph s. of, 242
Warner (*al* Warin), Ralph s of, 77, 80, 217, 291

Warwick, John, earl of, 144
——, Rich. de, 343 ; Rog., 278
Waterman, Rob., s. of Wm., 340
Waulon, Rog. de, 144
Waverton, 3, 19, 33, 56, 110, 319, 454-5
——, Hugh de, 323, 326, 412, 455
Weaverham, 7, 17, 55, 110, 282-4
——, Hervey, rector of, 283
Weedon (Bec), viii-x
" Wentala," 282
Weonger, Arnold de, 158
Wepre (co. Flint), xx, 16, 18, 29, 54-5
Werburgh. See St. Werburgh
" Werewelle," " Wirwella," 40, 44, 57
Werrestona. See Worleston
Wervin, xx, 3, 16, 28, 54, 81, 110, 112, 118, 131, 133-5, 252, 259, 271, 459-60, 473
West Kirby (Kirkeby), (xxxii-iii), 4, 7-8, 115, 137, 247, 250, 288-96
——, Bordland tithes of, (xxxiii)
——, church of St. Bridget of, 296
——, rectors of : Ralph de Mold, 247 ; Rich. de Coudray, (xxxiii). See Coudray ; Wm. s. of Rich., 296 ; Wm. (?), (xxxiii), 296
——, Kirkby fam. of, 295. See Kirkby, Rich. de
Weston, Hen. de, 450 ; Rob., 367
Weston (upon Trent), xxiv, 6, 7, 17, 20, 30, 35, 55-6, 87, 110, 136-7, 142 ff., 149-50, 160-61, 163-4, 171-3, 180-83, 187, 214, 231, 252, 475-6
—— Field names, etc. : Balilondes, 181 ; Copyornhul, 182 ; Couholm, 144-5, 182-3 ; Elmishul, 182 ; Holmdale, 171 ; Morshul, 173 ; Mucheledale, 171 ; Pastineslond, 173 ; Smaledale, 182 ; Sotindale, 171 ; Tachemedewe, 173
——, charter of liberties of, 142-3
——, court of, 173-4, 177, 190
——, oratory of, 164
——, Martin de Sibsey, rector of, 137, 164
——, Master Nicholas de, 121
——, Agnes de, 180-81 ; Ellis s. of Thos. de, 171 ; Hen. s. of Ellis, 171-3 ; Hen. s. of Wm., 150 ; Matilda d. of Ellis, 171 ; Matilda d. of Hugh, 160 ; Ran. s. of Rich., 180-83 ; Rich. s. of Gilb., 160 ; Thos., s. of Ellis, 171-3 ; Wm. s. of Lambert, 149, 157, 160, 169

Wettenhall, 48
——, John de, (xxxii), 205, 208, 311, 318, 322, 324, 328-9, 349, 403, 411, 414, 423, 428, 433, 435, 453 ; Pet., 228, 230 ; Ralph, 479 ; Rich., 228, 230 ; Rob., 230 ; Sweyn, 48, 58
Whitby, 18, 55, 110, 197-9, 207-9, 386, 473
—— Local names : Fliddale, 207 ; Whitebypul, 197-9 ; Portway, 207 ; Stanladeheth, 384, 386
White, Emma, 362, 364
Whitley, Nether, 69, 246
Wicebern (Wythebern, Wibern (?)), 40, 43, 234
Wich (Malbank). See Nantwich
—— judices de, 106 ; laws of, 106
Wichfeld, Wicesfeld, le, (xvii), 19, 34, 56
Wichtricheston, Wightreston (in Willaston by Nantwich), 20, 36, 61
Wiger', Steph., 440
Wilbraham, Sir Rich. de, (xxxi), 318, 349, 402-3, 423, 435
Wild, Sibilla, 184, 186 ; Wm., 184, 186
Wilfric. See Chester, bps. of
Willaston (Wirral), 3, 97-9
William the butler (pincerna), 21, 57-8 ; Wm. (c. 1215), 106
—— of the cellar, 271-3 ; Marg., his wife, 273
——, chaplain of the earl, 69 (?), 70, 77
—— the chaplain, 336
—— the cook, 245
—— the cutler, 239, 268, 271
—— the serjeant, 185
—— the smith, s. of Wulfric, 242
——, Andrew s. of, 59 ; Ralph s. of, 263 ; Rich. s. of, 330 ; Sim. s. of. See Kyme ; Thos. s. of, 315 ; Walt. s. of, 190-91
Willilegh, John de, 479 ; Nich., 408-9
Wilne (co. Derby), 6, 20, 30, 35, 56, 164-5, 187-95, 231, 475-6
——, le Bargeford in, 475-6 ; Herlisholm in, 195
——, Arnold de, 192, 194 ; Isabel, 192, 194 ; Isabel, 194 ; John s. of Walt., 190 ; Rob., 194 ; Rob. s. of Thos., 161, 193 ; Walt. s. of Wm., 190-93 ; Wm. s. of Reg., 191, 193 ; Wm. s. of Walt., 192
Wilym, Rog. s. of, 374
Winchcombe, prior of, 473
——, Wm. de, 466
Winchester, Pet. des Roches, bp. of 143

Windgates (nr Rudheath), (xxxv), 400, 404-7
Winebaud the sheriff, xlix, 49, 59
Winnington, 5, 315-18, 410-11
——, Rob s of Wm de, 315, 317, Marg d of Rob s of Wm, 315, Rob s of Rob, 319, Rob, 316-18, 328, 394, 404, 410, 433
Windsor, Cheshire MSS at, (xviii), xxxi
Wintershill, Wm de, 144
Wirral, I, 202, 205, 236, 270, chapel, 126
Wisdeleth See Lea
Wistanston (Wystanton), Sir Wm de, (xviii), 90, 196, 362
Withington, Old, 5, 319-25, 424
——, Wm de, 324, 411, 414
Withod, Agn, 389, Hen, 389
Witton, 216
Wlfricus See Wulfric
Wlvere, Duning s of, 234, Rob s of Duning s of, 234
"Woderston," 282
"Wodinton," 280, 282 (Dr Farrer suggests Wotton, Surrey It was in the honour of Clare)
Wombe, Orm, 351, Osbern, 350
Wood (de Bosco), Hen, 441-2, Rich., 89
Woodchurch, 4, 7-8, 19, 137, 359-66
——, tithes of, 366
——, Ad s of Hugh, dean of, (xxxiv), 362, 364, Emma (Walsh) d of Ad, 362, 363, Hamon, 251, 363, Leuca d of Hamon, 251, 363, Marg d of Hamon, 251, 364, Madock s of Leca, 359, 363

See Other, Rog s of Norman, 359, 363, Wm s of Hugh, 363
Woodcote, chapel of, (xxxii)
——, Wm de, 175
Woodford (in Stockport par), chantry at, 5, 7, 334
Woodward, Wilde le, 391
Worcester, Walter (de Cantilupe), bp of, 139
Worleston, 7, 19, 34, 56, 280, 282, 285
——, chapel of, 285
——, Hen de, 474
Worth, Jord de, 87, Rich, 329, Rob s of Jord, 87, 319-22
Wulfric, Wlfric, grandfather of Liulf de Croxton (Twemlow), (xxxvi) See Lache
——, man of the abbey, (xxxv), 404
—— the reeve, 40, 57
—— of Storeton, 280
——, Wm s of, 242
Wulmar, archdeacon (of Chester?), 56
——, Dunu[n] s of, 71, 234 (?)
Wulphere, King of Mercia, viii, xv
Wybunbury, Rich (I) de, (xxxiv), 82, 317, 401, 408-9, 410, 420, Rich (II), 318-19, 335 (?), 453

Yarndus, Yorwerth, 462-3
York, Thos (I), archbp of, 15, 54
Young (Juvenis), Master Hugh, 367
Yraduc See Hiraddug

Zacharias, Master, 131
Zouche, Wm de la, just of Chester, v, 213

INDEX II · SUBJECTS

See also under " Cheshire " and " Chester " in Index I

Acreswast, 171 , a portion of meadow land
Alienation, letters obligatory, etc , renouncing, 404, 440
Altarage, 133, 135, 249
Anniversaries, 211, 249, 335
Assart, license to, 393
Assizes, 138, 171, 192, 218 *n* , 219, 410 *See* Writs
——, great, 221
Astrum, 418 A hearth, house
Attornment, letters of, 428, 459-60
Avowries, 103, 108

Bacones, 419
Bancum, infra, 460 Into court
Battle, trial by, 178, 190, 246
Baya, 377 A creek A confusion between " haya " and " baya " in this abstract is possible
Bersare, 106 To shoot (with a bow)
Best beast, 388 , second best, 432
Bishop's visitation fees, 8 , rights in abbey churches, 110-11
Boat, liberty of, for fishing, 17, 466
Botta, 248, 254 Strip in a field abutting another strip or a boundary at right angles
Brevitor, 271 An engrosser of writs ? Not in Ducange Perhaps for *breviator*, " bearer of a monastic mortuary roll "
Bridges, 204, 376, 378, 478
Bruche(s), 314, 381 Broken-up ground, newly cultivated land
Bulliones, 106
Burgages, 245, 253, 255, 268-9, 468
Burgesses, 17
Burial, rights of, 300-301

Cannae, 381 Reeds, rushes

Champion (*pugil*), 178
Chantries, 7, 137, 162, 251, 334, 337, 469
Chapel, license for, 417
Charters, penalties for non-observance of, 383 *See* Manuscript
Churches, appropriation of, 115 - 16, 118, 120-22, 128, 130-35, 236, 288, 304
——, collegiate, xxi
——, disputes over advowsons of, 138, 218, 236, 294 f , 304 f
——, enfeoffment with, (xxx), 138, 142
——, farm of, 142 (?), 304
——, mother, 126, 195, 299-301, 309, 321, 331-2, 334, 474
——, duties of parishioners to, 331
——, presentation to, 94 (?), 110, 112, 116, 124-5, 138-9, 303 ff , 309
—— *See* Pensions
Claviger, 299 Butler, or perhaps rather sacristan (Ducange, s v *Clavarius*)
Clives, 172 ? Turf balks between strips in open fields
Coals, sea, 176-7
Corvesarius, 53 Shoemaker
Court *See* Chester, Abbey of St Werburgh and Weston in Index I *Also* Suit below
Crannoc, 267 A Welsh (and Irish) measure of corn
Creancia, 466 Lord's right of credit from tenant
Crenellation, 230
Curia abbatis, 137, 246 , *c comitis*, 247

Darrein presentment, assize of, 138 *See* Writs
Devise of goods, 92
—— of land, 273, 276-7

507

Doetum, 418. Watercourse. *See* Gode-
    froy, *Dict. de l'ancienne langue
    française, s.v.*
Domesday Book of Cheshire, deeds in,
    (xxx), (xxxii), (xxxiii), (xxxiv),
    (xxxvi), 91, 138, 197, 205, 208,
    219, 224, 296, 328-9, 359, 364,
    382 *n.*, 394, 411, 432-4, 454 (*bis*),
    457-8, 466, 477-8
———. See *Eng. Hist. Rev.*, xxxvii
    (1922), 481, xxxviii (1923), 240
Doomsmen (*judices, judicatores*), 104,
    106, 341
Dower, 17, 30, 55, 302, 421

Eyes (*insulae*), 332, 418, 424-5, 446.
    Riverside meadows

Fabrica, 349. Workshop
Feast, double, 249
Fermeso, 89
Fee farm (*perpetua firma*), 252, 255-6,
    276, 284, 340-41, 345, 350
Ferry rights, 475-7
Field (arable) system of Cheshire, 261,
    386, 388-93, 395, 398-9, 418-19,
    424, 434, 439-40, 444-5, 447-9,
    451-2, 456, 461-3
Fishing rights, 17, 20, 57, 201, 247, 383,
    466, 476. *See* Salmon
Forests, 2, 88, 90, 101, 104, 106, 236,
    319
Forarium, Forera, 173, 399. Headland
    in open field
Forinsec service, 362, 469
Fulling mills, 201

Gifts, *Post obit*, 17, 30-31, 47, 51, 55
Gorstae, 381. Gorse
Graveyard, consecration of, 309

Hard years, 423
Hay (*haya*) in forest, enclosure of, 319
Hayas, 377. ? Hags, cuts in peat
    mosses (N.E.D.). But see *Baya*
Herbarium, 467-8. Herb-garden ?
Herbergacio, 104
Hesa, 327. A hedge or hay
Historia charters, xxxix, 22-8, 32, 43
Hostillagium, 237, 239-40, 247, 465-6.
    Lodging right reserved in en-
    feoffment of a tenant

Iaun, Iampnum, 384, 453-4, 457.
    Furze, whin, gorse. Cf. Du-
    cange s. *Iampnum*
Incisor, 273. Carver or possibly gelder
Inspeximus of charters, 2, 25, 83-7

Insulae. See Eyes
Intercommoning of vills, 312
Interdict, 111
Isaiah, quotation from, 307
Iter of the Justice, claim to exemption
    from, (xxxii)

Jews, prohibition of alienation to, 156
Joint tenure of land, 33, 40, 56
Judicatores. See Doomsmen
Judices de Wich, 106
Knight's Service, 103, 105

Lada Cestrie, 161. Carrying service to
    Chester
Landgable, Longable, 255, 268-9, 341,
    345, 347-8, 466. The earl's
    burgage rent
Leper hospitals, 96, 126, 211, 381, 387
Leaseholders. *See* Termors, Leases,
    "Perpetual." *See* Fee farm
Loaves paid to Tower of Chester
    Castle, 81
Lodesmur' (?) Query for Lodesilver.
    See Lada
Loges mercatorum, 59. Booths, stalls.
    See *Mentoria*
Lordship, grant of, 400-401, 404, 406, 459

" Magna Carta " of Cheshire, 6, 101-9
Mandatum, 249
Manuscript sources for charters: Public
    Record Office — Charter Rolls,
    No. 66 (1278), 212, and No. 73
    (1285), 15, 25, 47, 52, 70, 74, 76-
    80, 88, 142-3, 231-5, 320, 338;
    Patent Roll, 28 Edw. I., 102;
    Transcripts, Series II., 291-2;
    Chester Plea Roll, No. 125, 336;
    Duchy of Lancaster Miscellane-
    ous Books, 12, 102. British
    Museum — Additional Charters,
    49974, 367; 51525, 209; Harley
    MSS., 1965, xxxii-iv and *passim*;
    2062, xxxi-xxxiv, 228, 477;
    2071, 67-70, 72, 74, 81-2, 90, 96,
    102, 113, 115, 120-21, 133, 135,
    221, 226, 307, 309-10, 349, 479;
    2074, 309-11, 315, 318-20, 322,
    325, 407, 410, 414-16, 425, 430-
    31; 2102, 115; 2119, 315; 2148,
    (xxxii), 293; Wolley Charters, v,
    27, (xxxii). College of Arms—
    MS. I. D 14, (xxxi). St. George's
    Chapel Windsor—MS. xi. E 5,
    (xviii), xxvii, 15, 25, 67, 70, 77-8,
    81-2, 85-6. Private Collections
    —Eaton Hall, (xvii), (xxx), xxv,

\l f , 38, 47, 51, 53-67, 75, 231-3 ; Farrer (Whitbarrow Lodge, Grange over Sands), Reg of Shrewsbury Abbey, 73 , Mainwaring (John Rylands Library), 323, 327, 394-6, 409, 412-13, 417-19, 420-23, 426-34   Shakerley (Vernon), (xvii), 295, 314, 320, 329, 434-5, 453, 477 Tabley Hall—Leycester's Liber H, 217, 219   Wood (Burnham, Bucks), 400-403, 408, 411-12

Maritagium, liberum, 184, 190, 253, 326, 355, 366, 390, 451, 459, 466

Marriage, lord's right of, 105, 162 (abbot), 179

Maundy Thursday, 249

Mentoria, 53   *See* Loges and Ducange, s v

Mills, 17-18, 40-41, 55, 58-9, 67, 76-7, 91, 110, 112, 137, 141-2, 201, 204-5, 229, 269, 319-20, 325, 378, 415, 420, 422-3, 445-6

Mortuaries, 129

Nativi, 4, 74, 76-7, 103, 105, 169, 186, 211, 387

Nota, 469   *Cum nota,* " with musical modulation " (Ducange)

Novalia, 110, 195, 457-8, 474   Land newly taken into cultivation, " Intakes "

Oblaciones, Obvenciones, 195, 286, 299

Oratories, 7, 334, 417, 471

Ostucarius, Auceps, 67, 75, 232   Hawker, falconer

Pannage, 86, 333, 338, 376, 384, 426

Parmenter, 53, 245

Parochial rights, 299-301

Pastura, 362   *See* Puture

Pelliparius, 53, 331   Skinner

Pensions from churches, 126, 134, 136, 164, 247, 250, 252-3, 271, 282

Pessona   See Pannage

Pinguedo, 89

Placita ad gladium pertinentia, 103

Plea of covenant, 155

Ploughing service, 149-50

Portmoot, 239, 341

Post obit grants   *See* Gifts

Preemption by lord, 447

Priest, married, 309

Procuracio, 247

Procurium domus, 94-5

Pulmentum, 353

Puture of abbot, 439, 440-41

—— of foresters, 236, 362, 364

—— of serjeants, 1, 81, 105-6, 236, 319, 439

Reaping service, 217

Relief, heir's, 105

Reptorf, 229

Rotuli matriculares (of bishop), 139

—— *regii,* 272, 471

Salmon, tithe of, 41, 43, 70, 91

Saltworks, (xxxv), 18 (*bis*), 32, 41, 44, 57, 106, 110, 215-16

Sanctorum Prisca, xxxvii, 15, 22 ff , 86, 217

Seals   (1) of the abbey, 293, 367 , (2) of the earls, (xvii), 69, 72, 97, 216, (3) of the justice, (xviii), 86, 219 , (4) of the prior and convent of Coventry, 134 , (5) of private persons, (xviii), (xxx), (xxxvi), 63 (?), 218, 328, 394, 396-7, 412, 423, 425, 427, 432, 434

Seisin by ear of corn and knife placed on altar, 40, 43

—— by fragment of soil, 31, 55

—— in part, 17, 31, 55

Selda lapidea, 340

Selions, naming of, 261

Sheaf, the third, 183

Sheriff's Stuthe, 104

Sichetum, 327 *et passim*   Syke, a small watercourse

Slaccum, 407   Slack   " A small valley "   From O N *slakki*

Stabilee in venacionibus, 217

Suit of court, 217, 466

Suitors (*sectarii*), 104, 161, 173, 176-7

Termors, 174, 177, 183, 192, 254, 442-4, 449

Terra tributaria, 76-7

Terricidium, 98, 229   Peat

Testament   *See* Devise

Testimonium of Anselm, 38

Thwertnic (Thwertulnay), 103

Tithes (*decimae*), 6, 17, 37, 55, 134, 137 139, 282-5, 305, 338, 437, 451 457, 473-4

——, Bordland (West Kirby), (xxxiii)

—— paid to St Werburgh's in Chester, 299

——, *hospicii,* 162

——, *procurii domus,* 94-5. See *Procuracio*

Tithes of venison, 91

Torale, Torellum, 351, 389, a kiln (Ballard, *British Borough Charters,* 1042–1216, p. 96 ; *Eng. Hist. Rev.,* xv., 508)

Tremium, 423. Hopper (of mill)

Trinoda necessitas, 11

Tuisio, 353. Not in Ducange. No satisfactory explanation seems as yet to have been suggested

Turbary, 264

Vaccaries, 332. Cow farms in forests

Vicars, 119, 128, 130, 133

Village hedge, 434

Villeins. See *Nativi*

Villeinage, land in, 285

Volatus, 381. A falconry

Warren, grant of, 2, 230-31

Waste, approvement of, etc., 227-9, 397-8, 424-5, 434, 439, 442-3, 451, 453, 455-7

Watch, 251

Wiches, laws of the, 106

Wills. *See* Devise

Wreck, right of, 106

Writ of reasonable bounds, 196

—— cosinage, 194

—— *darrein presentment,* 219

—— *mort d'ancestor,* 192, 410

—— *novel disseisin,* 453

—— *quare impedit,* 296

—— *quod permittat,* 365

—— right, 160, 163-4, 185, 224, 239

—— claim to villein, 169

——, revocation of, 195

THE END

Printed in Great Britain by R. & R. CLARK, LIMITED, *Edinburgh.*

The
Chartulary or Register
of
The Abbey of St. Werbur Chester

EDITED WITH INTRODUCTION AND NOTES

BY

JAMES TAIT, M.A., Litt.D., F.B.A.

President of the Society

MANCHESTER:

PRINTED FOR THE CHETHAM SOCIETY

1923

Ingram Content Group UK Ltd.
Milton Keynes UK
UKHW020738280323
419292UK00006B/286